THE REVOLT OF THE PROVINCES

DISLOCATIONS

General Editors: August Carbonella, *Memorial University of Newfoundland;* Don Kalb, *University of Bergen & Utrecht University;* Linda Green, *University of Arizona*

The immense dislocations and suffering caused by neoliberal globalization, the retreat of the welfare state in the last decades of the twentieth century, and the heightened military imperialism at the turn of the twenty-first century have raised urgent questions about the temporal and spatial dimensions of power. Through stimulating critical perspectives and new and cross-disciplinary frameworks, which reflect recent innovations in the social and human sciences, this series provides a forum for politically engaged, ethnographically informed, and theoretically incisive responses.

For a full volume listing, please see back matter

THE REVOLT OF THE PROVINCES

Anti-Gypsyism and Right-Wing Politics in Hungary

Kristóf Szombati

berghahn
NEW YORK · OXFORD
www.berghahnbooks.com

First published in 2018 by
Berghahn Books
www.berghahnbooks.com

© 2018 Kristóf Szombati

Library of Congress Cataloging-in-Publication Data

A C.I.P cataloging record is available from the Library of Congress

British Library Cataloguing in Publication Data

A catalogue record for this book is available from the British Library

ISBN 978-1-78533-896-0 hardback
ISBN 978-1-78533-897-7 ebook

To my parents, Zsuzsa and Béla, who taught me the virtue of endurance.

CONTENTS

List of Tables and Maps   viii

Foreword   ix
  Ivan Szelenyi

Preface   xiv

Introduction   1

Chapter 1   Historic Contextualization:
                "Gypsies," "Magyars," and the State   25

Chapter 2   Popular Racism in the Northeast:
                The Case of Gyöngyöspata   55

Chapter 3   Redemptive Anti-Gypsyism:
                The Transposition of Struggles from
                the Social to the Political Domain   98

Chapter 4   Right-Wing Rivalry and the Dual State   143

Chapter 5   The Limits of Racist Mobilization:
                The Case of Devecser   173

Chapter 6   From Racism to Ultranationalism:
                Jobbik's Transformation through an
                Ethnographic Lens   210

Epilogue   232

References   242

Index   255

Photographs follow page 126

TABLES AND MAPS

Table 2.1. *En gros* price of grapes as compared to inflation
and other fruit items (1991–2010).   60

Table 2.2. Number of individual agricultural producers
by region (1991, 2000, 2007).   61

Table 2.3. Number of viticultural producers by region
(2000, 2007).   62

Table 2.4. Number of people unemployed in Gyöngyöspata
(2000–2013); growth years in italic and inflection point
underlined.   63

Table 2.5. Criminal statistics for Gyöngyöspata (1990–2012);
years when the military post was dismantled (1995) and
the "criminal report" was published (2006) in bold.   69

Table 5.1. Number of people unemployed in Devecser
(2000–2013); growth years in italic and inflection point
underlined.   185

Map 2.1. Map of Hungary featuring Gyöngyöspata.   57

Map 2.2. Map of Gyöngyöspata featuring the "border zone"
(marked with stripes) and other landmarks.   85

Map 5.1. Map of Hungary featuring Devecser.   175

Map 5.2. Map of Devecser featuring the area contaminated
by the "red mud spill" (marked with stripes) and other
landmarks.   192

FOREWORD

Ivan Szelenyi

This is a carefully researched book and may be the best one I have read about the rise of the New Right—not only in postcommunist Europe, but in Europe as such. Its empirical focus is on the last twenty-five years in Hungary and on how anti-Roma sentiments were exploited by the political Right to build its base and establish a political hegemony, which at this point looks unchallengeable. Szombati shows that it is not "eternal racism" that is being appealed to. The racist component of far-right politics cannot be taken for granted. Using Roma as the enemy served a purpose at one time, but when it did not do so any longer the Right broadened its scope, found new "others" beyond Gypsies, and launched into what the author calls "ultranationalism."

With two well-documented local case studies, Szombati shows how anti-Roma prejudices may or may not lead to anti-Roma mobilization. In both cases, the structural preconditions for racist mobilization were present (namely, the devastating impact of neoliberal globalization), but what made the difference was a micropolitics embedded in slightly different trajectories and experiences. These are interesting cases and the conclusions are persuasive. The "Gypsy problem" can be "solved" (or perhaps better put, "managed") with "appropriate" policies.

The author elegantly links the success of racist mobilization to political economy: racism is a useful tool for mobilization where an "ethnic majority" feels itself to be on the "losing side," even if the "ethnic minority" is no winner at all. Under such conditions it becomes possible to blame "others" for "our" suffering.

I agree: the unspeakable conditions many Roma live in since the mid or late 1980s in former communist countries are not the same "as they have always been" and cannot be attributed to "eternal racism." Although we have solid evidence that Roma were since time immemorial discriminated against, at least in Europe, their social standing varied in different historical periods. They could be lower class, lower caste, or pariah caste, or, as I showed with János Ladányi for the postcommunist period, Roma (and who Roma are is a hotly debated issue) could also constitute an "underclass."

But the main purpose of this foreword is not to dwell on Roma but to suggest that this book has implications far beyond Hungary or Eastern Europe. Let me begin with the United States. While Donald Trump (having no experience, no knowledge of world affairs, and a terribly unpredictable temperament) was clearly unfit for the presidency and lacked a coherent ideology or world view, he knew what enough people in the United States wanted to hear to win the election: "Your problems are illegal immigrants. I will build a wall and expel eleven million of them." This was obviously nonsense. Of course, there were some "drug dealers" and "rapists" (as Trump said) among Latino immigrants, but arguably no more than among white Americans. Most of these "illegal immigrants" were maids, babysitters, gardeners, nurses, agricultural laborers—representatives of badly needed professions in the US economy. But they were easily identifiable as "enemies," and the identification of the "enemy within" satisfied millions of working-class Americans who feel deeply alienated from Washington elites and believe that their tax dollars are being poured into the purses of the "underclass," which they fear slipping into. This was especially true in a situation wherein the Democratic candidate failed to talk to the party's traditional base. These "insurgents" swayed the electoral votes in key Midwestern states, which won Trump the presidency. In my reading, the 2016 US election was the "counterrevolution of the white working class," whose members revolted against everything that the 1960s stood for (political correctness, affirmative action, redistribution, free trade) and were dreaming of bringing back "the good old days" when there were plenty of well-paid manufacturing jobs and no competition from China, India . . . or Latino immigrants. The dream of an ethnically homogeneous white America is of course impossible to achieve. But it is still possible to win an election based on this dream when 60 percent of the electorate is still white.

And now let's turn briefly to Brexit, which is another case of the "revolt of the provinces." London (whose mayor is Muslim and of Pakistani descent), along with cities that benefited from globalization, massively voted for Europe. "UK independence" was won by the votes of Eastern England's "counterrevolutionary working class." The story is frighteningly similar to the United States, with the major difference being that the enemies are not Latino immigrants but Eastern Europeans. The latter, taking advantage of free movement and European Union (EU) labor laws, left their rural homelands (which bore the brunt of neoliberal restructuring) behind in the hope of higher wages and prospects for the future. While working-class Brits have indeed lost jobs to these immigrants, they have primarily suffered from the shift from an industrial to a service-oriented economy, as well as from the privatization of the social housing sector. While these ills (as well as the advantages of EU membership) are invisible, "Polish plumbers" and "Hungarian waitresses" are easily identifiable. As in the United States, the "native" working class has turned away from the Labour Party (which embraced multiculturalism and meritocracy at the expense of working-class dispossession and anxiety) and toward parties that speak to their concerns—even if they do not do much more than that.

Finally, let me return to the somewhat parochial site of this book: Hungary. It is by now a commonplace to claim that the postcommunist transition—just as deindustrialization in the United States and Western Europe—had not only winners but losers too. The "post-peasants" Szombati is writing about did well in the 1960s and 1970s, much better than in earlier decades. They built new houses for themselves, bought cars, cultivated their gardens, and took their products to urban markets, earning higher incomes than they ever dreamed of. They prospered and did not attach particular value or importance to the fact that their neighbor was Roma. But in the 1990s, everything changed when these same people found themselves forced to compete with Dutch or Danish farmers under standards set by the European Union. This is when neoliberal globalization began to produce its nefarious effects in Eastern Europe. Younger people, especially those who had marketable skills, left the countryside, leaving behind those who had invested all their capital in the land, retired people, and "the underclass." So whom do you—if you identify as one of the former—blame for your worsening predicament and hopelessness? Of course, you will not blame those invisible "forces of globalization," which you cannot possibly fight anyway. You will blame your neighbor: the "Gypsy" who steals your tomatoes. This is why the far-right Jobbik Party's paramilitary actions, which this book so vividly describes, fell on fertile soil in villages threatened by "Gypsyfication."

While in the West we are just beginning to decipher the contours of the politics of the New Right when it comes to power, Eastern Europe and most notably Hungary serve as a kind of laboratory for testing the possibilities of rightist rule. Szombati's analysis is, again, cutting edge on this front. After showing us how far-right activists and politicians crafted a strategy that allowed the previously marginal Jobbik Party to entrench itself as the voice of the "abandoned countryside" and to firmly place the "Gypsy issue" at the top of the political agenda, he shows that the main right-wing Fidesz Party adopted elements of the new racist common sense to outmaneuver Jobbik. Fidesz achieved this with the help of an analogous strategy. Its talented and charismatic leader, Viktor Orbán, identified refugees (whom he mislabeled as "migrants") arriving from Syria as the Hungarian nation's dire enemies. The script of this campaign was written well in advance of the first refugees' arrival at the country's southern border. Fidesz put up billboards carrying the messages "Do not take away our jobs" and "Respect our laws." The fact that these messages were written in Hungarian (not Arabic) shows that they were intended for a domestic audience. Once refugees started to arrive in large numbers, the government allowed them to come by train to Budapest's Eastern Railway Station but then prevented them from boarding trains bound for Vienna and German cities. Tens of thousands of people thus found themselves stranded in miserable conditions in the middle of Budapest, generating stories of aggression and rape that found their way into the government-controlled media. The result was a surge in xenophobic attitudes and a receptivity to Orbán's promise to defend Hungary against "migrant hordes" and uphold the nation's "ethnic homogeneity."

Since the dissertation this book is based on was written and defended at Central European University (CEU), it is appropriate to end this foreword by highlighting that after the refugees were allowed to leave for Austria and Germany, Fidesz turned on global investor and CEU founder George Soros, making him public enemy number one. For a while, I thought that this was a nonstarter. After all, very few Hungarians knew of CEU. But I was wrong. Soros is Jewish, rich, American, and liberal. For the majority of Hungarians, these are negative labels. So the billboards posted all over the country carrying the message "Let's not let Soros have the last laugh!" were far from being a stupid mistake. Identifying a plausible enemy is what drives the far right in Europe and North America today (and what probably drove it all along).

Are we witnessing the death throes of xenophobic ultranationalism or will its specter be haunting the West for the foreseeable future? Can liberal democracies survive illiberal rule? These questions remain open to debate, but analyses like this one help us better understand the nature of the problem and what is at stake.

Ivan Szelenyi
Budapest, 11 September 2017

Ivan Szelenyi is William Graham Sumner Emeritus Professor of Sociology and Political Science, Yale University, and Max Weber Emeritus Professor of Social Sciences and Foundation Dean of Social Sciences at New York University Abu Dhabi. He is former president of the Hungarian Sociological Association and former vice president of the American Sociological Association. His authored and coauthored publications include *The Intellectuals on the Road to Class Power* (1979), *Urban Inequalities under State Socialism* (1983), *Socialist Entrepreneurs* (1988), *Making Capitalism without Capitalists* (1998), and *Patterns of Exclusion* (2006).

PREFACE

The research that underpins this book grew out of an ambition to come to terms with a deeply unsettling phenomenon, which I came into contact with as a community worker. In 2008, the first two victims of the politically motivated "Roma murders" were killed in a village that was twenty kilometers from the one where I helped local Roma establish a cucumber-growing cooperative. The thing I found most disconcerting about these tragic episodes was the silence that surrounded them. Most of my non-Romani interlocutors were unwilling to discuss them at any length. The few who were sought to relativize the murders by juxtaposing them with criminal acts committed by Roma or by highlighting the putatively legitimate motivations of the perpetrators. These unsettling encounters compelled me to probe more deeply this new preoccupation with "Gypsies" as a "problem population" by engaging in an open-eyed effort to understand popular experiences, discourses, and practices without recurring to the clichés that were plaguing public debate. The same year, I submitted a successful application to Central European University's (CEU) Ph.D. program in sociology and social anthropology. I finished the first preparatory year but then took a leave of absence to campaign for the green LMP (Lehet Más a Politika, "Politics can be different") party, which I had cofounded with fifteen other activists in 2007. I coordinated the writing of the party's Roma Integration Strategy and was elected to the party's steering board. After the elections of April 2010, I stepped down from my party functions and returned to CEU to pursue my research project. In the next five years I delved into the history of Romani groups in Hungary, invested considerable effort into dissecting the strategies of racist activists and far-right "political entrepreneurs," followed the unfolding of contentious episodes revolving around "Gypsies" in the political public sphere, conducted interviews with politicians, took part in political debates on the "Gypsy question," and, last but not least, conducted fieldwork in two localities where the emergent far-right Jobbik Party sought to escalate tensions between Roma and non-Roma. I submitted my thesis in July 2016 and defended it in September of the same year.

This research process was not only unconventional because of its length (2010–2015) but more fundamentally because it started out as a social experiment: an action research that aimed to test the workability of addressing ethnic tensions through peaceful conflict-resolution methods in rural communities. I persuaded LMP's political foundation to support a pilot project in the village of Gyöngyöspata, where far-right paramilitaries allied with the Jobbik Party had staged an anti-Romani mobilization campaign in the spring of 2011 (see chapter 4 for a description and analysis). Together with a handful of sociologists and anthropologists (whom I persuaded to take part in the initiative), we invited local councilors to address tensions between local Roma and non-Roma (which had already been bubbling to the surface but exploded after the arrival of paramilitaries) through a process of dialogue and negotiation involving opinion leaders from both sides. We proposed to first put together a "problem map" of Romani and non-Romani grievances as a means of offering a point of departure for dialogue and then to bring opinion leaders together with the aim of having them work on solutions to the obstacles to peaceful coexistence. The project, however, never got off the ground. By the time we tabled a detailed proposal, representatives of the local elite who could have supported our conciliatory approach had already been outmaneuvered by more radical competitors and found themselves forced to withdraw from public life. Faced with this failure, anthropologist Margit Feischmidt and I decided to continue research with the aim of deepening our understanding of the local conflict and documenting the—by then palpable—surge of the far-right in the locality.

By stepping into the fray as the advocates of social peace and dialogue, we had—on a conventional understanding of social scientific research—perturbed the social field and hopelessly contaminated the data we hoped to extract from it. Against this interpretation I put forward the claim that our experimental methodology allowed us to gain access to a community that would at that time have been extremely difficult to approach through conventional research methods. Our intervention was an effort at "reflexive social science" (Burawoy 1998): an attempt to interrogate the social order by subjecting it to a particular kind of pressure in the hope that the response would reveal key qualities of that order. We thus found ourselves compelled to repeatedly reflect on the way in which our experiment was coloring our data and interpretations. We recognized that by taking a stand against violence (and, by extension, against the proponents of violence) we were prone to overstate the salience of the Roma/non-Roma (and pro-Roma/anti-Roma) divide and to overlook blurred forms of identification and unconventional views and commitments. Our response was a deliberate effort to seek out people who occupied in-between positions until we could confidently establish that while there were many individuals holding heterodox views, they were not only unable to forge a common platform but had effectively been silenced by emergent actor-networks wielding significant symbolic power. Our experimental method did, of course, come with its own costs. We were, for instance, unable to approach the most diehard local supporters of the far-right party. Nevertheless, we found ways of addressing most of these shortcomings, in this case by convincing equally radical but politically less committed individuals to enter into a kind of "polemical dialogue" through which we sought to elucidate the deep-seated roots of our contrastive normative views. This strategy, I claim, allowed us to decipher the underpinnings of racist discourse with a degree of precision that was superior to what we could have achieved through conventional interviewing.

This first—experimental and reflexive—phase of the research ended in March 2012, seven months after the Jobbik candidate's electoral victory, when we found out that Gyöngyöspata's new mayor had labeled us "Zionist troublemakers" and declared us *personae non grata*. Having been forced to retreat from the field, Margit and I produced a policy study (see Feischmidt and Szombati 2012) that offered a comprehensive interpretation of the events that had taken place in the village and formulated a more tentative interpretation of the wider far-right mobilization strategy. This was followed by an effort to publicize our findings by organizing discussions and a conference at CEU, and by giving interviews to the mainstream media. We then wrote several scientific articles in Hungarian, German, and English, highlighting different aspects of the "Gyöngyöspata case" (see Feischmidt and Szombati 2013a, 2013b, 2014, 2016) and tracing the contemporary racialization of Roma in both Eastern and Western Europe (Feischmidt, Szombati, and Szuhay 2014).

Having closed the "Gyöngyöspata case," I decided to follow Jobbik into Western Hungary, where it sought to pursue its racist mobilization campaign with a view to embedding itself in a region where it had failed to make significant inroads. I opted to pursue fieldwork in the small town of Devecser, where Jobbik staged a large racist rally in August 2012. In Devecser, I adopted a more conventional research methodology (interviewing combined with participant observation)

but decided to retain the polemical approach we had used in Gyöngyöspata. Instead of positioning myself as a neutral observer (which
I considered impossible given my background), I identified myself as
a former activist looking to expand his intellectual horizon by engaging with the views of people whose circumstances differ substantially
from his. The intention, as in Gyöngyöspata, was to create space for
a kind of dialogue that invites both interviewer and interviewee to
leave their comfort zone in order to clarify their divergent positions
and allegiances. However, as time progressed, I ended up veering
toward a more conventional approach to participant observation and
(unstructured) interviewing based on the realization that members of
this community—where ethnicity cuts across class instead of overlapping with it—were far less suspicious of my former political activities.

My research in Devecser gave the project a comparative dimension
and forced me to engage in a more sustained manner with questions
related to territoriality and political economy (see the introduction
for details). This, in turn, shifted my attention to the social reproduction of class, a theme that ended up occupying a central place in my
interpretive framework. At the same time, I continued to greatly benefit from discussions with Margit, with whom we continued to share
thoughts after our collaboration ended in Gyöngyöspata. It was she
who helped me grasp the importance of symbolic politics and who
alerted me to the remarkably ambivalent nexus between racist and
nationalist ideas and the ways in which they have shaped the cultural outlooks of rural citizens. The final text is an integrated study
of the shifting economy, the rise of a far-right political movement, anti-Gypsy racism, and the dominance of the right-wing Fidesz Party in
Hungary. I seek to offer a nuanced approach to these interconnected
issues by engaging space, scale, history, racism, and class. And I look
closely at the intersections of local, regional, national, and global processes in making distinct political movements and environments.

I am grateful to staff and colleagues at the CEU's Department of
Sociology and Social Anthropology who read and commented on
drafts of chapters 2 and 5. Their questions and suggestions allowed
me to substantially improve the arguments I present in these key
parts of the book. My greatest debt is to Don Kalb, under whose gen-
tle but sure-handed supervision I was able to weave the divergent
threads of my research into a coherent fabric. Don also commented
extensively on the draft of the manuscript I prepared for Berghahn—
ruthlessly highlighting logical gaps and pushing me to clarify ideas
and sharpen formulations. His relational take on class was a major
source of inspiration for the project as a whole. I am also grateful to

him for forcing me to abstract (more on that key term below) my material from the Hungarian context and for providing precious advice on how it could be presented in a way as to make it intelligible to an international audience. I would also like to thank Judit Bodnár for highlighting a few annoying mistakes and suggesting that I rework some parts of the argument, and Dorit Geva for encouraging me to think strategically about the comparative dimension of this research.

This book would not be complete without the accompanying visual material that is the work of Polina Georgescu. Besides shooting great photographs, Polina also provided emotional comfort in moments of distress. The clarity of thought she brought to our conversations helped me "tame the beast"—that is, to finally pin down the constantly moving object of this research. The beast has, of course, only been pinned down in writing. It remains the task of others (and future selves) to tame it in the real world.

INTRODUCTION

This book aims to contribute to our understanding of the making of right-wing hegemony in Hungary, a country situated on the European Union's eastern periphery. It seeks to do this by shedding light on a popular racist movement that took shape outside the party-political arena in the 2006–2010 period and then went on to play a key role in the unmaking of left-liberal hegemony through its connection to right-wing agendas. This movement has not altogether been neglected by scholars and analysts, but its connection to broader economic and political dynamics and its impact on party politics remain largely misunderstood. Students of racism and xenophobia have failed to recognize the novelty of political anti-Gypsyism, seeing it as an extension of prevalent racist sensibilities, prejudices, and patterns of discrimination into the political domain at a time of economic and political upheaval. This perspective misses the crucial link between the rise of anti-Gypsyism and the crisis of social reproduction suffered by particular segments of the rural population as a result of capitalist transformations connected to global economic trends and, more particularly, Hungary's accession to the EU. Those who have called attention to the rise of racism and xenophobia in Hungary have, in other words, failed to see how anti-Gypsyism evolved out of social struggles and reacted to the real and imagined projects of ruling elites. As for political scientists and analysts, they have recognized how anti-Gypsyism fueled the rise of the far-right Movement for a Better Hungary (Jobbik) but have neglected its impact on mainstream politics and its role in the reconstruction of the state in the period following the right-wing Alliance of Young Democrats's (Fidesz) ascent to power in 2010. I fill these gaps by performing two broad analytic moves: (1) situating ideas about "race" and ethnicity within everyday relations, experience, and agency, and showing how these are themselves shaped by broader political economic processes and pressures; and (2) identifying relational strategies and processes that connected local sites of contention and allowed for the transposition of social antagonisms into regional and nationwide political struggles. These moves shift attention away from Gypsies and the far-right to historical processes unfolding over time and through space in two interconnected relational fields: everyday life and the political public sphere. The intention is to move beyond the unsurprising claim that xenophobia fosters xenophobic politics and to create analytic space for identifying the conditions of the emergence of racist movements and the processes shaping the trajectories they take.

The Argument in Brief

The argument I present can be portrayed as an effort to extend the analysis of scholars working in the political economy tradition who have attempted to theorize the making of right-wing hegemony in Hungary. This heterogeneous group of anthropologists, sociologists, and historians has highlighted structural tensions between markets and democracy in semiperipheral countries situated outside the European currency union (see Greskovits and Bohle 2012; Scheiring 2016), emphasizing in particular how pressure from international creditors and the European Commission to decrease the budgetary deficit pushed the pro-European left-liberal Gyurcsány government's policies in a neoliberal direction: toward the championing of growth and social mobility at the expense of national solidarity (see Éber et al. 2014). The cracking of the social democratic welfare agenda should, they argue, therefore be seen as a key condition of possibility for the reenergization of right-wing nationalist politics (see Kalb and Halmai 2011).

This body of work draws inspiration directly or indirectly from Karl Polányi's (2001) analysis of the fall of liberal capitalism, in which the renowned economist argued that the commoditization of money in the form of the international gold standard proved intolerable in countries that accumulated a large trade deficit, and called forth protective movements of various kinds in the interwar period. I have myself been inspired by Polányi's conceptualization of the "double movement"—that is, the expectation that economic shocks generated within a "disembedded economy" will generate "countermovements" in the political sphere if the state fails to protect "society" from the advance of the "free market." I have found the concept of the double movement a useful heuristic device in that it highlights the need to study the ways in which social actors respond to pressures created by capitalist transformations. This book will advance the argument that the decline of agricultural prices and production in connection to the process of European integration (which forced Hungary to open its doors to import products) contributed to the emergence of anti-liberal sensibilities among independent agricultural producers who bore the brunt of "Europeanization" in rural areas. It will, however, also highlight the limitations of Polányi's conceptualization by showing that his focus on markets is too narrow and arguing that in order to explain the ideological orientation and political thrust of countermovements, we need to develop a conceptual apparatus that is more sensitive to social experience and practice and that allows us to link antagonisms and rivalries that emerge in particular sites at particular moments in time to wider political and economic trends. To do this, I will draw on a recent impulse from anthropologists working in the political economy tradition who have opened new analytic vistas for studying the conjunction of global forces and local expressive universes in a way aimed at safeguarding the autonomy of everyday actors, while also avoiding the trap of privileging structure over dynamics and meaning over praxis.

My research highlights two key preconditions for the emergence of a racist countermovement in Hungary. The first was the "double crisis" of social reproduction: of the non-Romani "post-peasantry" whose social reproduction partially depended on small-scale agricultural production; and the ethnicized "surplus population" whose social reproduction partially depended on rewards distributed by post-peasant patrons and public goods allocated by local power-holders. I show that the "de-peasantization" of agriculture not only undermined livelihoods but also eroded the local hegemonies that guaranteed mainstream groups privileged access to collective goods and public services while also ensuring the subservience of the marginalized surplus population.

The second precondition I highlight is the ruling left-liberal elite's effort to emancipate the surplus population by disaggregating local mechanisms of segregation and control through the centralization of welfare and education programs. This effort generated feelings of "abandonment" among mainstream groups whose social reproduction increasingly depended on institutionalized forms of solidarity.[1] Taken together, these preconditions help explain why the countermovement emerged on the country's northeastern periphery and why it targeted both "unruly" Gypsies and "unpatriotic" elites.

Although de-peasantization and emancipation were institutionally independent of each other, both were intrinsically connected to the process of European integration. The liberalization of trade and the emancipation of ethnic minorities formed part and parcel of Europeanization—and this was not lost on representatives of the post-peasantry who came to play a prominent role in the articulation of popular grievances in the Northeast. While the interests and aspirations of the post-peasantry gave the countermovement a particular ideological orientation, the projects pursued by left-liberal elites gave it a particular political thrust. This explains why its representatives pressured the state to reallocate discretionary powers back to the local level and why this demand was formulated in anti-liberal and racist idiom. It also explains why (although not how) the movement could later become connected to anti-egalitarian right-wing political projects that championed ethnonational solidarity at the expense of "unworthy" others. Finally, the preconditions my research highlights also help explain why anti-Gypsyism could not gain so much traction as a generalized redemptive discourse (that laid the blame for communal decline on an alliance of Roma and liberal elites) in rural regions where the double crisis was evaded thanks to the availability of economic opportunities and the efforts of local power-holders.

While a reworked Polányian approach can help us explain *why* popular anti-Gypsyism emerged, it does not help us account for *how* it evolved into first a regional, then a nationwide, movement that exercised a demonstrable influence on both the politics of "electoral support" and of "governmental power." Hungary stands out in the region as the only country where anti-Gypsyism became a key dimension of party political struggle as a result of popular racist mobilization. Anti-Gypsyism also emerged as a regional movement in the Czech Republic, but it did not become a salient dimension of party politics in this country (see Albert 2012). Slovakia is similar to the Czech case, with the exception of an episode when the ruling conservative liberal government sought to disaggregate opposition to its neoliberal welfare reform plan by presenting it as an effort to redistribute rewards from "Gypsy welfare-scroungers" to "hard-working citizens" (Makovicky 2013). I have drawn on the work of social movements scholars to account for the transposition of local antagonisms into a coherent national movement. In my analysis, I highlight sets of actors and relational strategies that played a central role in the politicization of "everyday racism" (Essed 1991). I argue that local politicians, right-wing intellectuals, and the mainstream media played a key role in constructing a phantasmagoric image of the "dangerous Gypsy" through strategies of "abstraction" that stripped local events from their contexts and repackaged them together with historic anti-

Romani prejudices into a generalized redemptive[2] discourse that portrayed "the Gypsy"—in the singular—as the chief obstacle to the material prosperity, social cohesion, and cultural renewal of the national community.

I then trace the process whereby "redemptive anti-Gypsyism" went from gripping local imaginaries to spawning a nationwide "moral panic" in 2009–2010. I conceptualize this period as a "critical juncture" (Collier and Collier 1991) when important processes were launched through the selection of a particular option from a range of alternatives. This channeling occurred through the narrowing of the range of possible future outcomes through a chain of temporally ordered and causally connected events that pushed public opinion and political actors to take an increasingly radical position against "Gypsies." I establish that this "reactive sequence" (Mahoney 2000: 526) began at/with local contentious episodes that polarized deprived communities along ethnoracial lines. These episodes were conditioned by de-peasantization but emerged more directly in response to the—partially real, partially imagined—breakdown of local hegemonies. I show in detail how far-right political entrepreneurs sought to take advantage of these local conflicts, highlighting how Jobbik party leaders deployed a paramilitary proxy organization called the Hungarian Guard with the intent of creating situations wherein citizens were forced to side with either "Gypsy criminals" or "victimized Magyars." This strategy of polarization contributed to the emergence of a (counter)movement dynamic wherein "single episodes of collective action are perceived as components of a longer-lasting action, rather than discrete events; and when those who are engaged in them feel linked by ties of solidarity and of ideal communion with protagonists of other analogous mobilizations" (della Porta and Diani 2006: 21). Relying on social movement scholars' insistence that this kind of crystallization takes place in the "political public sphere,"[3] I argue that mainstream media inadvertently fostered this process by providing visibility to far-right mobilization campaigns and framing these (and other) episodes in a way that fostered perceptions of social breakdown. Strategies of abstraction and polarization thereby played a key role in upward "scale shift": an increase in the number of contentious episodes and of the visibility of the "Gypsy issue" in the political public sphere. One of the main lessons to take away is that we need to pay more attention to noninstitutionalized forms of political agency, which tend to fall below the radar of political scientists but may exercise a decisive impact on political struggles. At the same time, however, I heed political scientists' insistence on studying the interaction between radical and mainstream parties as a key element of political opportunity structures by showing how the right-wing Fidesz Party's espousal of a strategy of "adoption" (see Bale et al. 2010) played into the process of radicalization: the shift of both politicians and the electorate toward increasingly exclusionary and authoritarian demands and initiatives.

Having traced the transposition of "everyday racism" into "political racism," my analysis ends with an effort to capture key ways in which anti-Gypsyism shaped the politics of governmental power and of electoral support after Fidesz's historic victory at the parliamentary elections of 2010. I highlight the "dualization" of the Hungarian state, which progressively rescinded its obligation to combat poverty and exclusion, and redistributed resources and opportunities toward middle-class formation. This transformation already had precedents in the 1990s but emerged as a political project under Ferenc Gyurcsány's second government (2006–2009), which began to implement a new workfare program with a view to preventing the crumbling of the Socialist Party's voter base in its northeastern bastions. The transformation picked up pace after Fidesz's victory in 2010. Relying on Stuart Hall's (1983) insistence on "authoritarian populism" as a prime ideological strategy for enlisting heterogeneous popular constituencies and generating mass electoral support for right-wing political projects, I argue that Viktor Orbán harnessed the moral panic on "Gypsy criminality" to his own hegemonic project by deriding claiming behavior and embracing regional mayors' "anti-egalitarian populist" vision of the "work-based society." The Dual State (see Fraenkel 1969) emerged out of a "passive revolution" in response to the electorate's radicalization (itself a reaction to global economic pressures and the governmental record of left-liberal predecessors) and competition from a far-right rival. It is the result of a political alliance between a New Right (that has dissociated itself from the previous left-liberal consensus) and a popular movement (that has come to see itself as a victim of liberal elites and the "dangerous classes"). Although Hungary's Prime Minister portrayed the state's transformation as an effort to boost economic competitiveness in an era of heightened global competition, it primarily served as a political tool to buttress his power. Fidesz's second landslide victory at the parliamentary elections of 2014 can be attributed to a multiplicity of causes. I nevertheless argue that the ruling party's ability to maintain hold over a radicalized political center has at least partly to do with the recodification of rights and obligations, which allowed Orbán to take credit for rewarding "hard-working," and disciplining "work-shy," citizens. In the final part of the book, I show that the transformation of the Hungarian state also helps account for the demise of political anti-Gypsyism as well as a decisive shift in Jobbik's political program and strategy in the course of the last electoral cycle.

A Reworked Polányian Approach

One person who has greatly contributed to the analysis of local struggles within wider fields of power is a scholar whose name does not usually feature in analyses of racism and radical right-wing politics. This is none other than the great Hungarian political economist, Karl Polányi, who some seventy years ago advanced a theory of the rise of interwar fascism. In *The Great Transformation*, his magnum opus dealing with the rise of free market economics, Polányi (2001: 3) argued that fascism constituted a "protective countermovement" that was set in motion when efforts to extend the scope of the market through the commoditization of land, labor, and capital threatened to annihilate "the human and natural substance of society." The book connected the rise of fascism more directly to the ravages of the "gold standard"—an institutional innovation that put the theory of self-regulating markets for the first time into practice in the domain of international trade. He offered an analysis of fascism as a pan-European movement that became allied with nationalist and counterrevolutionary tendencies but drew its vital energies from "a market society that refused to function" (Polanyi 2001: 248). While seeking to retain a materialist view of world history, Polányi (2001: 138–139) replaced Marx's focus on production and exploitation with an emphasis on the contradiction between a "disembedded market" and "society":

> [The double movement] can be personified as the action of two organizing principles in society, each of them setting itself specific institutional aims, having the support of definite social forces and using its own distinctive methods. The one was the principle of economic liberalism, aiming at the establishment of a self-regulating market, relying on the support of the trading classes, and using largely laissez-faire and free trade as its methods; the other was the principle of social protection aiming at the conservation of man and nature as well as productive organization, relying on the varying support of those most immediately affected by the deleterious action of the market—primarily, but not exclusively, the working and the landed classes—and using protective legislation, restrictive associations, and other instruments of intervention as its methods.

Polányi's conceptualization of the double movement offers a number of opportunities for explaining how societies respond to macroeconomic pressures. First, it shines light on temporality as a key dimension of social and political change. Interwar fascism emerged at the moment when the "market system" entered a phase of "general crisis"—not before. This highlights the need to study the effects of capitalist transformations through time. Second, Polányi highlights the state's central role in generating the double movement. He argues that fascism resulted from European states' failure to protect the livelihoods of workers and peasants from destructive market forces. This underscores the importance of linking the emergence of social movements to a crisis of livelihoods or "social reproduction" (suffered by particular social categories) and popular appeals to institutionalized forms of solidarity. Polányi's analysis also highlights the need for a multi-scalar perspective that offers insights into the ways in which transnational economic and political processes—mediated by regulatory agencies (such as the EU and the nation-state)—create particular kinds of pressures for particular kinds of people in their everyday lives. Finally, his concrete historical analysis accentuates the interaction between a protective countermovement and ideological currents. Polányi's (2001: 250–251) remarks on the political dimension of interwar fascism show that he regarded the "symbiosis between movements of independent origin" as a necessary precondition for countermovements' success.

To be sure, Polányi's framework suffers from a number of shortcomings. His model is weakened by the location of contradictions between market forces and society. Although he clearly recognized that the response to the advance of the free market "comes through groups, sections, and classes" (ibid., 160), he does not provide an analysis of the situated struggles out of which countermovements are born. Polányi also underestimated the possibility and relevance of regional differences. While he recognized the importance of the national scale, he underestimated the relevance of the local in a double respect. First, local hegemonies may play a key role in the emergence of countermovements through confrontation or collusion with projects formulated by actors on the regional, national, and European level. Second, it is also on the local level where social antagonisms first acquire meaning and direction, and this shapes "classification struggles" (Bourdieu 1984) in regional and national arenas. Polányi, in other words, does not have the analysis of ideological and political conjunctures as fully worked out as other theorists (see Burawoy 2003).

In what follows, I draw on recent theoretical and methodological advances in the political economy tradition in anthropology and in the field of social movement studies to complement and improve Polányi's framework.

On the one hand, I take inspiration from anthropologists who have opened new vistas for studying the conjunction of global forces and local universes in a way that aims at safeguarding the autonomy of everyday actors, while avoiding the trap of reductionism and mechanical causality (Burawoy 2000; Burawoy and Verdery 1999; Friedman 2010, 2015; Kalb 1997, 2015; Mintz 1986; Sider 1986; Sider and Smith 1997; Wolf 1990). Don Kalb and Herman Tak have labeled this strategy a "critical junctions" approach (see Kalb 2011, 2015a; Kalb and Tak 2005), which they portray as a middle-road between the postmodern vision of radical historical contingency (i.e., local communities are free to choose their trajectories from the abundant menu of global offerings in economics, politics, and cultural images) and the rigidity of the core-periphery schema of Wallerstein's version of class theory (i.e., economic, political, and cultural programs travel in fixed packages that are imposed on local actors). Although scholars who subscribe to this agenda have come up with different ways of researching and conceptualizing the systemic constraints under which local actors operate, they all agree that local action is constrained by relations of power and dependency and that these relations exercise their effects through time (see social historians' interpretations of "path dependence"[4]) and space (see Harvey's [2005] concept of "uneven geographical development"), as well as "the interstitial relations between nominally distinct domains such as economics, politics, law, the family etc." (Kalb and Tak 2005: 3), which are nowadays overdetermined by the actions of modern nation-states and supranational entities such as the European Union. I draw on this body of literature to analyze the restructuring of the agricultural sector and to trace how this process galvanized frictions between two reemergent social categories in rural areas that suffered from the decline of the agricultural sector in the aftermath of Hungary's accession to the EU: the post-peasantry and the surplus population. I do this by reconstructing the history of economic, cultural, and social relationships in two localities (see below) after the "change of regime" of 1989. This allows me to establish a causal connection between large-scale political-economic transformations and the transformation of microrelationships in rural communities; to situate the emergence of "popular anti-Gypsyism" at a particular moment in time, and to link it to particular frictions between representatives of the post-peasantry and the surplus population.

On the other hand, I take inspiration from social movement scholars to explain how anti-Gypsyism evolved from an ideology that explained certain contradictions and problems emerging on the horizon of everyday lifeworlds into a political movement that decisively reshaped the priorities of decision-makers as well as the program of political parties. These scholars (see, for instance, della Porta and Diani 2006; McAdam, Tarrow, and Tilly 2001; Tilly 2008) have offered a robust critique of the structuralist and rational choice approaches that dominate political science and have exhorted researchers to see politics as an ensemble of contentious processes. McAdam, Tarrow, and Tilly (2001) have greatly advanced this agenda by highlighting how key processes such as political mobilization are driven by "relational mechanisms," which "alter connections among people, groups, and interpersonal networks" (26). Following their cue, I explain the emergence and impact of political anti-Gypsyism and its role in the rightward—anti-egalitarian and authoritarian—drift of Hungarian politics by focusing on a chain of causally interconnected contentious episodes that unfolded on the local, regional, and national level[5] and created space for the constitution of new political visions, identities, actors and alliances; the polarization of political groups; and a scale shift in political contention from local arenas to the national political arena. More specifically, I highlight a strategy of abstraction whereby regional mayors and right-wing intellectuals extricated local episodes from their contexts and reworked them—with the help of mainstream media outlets—into a generalized discourse that explained the failures of the left-liberal modernization project and simultaneously offered a model for redemptive action against "Gypsies." I then extend this analysis in time, focusing on the racist mobilization campaigns that were organized by the far-right Jobbik Party and its paramilitary allies. I argue that the main intention of far-right activists was to force "previously uncommitted or moderate actors [to gravitate] toward one, the other, or both extremes" (McAdam, Tarrow, and Tilly 2001: 322). Finally, I show how the dominant right-wing party took advantage of this process of polarization to derail left-liberal policy initiatives and disaggregate the ruling coalition.

What this amounts to is a move toward a relational and process-oriented framework that combines a focus on regional process and the social reproduction of "class" with an analysis of struggles within the political public sphere. The approach I develop can thus also be portrayed as an effort to renew one of the three dominant approaches (see Omi and Winant 2015) to racism:[6] the "class paradigm," which provides a useful correction to both of the depoliticized sociological interpretations forged within the "ethnicity"[7] and "nation-based"[8] approaches. This is especially important in light of the fact that the reemergence of political racism in Eastern Europe has often been interpreted in the context of historical legacies.[9] I follow class analysts in contesting approaches that portray anti-Gypsyism and/or the Jobbik Party as manifestations of lingering prejudices and authoritarian legacies by linking mobilizations around ethnicity and "race" to contemporary social antagonisms and interpreting "ethno/race-talk" as a proto-political speech-act that intervenes in the reproduction of social hierarchies and the distribution of symbolic and material rewards and opportunities (see Miles 1982; Miles and Brown 2003; Wimmer 1997, 2002). Like them, I also use "class" as a theoretical vista to highlight the intertwined development of racism and nationalism and to show how this creates favorable conditions for excluding non-national others from citizenship-based rights and resources (Balibar 1991). However, I seek to do this without reifying the notion of class.[10]

While I distance myself from authors who emphasize the centrality of prejudices and legacies, I do this without questioning the relevance of either sequentiality or historically sedimented cultural tropes for the analysis of political racism and far-right politics. These phenomena, I argue, are, however, best studied in relation to the formation of "class," "race," and politics in relational and embedded ways, rather than as instances of cultural overdetermination. In this I follow in the footsteps of anthropologists who have claimed partial autonomy for local actors by drawing on the by now well-established critique of culture as a shared and coherent system of meanings (see Kuper 1999) and by recasting the domain of culture as a cognitive and emotional field of interactions wherein actors engage in meaningful and materially consequential ways the impositions of (dis)order from above and without (see Kalb 1997; Sider 1986; Wolf 1990). I build on Eric Wolf's concept of the "engram"[11] and the example set by students of modern anti-Semitism[12] to construct a vantage point that allows for the identification of the specific circumstances under which ideas about "race" and ethnicity come to serve particular purposes and acquire specific meanings in particular places and moments in time. My key analytic strategy is to show how these ideas are embedded in comprehensive, temporally and spatially situated social relationships through the method of "retrospective micro-historical reconstruction" (Handelman 2005). Then I proceed to show how popular (everyday)

racism can be converted into political racism—instrumental struggles to transform the polity—by becoming disconnected from local
lifeworlds, embedded in ideological struggles, and by acquiring a
particular political thrust aimed to deal with the contradictions generated in everyday life. I contend that this approach answers racism
scholars' somewhat frustrated call to move beyond accounts that derive contemporary forms of racism from public political discourse(s)
and then use these as evidence to generalize about broader trends
within society (see Back and Solomos 2000: 24). It achieves this by
situating racism within particular settings before moving toward a
more general account of its wider significance.

The Project: Design and Methods

My initial idea was to frame the project as a comparative analysis of
the far-right's capacity to mobilize popular constituencies in two localities that I wanted to portray as exemplary of their wider regions:
Northeastern Hungary and Transdanubia (Western Hungary). Although in chapters 3, 4, 5, and 6 I will offer a detailed description of
both of my field sites, it may be useful to offer readers a brief overview already at this point.

Gyöngyöspata is a village[13] in the foothills of the Mátra Mountains,
approximately an hour's drive east of Budapest. Although it is situated in Northeastern Hungary—a region which has been particularly
badly hit by postsocialist deindustrialization and by the decline of
the agricultural sector after European accession—it does not figure
among the country's most deprived microregions. This is thanks to
the preservation of industrial capacities in and around the neighboring town of Gyöngyös where many locals work. Grape-growing and
wine-making have played a major role in the local economy since
the late Middle Ages, with output reaching its peak in the period of
export-oriented socialist viticulture. However, the economic transition of 1989 brought about the collapse of export markets, and the
sector underwent a severe crisis. The state-owned cooperative was
privatized and properties were handed back to the families who had
owned them before collectivization. Today, there are about ten active medium-sized family businesses in the sector and a higher number of self-sustaining agricultural producers. While the former are
relatively secure, the latter had to combine small-scale agricultural
production with low-paid industrial employment to sustain their
livelihoods. These post-peasants have forged narratives that make

sense of the failure to realize dreams of autonomy and upward mobility by laying the blame on local Roma, whose "thievishness" and
"scrounging" stand opposed to their "hard work." These families
welcomed the Hungarian Guard, a paramilitary organization whose
uniformed members conducted patrols in the village in March 2011
with a view to intimidating "Gypsy criminals." While this important
episode—which made national and international headlines—reas-
sured post-peasants and allowed Jobbik to take control of the village,
in the long run the local economy, which relies heavily on tourism,
suffered from the far-right intervention. This, along with other events,
allowed Fidesz to take back control of the village in 2014.

Devecser is a small town that lies on the Transdanubian Plain at the
foot of the Somló Hill, a former volcano that offers ideal conditions
for viticulture. Although wine made by peasants from the local Juhfark variety had for centuries attracted merchants from Budapest and
Vienna, the small size of the area suited for grape-growing prevented
viticulture from acquiring the role it played in the Mátra region.
Large-scale cereal and meat production, on the other hand, played
an important role in the local economy until the dismantlement of
the Blooming Cooperative after the change of regime. Thanks to the
entrepreneurial flair of the cooperative's former president and local
Roma entrepreneurs, Devecser managed to safeguard most of its
productive capacities *and* to convert itself into a regional market for
second-hand household items. The "cushioned transition" partially
explains why in Devecser the postcommunists managed to evade the
kind of wipe-out they had suffered in many other rural areas, including Gyöngyöspata. Although the Socialist Party performed poorly at
the parliamentary elections of 1990, it recovered lost ground in the
subsequent years, arriving in first place in 1994, 1998, and then in
2006. This, however, was followed by a decline in the party's fortunes,
partly as a result of the decline of both the local and national economy. In October 2010, the town suffered a major industrial disaster
that led to the departure of hundreds of families and strained social
relations in the locality. In 2012, Jobbik conducted its last high-profile
anti-Gypsy mobilization campaign in Devecser. While the effort to
polarize the local community along ethnoracial lines was successful
in Gyöngyöspata, it failed in Devecser, prompting Jobbik to revise its
political strategy and program.

Drawing inspiration from Kalb's (1976) comparison of working-
class reproduction and politics in the central Brabant and the Eind-
hoven regions and Tilly's (1976) comparison of two regions in Western France—the Val-Saumurois, which supported the revolution

of 1789, and the Mauges, which supported the counterrevolution known as the Vendée revolt—my initial idea was to rely on statistics published by the Central Statistical Office to highlight key sociogeographic differences between the two localities in order to explain the divergent outcomes of the two local mobilizations, which took place in March 2011 and August 2012 respectively.

Poring over the notes that I produced during the two successive periods of fieldwork (between March 2011 and March 2012 in Gyöngyöspata, and between January 2013 and December 2014 in Devecser), I reached the conclusion that the theoretical assumptions that underpinned this rudimentary comparative framework were flawed. The first lesson I drew was that the structuralism pervading my thinking hindered the explanation of the political outcomes I initially sought to explain. Jobbik did not "succeed" in Gyöngyöspata and "fail" in Devecser simply because of the ready-made co-presence of deprived "peasants" and marginalized "Gypsies" in the former and the lack of class-cum-ethnic polarization in the latter. The outcomes of the two mobilization campaigns had more directly to do with ordinary citizens' perception of their own predicament, of Roma, and of the intentions of local and national elites. A deeper engagement with my field notes also suggested that these perceptions emerged out of first-hand experiences with the negotiation of social relationships, events unfolding in nearby localities, and the initiatives of elites. This realization shifted my attention from structures to experiences and struggles and highlighted the importance of elucidating micro-macro linkages between the domains of "everyday life" and the "political public sphere."

Shifting my attention to classification struggles waged by actors operating on different scales led to another realization. It dawned on me that my initial comparative framework was weakened by an important "event" that influenced the outcome of the Devecser blitz campaign. Although the two cases of racist mobilization I initially became interested in were separated by only seventeen months, it was in this critical period that the new right-wing government introduced a number of key reforms with the intention of defusing tensions around the "Gypsy issue," which the far-right Jobbik Party had instrumentalized to mount a powerful offensive in the national political arena. Fieldwork in Devecser—as well as information trickling in from informants in Gyöngyöspata—highlighted the relevance of these reforms for understanding the outcomes of the Devecser campaign and the waning of the moral panic on "Gypsy criminality,"

which had been at the center of public attention and political contention in the 2006–2010 period.

The shift from structure to experience and to multi-scalar struggles that both shaped and captured experiences made me realize that
there were more interesting questions to be asked than why Jobbik
succeeded in Gyöngyöspata and failed in Devecser. It led me to re-
envision my project as an attempt to study different manifestations
of racism and trace its transposition from a set of sensibilities into an
ideology, then into a (political) movement, and then back into a looser
current. To achieve this, I combined the "extended study" (Burawoy
1998) of two local cases with an analysis of contentious episodes that
took place on the regional and national scale. This kind of analysis
started out from locales and relationships that a "critical junctions"
agenda reveals as sites and objects of contention. I then worked my
way "up and outward" by following the actors who made an effort
to symbolize locally significant episodes with a view to creating political effects. The advantage of this approach is that it allowed me
to simultaneously unearth the microfoundations of political racism,
capture how large-scale transformations pushed the political process
in a particular direction, and show how this shift led to the structural
transformation of party politics and the state.

The final draft of the manuscript reflects this shift from a syn-
chronic toward a diachronic perspective. I rely on my fieldwork in
Gyöngyöspata to explain the emergence of popular anti-Gypsyism
in the Northeast in the 2006–2010 period, and use material collected
in Devecser to show how a local community responded to racist mobilization after the dissipation of the moral panic on "Gypsy criminality." This differential treatment of my two cases ("exemplary" in
the case of Gyöngyöspata, "exploratory" in the case of Devecser) also
requires a different methodological toolkit: I rely primarily on "retrospective micro-historical reconstruction" (Handelman 2005) in the
former case and on "political ethnography"[14] (Baiocchi and Connor
2008) in the latter.

My cases are clearly not representative. They resemble each other
in that they both emerged as sites of "unsolicited interventions."
While the inhabitants of Gyöngyöspata saw themselves as either the
victims of the far-right or the media (which, in their view, had soiled
the town's reputation), the inhabitants of Devecser were united by the
experience of suffering an unprecedented industrial disaster. Hence,
far-right mobilization in Devecser did not leave such a powerful mark
on the local community of memory. While these two interventions

radically differed, they transformed the two localities into symbols of the "suffering countryside," making their inhabitants witnesses of this suffering. This, I contend, makes them prime sites for social scientific investigation, first because the experience of victimhood made the issues that interested me more amenable to scrutiny. The people I encountered in my field sites were uncommonly willing to let a researcher peek into their lives and talked openly about their views on ethnicity/"race" and politics—issues that are notoriously difficult to research in normal settings. Second, because the radical and unprecedented nature of these interventions caught local actors off guard, forcing them to come up with innovative responses. In the core of my analysis, I will take pains to highlight the innovative character of the strategies that far-right activists and politicians elaborated and show how this contributed to the success of their initiatives. Both fieldwork experiences felt very much like being part of social experiments. Although the volatility of the social situation rendered the construction of interpretations more difficult, I could not have asked for a better opportunity to study how people respond to the unfolding of the historical process in unexpected directions (such as when the police allowed paramilitaries to control Gyöngyöspata for two weeks or when the government allowed inhabitants of the Dankó settlement to move into the center of Devecser).

While the uncertainty of the social situation and certain developments made these localities nonrepresentative in the classic sociological sense, this does not detract from the value of my findings or undermine my effort to formulate wider claims. Based on a close reading of secondary sources and my previous work in rural environments, I claim that the agencies and strategies I encountered and the mechanisms and processes I unearthed were not unique to my two field sites but reflected wider trends (and were "representative" in this sense). My ethnographic locales, as advocates of the extended case method convincingly argued, can therefore be studied as simultaneously shaped by and shaping an external field of forces, which operates with its own principles of coordination and its own dynamics (Burawoy 1998; Handelman 2005; Kalb 1997, 2005). Finally, I would also like to highlight that the symbolic (and political) value attached to these rural localities was fortunate in that it attracted the attention of actors who operated on the national level. This facilitated the analysis of the ways in which the state is implicated in processes unfolding on the local level and the ways in which local events can be elevated into the national arena—linkages that occupy a central place in my research design.

The decision to pursue multisited fieldwork in two regions that greatly differ from each other made me reflect on the interaction between slow-moving structural forces, more dynamic cultural practices, and quick-paced political maneuvers throughout the study. This volume constitutes an attempt to combine these two—comparativist and diachronic—lines of inquiry. I do not claim to have fully succeeded in combining insights gleaned from comparison and those gleaned from the study of the political process within my research design. The limitations of this approach will become most clear in my analysis of the Devecser blitz campaign. Nevertheless, I hope to show that researchers should take into consideration the ways in which cultural and political agencies play out unevenly across salient territorial divides.

This book will therefore probe the relevance and potential of a multi-scalar relational approach to racism. I hope to show that a focus on contentious relations in everyday lifeworlds and the political public sphere (and their intended and unintended consequences) can help us

- explain the emergence of popular racist sensibilities in the Northeast in the 2006–2010 period;
- account for the transposition of popular anti-Gypsyism into political anti-Gypsyism and the latter's impact on the politics of electoral support in the 2006–2010 period;
- highlight the impact of political anti-Gypsyism on the politics of governmental power (in the 2010–2014 period); and
- identify some of the ways in which the latter reconfigured social antagonisms on the local level and shaped the politics of electoral support in the 2010–2014 period.

These four lines of inquiry will be pursued through divergent methods and rely on the following types of evidence.

I rely on ethnographic fieldwork conducted together with Margit Feischmidt in the village of Gyöngyöspata between March 2011 and March 2012 to pursue the first line of inquiry. The argument I present relies on semi-structured interviews (conducted with members of the local elite), oral history interviews (conducted with "commoners"), and the analysis of archival resources and field notes taken during the eighteen field visits (that lasted between two and twelve days) in the above-mentioned period. Building on secondary sources and statistical analysis, I will seek to present this locality as an "exemplary" case that allows us to shed light on wider regional trends on the country's northeastern periphery.

I use semistructured interviews (conducted with members of the local elite) in Gyöngyöspata, secondary sources focusing on the representation of Roma and "ethnic conflicts" in the 2006–2010 period, and archival resources (news items published in the main online news portals in the same period) to analyze the politicization of popular racism.

I conduct a critical analysis of the transcripts of the speeches of Prime Minister Viktor Orbán and of the secondary literature dealing with the second Orbán government's (2010–2014) social policy reforms to highlight the impact of political racism on the politics of governmental power pursued by the New Right.

I rely on ethnographic fieldwork conducted in Devecser between January 2013 and December 2014 (fifteen field visits that lasted between two and twenty-two days), as well as evidence provided by key informants in Gyöngyöspata, to assess the impact of the new politics of governmental power on local social and political struggle (and the role that ideas about ethnicity/"race" played within these). I treat Devecser more as an "exploratory" case to analyze the failure of the last important racist mobilization campaign that Jobbik organized in August 2012. In other words, while I use my research in Gyöngyöspata to study the phase of emergence and diffusion of what I see as a racist "mobilization cycle" (2006–2012), my work in Devecser will serve to explore the consummation of that cycle.

The Structure of the Book

The role I attribute to sequentiality and my emphasis on racialization/ethnicization necessitate an effort of historical contextualization. In the first chapter I will therefore focus on the secondary literature to show how the "Gypsy/Magyar" dichotomy emerged as the dominant framework for signifying tensions and rivalries between people who occupy different positions in social space, are bound by particular social relationships, and have historically entertained different types of relations with the nation-state. I will focus my sights on the 1980s and 1990s, which I consider of key importance. I emphasize economic and political processes ("de-peasantization," welfare reform, decentralization) that explain the divergence of trajectories taken by the post-peasantry and the surplus population, and the rise of antagonisms between these emergent groups; important changes in social relationships after regime change; the asymmetric character of the process of identity and group-formation ("racialization"); and the influence of both the liberal state ("codification") and local hegemonies on this process. This historic analysis allows me to elucidate how regime change influenced the self-understandings, emotional economy, cultural outlooks, and practices of ordinary citizens who—liberated from the yoke of official discourses that categorized them as belonging to a putatively unitary working class—found themselves both inwardly compelled and outwardly incentivized to highlight their differences and formulate their particular claims in the idiom of "race"/ethnicity.

In chapter 2, I reconstruct the process whereby these emergent groups came into friction in the course of the last decade in connection to broader economic and political processes of "neoliberalization" and "Europeanization." I do this through a retrospective microhistory of Gyöngyöspata, where popular anti-Gypsyism emerged relatively early. This analysis highlights the double crisis of social reproduction as a key source of frictions. The latter emerged in the domain of culture and eroded the regime of "hegemonic Hungarianness" from "below," thereby encouraging the search for alternatives. In a second move, I show that this assimilationist regime was—metaphorically speaking—also eroded from "above." The key claim is that post-peasants' growing intolerance of the surplus population was enhanced by local authorities' unwillingness to clamp down on petty forms of criminality and the left-liberal government's effort to emancipate Roma (qua ethnic group) under the banner of its "integration politics." The crux of the argument is that abandonment in relation to elites deepens fears of social breakdown and fosters the appetite to tame "unruly" social elements. Through an effort of extension I will argue that out of these two conditions of possibility of the emergence of popular racist sensibilities—double crisis and abandonment—the first was absent outside zones of deprivation, and this offers a partial explanation for the emergence of popular anti-Gypsyism in the Northeast.

In chapter 3, I highlight the actors and strategies that played a key role in upward scale shift: the transposition of local ethnic frictions (microhistories) into a nationwide movement to contain the "Gypsy menace" (macrohistory) in the 2006–2010 period. I argue that two relational strategies—"abstraction" and "polarization"—played a key role in the emergence of political racism: the public formulation of demands to clamp down on Roma and inscribe the principle of ethnic preference into law and policy. These strategies were elaborated and implemented by a heterogeneous set of politically oriented actors who shared an interest in increasing the visibility of the "Gypsy issue" in the political public sphere. Together, their actions led to the emergence of a moral panic on "Gypsy criminality" in the run-up to the European and national parliamentary elections of 2009 and 2010.

In chapter 4, I analyze the impact of the moral panic on the "politics of governmental power" and argue that it played a key role in the liberal state's transformation in an authoritarian direction under the new Fidesz government in the 2010–2014 period. I show that the leader of the main right-wing opposition party sought to incorporate elements of the new racist common sense into his own hegemonic project by espousing an anti-egalitarian vision of the "work-based society" that had been promoted by mayors in the Northeast. Once in government, the Fidesz Party went on to implement this vision by separating the "Normative State" (which holds jurisdiction over "homogenous society") from the "Prerogative State" (which is provided special means to discipline "heterogeneous groups") under the banner of the System of National Cooperation (henceforth SNC).[15] In this chapter I also address one of the prevalent shortcomings of studies dealing with political racism by seeking to account for "downward scale shift." Taking inspiration from the debate around "authoritarian populism," I argue that the dualization of state functions decreased both the possibility of and demand for racist mobilization and thus helped the ruling party retain its hold over a radicalized political center.

In chapter 5, I move back from the national to the local level to highlight differences in the reconstruction of social collectivities in a region where the double crisis was evaded. In an effort to build my material into a contrastive case, I argue that an organic racist countermovement failed to emerge in the critical 2006–2010 period in an environment where access to Western commodity and labor markets allowed some "Gypsies" and "Magyars" to shield themselves from the negative impacts of economic restructuring in the period of European accession. My material also highlights mainstream groups' positive reaction to the local mayor's effort to mitigate feelings of abandonment through a combination of compensatory and repressive measures that followed the logic of anti-egalitarian populism and relied on the dualization of state functions after 2010. These two factors—the absence of the double crisis and the new politics of governmental power—helped local actors prevent Jobbik from embedding its racist-extremist agenda in Transdanubia.

In chapter 6, I turn to political ethnography to provide a window onto the consummation of the racist mobilization cycle in the 2012–

2014 period. Relying on material collected in Devecser, I show how the local Fidesz chapter progressively lost its credibility in the eyes of local citizens and how Jobbik took advantage of this to mount a challenge with the help of a revised political strategy. I identify two key conditions of possibility for Jobbik's transformation into an ultra-nationalist party: the delegitimation of Fidesz and the collapse of left-wing political-economic networks on the local level. I then go on to highlight the ideological, programmatic, and stylistic innovations that allowed Jobbik to project the image of the "true nationalist force" and successfully woe orphaned left-wing and disillusioned right-wing constituencies. I focus more particularly on ideological innovation by highlighting the way in which a supremacist form of redemption offered an alternative to "Gypsy-talk" in a relatively deprived environment where Roma could not be straightforwardly blamed for the plight of the "hard-working majority." It appears that while "Gypsy-talk" expresses discontentment with the unjust redistribution of material and symbolic rewards in a liberal polity, "Trianon-talk" can be used to highlight the ways in which the new right-wing elite ravages the local (and, by extension, national) community. This allowed Jobbik to unite disaffected voters of all colors and stripes in a former left-wing bastion. The party then successfully replicated this strategy in another Transdanubian town as well as other localities. Jobbik, however, has so far failed to mount a serious challenge to the ruling Fidesz Party in the national political arena. This key development falls outside the scope of my analysis, but I will nevertheless attempt to address it in the book's epilogue.

Notes

1. Bustikova (2014) develops a similar line of reasoning by noting that support for radical right-wing parties originates in opposition to policy changes in the status quo of ethnic relations. My analysis differs from hers in that I situate "abandonment" on the level of everyday life and argue that it did not foster the rise of the radical right on its own.
2. Friedländer (1997) maintained that Nazi anti-Semitism was distinctive for being "redemptive anti-semitism," namely a form of anti-Semitism that could explain all in the world and offer a form of redemption for the anti-Semitic. Writing about Bulgaria, Efremova (2012) recently argued that redemption is also a key feature of contemporary anti-Gypsyism in this country.
3. The concept was developed by Habermas (1974: 49): "We speak of the political public sphere in contrast, for instance, to the literary one, when public discussion deals with objects connected to the activity of the state. Although state authority is so to speak

the executor of the political public sphere, it is not a part of it. To be sure, state authority is usually considered 'public' authority, but it derives its task of caring for the well-being of all citizens primarily from this aspect of the public sphere. Only when the exercise of political control is effectively subordinated to the democratic demand that information be accessible to the public, does the political public sphere win an institutionalized influence over the government through the instrument of law-making bodies." In what follows I will rely on Habermas's loose definition, which allows for the joint treatment of formal and informal discussions related to the state and the public good.

4. For a useful discussion of a diverse set of interpretations, see Mahoney and Schensul 2006.

5. Berezin (2009) studies right-wing populism in France and Italy through contingent events that pushed the political process in a certain direction. While my analysis also takes account of events that "emotionally engaged the national collectivity" (ibid., 11), I primarily focus on local and regional episodes to account for the transposition of "everyday racism" into "political racism" (on which more below).

6. I follow Robert Miles, who defined racism as combining (1) the signification of some biological and/or somatic characteristics as the criterion by which populations are identified (and the attendant representation of these populations as having a natural, unchanging origin and status, and therefore as being inherently different from others); and (2) the attribution of one or more of the groups so identified with additional (negatively evaluated) characteristics and/or their representation as inducing negative consequences for (an)other group(s). See Miles and Brown 2003: 103–104.

7. Omi and Winant (2015: 22) argue that in "ethnicity-based approaches, the race-concept is . . . reduced to something like a preference, something variable and chosen, in the way one's religion or language is chosen." Racism, too, is seen as a matter of attitudes and beliefs, involving such issues as prejudice, beliefs about others, and individual practices. Such "culturology" (see Wolf 1999: 61) obfuscates the "ocular" and ascribed character of "race," divorcing its analysis from questions of power and inequality. By lodging "race" and racism in the individual psyche, it also divorces explanations of identity and identification from social interaction and practice. Despite these shortcomings, the approach remains influential in sociology and has informed studies of racism and right-wing politics in Hungary, so much so that one of the dominant explanations that has been proposed for the rise of radical right-wing politics in Hungary is an increase in the level of ethnic prejudice in society (see Csepeli 2012; Krekó, Juhász, and Molnár 2011).

8. The nation-based paradigm originates in seizures of territory by modern empires. Nation-based theories treat race as a manifestation of the presumptively deeper concept of the nation, and project "internal colonial" relations of domination and resistance forward into the present (see Omi and Winant 2015: 12). While such an approach may be useful for analyzing the predicament of racialized minorities in territories once dominated by "settler colonialism," it is problematic for analyzing constructions of "race" and ethnicity in societies that lack a history of racial despotism and where the state has actively promoted the assimilation of ethnic (i.e., non-racialized) minorities. In such environments, racism and related phenomena—such as discrimination and ethnic violence—cannot be straightforwardly treated as the expressions of durable ethnic supremacy. While supremacist tropes may in fact be present in society, they may—as I will indeed show—also serve as rivals to racism.

9. See the *Communist and Post-Communist Studies* journal's special issue on "Legacies and the Radical Right in Post-1989 Central and Eastern Europe" (vol. 42, no. 4, December

2009). Guest editor Michael Minkenberg (2009: 450) formulated the claim that "in contrast to its Western European counterpart, whether it is catching up or not, the Central and Eastern European radical right is particularly conditioned by the force of history ... [T]he histories of state socialism and of pre-socialist (non-democratic) experiences can be seen as major forces in shaping both the contents and the opportunities of the radical right in these new or emerging democracies."

10. While linking ethnoracial identity and identification to the most material human question ("How do we sustain and reproduce ourselves practically?") is welcome, class analysis has been hindered by structural Marxist influences. This is true for political scientists who attempted to find a "sustainable class aspect" in far-right voting behavior in Eastern Europe (see Minkenberg and Pytlas 2013) and for sociologists who have sought to compare the positions of "minorities" and "natives" in different economic spheres: in markets, in systems of distribution, and in the production process.

11. Wolf (1969) developed the concept to contrast two approaches to culture: a "culture-as-template" approach, which some social historians (e.g., Sewell 2005) have relied on to account for self-reproducing historical sequences; and his preferred approach, which relativizes the explanatory power of "moments of origin" and "cultural foundations" and looks instead at how "foundational moments are ... manipulated by elites and contenders through time" (Kalb and Tak 2005: 11). Rebel deployed Wolf's concept in his investigation of Holocaust-forms in Austria to argue that the historical reproduction of "inheritance and dispossession figures" in everyday lifeworlds pointed toward organized forms of terminal exclusion and organized disposal (see Rebel 2010: 115). I will draw on his conceptualization of "engrams" as articulate and institutionalized memories "stored" within a "community of memory" to argue that representatives of the post-peasantry relied on "old" ideas about "Gypsyness" (including the use of exclusionary practices) to elaborate a novel redemptive discourse that spoke to the experiences and aspirations of wide segments of rural society and successfully dislodged an old assimilationist discourse, which constituted the ideological bedrock of local hegemonies (see chapter 1).

12. An approach pioneered by "realist strain theorists"—which emerged out of a polemic involving German scholars who sought to make sense of the obstinacy of anti-Jewish sensibilities in European publics—has gone some way in outlining the contours of an approach to racism that avoids the twin traps of culturalism and structuralism. Led by historians and sociologists, this group of scholars contested the claim that anti-Semitic sentiment was rooted in the cultural memory of the historic antagonism that pitted the Christian against the Jewish faith (see Langmuir 1990; Smith 1996) based on the observation that anti-Semitism had historically waxed and waned and had also exhibited a remarkable geographic variability. These scholars, without contesting the power of cultural stereotypes, highlighted the salience of tensions, conflicts, and rivalry between "Jews" and "natives"; argued that in a period of deep social crisis, anti-Semitism could be forged into an ideology that explained the failures of the prevalent sociopolitical system; and offered a model for redemptive social action (see Kovács 1999; Rürup 1987; Volkov 1978; Wistrich 1990). The main advantage of this approach, as I see it, is that it seeks to historically contextualize the emergence of modern anti-Semitism by linking it to antagonisms generated by capitalist transformations while also taking pains to show how popular representations were combined with elements of scientific racism to forge a doctrine that promised to resolve these antagonisms through political action.

13. In 2013, Gyöngyöspata was officially recognized as a town, but in what follows I will continue to refer to it as a village.

14. The kind of political ethnography I conducted combined two of the three approaches identified by Baiocchi and Connor (2008: 140): the "ethnography of political actors and institutions" and the "lived experience of the political."
15. The concepts of the "Normative State" and the "Prerogative State" are derived from Fraenkel (1969).

– Chapter 1 –

HISTORIC CONTEXTUALIZATION
"Gypsies," "Magyars," and the State

In this chapter, I heed Charles Tilly's (2008: 420) argument that "all political processes occur in history and therefore call for knowledge of their historical contexts." I highlight key elements of the historical process wherein ideas about race/ethnicity reemerged in Hungary after regime change. This historical contextualization focuses on one question: how to account for the figure of "the Gypsy" taking center stage in public life from the middle of the last decade. Some would say that this question is misplaced, given that Roma have been persistently subjected to persecution and discrimination over the centuries. I beg to differ. A recent effort to write a relational history of Romani groups in Hungary highlighted key differences in relation to the social relevance of ethnicity in different historical periods. This underscores the need to separate periods of "de-ethnicization" and "re-ethnicization" and to offer explanations for these historical dynamics. In what follows, I focus on two periods—late socialism (1961–1989) and liberal democracy (1990–2010)—in order to highlight economic and political forces that created space and incentives for the reconstruction of communal relations along ethnic lines. This contextualization will show that state-sponsored integration efforts generated racist sensibilities and that these were mitigated through informal mechanisms of segregation and control that relied on a discursive regime—which I propose to call "hegemonic Hungarian-ness"—which placed a taboo on the evocation of ethnicity in public discourse. I argue that the decentralization of the state after regime change allowed for the survival of these local hegemonies. In the final part of the chapter, I rely on secondary sources to highlight processes that may have plausibly eroded these hegemonies from the beginning of the new millennium. The first was the de-peasantization of the countryside (in connection to European enlargement) and the concomitant crisis of social reproduction of two reemergent social groups: the "post-peasantry" and the surplus population. These secondary sources also show that the dualization of the welfare state (which I discuss below) played a key role in the emergence of this social divide—in both fact and fiction—and that relations between the two groups were most acute in regions where the "post-peasantry" came to depend on institutionalized forms of solidarity. It will be the task of the next two empirical chapters to show how these groups came into friction and how this led to the "naming and blaming" of "Gypsies."

Roma in History: In Defense of a Relational Realist Approach

In Hungary, where the discipline of "ethnology" has largely failed to reflect on its implication in the Orientalization of the other (see Prónai 2008), the task of analyzing the production of ethnic difference in history was taken up by a few sociologists and historians. Csaba Dupcsik, author of a monograph titled *The History of Gypsies in Hungary* (2009), used secondary sources to reconstruct the historically variable meanings that have been attributed to "Gypsyness" (a shorthand whereby he refers to the dominant representation of people categorized by others as "Gypsy" or, more recently, as "Roma") and the transformation of Romani forms of life in the twentieth century. Dupcsik's key point is that the policies of the nation-state have had an overdetermining influence on the cultural strategies of Roma and that those labeled "Roma" have had even less power over their representation in public life. Dupcsik blames nationalist elites—and the social scientists who supported their projects—for both participating in and fueling the stigmatization of the Romani minority.[1] In a less direct form, he also accuses elites of enforcing an assimilationist politics that consistently hindered the project of Romani nation-building, thereby robbing Roma of the power to claim cultural and political rights based on an imagined collective identity. Although his monograph suffers from a lack of theorization and conceptual clarity, Dupcsik's account is valuable in one important respect. By drawing a link between the cultural strategies pursued by Roma and the intentionality of the groups controlling the state, he indirectly questions the key claim of culturalist scholars who have exoticized Roma by investing them with the ability to transcend the constraints imposed by mainstream groups. While, as Michael Stewart (2002, 2013) argued, there clearly are Romani groups who have been successful in carving out spaces for economic and cultural autonomy, these groups represent a fraction of the people who are categorized as "Roma." Moreover, even Vlach Romani entrepreneurs, who have been the most successful in maintaining cultural distance and autonomy, are limited by constraints imposed by mainstream groups. "We play the same games as other Roma," one of my Vlach Romani informants told me; "the only difference is that we have been dealt a better hand." This, I claim, was a particularly insightful way of saying that although they have different aspirations and strategies, traditional Roma must also take part in the struggle for symbolic recognition and material rewards controlled by non-Romani actors.

The implication is that we must pay attention to the ways in which Romani culture is objectified and contested in public life. Dupcsik's (2009) monograph singles out one terrain of symbolic struggle. Relying on Foucault's insistence on studying the nexus between knowledge and power, he asserts that ruling elites have—with the help of nationalist sciences—offered a particular type of mirror for Roma to look at themselves in. This mirror reveals the other through the lens of adaptability. It portrays those who deviate from "homogeneous society" (Bataille 1993) as backward and potentially dangerous. Dupcsik (2009: 20–26) stresses the ideological-political function of this "deviancy-oriented perspective," which is most often manifested in a specific speech-act: the act of "naming the Gypsy" (ethnic categorization). He exhorts us to recognize that this speech-act serves an ideological function: to naturalize socially produced inequalities and hierarchies and thereby obfuscate the forces, mechanisms and agencies that are responsible for their reproduction. Dupcsik highlights the role of the state, more precisely its penal and scientific apparatuses, in the reproduction of ethnoracial boundaries and hierarchies. This is rendered apparent by the book's cover photograph (taken in 1909), which depicts a Vlach Romani man and his two children standing in front of their tent in the company of two gendarmes and a female representative of a charitable organization. In the main text, he cites one of the few representatives of "critical ethnology," who originally published the photograph with the aim of highlighting "the alliance between the state's punitive apparatus, charitable bourgeois organizations and science" (Szuhay 1998: 95, translation mine). Although Dupcsik recognizes the historically contingent nature of this alliance as well the historically variable strategies of the nation-state, his text nonetheless gives the impression that the history of the interethnic relationship is similar to a *perpetuum mobile*: a musical piece that is intended to be repeated over and over again without modification.

Dupcsik is not alone in seeing Romani history as a self-perpetuating cycle of exclusion. Pál Nagy, one of the few historians who has made an effort to integrate this "people without history" into Hungarian history, claims that most modern accounts focusing on Roma fit into a moral-cum-heuristic approach he labels the "affliction and persecution paradigm" (Nagy 2007). On this view, "the dominant principle that guides Romani history is [the external environment's] contempt towards Gypsies. . . . Romani history is the history of resistance to and escape from . . . the constraints imposed by a hostile environment" (Nagy 2007: 1–2, translation mine). Considering the many instances of state-induced oppression and violence that have targeted Roma in the twentieth century, it is easy to see why researchers sympathetic to the plight of a stigmatized minority may be prone to representing Romani history as a history of persecution encouraged or organized by the state—that is, to reduce it to the history of the "Gypsy question" (see Binder 2009).

This approach, much like analytic efforts that define the modern state as a "racial state" (Goldberg 2002), fails to situate exclusion, persecution, and violence within the larger historical process based on the conviction that the (national or colonial) state has an invariable interest in reproducing ethnoracial privilege and hierarchy. Nagy has convincingly shown such an approach to be untenable for the Hungarian case. In an overview of the history of Roma in Hungary, he highlights two historical periods wherein a process of "acculturation"—evidenced by the mixed marriages, the spread of residential cohabitation, and the rise of a shared material culture—was underway, as a result of which Roma were provided the opportunity to pass to the other side of an increasingly blurred and weakly policed ethnic divide. He stresses that in both cases—the period of enlightened absolutism (spanning the second half of the eighteenth century) and late socialism (1961–1989)—the central state actively sought to undermine the previously entrenched ethnic hierarchy through economic and social policies as well as the promotion of forms of representation that emphasized the "social dimension" of Gypsyness:

> Some [historical] sources define "Gypsyness" in ethnic terms with reference to the Latin terms gens or natio . . . . Other sources emphasize the social dimension of "Gypsyness" with reference to the Latin terms conditio or professio. The equivalent for this in Hungarian sources is the word *"állapottya"*

(referring to social situation or occupation). Professio can thus be taken to mean: craft, occupation or means of subsistence . . . . In the 18th century it is this latter definition that became dominant. (Nagy 2007: 6–7, translation mine)

The elites controlling the central state pursued similar goals in the two mentioned periods: they sought to convert Roma into wage-earning and tax-paying laborers and to promote their social inclusion by renaming them "new Hungarians." Nagy (2007: 6, 10) suggests that concerted state action responded in both cases to powerful social and economic dislocations that generated antagonisms between Roma and other groups. In the eighteenth century, frictions were mainly caused by the effort of non-Romani members of guilds (which had been resurrected after the Turkish occupation) to exclude Romani blacksmiths and metalworkers (by far the most popular Romani professions) from the labor market. In the postwar period, it was the rise of petty criminality as a result of the collapse of Romani livelihoods (itself connected to declining demand for traditional products and services and stringent constraints on petty trade) that necessitated state intervention. This insight leads Nagy to offer an alternative to the "affliction and persecution paradigm." This alternative, which he labels the "co-existence paradigm," calls on researchers to analyze the impact of large-scale economic and political forces on the inter-ethnic relationship (Nagy 2007: 2). Instances of discrimination and persecution should, he argues, be seen as responses to large-scale crises, which are most likely to manifest themselves in (ethnic) competition for economic opportunities and symbolic rewards. Although Nagy does not attempt to situate his approach in the wider body of literature on ethnicity, his take clearly echoes realist approaches to the study of ethnicity, which have identified large-scale historical processes and power differences within societies as determinants of ethnicity.[2]

The main strength of Nagy's (2007) approach is that it historicizes the study of ethnoracial exclusion and decenters it by recasting the state as just one—albeit powerful—actor involved in a complex process of negotiation and struggle that takes place on a number of scales (local, regional, national, and, recently, European) that are connected through the agencies of social actors who have a stake in ethnic categorization. This approach is better equipped to deal with historic shifts than Dupcsik's state-centered approach. It is also more encompassing than anthropological and microsociological studies of Roma, which have failed to question the ways in which the state may influence classification struggles and also become involved in the reproduction of complex forms of ethnicized (or racialized) exclusion. This is not to say that Nagy's approach—inspired, I believe, by Weber—is free of problems or limitations. In what follows, I will argue that his narrow focus on the ethnic division of labor needs to be expanded in order to gauge the impact of large-scale historical transformations on social relationships in particular sociogeographic settings. His analysis, moreover, remains wedded to a unitary conception of the state, which, for instance, precludes the possibility that local power-holders may not always follow codified protocols but at times follow alternative agendas. Nagy, moreover, fails to take note of the fact that the state may itself become the object of social struggles, as when emancipatory movements push for antidiscrimination, desegregation, and cultural emancipation, or when nativist movements seek to overturn such policies. His framework, in other words, lacks a focus on process and, more particularly, struggle. The list of shortcomings could be continued. Nevertheless, the approach he outlines offers the advantage of foregrounding large-scale socioeconomic processes. This shift in perspective forces us to denaturalize the emergence of racism at a particular moment in time and to ask which kinds of structurally generated antagonisms it may respond to.

The task of rewriting the history of Romani groups in Hungary in the context of a realist relational theoretical framework obviously transcends the scope of this book. Therefore, I will limit myself to a limited number of remarks on the historical periods that are directly relevant for the study of the contemporary racist countermovement: the state socialist (1947–1989) and the liberal democratic (1989–2010) periods.

The Late Socialist Era: Proletarianization and De-ethnicization

I begin by noting that the capitalist mode of production exercised a powerful impact on the interethnic relationship from the end of the nineteenth century. Growing industrial output, and the development of light industry in particular, led to a steady decline in demand for traditional Romani products (e.g., tools and household appliances made of metal and wood). This trend hit rural Romani communities—who were directly dependent on peasant households for their subsistence—hardest. While Roma living in cities could rely on persistent demand for "Gypsy music"[3] or take up industrial work, such options were not readily available in the predominantly agricultural countryside. Although we know surprisingly little about the history of Gadjo/Gypsy relations in rural areas—where the majority of those categorized as "Gypsy" lived—available studies suggest that a crisis of social reproduction was unfolding in many rural arenas and that this was worsened by the physical relegation of "Gypsies" to the margins of local communities (see Ladányi and Szelényi 2006: ch. 2). Capitalism, in other words, functioned as an invisible but nonetheless powerful "difference-making machine." While encouraging economic integration and cultural assimilation in industrializing cities, it fostered the socioeconomic exclusion of the surplus population and its cultural differentiation from peasants in rural areas. It was also in this period that a discourse that portrayed "the Gypsy" as inferior emerged for the first time. Dupcsik rightly emphasizes the relevance of the "Dános case" (1907), which made the headlines of the country's main newspapers. The murder of the owner of a roadside inn by a group of "Gypsies" led to calls for the severe punishment of perpetrators. Although a link between Gypsyness and criminality had already been established in an earlier period (Binder 2010), the case played a pivotal role in the emergence of a discourse that condemned Roma collectively and called for a radical solution to what journalists began referring to as "the Gypsy question," as in this example from the *Budapest Gazette* of 20 May 1908:

> Based on the lessons of the case we call for putting an end to truculence and for a radical solution to the Gypsy question. . . . What sympathizers say is not true; these are not humans or our fellows. The Gypsies from Dános— like their *race*—have been stalled in their development and now constitute an intermediary *race* between man and animal. They are, however, not like monkeys—who are gentle and mild in comparison—but more like wolves or jackals in that they are vicious, ferocious, thievish and murderous. (Pomogyi 1995: 36–37, translation and emphasis mine)

This novel representation of Roma within a racialized exclusionary discursive framework drew inspiration from the transnational discourse of "scientific racism" (see Miles 1982). This is an important development. Omi and Winant (2015: 13) have rightly noted that the race concept carries a crucial corporeal dimension: race is "ocular in an irreducible way. Human bodies are visually read, understood, and narrated by means of symbolic meanings and associations." While the typologization of Roma clearly differed from that of black people—commonly called "Blacks"—in many regards, it was also dominated by an insistence on biological inferiority and on genetically coded proneness toward social aggression and criminality. The racialization of Gypsyness was significant in that it counterbalanced the previously hegemonic image of the "noble savage," which had been promoted by ethnologists who wanted to preserve traditions they saw as being on the verge of disappearance.[4]

Although the practical effects of racialization are still not well understood, the new topos of the "Gypsy criminal" clearly exercised an impact on the policy domain, especially penal policy.[5] The nexus between racial discourse and policy became more apparent in the 1930s, when "race experts" inspired by Nazi ideology established a link between the "Jewish question" and the "Gypsy question." While the most drastic measures proposed by these experts—such as the deportation of "vagrant Gypsies" to concentration camps—only began to be implemented at the end of the Second World War, the previous decade saw the progressive curtailing of Romani citizens' social and economic rights by increasingly authoritarian state authorities. Although the Hungarian state did not invest the same kind of effort into the codification of their exclusion from the political community as it did in the case of Jews, in practice it also treated Roma as second-class citizens.[6] The interwar period ended with the deportation of thousands to concentration camps and a small number of spontaneously executed mass murders by local gendarmes.[7]

The foundation of the people's democracy removed the threat to "bare life" that the authoritarian right-wing state posed to the Romani population. The new constitution, adopted in 1949, officially forbade all forms of "discrimination of citizens based on gender, faith or nationality" (section 49. §2, translation mine) and granted all nationalities the "possibility to receive education in their native tongue and to develop their national culture" (section 49. §3, translation mine). However, based on the observation that the Roma had no written language or territory, the Communist state denied them the right to form their own cultural associations.[8]

The legal integration of Roma was not paralleled by measures that could have allowed them to exercise the new economic and social rights they were awarded on paper. To the contrary, strict regulations on itinerant trade and service provision prevented them from reaping income on the commodity and services markets, pushing an even larger number of communities into the poverty trap that had emerged in the period of capitalist expansion. The situation was probably even worse than before because the Communist elite's effort to extract income from the peasantry (with a view to rebuilding a war-torn country and improving the life conditions of the industrial proletariat) had serious repercussions for the vast majority of peasant "patrons" on whom Roma "clients" depended. While petty criminality remained a source of tensions, the first decade of state socialism saw the spread of state-administered "disinfection campaigns" that targeted areas where epidemics such as typhus and cholera had broken out. These campaigns—which lasted until the 1970s—exercised a long-lasting impact on the Romani psyche[9] and entrenched the adjectives "lousy," "stinky," and "dirty" as key markers of Gypsyness in public discourse.

The campaigns carried out by doctors and policemen are indicative of the socialist state's initial response to the "Gypsy question." This response was centered on the punitive apparatus that had been developed in the interwar period to deal with the problem of so-called vagrancy. Historian Barna Purcsi recently revealed that the Interior Ministry drew up plans as early as 1952—following the example set by the Soviet Union—to sedentarize and educate approximately forty thousand vagrant Roma based on the claim that "in our people's democracy it is not permissible to allow vagrant Gypsies who are capable of working to continue living forlorn based on loose moral standards or to threaten the property and health of our working people" (cited by Purcsi 2001, translation mine). Equally noteworthy was the ministry's decision (dated 17 June 1955) to provide "vagrant" and "work-shy" individuals with temporary black identity cards. These black identity cards remained in use until 1961, when they were exchanged with permanent cards identical to the ones that had been issued to "normal" citizens following the decision of the Council of Ministers on 16 October 1953.[10]

The removal of black identity cards was only the first step toward the racial destigmatization of citizens of Romani descent. In 1961, the Political Committee adopted a decree titled *Tasks in relation to improving the circumstances of the Gypsy population*. The document officially recognized the persistence of prejudice (citing "a superstitious aversion to Gypsies" and the generalized belief that most Roma are criminals) and outlined the fundamental principles of policy, declaring that measures "directed at the Gypsy population shall start from the principle that—despite certain ethnological characteristics—it does not constitute a nationality" (*Tasks* II/1, translation mine). The decree, in essence, amounted to an "assimilationist offer" built on the foundational promise of material benefits and the prospect of gradual integration into homogenous society. In exchange, the state required Roma to leave their "backward" traditions, language, and communities in order to embrace the values and way of life of the (ethnic) majority. This assimilationist offer was underpinned and policed by a discursive regime—which I propose to call "hegemonic

Hungarianness"—that placed a taboo on the evocation of Romani ethnicity in public discourse. While the regime denied Roma cultural rights, it also placed a taboo on ethnic stigmatization. That, at least, was the aim of the Communist leadership. In reality, certain Romani groups—especially Vlach Gypsies and Beash—managed to maintain ethnic forms of self-identification through the performance of cultural practices in the private realm (see Stewart 1997). At the same time, as I explain below, practices of ethnic discrimination were transposed into more subtle informal strategies that allowed the ethnic majority to maintain its distance and safeguard certain privileges.

A fair assessment of the assimilationist integration policy must start with the recognition of the socialist state's much boasted success in the domain that touched on the foundation of its ideology: the eradication of unemployment. Responding to the labor scarcity that characterized the socialist economy, the state managed to put Romani men to work in a record amount of time by mobilizing them in a small number of economic sectors: construction and road building, mining and metallurgy. By 1971, the ratio of economically active Romani men had reached the ratio of non-Roma. The Communist state experienced more difficulties in mobilizing Romani women, but this was less important because of the official emphasis on women's procreative role.

Internal party documents show that economists were concerned with Romani "work morale," which was apparently below average. Even these critical voices conceded, however, that integration through work had made a significant positive impact on the "culture" of the new Magyars. Dissident intellectuals also recognized the achievements of the party state in the domain of employment. Reflecting on the difference between poverty in the 1930s and 1970s, antipoverty activist Ottília Solt (1998: 243) highlighted the importance of regular income for Romani families, remarking, "Even the poor get to eat more than once a day in most days of the month. . . . Almost all poor people have a change of decent clothing and a pair of shoes" (translation mine).

The other measures whereby the state sought to promote social integration were far less successful. The push to eradicate rural settlements where the majority of Roma lived in segregated, crowded, and unhealthy conditions led to the building of approximately twenty-three thousand new homes (Domokos 2010: 32). According to the estimation of one study, the effort improved the housing conditions of one-third to one-half of Roma living in Hungary between 1965 and 1985 (Lengyel 2006: 80). However, the comprehensive "Gypsy survey" conducted by sociologist István Kemény and his colleagues found that *all* resettlement projects they surveyed had resulted in the creation of a new settlement (Kemény 1976: 27). In other words, "settlement liquidation projects" only went as far as demolishing huts and erecting slightly better buildings in their place, instead of offering Roma the opportunity to integrate into mainstream society.

The situation was no rosier in the domain of education. Although the socialist regime had successfully integrated the youngest generation of Roma into the school system, it failed to provide it with the knowledge and skills needed to enter high school or acquire a vocation. In 1971, for instance, only 0.5 percent of Roma age fifteen or up held a high school degree (while 30 percent of the non-Romani population were enrolled in high school). The late socialist period produced better results on paper (through the enrollment of Roma into vocational schools providing high school degrees). In reality, however, only 10 to 15 percent of a given cohort managed to obtain skills that provided an opportunity to find work outside the sphere of unskilled manual labor.[11] Sociologists blamed this state of affairs on the emergence of practices of segregation. A study revealed that in the 1985/86 school year every sixth Romani student was enrolled in "special needs" classes where pupils were taught separately from their peers (Havas, Kemény, and Liskó 2002: 14). Although selection criteria were not in any apparent manner related to ethnic background, they disproportionately affected Romani families.[12] Parallel to the rise of the ratio of Roma in the school system, local bureaucrats came up with more subtle strategies—such as the creation of special classes for gifted students—that allowed for the segregation of Romani students. My discussions with a former school principal in Devecser revealed that such strategies were carefully kept from the public ear. "The existence of Gypsy classes," he told me, "could not be acknowledged in public." He himself learned this the hard way. After referring explicitly to "Gypsy students" in the inauguration speech he gave after being nominated for the position of principal (in the second half of the 1970s), he was confronted by angry Romani parents and had to be escorted out the building through the back door. The same parents, however, accepted the creation of separate classes for their children based on the argument that they had different needs (and, later, the creation of special classes based on the argument that gifted children deserved special treatment too).

This shows that—contrary to Stone's (1995) claim that racist discourses play a key role in maintaining inequality and domination in societies where the law supports equality—social hierarchies could also be reproduced through obfuscation mechanisms that relied on alternative cultural codes (see also Tilly 2001). To be sure, social closure based on claims of need and merit differed from racialized discrimination in that it allowed for the contestation of decisions (such as who would attend which class) and compelled decision-makers at all levels to avoid "black-and-white outcomes." This social logic created space for a specific type of social game wherein decision-makers would reward, by providing them with access to opportunities, those who could best demonstrate their worth and merit. By performing this gate-keeping function they also sought to reassure the non-Romani population (by demonstrating that only the truly worthy would be allowed to pass the gates) and to maintain pressure on Roma who were not so eager to espouse assimilation. Above I referred to this game as following the logic of "hegemonic Hungarianness" to highlight the fact that the definition of social merit clearly relied on the cultural codes of what Georges Bataille (1993) called "homogeneous society": the society of work, exchange, usefulness, sexual repression, fairness, tranquility, and procreation.

Zsolt Csalog, one of the few sociologists who conducted participant observation in the 1980s, was the first to arrive at the conclusion that the socialist regime had added a new dimension to the Gypsy/Gadjo relationship. By centralizing the redistribution of symbolic and material rewards and leveling the social playing field (at least in legal terms), the Communist elite had introduced a previously inexistent element of competition into the interethnic relationship. Although the new code of merit was far from being colorblind, the state's assimilationist politics began to erode local hegemonies. Socialism constituted a radical break with a past in which "the relationship between Roma and non-Roma was governed by decades—if not centuries—of old rules. Every village, town and district used to have its own 'Gypsy policy'" (Szalai 2000: 534, translation mine). Csalog (1984: 123–124) was the first to highlight the ramifications of the new unitary "Gypsy policy":

> The second stage of the agricultural reform [which was initiated in the early 60s] created the impression—for both Roma and the peasantry—that the beneficiaries of the land reform had few reasons to be content. The "settlement Gypsy" could aspire to the same job, wage and treatment as the peasant who had sought refuge in the industrial sector after having been forced to hand inherited land [over to the newly created cooperatives]. While this state of affairs was perceived as a historical injustice by rural non-Roma, it provided Gypsies with a sense of epicaricacy together with a false sense of victory. Confrontation could therefore take on sharper forms *because the interests of Roma*

and non-Roma no longer bypassed each other [but collided]. (translation and emphasis mine)

In this seminal—and largely forgotten—article, Csalog (1984) went on to argue that antagonisms generated by a zero-sum struggle for material and symbolic rewards controlled by the central state did not spill into ethnic conflict because the Communist elite failed to muster the political will to push through the integration policy in the crucial domains of residence (i.e., relegation to rural settlements and the margins of villages) and education (i.e., segregation and exclusion from higher schooling), which remained to a large extent under the control of local communities. This is a crucial insight that calls for shifting the analytic gaze from the national to the local scale and from the central state apparatus to local municipalities. Csalog's analysis underscores the need to analyze the ways in which local apparatchiks can sabotage official policies and create space for informal mechanisms of segregation and control that can function under the guise of "hegemonic Hungarianness."

Building on his ethnographic observations, Csalog (1984) presciently remarked that the discrepancy between the integration promise made by representatives of the central state and the everyday experience of being refused access to channels of mobility and being treated as social parasites led to the emergence of cultural alternatives to the project of assimilation among the Romani population. Vlach Gypsies felt vindicated in their effort to maintain a degree of distance vis-à-vis mainstream society, while a small group of radical intellectuals began to elaborate an overarching ethnonationalist project and other groups began to orient themselves toward religious groups that radiated an open and potentially emancipatory atmosphere. Csalog noted that at the time of writing, the majority of the country's Romani population had not embraced any of these alternatives but opted for a middle road that combined a yearning for assimilation with a cultivation of grievances and rancor. He ended his text with the warning that the peasantry—which he portrayed as moving in an increasingly intolerant direction due to the fear of villages being inundated by Roma but also to the dissipation of the culture of "peasant humanism" (Csalog 1984: 132)—could respond with violence to this novel oppositional orientation. Csalog believed that such a scenario was all the more likely because the Communist leadership was feeding the false myth that the state had been forced to shoulder the heavy material burden of integration and failed to counter emergent popular narratives that blamed the erosion of material security on Roma.

Postsocialism: Deproletarianization and Marginalization

Csalog obviously did not take into account the possibility that the socialist regime would enter a phase of acute crisis and collapse a couple of years later. The paper I cited was actually written just before
a crucial period when large industrial conglomerates and export-
dependent collectives began to lay off workers under the pressure of
a new economic policy that sought to reduce the indebtedness of state
enterprises.[13] The main losers of this policy turned out to be unskilled
workers who not only lost their jobs but also had to face the prospect
of impoverishment due to the lack of welfare policies helping the unemployed. Since Romani men, whose level of education was far below average, were heavily overrepresented among this new surplus
population,[14] it was primarily they (and their families) who bore the
brunt of the economic crisis. On top of facing a crisis of social reproduction, these workers also found themselves confronting a wall of
silence. Representatives of the party-state were not only reluctant to
acknowledge the existence of unemployment but—as Csalog (1984:
131) observed—privately also blamed the Roma for their predicament
based on the claim that they had been unable to strip themselves of
a lumpen culture that fostered hedonism and foot-dragging. Ethnographic evidence[15] suggests that this "private transcript" gained
widespread currency, resulting in the circulation of narratives that
portrayed the Roma as unworthy of assistance. These narratives
negatively affected not only those who had lost their jobs but also
those who were seeking to hold on to their workplaces. In situations
where employers had to make a decision between firing a Romani or
a non-Romani worker, they would have a strong incentive to fire the
Romani individual.[16] Because of these factors, the majority of Romani
men found themselves trapped in long-term unemployment. Their
predicament was especially acute in the northeastern part of the
country, where the unemployment rate was three times higher than
in Budapest and where close to half of the Romani population is concentrated.[17] The strong ethnic dimension of economic exclusion can
be highlighted with the help of one single statistic. While in 1971 the
employment ratios of Romani and non-Romani men nearly matched
each other (85.2 versus 87.7 percent), by 1993 they had grown miles
apart (28.6 versus 64 percent).

From the perspective of affected individuals, the process of marginalization was of course traumatic everywhere. However, from a
societal perspective, it was most damaging in the industrial areas
where Roma had been relocated en masse, and the villages of de-

pressed regions where poor Roma who had lost their livelihoods moved in to occupy the houses that their non-Roma owners had left behind. This sudden and quick change in composition of the population led to the eruption of local conflicts in the 1990s. Of these, there were two that were reported in the national media: the Kétegyháza "ethnic war" (September 1992) and the "Western exodus" of Roma from the village of Zámoly (1999–2000).[18] The eruption of conflicts was predicated upon three factors: (1) the socioeconomic marginalization of Roma; (2) the persistence of negative stereotypes and animosities harbored by non-Roma; and (3) the inefficiency of the state's penal apparatus during the period of transition[19] (see Feischmidt, Szombati, Szuhay 2014).

Interestingly, the eruption of ethnic conflict did not prompt Hungarian sociologists to engage in analyses that could have elucidated the ways in which microhistories and macro forces came together to generate such conflicts. In my view this has partly to do with the development of sociology as a discipline in the postsocialist period. Sociological research focusing on questions related to ethnicity became split between scholars who formed an interest in uncovering the novel predicament of Roma and the shifting meaning of Gypsyness, and others who were mainly concerned with the predicament and self-understanding of non-Roma. This epistemological split could only develop because the Hungarian sociological research community had developed a preference for objectivist and empiricist epistemological approaches, which neglected the relational aspects of group and identity formation. This is not the place to identify the complex reasons underpinning this particular epistemological history. What I find important to note is that the survey approach pioneered by István Kemény (1972, 1976) and his colleagues (Kemény, Janky, and Lengyel 2004)—who conducted three rounds of surveys on the predicament of Roma[20] between 1971 and 2003—played an important role in relegating the approach that began to be developed by Csalog to the sidelines of sociological inquiry. Instead of situating the struggle over the definition of Gypsyness within the broader struggle for material and symbolic rewards, and social and political power, these surveys took as their axiomatic point of departure the claim that the negative representation of Gypsies is a historically sedimented mental construct lodged deep in the psyche and that its eradication can only be achieved through colorblind public policy. Adopting the assimilationist stance of the Communist elite, the team led by Kemény—who was first ostracized, then tolerated before being cautiously supported by the Communist leadership—thus believed that ethnic traditions no longer constitute a point of reference for individuals of Romani descent and that the latter should therefore be conceptualized as would-be members of the proletariat whose integration can be guaranteed by eradicating the causes of poverty, tackling everyday forms of discrimination (tacitly tolerated by the state), and slowly replacing the "culture of poverty" (that had allowed Roma to cope with marginality) with the values of homogeneous society (Kemény, Janky, and Lengyel 2004).

Although the empiricist corpus created by the "Kemény camp" became the standard textbook knowledge on Roma (and many of Kemény's students went on to occupy key positions in the academic field), it emerged as the object of criticism both inside and outside sociology in the last decade of the party state. Kemény attracted the ire of a handful of Romani intellectuals who claimed that he promoted cultural genocide. Some of these intellectuals had already played a role in the short-lived Cultural Association of Hungarian Gypsies and later went on to play a key role in the emergent civil rights movement that saw the cultivation of ethnic pride as a precondition for social integration and believed that mainstream society had to make significant efforts to make space for Roma. Within the academic field, the group was criticized by János Ladányi and Iván Szelényi (1997, 1998), who—taking inspiration from Bourdieu's scholarship (more particularly his conceptualization of social groupness as the inherently unstable outcome of classification struggles)—argued that sociology's main task was not to take sides by adopting a certain definition of Gypsyness but to analyze shifts in that definition and to reveal the largely invisible social forces that render such shifts possible.

The duo did not content itself with formulating this critique but went on to offer its own macrosociological view on the transformation of the interethnic relationship after regime change. This interpretation relied on the key observation that the neoliberal social model promoted by left-liberal (and conservative-liberal) elites allowed for mobility into the middle class, while also fostering the emergence of spatially concentrated surplus populations who were unable to escape the trappings of structural unemployment and social marginalization (Ladányi and Szelényi 2006). This economic-cum-social process, they argued, resembles the shift from a Fordist to a post-Fordist regime of production in the United States, which fostered the emergence of pockets of poverty in inner city areas.[21] Poverty and exclusion became in both cases closely intertwined with race/ethnicity because mainstream society—which showed some willingness to incorporate upwardly mobile segments of a historically stigmatized "pariah caste"—interprets poverty-induced social banes (such as "welfare dependency," criminality, domestic violence, and so on) as the products of a deviant subculture. The terms "Black" and "Gypsy" not only carry a moral stigma but are also infused with historically sedimented racist tropes that further naturalize the exclusion of the emergent "underclass,"[22] limiting public discussion of the structural forces that, in the duo's view, ultimately drives this process of group formation. While the neoliberal state is not directly implicated in the naturalization of structural violence (seeking to counter it with robust antidiscrimination legislation), it is indirectly complicit in the marginalization of a subproletariat whose labor is no longer required in a postindustrial economy through the promotion of "prisonfare" and a laissez-faire approach to the production of spatial inequalities (see Wacquant 2008, 2009).

The bulk of the empirical studies on ethnicity that have been produced in the last ten years in Hungary have taken inspiration from these divergent—yet not wholly incompatible—lines of investigation. A malicious observer would even claim that most of this research has produced disconcertingly familiar and simplified reiterations of two competing core claims: (1) that "Roma are the victims of discrimination" or (2) that "the liberal state refuses to address the structural forces underpinning socioeconomic exclusion and marginality." A less malicious observer would note that some studies that have taken inspiration from these pioneers have actually nuanced and advanced our understanding of the "Romani predicament." Risking committing an injustice, I would like highlight the work of Júlia Szalai, who has thoroughly studied the liberal social policy regime that emerged in response to the unemployment crisis of the early 1990s. Her work shows that postsocialist elites channeled public resources into the alleviation of acute crisis situations (such as sickness, a temporal loss of income, other shortages, etc.) instead of seeking to address the chronic problem of long-term unemployment (see Szalai 2002, 2005). Although the postsocialist state protected the newly created surplus population from the worst calamities (such as chronic hunger), the "dual welfare regime" that prioritized the needs of the lower-middle class actually reinforced the "poverty trap." Szalai does not simply show that this regime was founded on false assumptions—namely, that poverty and exclusion were generated by the economic crisis that sunk socialism's ship and that these ills would automatically disappear once that crisis was overcome—but also argues that it powerfully contributed to the entrenchment of an individualistic conceptualization of poverty among the public and the symbolic division of society into the camps of the "striving" and the "lazy" (Szalai 2007). She notes that the key policy mechanism responsible for this outcome was the decentralization of the welfare regime based on the liberal credo that local communities are best placed to assess and address poor people's needs. Summarizing the unintended outcomes of decentralization, Szalai (2002: 39) argued that

> social policy legislation left the definition of poverty and the principles of its alleviation to local communities. This automatically transformed a societal problem into a communal one through the redefinition of [distributive] conflicts pitting the poor against the non-poor as a problem of social (dis)order. ... This re-orientation [of social policy] attenuated social conflict and ... ensured social peace. This, however ... was achieved at the expense of the poor. (translation mine)

Szalai's claim echoes Csalog's (1984) interpretation of the way in which the late socialist state managed to secure social peace in the countryside in a moment of economic crisis. However, while Csalog stressed the efficacy of informal mechanisms of segregation and control, Szalai highlights the unintended consequences of the formal decentralization of key discretionary powers after regime change. Her claim is that local power-holders took advantage of their newly gained distributive powers to secure the privileges of the ethnic majority at a moment when mainstream groups were gripped by fears of *déclassement*. This strategy was not unique to Hungary. Political elites in the whole postsocialist bloc addressed the "social issue" by decentralizing social policy structures and thereby shifting the burden of care to local municipalities, which did not have the capacity to affectively address chronic social problems linked to unemployment. Lacking methods and financial instruments to foster the socioeconomic integration of the surplus population, local power-holders responded in the majority of cases by introducing mechanisms of segregation with the intention of separating the surplus population from mainstream groups. One such model case was the local council's attempt to physically separate Roma and non-Roma in the Czech town of Ústí nad Labem by erecting a concrete wall between the so-called Gypsy settlement and the part of the town inhabited by the ethnic majority. Since the Ústí incident, walls dividing the ethnic majority from ethnoracially stigmatized social outcasts have sprung up in different corners of the region. There are walls in Eastern Slovakia (Ostrovany, Lomnička, Trebišov, Vrútky) and in Romania (Baia Mare). Sonia Hirt (2012) has conceptualized walls as tools of "difference-making," which enable local elites to reinforce distinctions between "us" and "them" and thereby buttress social hierarchies through planning and other forms of spatial politics.

Recent work carried out by sociologist Tünde Virág (2010) has yielded further insights into the production of space in postsocialist Hungary. Having conducted fieldwork in two microregions that figure among the most depressed in the country, she highlighted the emergence of "ghetto-villages" as a result of a large-scale population exchange in regions that are situated at a distance from centers of economic activity as well as administrative centers (Virág 2010). These localities have been abandoned by skilled manual workers and white-collar professionals who possessed enough cultural and economic capital to move residence to more dynamic regions. Their place was mostly taken by people who found themselves excluded from the primary labor market and forced to sell their flats or vacate social housing due to chronic shortages in disposable income. Virág (2010: 7–22) notes that these migratory flows resulted in the emergence of "ghetto-regions" in the Northeast (the Cserehát region) and in the Southwest (the Ormánság region).

While this process is mainly driven by invisible socioeconomic forces, local mayors have in some cases been directly responsible for the expulsion of the surplus population. Virág's (2010: 129–176) analysis shows that those who find themselves relegated to geographically peripheral and infrastructurally deprived zones also have to confront an array of invisible walls that prevent them from ever leaving these places. She notes that the inhabitants of "ghetto-villages" find themselves relegated to "ghetto-schools" that function as warehouses for the surplus population, relieving other schools from the burden of integrating children who may hinder the development of "normal" students (ibid., 159–176). This kind of segregation, Virág (ibid.) notes, lacks codification and relies on the same kinds of informal—yet closely coordinated—arrangements that Csalog had already highlighted in the 1980s. Due to the extreme scarcity of public resources in these localities and microregions, the surplus population can no longer subsist on welfare benefits and is thereby compelled to take up badly paid agricultural work on lands that are owned by non-Roma who reside in villages or towns situated in the vicinity of ghetto-villages. This dependence on "peasant patrons" (see Durst 2015) not only ensured a steady supply of cheap labor to a sector that suffered after European accession (on which more below). It also has been instrumental in quelling dissent among the ranks of the surplus population. The only alternative to clientelism—which can take on a number of forms ranging from occasional "day labor" to everyday work as a "family slavey" (see Kovács, Vidra, and Virág 2013)—is the "subsistence economy," the gathering of mushrooms, snails, and other natural resources that are valued in Budapest and Western Europe. The latter has, however, been impaired by authorities' increasing effort to clamp down on environmentally destructive behavior, as well as the lack of middlemen who ensure the transport of products to far-away markets.

Although Virág's (2010) book deals with the spaces that I will call "zones of deprivation," at one point she takes a detour to note that it was during her fieldwork that anti-Gypsy popular sensibilities burst into the open in a northeastern microregion that bordered on the Cserehát region (where she conducted research). Relying on anecdotal evidence, she suggests that this eruption of popular racism may have responded to the left-liberal government's attempt to reform the "illfare state" (Dupcsik 2009) in 2007 through the introduction of a guaranteed minimal income for all families in order to alleviate the plight of the surplus population:

> Although studies revealed that only a fraction of unemployed welfare claimants were entitled to a level of benefits that approached the minimal wage, in these exceptional cases the rational course of action was for claimants to refuse . . . to take up a job that only paid the minimal wage. This led to heightened animosity towards the unemployed . . . amongst whom Roma were overrepresented. Accordingly, animosity towards welfare claimants takes on an ethnic guise. (Virág 2010: 148–149, translation mine)

While distributive conflicts may have contributed to a popular backlash against a social category whose members were perceived as lacking in social merit and moral worth (see Huszár 2011), evidence provided by the small number of fieldworkers who conducted participant observation in villages that were struggling to contain the influx of "Gypsies" suggests that it would be wrong to narrowly focus on the role that the struggle for material rewards played in the emergence of popular racism. András Vígvári's (2013) brilliant description of social tensions in one single street in the northeastern village of Tiszakerecseny highlights the symbolic struggle between self-identified "natives" (*őslakos*) and an ethnically and culturally heterogeneous group of precarious immigrants who have no name for themselves but are called "Gypsies" by representatives of the previous group. In his microstudy, Vígvári (2013) interprets symbolic power struggle between a culturally coherent but decaying "old" and a culturally incoherent but emergent "new" world that revolves around the key question of who gets to impose their rules and values. Representatives of the "old world" are united by an adherence to agricultural production and peasant values (welfare, order, cleanliness), an unbroken allegiance to the Reformed Church, and nostalgia for both pre-Communist times and state socialism. They see regime change as an irrational event that triggered economic decline and moral chaos. This group perceives its leading cultural, social, and political role as being threatened by the influx of poor newcomers who now constitute a numerical majority. This threat is partly imagined but partly real in that "natives" have witnessed the metamorphosis of their street. They describe this process as "Gypsyfication" despite the fact that non-Roma are also to be found among "welfare scroungers" and the "idle." Vígvári (2013: 329) concludes his essay thusly:

> Selective migration—the departure of middle strata and the influx of lower strata—which has only been worsened by the social and territorial disadvantages brought by regime change, signals the twilight of the old world. Native parents try to persuade their children to leave the village and this shows that the idealized lifestyle [of natives] is no longer seen as sustainable in this space. The native world has thereby compromised its own future . . . . Its place is being taken by a culturally heterogeneous group whose members . . . cannot yet come to an agreement on common norms. (translation mine)

Vígvári's insightful description provides a point of entry for my analysis of popular anti-Gypsyism in Northeastern Hungary. It highlights the loss of confidence of a group that I will identify as the "post-peasantry," and the—partially real, partially imagined—"inundation" of villages by heterogeneous elements of the surplus population as a key cause of popular racist sensibilities.

Losing Ground: Depeasantization and the Post-Peasantry

The concept of "post-peasantry" was elaborated by European anthropologists to refer to either family-run agricultural enterprises or the workers of large-scale agricultural firms (see Tamanoi 1983). This definition was modified by Henri Mendras (1970), whose widely cited study emphasized the vanishing of traditional peasant modes of production and forms of life under the impact of industrial civilization. Mendras's conceptualization was adopted by Hungarian sociologists to refer to the predicament of "peasant-workers" who worked in urban factories. Kemény (1972) and Márkus (1973) argued that these rural residents were going through a process of proletarianization and that subsistence production was part of this strategy, not a vestige of peasant traditions. Szelényi (1992) later argued that participation in the "second economy"—which mostly involved the sale of agricultural commodities that were produced on so-called "household plots" (*háztáji*)[23]—served as a means of accumulating capital that peasant-workers could invest in the tuition of their children in order to promote their social mobility.

Imre Kovách (2003), one of the leading figures of European rural sociology, adopted the concept of "depeasantization"[24] to describe the transformation of rural society in the aftermath of regime change. He used the term to capture the declining sway of the post-peasantry over the economic, social, and political life of villages and small agricultural towns. In his latest monograph, he offers a detailed account of this multidimensional process, arguing that it was the most salient feature of the transformation of the countryside in the 1990s (see Kovách 2012). He highlights "structural," "social," and "cultural" dimensions of depeasantization. In structural terms the process refers to "deagriculturalization" (agriculture is no longer the dominant sector of the rural economy, although the majority of rural inhabitants continue to take part in food production); and the disappearance of the "historic peasantry," which was the dominant social class until collectivization and survived until the 1990s; and the decline of "socialist petty entrepreneurs," the majority of whom proved unable to convert themselves into successful farmers despite the promises of "reprivatization." In social terms, depeasantization refers to the rural population's declining ability to resist or take control of external pressures and the concomitant shift of control over resources and norms to non-place-based actors through the process of globalization. Finally, in cultural terms, depeasantization refers to the loss of traditions of the historic peasantry and the spread of consumer culture (see Kovách 2012: 199–201). Kovách's (2012: 195) conclusion is that

> the rebirth of family-run agricultural production [after regime change] did not reproduce the peasant condition . . . . Proletarianization en masse, the embourgeoisement of the owners of mid-size and large private enterprises, the prevalence of aspirations to social mobility among the younger generation have overwritten elements [of historic peasant heritage] that survived socialism. (translation mine)

This interpretation builds on one of Kovách's (1997) earlier analyses in which he observed that the agricultural sector was suffering from a lack of investment capital and unequal access to national subsidies, which had caused a "crisis of overproduction" in the first decade following regime change. This crisis was prolonged by the process of European enlargement, which exposed petty agricultural producers to international competition under highly unequal terms, resulting in a steep decline in the number of "individual enterprises" from 958 thousand (in 2000) to 567 thousand (in 2010).[25] One of Kovách's (2012: 156–164) most astute observations is that small-scale agricultural production entered a phase of crisis at the same moment when local mayors (who had been granted key powers in the course of the above-mentioned decentralization drive) began to lose ground against newly formed clientelist networks that were dominated by agribusiness and the regional representatives of mainstream political parties. His analysis highlights the nexus between economic decline and the shift of the locus of economic power and political influence away from the local scale.[26] This highlights a fourth—political—dimension of depeasantization and highlights the way in which political elites fostered the demise of the "historic peasantry" and prevented petty agricultural producers from playing a leading role in rural communities by excluding autonomous civic organizations from key decisions and actively creating space for external capitalist pressures.[27]

Other researchers have contested Kovách's claim that the peasantry has ceased to exist as a social group in the postsocialist period. Harcsa (2003) called attention to the fact that tens of thousands of family-run agricultural enterprises work under conditions that resemble the peasant mode of production and form of life—deriving the bulk of their income from agricultural production based on privately owned land, combining self-reliance with market-oriented production, exhibiting an ability to resist external pressures, and expressing allegiance to cultural networks that seek to revitalize historic peasant traditions. In a similar thrust, Kovács (2006) argued that the processes under way should be conceptualized as the transformation rather than the disappearance of the peasantry. Another researcher proposed the concept of the "involuntary peasantry" to highlight the predicament of landowning families who do not have enough economic and cultural capital to exit depressed rural areas and therefore find themselves forced to toil the land and market their agricultural products (Molnár 2005). The enforced reliance of the majority of the rural population on agricultural production[28] (which they combine with other income-generating activities) has apparently gone hand-in-hand with the preservation of "certain elements of peasant traditions, which are palpably present in contemporary life" (see Kotics 2011: 177). None of these critics contested Kovách's claim that independent agricultural producers hold declining sway over the social, cultural, and political life of villages and small agricultural towns.

I myself do not see a contradiction between Kovách's effort to capture the decline of petty agricultural production under economic and political pressures and his critics' focus on petty agricultural producers' "ongoing struggle for autonomy and progress in a context characterized by multiple patterns of dependency and associated processes of exploitation and marginalization" (van der Ploeg 2008: xiv). While rural society may no longer be dominated by the descendants of the "historic peasantry," we have witnessed the emergence of disparate efforts to safeguard what I would call the peasant mode of production and form of life,[29] to buttress producers' sense of self-worth, and to exercise greater influence over the cultural and political life of rural communities. I propose to call these independent agricultural producers "post-peasants" in order to differentiate them from the "historic peasantry." While Hungarian law has established a difference between "family farms" (who have the status of juridical persons) and "primary producers" (who are considered natural persons), I will subsume both under the concept of the "post-peasantry." This is because representatives of both categories are dependent on the land and the local community for their social reproduction, and because this reliance is coupled with a sense of pride that is rooted in—partially successful—efforts to safeguard some form of autonomy and preserve certain elements of traditional peasant life.

Such a broad delineation of the post-peasantry would obviously be problematic if I wanted to highlight the internal socioeconomic and sociocultural differentiations of those who depend to some degree on the land for their social reproduction. (Pensioners who work microplots to supplement income derived from the state obviously differ in terms of social autonomy and power from those who derive the bulk of their income from market-oriented agricultural production.) Such a broad definition, however, serves the purposes of an analysis that seeks to decipher the emergence of social collectivities and antagonisms in rural regions. It allows us to differentiate this category from "agribusinessmen" who own sizable enterprises where production is highly specialized and completely oriented toward markets and dependent on financial and industrial capital (embodied in credit, industrial inputs, and technologies). Van der Ploeg (2008: 1–2) notes that forms of entrepreneurial farming often arise from state-driven programs for "modernization" of agriculture and "entail a partial industrialization of the labour process." He argues that in the current conjuncture, expansion—through scale enlargement—is a crucial and necessary feature of these enterprises. Their strong reliance on the state and globalized markets differentiates agricultural entrepreneurs from post-peasants, who are often more successful in distancing themselves from economic and political dependencies thanks to pluriactivity strategies. Agribusinessmen are, however, less "embedded" in and hence less dependent on—in both ecological and social terms—territorially organized social arrangements. In contrast to place-based agricultural producers, they are not dependent on local labor and social networks of trust and reciprocity. This has obvious repercussions on their willingness to take responsibility for the well-being of local communities. One of the most salient—although seldom remarked—features of regime change from the vantage point of rural communities has been the withdrawal of agribusinessmen from local public life (see Váradi 2007) and—in more practical terms—from the financing of local public institutions and services. This took place in a period when the political class took decisive steps to weaken the clout of local municipalities. One of the key measures whereby it achieved this was the gradual reduction of the ratio of personal income tax left in the hands of local municipalities from 100 to 5 percent in the 1990–2002 period.[30] While the central state also took greater financial responsibility for certain public services, this was not proportional to the loss of revenue on the local level.

The decline of the post-peasantry's economic position and social power had two important consequences. First, its representatives became increasingly reliant on services offered by the state in terms of social reproduction and social mobility. Second, decline generated a crisis of self-confidence. This explains why questions related to the control over collective resources and to cultural hegemony became pronounced in the countryside after the new millennium. A focus on decline also shines light on "zones of deprivation," where the threat of losing ground was most palpable and which the post-peasantry could not exit, which may explain why its representatives turned to the alternative strategy of "voice" (Hirschman 1970). Kovách's (2012) effort to connect decline with key political processes—most notably the declining power of municipalities—also sheds light on the hidden ways in which policies pursued by ruling elites contributed to the emergence of social antagonisms in deprived rural regions. Although the reallocation of economic resources and political power from place-based to non-place-based actors was largely invisible from the vantage point of everyday lifeworlds, it generated minor yet recurring and highly personalized frictions between people who found themselves pitted against one another in local schools, welfare bureaus, and municipality halls. This goes some way in explaining why it was this particular social boundary and relation that became the object of concern and contention in the last decade in peripheral rural communities.

In the next chapters, I will strive to nuance, extend, and dynamize this rudimentary interpretation through a retrospective microhistory of the Northeast where socioethnic frictions emerged. In chapter 2, I rely on our collaborative fieldwork in Gyöngyöspata to reconstruct the process whereby these categories came into friction in the course of the last decade in connection to broader economic and political processes of "neoliberalization" and "Europeanization." In chapter 3, I extend this analysis into the political domain and show that "naming and blaming Roma" not only provided an avenue for expressing the post-peasantry's experience of losing ground, but also entrenched the suffering of the "abandoned countryside" as a key political issue, allowing regional elites to pressurize the government into repatriating financial resources and discretionary powers to the local scale.

Notes

1. Dupcsik's (2009) argument recalls Balibar's (1991) claim that racism emerged in conjunction with the ideology of nationalism. The latter argues that representatives of the "nation" will inevitably identify themselves through racial idiom because historical, cultural, political, and other distinguishing factors of a "nation" are ultimately subsumed under the idea of "race" (see Balibar 1991; also Miles and Brown 2003: ch. 6). Without entering this debate, I would nevertheless note that it holds less relevance for territories and periods when and where political—rather than ethnic—conceptions of nationhood prevail.

2. Nagy's (2007) framework reminds me of Leo Despres's (1975) effort to integrate the analysis of societal power relations with an analysis of interpersonal ethnicity by distinguishing between three levels where ethnicity is negotiated: the level of the "overall social system," the level of "organized ethnic group relations," and the level of "interpersonal encounters."

3. Klára Hamburger (2000: 25) makes an interesting observation in connection to the strong and persistent demand for "Gypsy music" (which, in fact, had nothing to do with the traditional music of Romani groups and was only called by that name because it was played by Roma): "[in a period when] the practice of the Hungarian language—the foundational stone of Hungarian identity—was officially banned . . . Hungarian tunes played by Gypsies became primary vehicles for the expression of Hungarian national identity" (translation mine).

4. Antal Herrmann (1851–1926), the founder of the Society of Hungarian Ethnologists and of the *Ethnologische Mitteilungen aus Ungarn* journal (which was the official organ of the international Gypsy Lore Society), played a key role in this "benign exoticization" of Roma.

5. Dupcsik (2009: 92) relies on historian Barna Purcsi's (2001) work to highlight this impact, noting for instance that in 1921 the officials of Győr county suggested the incarceration of "Gypsies presenting a threat to public security" to the interior minister.

6. There is a disagreement between historians as to whether Roma were—similarly to Jews—subjected to racialized forms of persecution (see Kenrick and Puxon 1995), or whether the Hungarian state implemented "discriminatory measures [against Roma] based on public security concerns" (Karsai 1992: 119, translation mine).

7. The number of Roma murdered remains an object of debate. The only monograph dealing with the history of the *Porajmos* (Roma Holocaust) in Hungary puts the number of victims between five thousand and ten thousand (Karsai 1992).

8. The Cultural Association of Hungarian Gypsies—created in 1957—constitutes an exception. This organization was, however, short-lived. When Roma began to turn in significant numbers to President Mária László for help in fighting discrimination, she was removed from office (in 1958). The organization was officially disbanded in 1961. See Sághy 2008.

9. One of my elderly Romani informants in Devecser recalled with horror the sudden arrival of dozens of "Kalashnikov-toting" policemen who imposed an immediate quarantine on his community. He also told me that the fact that women were forced to undress in front of doctors and have their heads shaven violated a deeply-entrenched cultural norm (women were only allowed to appear nude in front of their husband), and that although they never spoke about the incident he was sure that the experience stayed with his wife for the rest of her life.

10. The Interior Ministry proposed that recipients of permanent identity cards be fingerprinted and suggested that all "vagrant" and (as a new measure) "semi-vagrant" individuals be forced to take part in a special census. This was complemented by the suggestion to indicate (in the "extraordinary remarks" rubric of the new identity cards) that these presumably untrustworthy citizens had taken part in a census. The Ministry—citing the sedentarization of "vagrant" and "half-vagrant" Roma as its leitmotif—thus proposed to criminalize a significant proportion (perhaps a third) of the country's Romani population. The proposal made it onto the table of the Political Committee but was torpedoed by first secretary János Kádár, who was in favor of adopting a "colorblind" policy toward Roma.

11. To be fair, one must also note that groups who sought to maintain their traditional skills and occupations managed to pass on relevant skills outside the domain of formal education. Of these skills, however, it was first and foremost entrepreneurial flair that proved useful, and its value was limited in an economy where tight restrictions were imposed on petty trade and other forms of entrepreneurial activity (see my analysis in chapter 5).

12. The same study revealed that while the ratio of Roma was 5.9 percent in elementary schools (in the 1974/75 school year), every fourth pupil attending "special needs" classes was categorized as "Roma" (Havas et al. 2002: 7–8). By 1985/86, the ratio of "Roma" children attending "special needs" classes had climbed to 38 percent.

13. Studies focusing on Hungary's spiraling into a deadly debt cycle revealed that the small, relatively open economy's export dependency and vulnerability to external shocks radically grew after the oil crisis—as a result of increasing natural resource prices within COMECON (Council for Mutual Economic Assistance) and the ensuing worsening of the terms of trade. Facing the prospect of a Latin-American scenario (indebtment followed by bankruptcy), Hungary's leaders opted in 1973 for a risky strategy—later coined "planned indebtment" (Földes 1995)—which foresaw the taking of relatively cheap mid- and long-term loans. These were to be used to develop the country's export capacities with a view to boosting income from international trade and using this income to pay back lenders. The strategy already showed signs

of faltering by 1976–1977, prompting economic decision-makers to adopt restrictive policies—for example, a drastic increase of the price of bread—in 1978. Before decision-makers could test the efficiency of belt-tightening, the US Federal Reserve began to aggressively raise interest rates in 1979. The fallout was a dramatic rise of the cost of debt repayment. While most researchers agree that the "Volcker shock" (1979–1981) was the moment when the door of the "debt trap" closed on Hungary, there is disagreement as to where the fault lies. For a discussion see Éber 2014.

14. See Kertesi (2005), who conducted pioneering quantitative studies on the impact of the socioeconomic transformation on the Romani workforce.

15. One of the most shocking documents of how the victims of regime change came to be blamed for their own predicament was produced by documentary filmmaker Tamás Almási. Almási produced a series of films that captured the collapse of industrial production in Ózd, a town that had been at the heart of the socialist modernization experiment and found itself facing an uncertain future. His films provide a unique and highly valuable vista onto the process of reckoning and transformation in the 1987–1997 period.

16. Kertesi (2005) found strong evidence of discrimination against Roma on the labor market in the country's northeastern industrial heartland. See also Kertesi and Kézdi 2011.

17. In 1993, 24.3 percent of Roma lived in the North (Borsod-Abaúj-Zemplén, Heves and Nógrád counties) and 19.8 percent in the East (Szabolcs-Szatmár-Bereg, Hajdú-Bihar, and Jász-Nagykun-Szolnok counties). Ten years later, respective ratios were 32.3 and 19.7 percent. See Kemény, Janky and Lengyel 2004: 16–17.

18. For an analysis of these two cases see Szuhay 2012 and Melegh 2003.

19. The third only applies to the first case.

20. These surveys were conducted in 1971, 1993, and 2003 respectively.

21. The duo draw on Julian Wilson's early structuralist work on inner-city poverty, especially his *The Truly Disadvantaged* (1987), *The Ghetto Underclass* (1993), and *When Work Disappears* (1996).

22. While Ladányi and Szelényi are right to argue that inequality-generating mechanisms—such as exploitation or opportunity hoarding—do not necessarily require self-conscious efforts to subordinate excluded parties, or explicitly formulated beliefs in the inferiority of excluded parties (see Tilly 2001), their claim that the underclass concept captures "the experiences of the Roma ghetto poor during particular historic periods" (Ladányi and Szelényi 2006: 9) is problematic. Portraying deproletarianized industrial and agricultural workers as representatives of the underclass actually conceals key aspects of their experience: social—and later racial—stigmatization and exclusion from channels of social mobility through the agency of local power-holders who have the means to prevent them from accessing resources that are critical for their social reproduction (see Stewart 2002; Wacquant 1996; and my own analysis in the next chapter).

23. The household plot was the only form of private (family) farming allowed during the socialist era. These plots (which were typically less than one hectare in size) were attached to a rural residence. Chris Hann (2013: 182) highlighted the rationale for allocating these plots: "In contrast to capitalist modernization, the socialist variant aspired to replicate industrial divisions of labour within the countryside. Especially in the form known as the State Farm (Russian: *sovkhoz*; in Poland the PGR), but also in the more widespread collective or cooperative farm (*kolkhoz*; *spółdzielnia rolnicza*), complex new hierarchies were imposed. It generally took some time before the members of agricultural cooperatives came to enjoy wages and pensions comparable to those of urban factory workers. In the interim, they were remunerated according to 'work points,' supplemented by the allocation of a 'household plot' for subsistence

gardening." Households could also sell agricultural products to neighbors and relatives, or at markets in nearby towns. This income-generating function became especially salient after regime change, which led to the dismantlement of cooperatives and generated massive unemployment in the countryside.

24. I note that Kovách adopted the concept from the international lexicon. Depeasantization is one of the major indices of the process of "social modernization." It can be defined as a "multi-layered process of erosion of an agrarian way of life, the increasing difficulty to combine subsistence and commodity agricultural production with an internal social organization based on family labour and village community settlement" (Vanhaute 2012: 317–318). Depeasantization includes a diversification of survival coping mechanisms on behalf of the rural poor, such as petty commodity production, rural wage labor, seasonal migration, subcontracting to (multinational) corporations, self-employment, remittances, and income transitions. Rural-urban migration patterns are often also part of rural household strategies (Johnson 2004: 56, 61). Johnson has argued that the biggest problem with the concept is that it leaves unexplained the link with concordant processes of urbanization, industrialization, development, and marginalization. Because of this, depeasantization is often supplemented with the concepts of deruralization (as a synonym of urbanization and the decline of rural areas) and deagrarianization (Bryceson 1996). The latter refers to the declining role of agricultural production within rural livelihoods. Bryceson (2000: 323) argues that "as the processes of de-agrarianization and de-peasantization combine, the vulnerability of peasantries deepens," and that in the neoliberal era, "peasantries are disappearing more rapidly than before" because governments in Asia, Latin America and Africa are largely powerless to implement policies that could ensure their survival (Bryceson 2000: 323). De-peasantization can therefore be seen "as a specific form of deagrarianisation in which peasantries lose their economic capacity and social coherence, and shrink in size" (Vanhaute 2012: 318). Others have, however, emphasized the viability of "re-peasantization" strategies. Jan Douwe van der Ploeg has argued that this century could even witness a new turning point, via a re-emergence of the peasantry. He grounds this claim in the observation that farming is increasingly being restructured in a peasant-like way in response to the agrarian crisis (see van der Ploeg 2010).

25. See Központi Statisztikai Hivatal 2008: 168; and Vidékfejlesztési Minisztérium n.d.: 27.

26. Kovách (2012) shows that lobby organizations that promoted the interests of "family enterprises"—which formed the economic backbone of the post-peasantry—lost ground to those that backed agribusiness. This shift in the balance of social power was most clearly manifested in agribusinessmen's success in appropriating the bulk of European agricultural subsidies.

27. I note that the shift in the balance of power away from the local level and away from the "countryside" took place despite the participation of the Independent Smallholders' Party in two center-right governments (1990–1994, 1998–2002). Although the party's post-1990 history waits to be written, I am convinced that its exit from parliament in 2002 had primarily to do with its inability to contain (much less reverse) this process.

28. A comprehensive survey conducted in the year 2000 found that half of Hungarian households worked a plot and/or raised animals. The same survey found that half of these households—that is every fourth household—reached a threshold of production that experts consider minimally necessary for the sustainability of microenterprises (see KSH 2008: 25).

29. I agree with van der Ploeg (2008: 1), who sees a continuity in the mode of production and social reproduction: "peasant agriculture . . . is basically built upon the sustained use of ecological capital and oriented towards defending and improving peasant live-

lihoods. Multi-functionality is often a major feature. Labour is basically provided by the family (or mobilized within the rural community through relations of reciprocity), and land and the other major means of production are family owned. Production is oriented towards the market as well as towards the reproduction of the farm unit and the family."

30. The first democratically elected (center-right) government led by József Antall already reduced the ratio of the personal income tax that the state left in the coffers of local municipalities to 30 percent. The center-left government led by Gyula Horn (1994–1998) further decreased that ratio to 20 percent, and Viktor Orbán's first right-wing government (1998–2002) reduced it to 5 percent.

– Chapter 2 –

POPULAR RACISM IN THE NORTHEAST
The Case of Gyöngyöspata

In this chapter, I will reconstruct the microhistory of one particular rural locality to highlight structural pressures and relational frictions that plausibly played a pivotal role in the rise of an organic racist countermovement in microregions situated on the country's north-eastern periphery in the middle of the last decade. Certain parts of the analysis I present rely on material I collected together with Margit Feischmidt between March and December 2011, while others make use of our joint interpretations (Feischmidt and Szombati 2012, 2013a, 2013b, 2014, 2016). What is novel in comparison to our earlier work is my effort to link the emergence of popular racist sensibilities to the structural forces that I highlighted in the previous chapter on the one hand, and to a particular set of left-liberal policies on the other. In the first part of the chapter, I will highlight the ramifications of the decline of the post-peasant economy in connection to Hungary's accession to the European Union, arguing that it fostered a sense of loss and disempowerment among the segment of the population that I identify as the post-peasantry. I will then argue that certain frictions between the post-peasantry and the surplus population provided an experiential avenue for laying the blame for these banes squarely on "settlement-dwellers." While these frictions were connected to wider socioeconomic trends, I will show that "culture" was the domain where "class"—the lines of antagonism—came together by high-lighting young settlement-dwellers' frustration with clientelism and their appropriation of cultural practices that contested post-peasants' effort to reinstate hierarchical bonds. These actions and counterac-tions eroded local mechanisms of segregation and control relying on the logic of hegemonic Hungarianness, thereby encouraging the search for alternatives. In the second part of the chapter, I will argue that these mechanisms were—figuratively speaking—not only eroded from "below" but also from "above." The key claim is that mainstream groups' growing intolerance of the surplus population was enhanced by local authorities' unwillingness to clamp down on petty criminality and the left-liberal government's effort to emancipate Roma under the banner of its "integration politics." This sense of abandonment was worsened by local power-holders' refusal to acknowledge the existence of frictions, and by the left-liberal politicians' attempts to justify petty criminality, which fostered the suspicion that elites were deliberately shielding criminals. Feelings of loss, relational frictions, and the spread of abandonment in relation to local and national elites strengthened the hand of a local elite group whose leaders proposed to prevent the further decline of the locality by espousing a confrontational approach towards Roma. In the last part of the chapter, I describe how the group's representatives became embroiled in episodes of collective violence that played a key role in the polarization of the community along the lines of ethnicity, simultaneously generating a demand for repressive measures against the criminalized surplus population.

The Polarized Transition:
When "Ethnicity" Overlaps with "Class"

Gyöngyöspata (see map 2.1) is situated in the foothills of the Mátra mountains, approximately ten kilometers northwest of the town of Gyöngyös in Heves County. The locality is situated within a microregion that does not figure among the most deprived ones but is bordered by two others that are among Hungary's thirty-three "most disadvantaged microregions."[1] At the time of the last census (2011), 2,586 people lived in the village, of whom 318 (12 percent) identified themselves as belonging to the Romani minority. The village, which had once been an important commercial center and enjoyed the same rights as Gyöngyös, is part of a historic grape-growing and winemaking region. Up until the middle of the twentieth century, the local peasantry dominated viticultural production, but the socialist period brought significant changes to the sector. In 1975, individually owned terroirs were collectivized and united under the umbrella of a new cooperative (the United Mátrai Cooperative), which successfully reorganized viticultural production in Gyöngyöspata and two

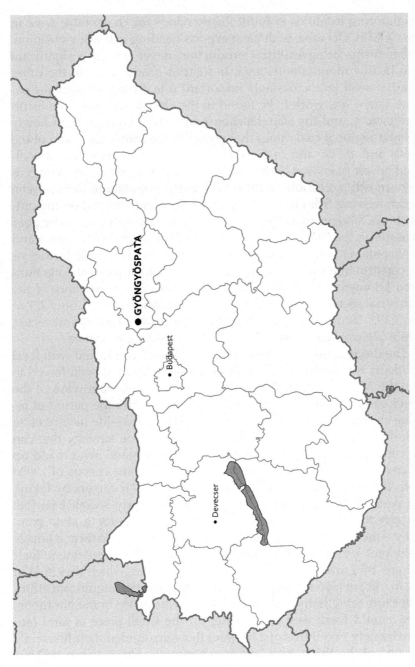

Map 2.1. Map of Hungary featuring Gyöngyöspata. © Wikimedia Commons, CC BY-SA license.

neighboring localities to fulfill the demands for cheap table wine in the COMECON area, with most exports heading to the Soviet Union. Other forms of agricultural production never played a significant role in this mountainous area. Industrial production, on the other hand, played an increasingly important role during the socialist period. There was work to be found in the electric company, the furniture factory, and the slaughterhouse in nearby Gyöngyös, in newly opened regional coal mines that powered the industrial boom of the 1960s and 1970s, and in Visonta, where the country's largest coal-fired power plant was opened in 1969. The jobs available in Gyöngyös were mostly accessible to the non-Romani population. Roma—who began moving from their segregated settlement situated on the outskirts of Gyöngyöspata into the streets that had been vacated by poor peasants in the 1950s—were encouraged to take jobs in the mines and in Visonta. Other Roma worked in the Goldberger textile factory or on construction projects in the capital city, which was only one hundred kilometers from the village. The increasing importance of the industrial sector was reflected in official statistics. In 1990, only 227 of the 1,193 "active earners" were employed in the agricultural sector, while 621 worked in the industrial and construction sectors.[2]

The discussions and interviews Margit and I conducted with local residents revealed that the peasant families who had been forced to join the Mátra Cooperative in the great collectivization wave of the 1960s came up with complex strategies to weather the period of regime change. The following—strongly condensed—life history of an elderly couple offers an insight into a conversion strategy that can be considered typical for the 809 "inactive earners" who made up 30 percent of the local population according to the census of 1990.[3] Both the woman and man in question began their careers by taking up work in a state-run grocery shop in the early socialist period. Thanks to their privileged status—they worked for a state company—they were among the first to obtain the right to farm a household plot (*háztáji*), which had allowed them to supplement their income by growing lettuce and other vegetables, which they sold at the market in Gyöngyös. Farming a háztáji required significant effort. After returning home from their official workplace in the afternoon, they would work well after sunset on the small piece of land (approximately two-thirds of a hectare) that surrounded their house. By the end of the 1980s, they had saved enough money to buy a Dacia car and a small orchard on the Goat Stone—a hill overlooking the village—where workers from the village and nearby localities began to build wine cellars and holiday houses[4] in the second half of the

1960s. In 1991, the couple used the remainder of its savings to buy more land, the price of which had fallen by 50 percent immediately after the adoption of the much-anticipated Compensation Law.[5] They were not the only ones to profit from this opportunity. While in many other (especially poorer) rural localities most of the land was obtained by the managers of the dismantled cooperatives, here the latter only managed to buy three hundred hectares (which they used to create a cereal production company that employs twenty people today). Buying land proved to be a prescient strategy as it allowed post-peasants to weather the period of regime change. The woman explained that "standing on two feet" allowed the family to compensate for the loss of formal employment after her husband was fired from his workplace. Capitalizing on their assets (the car, the small plot, and the orchard) they began selling lettuce and fruits on the wholesale fruit and vegetable market in Budapest (where prices were significantly higher than in Gyöngyös).

The census of 2001 registered only forty-three local people employed in the agricultural sector. The steep drop in the number of people employed in agriculture reflected the further diminution of the sector's share in the local economy, in line with national and regional deagrarianization trends.[6] It also attests to the concentration of vineyards in the hands of the family-run enterprises that dominate viticultural production. The sluggish growth of the price of table grapes in the 1990s (see table 2.1) forced many post-peasants to abandon the cultivation of small plots. Their terroirs were purchased by the owners of the ten to twelve medium-sized viticultural enterprises that are still active in the sector today. These businesses are run by "native" (*tősgyökeres*) local families, with the exception of the smallest, which was founded by a young man from the capital city who sold his assets to buy a plot and grow grapes in "the wonderful local soil made up of a rare mix of lime and andesite" (as he told me). These families were the real winners of the capitalist transformation. They not only dominated the most prestigious sector of the local economy but—as I will go on to show—also played a key role in communal life.

The widespread use of small land holdings to stabilize rural livelihoods in the period of regime change, followed by the concentration of land in the hands of the most competitive family businesses, was not only typical for Gyöngyöspata and the villages of the Mátra region but also for most Hungarian rural localities. Data published in a report dealing with the state of agriculture revealed that the number of individual producers dropped by a staggering 31.3 percent between 1991 and 2000, and then by another 35.5 percent between 2001 and 2007 (KSH 2008: 168). The trend was especially pronounced in the Northern Hungary region,[7] where their number declined by 36.3 and 39.9 percent respectively (see table 2.2). The same data set shows that Northern Hungary's dismal record partially resulted from a steep drop in the number of individual viticultural producers (who made up one-fourth of individual producers in the region). Almost half of individual viticultural producers who were active in the year 2000 went out of business by 2007 (see table 2.3). The main economic rationale for abandoning small vineyards was the sluggish increase of the price of wine grapes, which only grew by 30 percent, whereas inflation was 73 percent in the 2001–2010 period. This was below the rate of growth of the price of many fruits and also inferior to that of table grapes (see table 2.1).

Table 2.1. *En gros* price of grapes as compared to inflation and other fruit items (1991–2010).

	Average price in 1991– 1995 period (ft/kg)	Average price in 1996– 2000 period (ft/kg)	Average price in 2001– 2005 period (ft/kg)	Average price in 2006– 2010 period (ft/kg)	Average price increase between 1991–1995 and 1996– 2000 (%, 1991–1995 =100.0)	Average price increase between 2001–2005 and 2006– 2010 (%, 2001–2005 =100.0)
Table grape	22.92	38.36	72.88	127.74	**167**	**175**
Wine grape	17.88	41.30	50.76	66.24	**231**	**130**
Apple	13.80	20.28	16.26	29.46	147	181
Pear	19.12	37.78	48.66	62.54	198	129
Cherry	43.06	99.30	135.38	199.82	231	148
Sour cherry	39.80	149.30	100.70	105.76	375	105
Plum	20.66	28.46	45.96	54.94	138	120
Apricot	43.14	75.76	91.50	97.38	176	106
Peach	33.08	45.30	63.46	59.44	137	94
Raspberry	136.16	170.48	213.06	342.14	125	161
Strawberry	60.80	124.36	212.84	396.04	204	186
Inflation					**625**	**173**

Table 2.2. Number of individual agricultural producers by region (1991, 2000, 2007).

| | 1991 | 2000 | 2007 | Number of individual agricultural producers in 2000 as compared to their number in 1991 (%, 1991 = 100.0) | Number of individual agricultural producers in 2007 as compared to their number in 2000 (%, 2000 = 100.0) | Share of regions in relation to total number of such enterprises (%) |
	n	n	n	1991–2000	2000–2007	2007
Central Hungary	124,060	81,112	61,266	65.4	75.5	9.9
Central Transdanubia	151,489	89,803	55,163	59.3	61.4	8.9
Western Transdanubia	153,099	101,678	61,333	66.4	60.3	9.9
Southern Transdanubia	168,909	122,824	76,881	72.7	62.6	12.4
Northern Hungary	211,506	134,655	80,986	63.7	**60.1**	13.1
Northern Great Plain	302,815	220,191	148,938	72.7	67.6	24.1
Southern Great Plain	283,875	209,143	134,084	73.7	64.1	21.7
Sum / Average	1,395,753	958,534	618,651	68.7	**64.5**	100.0

Table 2.3. Number of viticultural producers by region (2000, 2007).

	2000	2007	2000–2007	2007
	n	n	Number of viticultural enterprises in 2007 as compared to their number in 2000 (%, 2000 = 100.0)	Share of regions in relation to total number of such enterprises (%)
Central Hungary	12,989	9,703	74.7	8.1
Central Transdanubia	29,045	20,396	70.2	17.1
Western Transdanubia	34,215	24,217	70.8	20.3
Southern Transdanubia	37,097	21,647	58.4	18.2
Northern Hungary	36,470	18,789	**51.5**	15.8
Northern Great Plain	19,923	8,645	43.3	7.3
Southern Great Plain	28,066	15,792	56.3	13.2
Sum / Average	197,805	119,189	60.3	100.0

The main factor that differentiates Gyöngyöspata from more depressed northeastern localities is that the village is situated in a microregion that weathered the economic crisis relatively well as compared to other industrialized centers in the Northeast.[8] The Mátrai Power Plant—whose majority shares were sold to German energy giant RWE in 1995—did not fire its skilled workers and continues to employ 2,100 people (while also indirectly supporting the jobs of another 1,500 people). This goes a long way in explaining why the majority of the 751 blue-collar workers who were registered as "commuting workers" in 1990 managed to retain their jobs.[9] It also explains the evolution of the unemployment rate between the three consecutive censuses (1990, 2001, 2011). While in 1990 Gyöngyöspata was among the twenty percent of localities where the unemployment rate was the highest in the country, in 2001 the local unemployment rate equaled the national average, and in 2011 it was below average (4.9 versus 6.5 percent).

Gyöngyöspata did, however, resemble the country's most disadvantaged localities in one particular respect. Local unskilled workers found themselves permanently locked out of the formal labor market. Layoffs began in the 1980s,[10] but the process accelerated in the aftermath of regime change when the Goldberger factory was closed (in 1993) and unskilled workers were laid off from Visonta. At the time of research, out of the approximately one hundred working-age local Romani men, only three held jobs and an additional five were employed by local grape-growers and winemakers on a more or less regular basis. (To our knowledge, all of the Romani women were unemployed.) Data provided by the National Employment Service (see table 2.4) show that unemployed Romani men constituted the majority of those whom the bureau registered as unemployed in Gyöngyöspata between 2000 and 2007. As described in the previous chapter, high unemployment rates among Roma in the post-1989 period were the result of the conjunction of structural disadvantages (i.e., the sharp decline in demand for unskilled labor in the capitalist economy) and ethnic discrimination on the restructured labor market. The unemployment crisis was most pronounced in northern and eastern regions, where one half of Roma lived and employment opportunities for unskilled workers were all but wiped out after the closing of mines and factories.[11] While news of the dramatic employment situation in cities like Ózd and Miskolc reached the wider public, the no less dire predicament of rural Romani communities living on the periphery of the country's industrial heartland largely evaded the public gaze. The predicament of the rural Romani population was especially dire in peripheral villages due to the lack of access to public services (see discussion below) and the lack of demand for real estate, which condemned the surplus population to geographic immobility (see my discussion of rural ghettoization in the first chapter).

Table 2.4. Number of people unemployed in Gyöngyöspata (2000–2013); growth years in italic and inflection point underlined.

2000	2001	2002	2003	2004	2005	2006
133	124	124	*137*	*146*	*153*	*161*
2007	2008	2009	2010	2011	2012	2013
156	*160*	*193*	<u>*216*</u>	190	157	166

Hegemonic Hungarianness in Response to Polarization

Microstudies of the surplus population highlighted that it was far from being ethnically homogenous (see Kovács et al. 2013). However, due to the large proportion of citizens of Romani descent in its ranks and the general perception that rural marginals lived a "Gypsy life," people living on the margins of mainstream society were labeled "Gypsies."[12] In Gyöngyöspata, the overwhelming majority of those who had lost their industrial workplaces were of Romani descent. These families lived in the "Gypsy settlement": a row of houses that had initially been inhabited by poor landless peasants. The time I spent talking to the families who lived there revealed that a number of them had moved back from Budapest to the settlement in the early 1990s after male members lost their jobs. Most of these families had roots in Gyöngyöspata, but there were also a few genuine newcomers who had had no prior relationship to the village.

In 2007, local representatives enacted a building regulation that prohibited the building of new homes (which, at that time, was actively supported by the left-liberal government), as well as renovations and improvements to built property in streets that higher status groups had abandoned. By limiting the supply of housing on and in the vicinity of the settlement, local representatives sought to prevent Roma from nearby villages and Gyöngyös[13] from moving to Gyöngyöspata in large numbers. Their aim, in other words, was to prevent Gyöngyöspata from becoming a "ghetto-village."[14]

Our discussions with the former principal of the elementary school revealed that settlement-dwellers[15] had routinely been relegated to separate classes or mixed with children requiring special care well before her tenure (1996–2006).[16] This separation involved spatial division as well. The special "B" classes were confined to the ground floor, whereas the "normal" classes occupied the second floor of the school building. These classes also used separate bathrooms, and children attending special classes did not take part in sporting activities organized at the local swimming pool. As for after-school activities, these were restricted to children whose mothers were employed. (As noted above, Romani women were all unemployed as a result of which their children were excluded from this service.) The former principal told us that this system was introduced to reduce interaction between children who came from different backgrounds and thereby prevent conflict situations that teachers were ill-prepared to handle. This, however, was only one part of the story. Segregation was also designed to prevent the flight of higher status families (i.e., the transfer of children to one of Gyöngyös's schools).[17] In order to prevent the "Gypsyfication" of the school, the principal—like her predecessors and successor—not only ensured the segregation of "problematic children" but also made sure that "clean classes" were taught by the best teachers. The unequal distribution of educational resources and the stigmatization of settlement-dwellers as "problematic" or "retarded" was powerfully consequential. In the last decade, the school has had only one "Gypsy" pupil (the son of the Gypsy Self-Government's president) who was able to earn a high school degree. This single statistic highlights better than anything else the educational disadvantages suffered by settlement-dwellers. It also explains why—due to their low educational skills—it was implausible for them to leave the village in order to take up work in economically more dynamic regions. Since the local economy had little need for unskilled labor, settlement-dwellers found themselves with only one viable option: to work in the vineyards and orchards of local post-peasants.

The most important feature of the two mechanisms of segregation I alluded to—residential and educational segregation—was that they were not legitimized through the language of ethnicity but through the idiom of merit. Choosing who got to attend "normal" classes was, as the former principal explained, based on the "capabilities" of children. Villagers, in the meantime, told us that they would be willing to consider selling their houses to "tidy" families. For the external observer, it was clear that differences of merit mapped onto different positions in the social hierarchy. The children of settlement-dwellers were rarely deemed "capable" and their parents "tidy" enough to be offered the prospect of social mobility. Still, the moral economy of merit allowed a few settlement-dwellers to escape mechanisms of segregation and control. We knew of four or five families where men were regularly offered work in orchards and vineyards. Their children, incidentally, also got to attend "normal" classes. Most of these families had also managed to purchase a house outside the settlement. By offering "adaptable" families the prospect of crossing the invisible ethnic-cum-class boundary, local power-holders had created a powerful tool for disciplining settlement-dwellers. The latter were given a viable strategy for escaping exclusion: playing the "worthy" ("deserving," "hard-working," "tidy," "normal") family better than others.

I am not the first to highlight the persistence of hegemonic Hungarianness (see previous chapter) in the postsocialist period. Two anthropologists who worked in a locality that is similar to Gyöngyöspata noted that competition for opportunities and resources controlled by "peasants" was waged by extended Romani families (Horváth and Kovai 2010). They also noted that the quasi-utopian prospect of assimilation prevented settlement-dwellers from developing durable bonds of solidarity. This was also the case in Gyöngyöspata where those who escaped from the settlement distanced themselves symbolically from those who stayed behind through the adoption of the hegemonic discourse of "unruliness" (*zsiványság*) and "untidiness" (*retkesség*). Such distancing was motivated on the one hand by the desire to free oneself from the burdens of helping distant relatives. (Practices of redistribution within these families helped members weather chronic shortages—of food, medicine, tobacco, etc.—and unexpected calamities—sickness, death or incarceration of a family member, etc.) By reneging reciprocal ties, these families stood a better chance of accumulating a minimum amount of savings, which was crucial for the successful implementation of mobility strategies. These "escapees" found themselves betwixt and between the two communities: they were no longer considered "Gypsies," but neither were they accepted as full-fledged members of the village community. This, however, did not dissuade them from harboring the hope that their children would be able to live like "normal people."[18]

The Decline of the Post-Peasantry

My discussions with settlement-dwellers revealed that there had been a drop in the demand for seasonal agricultural labor in the middle of the last decade (2000–2010). Up until then, several of my interlocutors had regularly worked in the orchards and vineyards of post-peasants. Although the latter preferred to employ poor peasants and seasonal migrants from Transylvania (who were said to be more hard-working), post-peasant households were also forced to rely on local unskilled Romani labor. This changed after Hungary's accession to the European Union. The "Romanians" disappeared (presumably because they could earn more in Spain and other countries). The producers we talked to also stressed that they could not keep pace with international food exporters, who made significant productivity gains through mechanization and took advantage of the scrapping of tariffs and the abundance of cheap migrant labor in the expanded European Economic Area. The elderly owners of small orchards and vineyards responded by abandoning and/or selling their plots and investing the money they received into the social mobility of their children. This is what van der Ploeg (2008) and Kovách (2003) called "depeasantiza-tion": the abandonment of the peasant mode of production and form of life. As noted above, this process, here as elsewhere, was part of a wider "deactivation" trend: the decline of agricultural output and the number of people employed in the sector. While some vineyards were purchased by the viticultural entrepreneurs, many were simply abandoned. It must also be noted that some viticultural producers sought to reduce their vulnerability to price shocks by combining the production of wine grapes with other economic activities, such as winemaking and the opening of bed-and-breakfasts. In the next chapter, I will have more to say about this particular "repeasantiza-tion" strategy.[19] At this point, I would simply like to say that depeas-antization outweighed repeasantization in terms of its impact on the demand for unskilled labor. While local winemakers (who strove to produce high-quality "hand-made" products) continued to employ one or two unskilled workers on a more-or-less regular basis, viti-cultural entrepreneurs who invested in mechanization need only a few farmhands to help them during the harvest. This explains why there were only four or five Romani men who were regularly offered agricultural work at the time of our research.

The decline of the post-peasantry had a number of important con-sequences. First, post-peasants (who had already been forced to in-vest large amounts of capital and physical labor into reconversion strategies during the period of capitalist transition) had to work even harder to maintain the profitability of their microenterprises. Many of the families we talked to had exhausted their resources and were also grappling with health problems by the middle of the last decade. This was, for instance, the case of the elderly couple whom I intro-duced in the beginning of the chapter. As I mentioned, the couple made use of their assets (a plot, "compensation coupons," a car) to supplement their meager income. The physical effort which allowed them to sustain their status and raise three children eventually took its toll. In 2013, the husband died of leukemia, and the woman de-cided to sell three hectares of land because she had lost the motiva-tion to continue the life of toil, which—she told us—had been built on the conviction "that it is hard work, and hard work only, that gets you ahead in life." Her children were not willing to follow their par-ents' example. Like the children of many other post-peasant families, they fled Gyöngyöspata to attend university (and then find work) in Budapest. Their departure left ailing parents wondering not only if it was worth it all but also who was to blame for the dispersion of their families and the demise of their way of life.

The declining demand for unskilled labor in the declining post-peasant sector also affected the surplus population. The already diminished stream of income trickling into poor households decreased even further. This created incentives for finding alternative means for ensuring social reproduction on a minimal level. Mothers told me that they had difficulties educating their children to become good, reliable workers. This was also true for "striving families" who had made important steps toward social integration. The result was the appearance of petty theft as an alternative means for securing income. Informants were in agreement that there were three "problematic families" in which young adults and children regularly stole small things from "peasants," especially elderly people living on their own (who offered an easy target to thieves). Our visits to these informants—women who lived in the vicinity of the settlement—revealed that many of them had entertained good relationships with one or two families who lived in the settlement. Most of them had owned an orchard or a vineyard on the Goat Stone, a "cellar-hill" (a hill that accommodates cellars where the grapes are processed into wine and then stored in bottles or barrels) where I was told that the best wine grapes were grown. In exchange for help in the orchards and vineyards, owners would offer a portion of the harvest or some other in-kind reward. Until 1995, the vineyards located there had benefited from the protection of a military camp that occupied the hilltop. (Soldiers, we were told, would on occasion fire warning shots in cases when thieves attempted to approach the grapevines.) Our informants remembered the departure of the military as having co-incided with a rise in petty criminality. This may have been true, if we are to believe the statistics I obtained from the Interior Ministry (see table 2.5, which shows that the number of "crimes against property" registered by the police and published by the Interior Ministry increased from 53 to 70 between 1994 and 1995).

Settlement-dwellers told us that the vineyards and orchards had been progressively abandoned by their elderly owners because the work was too hard and the benefits too meager. Post-peasants mostly disagreed with this. Most of them told us that local thieves were primarily responsible for owners' retreat from the Goat Stone. What both sides could agree on was that the cellar-hill's decay had been gradual, beginning in 1995 and ending in 2006.

Post-peasants were still extremely bitter about the destruction of their property when we interviewed them in 2011. The memory of once resplendent vineyards and orchards, and the sight of decaying cellars and holiday houses, reminded former owners of the difficulties

Table 2.5. Criminal statistics for Gyöngyöspata (1990–2012); years when the military post was dismantled (1995) and the "criminal report" was published (2006) in bold.

Year	Total number of crimes	Crimes against property	Unresolved criminal cases	Crimes committed by minors
1990	40	18	18	0
1991	63	38	35	1
1992	59	39	16	2
1993	46	35	18	0
1994	66	53	24	5
1995	**93**	**70**	**25**	**5**
1996	27	13	10	0
1997	49	34	21	0
1998	48	36	24	0
1999	81	63	44	1
2000	70	52	40	0
2001	54	35	30	0
2002	55	41	22	0
2003	74	45	36	1
2004	56	39	19	1
2005	47	29	21	2
2006	**99**	**42**	**28**	**0**
2007	71	46	29	1
2008	47	21	19	0
2009	37	21	15	0
2010	50	34	28	0
2011	97	44	30	1
2012	77	31	33	0

brought by regime change—the dissipation of material security after the collapse of socialism—and the shattering of peasant traditions: the unproductive toil on the land and the vain hope that it would earn hard-working families a decent living. Some of them mentioned that their feeling of loss was rendered unbearable by "the reappearance of roof tiles on the houses of settlement-dwellers." (In other words, they accused local Roma of stealing the tiles from the roofs of their cellars and using them to repair the roofs of their own shabby houses.) This story, which enjoyed wide circulation at the time of our research, is important because it shows that the Goat Stone had become a symbol through which experiences of decline were linked to the presence of a "problem population." Although the orchards and vineyards were abandoned in the period when the agricultural sector was undergoing a second phase of restructuring (in connection to Hungary's accession to the European Union), their decay came to be associated in the post-peasant imaginary with petty criminality.

The impact of the Goat Stone's devastation on communal relations was rendered apparent by the publication of a "criminal report," which catalogued "misdemeanors and other crimes" committed by the "local underworld" based on victims' testimonies in the autumn of the year when the last cellars were being abandoned by their owners (2006). The sixty-five-page report—published by a previously weightless local association, the *Friends of Gyöngyöspata Circle*—was composed of two parts: a short introduction wherein the association's president offered her own interpretation of the misdemeanors; and the anonymized transcripts of verbal testimonies, which had been offered by self-declared victims. In this chapter, I will mainly be concerned with the second part, which provides a unique insight into the nature of the grievances that had strained the relationship between post-peasants and settlement-dwellers from the middle of the last decade. In what follows I reproduce three testimonies to give readers an insight into the grievances of those who self-identified as representatives of the "decent majority," and into the idiom in which these were expressed:

> One day, this was two years ago, I noticed that 160,000 forints had disappeared from the house. We called the policeman because only this Robi had been inside the house. They caught him and he admitted to having taken the money. He promised that he would return it. He gave back 25,000 [forints] but we are still waiting for the rest of the money.
>
> This happened a couple of years ago on Easter Monday. My mother was at home alone, the gate was not closed properly and four Romani lads came in to "sprinkle" her, pushing her from the kitchen into the living room. In the meantime, the other lads stole her purse; there wasn't too much money in it. They also took the clock from the kitchen. Since the incident my mom's mental state has severely deteriorated; she is overcome by fears even during daytime.
>
> For some time I only knew the situation from local inhabitants' dreadful stories of the local underworld. I observed, first with astonishment, then with deep sorrow, the Goat Stone, one of the most characteristic cellar-hills of the country, which has been turned into an uninhabited wasteland by the thieves.

I heard of the old man who had desperately tried to protect his peach trees but was forced to run for his life after local criminal-seedlings started throwing stones at him. I heard the story of the owner of the neighboring cellar which was burglarized six times in the last ten years. . . . Three weeks ago it was our turn to experience the deeds of the local underworld on our skin. My mother was robbed in front of our cellar. The object of value could naturally not be recovered, but one of the perpetrators was identified. Despite the presence of witnesses and the fact that the damage inflicted was worth approximately one hundred thousand forints we saw the perpetrator in the village again. We also heard that he had robbed and beaten an older man since this event. Up until now we dreamed of moving to Gyöngyöspata in a few years' time. This is now in jeopardy because we bear responsibility for the lives of our future children. We don't want to live in a village where people leading criminal lives roam freely . . . . We don't want to live in a place where I cannot plant a tree in front of the cellar because the local underworld sends its children to cut it up for heating . . . . We don't want to live in a place where we cannot send our children to the local school. Who is the local underworld made up of? People who make a living by recourse to theft, robbery and, naturally, social benefits. There are hundreds of hectares of forest and orchards around the village that require manual labor. There is work for everyone here, everyone! But the local underworld is not willing to work like the "stupid peasants"—as they say. Instead, they live on social benefits, which are paid for by the "stupid peasants" and their urban kin. They ruin the life prospects of their own children. Four- or five-year-old children who, as we ourselves witnessed, still cannot speak are cajoled or coerced into stealing by their own parents. . . . In winter, I saw two two- to three-year-old children carrying a bucket of water with bent backs in the snow. In Africa evil people make killing machines out of five- to ten-year-old children. Those who teach their children how to lead a criminal lifestyle, instead of educating them, are committing an almost equally sinister crime. But the teachers here are not terrorists or guerrilla leaders, but parents! Parents who then use their children as shields because society has no answer to childhood criminality. They can't be reported to the police, the law offers no protection against them. These parents are the basest people.[20] (translation mine)

I begin by noting the obvious: by the time of the report's publication, settlement-dwellers had come to be perceived as menacing the peace, dignity, form of life, and livelihood of mainstream groups by dozens of local inhabitants. Although the victims were deliberately left unidentified, forms of self-identification (e.g., "I am an elderly lady") and the language of the testimonies warrant the assumption that, in 2006, discontentment with local Roma was still largely confined to pensioners and owners of orchards and vineyards who together made up approximately a third of the local population.[21] This is not to say that all pensioners and landowners were angry with "the Gypsies" (in the plural). Nonetheless, the testimonies make clear that the author did not weave the report out of thin air. In 2006, Gyöngyöspata witnessed a largely spontaneous wave of popular anti-Gypsyism.

This wave of popular resentment appears to have been directly fueled by the perception—shared by one part of the local population—that certain misdemeanors linked to "the local underworld" kept recurring and that this recurrence constituted a threat to "decent people." Out of these misdemeanors, petty theft was singled out as the gravest offense. In this regard I find important to quote the former vice-mayor, who told us that "petty theft did not use to be a problem because twenty kilos of fruit is not such a big deal. But the situation of peasants has changed for the worse and this also means that the people from here are not as tolerant as they used to be" (excerpt from interview, translation mine).

The vice-mayor's comment highlights the link between post-peasants' sense of deprivation (generated in the midst of economic restructuring) and their growing "intolerance" toward the surplus population. While proponents of the "relative deprivation thesis" have emphasized that feelings of deprivation are primarily caused by disappointing comparisons with one's own past or with social reference groups and that these tend to make people more anxious, insecure, and resentful toward "others" (see Rydgren 2007), my material highlights the centrality of theft in rationalizing individual loss and collective decline. While theft is most often discussed in the anthropological literature on postsocialism as a generic metaphor for expressing experiences of dispossession in connection to elite strategies of economic restructuring and welfare state retrenchment (see Kalb 2009), the criminal report and our subsequent fieldwork in Gyöngyöspata showed that it could also signify the post-peasantry's sense of losing control over "its" villages in the presence of a problem population. I included the last testimony to show that an abstract representation of settlement-dwellers as a dangerous collectivity presenting a threat to the wellbeing and future of the village community had spontaneously emerged in 2006.

Contesting Hegemonic Hungarianness

It is noteworthy that representatives of the post-peasantry had made an effort to integrate settlement-dwellers into the local economy in the period that preceded the report's publication. This effort was led by two women who played a pivotal role in the Friends of

Gyöngyöspata Circle. A woman who owned a vineyard and a bed-and-breakfast began to sell brooms that were made by the oldest Romani man and encouraged younger men to learn this traditional Romani skill. Although the arrangement lasted until the man's death, her efforts to revive the tradition failed. Another initiative—the promotion of microscale gardening among settlement-dwellers—which was promoted and managed by the local doctor—also failed to take off. Both women explained the failure of these initiatives by reference to the laziness of settlement-dwellers, claiming that they had become accustomed to living on social assistance that was paid from the pockets of taxpayers. The time I spent on the settlement convinced me that this explanation was completely oblivious to the viewpoint of the putative beneficiaries.

Broom-making had never occupied a predominant place in the skill set of the local Romani population. The grandfathers and great grandfathers of settlement-dwellers had either worked as musicians or agricultural laborers. (As noted above, the oldest living members of the community worked during the socialist period in regional mines and on construction projects in the capital city.) When I asked them about what they thought about broom-making, former industrial workers told me that they were absolutely uninterested in "going back to a past that never was," as one of them put it to me. "Me making a broom? You've gotta be kidding" was the mildest reply I received. My interlocutors were, moreover, also skeptical of the profitability of broom-making. Not only were there too many unemployed men in Gyöngyöspata, but also they had heard that several dozen local municipalities had organized broom-making courses for unemployed Romani men in different corners of the country and that these had achieved dismal results. There was simply not enough demand for hand-made brooms in a country that had liberalized trade with China in 2004.

When we asked settlement-dwellers about the failure of the gardening initiative, we received replies that pointed in a similar direction. Young women told us that they did not want to become "peasants" because that lifestyle did not suit them and because even families who had worked the land for decades were struggling to make ends meet. Romani families who had lived in Budapest did the most sneering about the project. Growing one's own produce was especially undesirable for these families, who had moved back to Gyöngyöspata only because they could no longer afford to live in the capital city. Having grown accustomed to life in a capital city, there was nothing appetizing in the (peasant) ideal of working the land.

One of the men who accepted work in the orchards and vineyards of post-peasants told me he would prefer other types of work but this was the only way for him to earn a decent income.

Discussing the two failed projects gave me a glimpse of the deep sense of injustice that proletarianized middle-aged men—who had accepted the socialist state's "assimilation offer" (see previous chapter) and worked hard to be accepted as the equals of non-Romani coworkers—harbored. What struck me particularly was not the experience of injustice and victimhood—which András Bíró (2013) had characterized as the defining element of Romani cultural outlooks in the postsocialist period—per se. It was rather that these men were at a loss when it came to expressing their grievances. The only language that they had at their disposal came directly from the liberal lexicon. My interlocutors mentioned "discrimination" and "racism" when they tried to make sense of their experience of being locked out of formal jobs and mobility. I found that these words did not address the key element of that experience—namely, that of having been excluded from workplaces that could sustain the dream of assimilation into the community of equal citizens. Still, this was the only language in which the experience of exclusion could be voiced. And this language was also useful because within particular institutional arrangements it could—as I describe below—serve as an instrument for claims-making. Yet, the language of antiracism remained largely inadequate within the most important social realm—everyday life—because it was easily countered by the hegemonic discourse. Representatives of the local elite were joined by upwardly mobile Romani families in branding those who refused to work as "lazy welfare-scroungers." The language of antiracism was ineffective against this discursive strategy because it did not offer an avenue for defending the rebuttal of well-intended employment schemes or for contesting the not-so-innocent assumption underpinning these projects: that Roma were only fit to become the clients of post-peasant patrons. Roma who refused to take part in the above-mentioned broom-making and gardening projects were labeled "lazy," and the failure of these initiatives was widely referred to in order to underpin the generalized claim that local Roma were work-shy.

Members of the younger generation came much closer to challenging common-sense assumptions formulated within the doxic universe of work and merit. The adolescents I got to know harbored the same sense of victimhood as their parents. These young men—who spent a great deal of time listening to rap music and watching music videos on the internet—had grasped that they only had the slimmest chance to realize the dream of escaping the "shitty settlement" where they felt imprisoned "as in a ghetto" (their word, not mine). But, instead of holding a largely repressed inner grudge against Magyars, members of the younger generation found avenues for publicly voicing their dissatisfaction with being relegated to the margins of society. It was the politically charged repertoire of urban "Gypsy rap" that provided the key source of inspiration for expressing the experience of marginality.

Munk (2013) recently noted that the genre's appearance can be linked to the Black Train (*Fekete Vonat*) band, which rose to fame in an incredibly short amount of time in 1998. Although the band remained at the center of public attention for only a short time, it provided a critical impetus to the development of a subculture that expressed experiences and ideas that had hitherto been absent from public culture. Another researcher noted that Gypsy rap "expressed a fundamental tension between power-holders and those who have been forced to live in positions of subservience" (György 2009: 131, translation mine), and that this antagonism was signified through the symbolic equation of Afro-American and Romani experiences of exclusion and marginality.[22] Writing in 2009, she emphasized that this "culture of resistance" was largely confined to the eighth district of Budapest, which had become a metaphor for ghettoization, criminality, and the refusal to accept the norms of homogeneous society.

By the time of my research, Gypsy rap had arrived in the countryside. The young settlement-dwellers I interacted with took advantage of the availability of free internet access in elementary schools and cheap internet access in private households to appropriate the incendiary music of the Black's Trains numerous followers. Although György highlighted that politically charged rap lyrics played a key role in the emergence and spread of a novel kind of identity politics, I do not see the reimagination of the settlement as a "ghetto" or the self-perception of young settlement-dwellers as the subjects of racialized forms of exclusion as the most consequential influence of the new genre. After all, the liberal discourse of antiracism (which was incidentally also shaped by the discourse of the US civil rights movement) already offered an avenue for criticizing racialized mechanisms of exclusion. Instead, I found that rap exercised a more powerful influence on the level of culture as ethos and practice than on the level of *Weltanschauung*. The main *differentia specifica* of young settlement-dwellers, compared to the generation of their parents, is that they have been injected with the ethos of revolt and that rap culture has offered a model for transforming this ethos into everyday practice.

Until most recently, one of the favorite pastimes of young settlement-dwellers was to hang out in the streets of the village, especially in the evening when everyone was expected to retreat to their (segregated) living quarters. "Hanging out" in public space was, in other words, considered indecent. Yet this is exactly what young settlement-dwellers liked to do because it allowed them to establish a degree of visibility and presence. The practice of hanging out reminded me of Benjamin's (1999) description of the flaneur: the idler, the urban explorer, the connoisseur of the street. Benjamin, drawing on the poetry of Baudelaire, made this figure an emblematic archetype of modern urban experience. Using his term as a reference point, we may construct the character of the "intruder": the rural idler whose intent is not to explore the well-known (and rather boring) world of the peasants but simply to remind them that the arbitrary rules they devise will not be respected by all, or at least not at all times.

"Intruding" was not the only form of symbolic action in the repertoire of young settlement-dwellers. They also played tricks on elderly ladies who (as the most vulnerable members of mainstream society) offered easy targets to bored adolescents. This kind of symbolic play on hierarchies was not taken lightly. Stories of old ladies being harassed on their way to mass—circulated through gossip—played a key role in spreading the message that Roma were beginning to exhibit "unruly" forms of behavior in Gyöngyöspata. Although petty theft was the most often cited grievance in the above-mentioned criminal report, victims' testimonies also contained numerous references to the harassment of elderly ladies, as evidenced by the second testimony I reproduced above. The author of the "criminal report" used this and other examples to claim that "public security is a thing of the past. . . . Children and adults cannot walk on the street without having to fear becoming the victims of atrocities. Romani adolescents shout obscene words at bypassers. Those who dare to respond are verbally threatened or simply spat on" (translation mine).

In the next chapter, I will have more to say about the discursive strategy of "abstraction" whereby the local counter-elite—led by leading representatives of the post-peasantry—sought to condense popular experiences and historically sedimented fears (see my discussion of historic representations of the Gypsy as "dangerous other" in the previous chapter) into a narrative that portrayed Roma (in the plural) as posing a threat to Magyars (in the plural too). Here, I would like to stick to the verbal testimonies to argue that the "naming and blaming" of settlement-dwellers was facilitated by the gradual disappearance of patron-client relationships. My discussions with settlement-dwellers who were in their forties and fifties revealed that they still remembered that their parents and grandparents had forged durable bonds with peasant families. These bonds began to lose their importance from the 1960s, when Roma men entered formal employment. I was told that this did not put an abrupt end to these relationships. Romani families continued to maintain friendly relations with their former patrons and would occasionally still help them out with certain chores (in exchange for small material rewards). During our fieldwork, I still found evidence for the survival of such reciprocal ties in the case of elderly ladies who needed help around the house. One possible reading of the above-cited second testimony is that the lads who stole money from the purse were members of a family whose older members had been the lady's clients. If that is true, it would explain why the theft of an almost empty purse would have caused such outrage. I may, of course, be wrong about this, but the story nonetheless lends itself to a broader interpretation—namely, that the disintegration of social relationships (and concomitant obligations) should be seen as a cause of the spread of unruly conduct among settlement-dwellers. This, however, is the ethnographer's reading. The victims—or, more precisely, those who cunningly portrayed themselves as their spokespersons—forged a different interpretation.

Abandonment

At this point, it is necessary to note that the president of the Friends of Gyöngyöspata Circle had sent copies of the report to the local notary, the police chiefs of the city of Gyöngyös and Heves County, and the (Socialist) parliamentary representative of the Gyöngyös electoral district. The choice of recipients shows that the association laid part of the blame for the spread of unruly behavior on local authorities and elected lawmakers. The claims formulated by the author in the report's introduction offer further insights into the intentions of the association's president:

> Recidivist offenders are not deterred by the actions of authorities; they live their lives as they please. They cannot be given meaningful sentences because the law protects them . . . . There are more and more instances of libel, minor bodily harm, slander and hooliganism despite the actions of the police . . . . Criminal proceedings are dropped due to the fact that the offenders are minors, could not be identified or for other reasons. While the weakness of the law makes honest men skeptical, it emboldens criminals. (translation mine)

This key passage reveals that the president primarily had an axe to grind with "the law"—or, more precisely, those who had been invested with the political authority to circumscribe the domain of criminality and codify punishment for criminal offenders. Although some of the testimonies reveal dissatisfaction with the work of the police, the president, citing the "weakness of the law," laid the blame for rampant criminality at the feet of national politicians. This conviction also found expression in another passage: "The local population unanimously requests the media and the courts not to accept *livelihood criminality* as a justification [for criminal acts] because work and opportunities are available to every Hungarian citizen. Vegetables and fruits can be grown in anyone's garden, irrespective of gender, race or religion" (translation and emphasis mine).

Although the sentence appears to lay blame on the media and the courts, there is more here than meets the eye, as revealed by the reference to "livelihood criminality." The term initially appeared in the specialized jargon of the socialist police in the 1960s as an indirect way of referring (in internal communication) to criminal acts that were attributed to Roma (see E. Z. Tóth 2012). It has since become linked in the public imaginary to a liberal politician—Gábor Kuncze—who acted as interior minister between 1994 and 1998. This linkage is the fruit of long years of painstaking work. Since the beginning of the millennium, intellectuals and politicians[23] associated with the right-wing power bloc have persistently accused the minister of condoning theft by reinterpreting it as "livelihood criminality" and of shielding thieves by weakening the penal code.[24] What we see here then is an oblique critique of the ruling left-liberal elite's attempt to justify petty criminality through a strategy that Cohen labeled "interpretative denial":[25] the attempt to justify an action (or series of actions) that may be seen by some as damaging and/or unjust by arguing that what happened was not what they think had happened. Although Kuncze had in fact never condoned petty criminality, he did voice his conviction that the use of the term "livelihood criminality" was warranted because perpetrators "steal money or items of value . . . in order to ensure their own survival."[26]

My broader claim is that the suspicion that the ruling elite was not only unwilling to clamp down on thieves but actively provided legal cover for petty criminals fostered a sense of abandonment, and that the latter reinforced post-peasants' intolerance toward the surplus population, together with their conviction that something had to be done to tame them. Although the report published by the association cannot be straightforwardly treated as a window onto the emotional life of the local post-peasantry, the claim that "the law offers no protection" against petty criminals may have been shared by many at the time of its publication. The interviews we conducted with people who lived close to the settlement and the former owners of orchards and vineyards five years after its publication underscored this assertion. Two of our informants specifically mentioned that they were still angry with the previous left-liberal government—and minister Kuncze in particular—for condoning petty theft and thereby promoting a culture of idleness and criminality among settlement-dwellers. A young man who had moved from Budapest to the locality to produce hand-made wine and had earned a reputation after being awarded the prestigious title of "Young Hungarian winemaker of the year" in 2011 summed up the opinion of local winemakers: "I often talk with the others about why it's so hard to find Gypsies willing to work nowadays. In these discussions someone will always mention that the political left committed a historical sin when it shied away from striking down at the right moment. Instead of answering force with force, it left the Gypsies off the hook" (translation mine).

While I use the term "abandonment" to describe popular feelings in relation to the ruling elite, locals talked of "treason," "guilt," or "betrayal" when (on the rare occasion) they spoke directly about what the young winemaker from Budapest alluded to as the left's "historical sin." The report's first key sentences underscore my interpretation that feelings of abandonment (caused by an unresponsive elite) fueled anti-Gypsy sentiment: "After that wonderful and hopeful beginning, the 1990s brought with them the first thefts of fruit perpetrated by Gypsy kids . . . [now] public security is a thing of the past [and] the inhabitants of the village are forced to stomach the whims of the hypersensitive Romani population, which immediately turns to the ombudsman [whenever it is pressurized].

The phrasing is interesting since the Ombudsman for the Rights of National and Ethnic Minorities had to my knowledge not intervened in Gyöngyöspata until the report's publication (autumn 2006). The reference can perhaps then be seen as the imprint of episodes where the institutions of the liberal state had intervened to help local Romani groups assert their rights and assist their struggle against local mechanisms of segregation and control.

In the perception of local power-holders, one of the main advantages of hegemonic Hungarianness was that it allowed them to formally adhere to the state-enforced principle of nondiscrimination while informally upholding privileges and mechanisms of exclusion that violated the spirit of the law.[27] Although Romani activists had sought to challenge this contradiction since the early 1990s, their calls to action were generally ignored by governments and authorities. This situation changed, however, after Hungary filed its application to become a full member of the European Community. Countries aspiring to membership were requested to demonstrate a tangible commitment to combating discrimination against ethnic minorities. In the changed geopolitical environment, previously powerless activists and organizations found themselves in a position to focus international attention on local issues and pressure nation-states into taking action in favor of disadvantaged Romani communities. In Hungary in the late 1990s and early 2000s, a coalition of Budapest-based human rights organizations and Romani activists carried out a number of successful interventions against local power-holders who had unilaterally imposed measures that undermined the rights of Romani citizens. After one such successful intervention, a prominent sociologist and the country's most prominent Romani activist noted,

> In our opinion, the most important consequence of the Székesfehérvár ghetto case[28] is that it put an end to an unhealthy process highlighted by the towns of Kétegyháza, Sátoraljaújhely and Tiszavasvári. These cases were silently pushing the country toward a situation in which the most blatant forms of discrimination would appear natural and remain unsanctioned. The Székesfehérvár case broke that silence and this may mean that social and ethnic problems will no longer be swept under the carpet. (Ladányi and Horváth 2000: 112, translation mine)

The most important domain in which the ruling left-liberal elite attempted to move forward was desegregation of public education in 2002. At the time the reform was introduced, the Hungarian school system was one of the most decentralized ones in Europe. Although the central state provided funds for maintaining schools, the latter had been managed by local municipalities since regime change. Municipalities also had the right to define schools' catchment areas and to design pedagogical programs and curricula. This regime allowed for the "spontaneous segregation" of children who came from disadvantaged and/or minority backgrounds. Two consecutive in-depth studies carried out by two sociologists on behalf of the Institute for Educational Research in 2000 and 2004 showed that approximately half of Romani elementary school pupils attended classes where Romani children were in a majority (Havas and Liskó 2005: 23–24). The duo's findings, moreover, provided clear evidence that segregation was not spontaneous but resulted from principals' deliberate efforts to create parallel—"clean" and "Gypsy"—classes with a view to channeling available resources (the best teachers, extracurricular activities,

etc.) into the social reproduction of privileged social groups. In a separate monograph in which they sought to interpret their findings, the
researchers pointed out that

> [mechanisms of] segregation do not function on the basis of ethnicity. What
> we see is the creation of classes offering high-quality teaching to children
> coming from high-status groups, which also provide space for children com-
> ing from the most integrated Gypsy families. In the meantime, children com-
> ing from poor, low-status non-Romani families are often grouped into classes
> that are created to segregate Gypsy children. To this we must add that as a
> result of patterns of migration and residential segregation and of competition
> between schools, certain institutions become the warehouses of socially de-
> prived groups. The ratio of Gypsy children is always high in these schools but
> there are only minor differences between classes because internal selection no
> longer serves any function. (Havas et al. 2002: 80, translation mine)

These findings exercised a decisive influence on the left-liberal
government's education policy. In 2005, the liberal minister introduced a new law on public education that sought to restrict principals' room for selection. This was achieved by changing the rules on
the establishment of catchment areas. Municipalities that maintained
more than one school had to establish catchment areas in a way as
to ensure that the difference in the proportion of severely disadvantaged pupils between schools would not exceed 25 percent. Another
rule sought to limit municipalities' freedom to admit children from
outside their catchment area by forcing them to make such choices
based on a lottery system.

In the northeastern town of Jászladány, the local mayor came up
with an innovative strategy for upholding segregation. His plan was
to facilitate the creation of a separate school for non-Romani students
by renting a building that belonged to the municipality to a newly
created foundation that would open a private school for privileged
pupils. In March 2002, the municipality passed a decree that allowed
the leasing of the building to the foundation. Speaking on national
television, the mayor defended the move by asserting, "It is not me
but life that segregates." He also claimed to "protect the children who
wish to learn and to . . . create an opportunity for them to stay in Jászladány" (quoted by Zolnay 2012: 36). In May, the ombudsman wrote
a letter to the county administrative office in response to the local
Gypsy Self-Government's complaint that the local council had not
sought its approval for leasing local government property. In August,
the county administrative office reversed the local decree whereby
the municipality had leased its building to the private school. This
led infuriated parents who had enrolled their children in the private

school to organize a demonstration. The parents also sent an open letter to the incoming left-of-center prime minister, Péter Medgyessy, protesting the limitation of their educational freedom. It is at this point that the local mayor had another ingenious idea. Relying on local support for the private school, he took advantage of a loophole in the legal framework regulating the procedure for electing ethnic minority self-governments to mount a campaign to elect non-Romani representatives to the local Gypsy Self-Government. The strategy worked. The newly elected Gypsy Self-Government voted to suspend the minority veto, forcing the ministry to grant the private school the license to operate.[29]

Although the tactics of the local mayor did not become a blueprint for local segregationist struggles, the Jászladány case catalyzed local efforts to find legal mechanisms for maintaining "spontaneous segregation." Zolnay highlighted that the mayors of peripheral villages banded together to agree on the allocation of "problematic" pupils in a way as to evade the eruption of similar conflicts. The solution in the majority of depressed microregions (where the surplus population was increasingly concentrated) was to designate one elementary school as a "depot" or "ghetto-school" where the children of marginalized rural families could be relegated (Zolnay 2012: 37). In exchange, neighboring municipalities provided financial assistance (and other advantages) to the locality that offered to warehouse the children of the surplus population.

The civil rights coalition struggled to come up with a counter-strategy to block this locally coordinated effort to subvert desegregation. Its representatives finally managed to persuade the government to pass the Act on Equal Opportunity in 2005, which qualified segregation in schooling as a violation of the principle of equal opportunity. The same year, a prominent Romani activist founded the Chance for Children Foundation (CFCF) with the aim of initiating test cases against local municipalities. The first such case was initiated in the autumn of 2005 against the municipality of Miskolc. The foundation claimed that the city had violated the requirement of equal treatment when the council voted to unite local elementary schools without amending the borders of catchment areas. The case was bound to set a precedent as to whether municipalities could be held legally accountable for indirectly promoting segregation. Zolnay (2012) noted that an eventual victory for the antisegregationist camp would have—paradoxically—been detrimental for local Romani pupils because in-school segregation would have been transformed into segregation among schools and that the latter would have been even more detrimental to them. But the outcome of the case baffled every-one. Although the court of appeal ruled in the foundation's favor, the municipality of Miskolc refused to adhere to the verdict because its enforcement "would have jeopardized the fragile system that had been elaborated by the council" (Zolnay 2012: 40).

Although he shies away from drawing this conclusion, Zolnay's account of the Miskolc test case shows that the legal enforcement of the "integration policy" was not only ineffective but also coun-terproductive. It was ineffective because "the Ministry of Education was not able to enforce crucial elements of its antisegregation policy" (Zolnay 2012: 41). It was counterproductive because it forced public opinion—first on the local, then on the national level—to take sides between the proponents of "free choice" and those of "enforced de-segregation." The left-liberal elite was not only marching against the very principle—free choice—that it was vindicating in all other pol-icy areas as the remedy to inefficiencies; the tactics it pursued—the legalization and bureaucratization of the conflict and the unwilling-ness to discuss the consequences of its policies with representatives of local communities—made its approach appear rigid, authoritarian, and disconnected from everyday concerns. The reactions of citizens in Jászladány and other localities show that this approach fostered a powerful sense of abandonment in relation to the ruling elite.

In Gyöngyöspata, local power-holders succeeded in upholding the local regime of segregated instruction until 2011, when CFCF launched a similar legal case (which it eventually won). Our inter-views with the former mayor and the former school principal re-vealed, however, that they were already troubled by the prospect of becoming the targets of CFCF in 2005 and had initiated contact with the foundation to avoid being dragged to court. Due to the lack of sound ethnographic evidence, it is hard to assess the impact of this prospect on the moods and sensibilities of mainstream groups. The report's reference to the ombudsman nevertheless highlights the Friends of Gyöngyöspata Circle's preoccupation with the liberal state as a potential source of threat.

Border Frictions

In Gyöngyöspata, it was not the struggle for the maintenance of priv-ileged access to key public resources that led to the collapse of the old regime of segregation and control, but a series of violent confronta-tions on the invisible border that separated the "settlement" from the "village" (see map 2.2). Our interviews revealed that the interethnic relationship had become most tense in the border zone delineated by the "Bajcsi" and Bem streets. This was an ethnically mixed area where non-Roma lived side-by-side with a few upwardly mobile Romani families. Discussions with informants from both sides revealed that the relationship between Romani and non-Romani families had been characterized by a fragile equilibrium in the last couple of years. The gardens of the houses lining the Bajcsi street—which flanked the creek bordering the settlement—had been "plundered" on a number of occasions. Both our Romani and non-Romani informants told us that these thefts had been committed by settlement-dwellers. Our Romani respondents stressed, however, that three "recalcitrant" (*renitens*) families" were to blame and that one of these had been forced to leave Gyöngyöspata. In the meantime, non-Romani residents of the Bajcsi street formulated the opinion that the Romani community and, more particularly, its leader bore the responsibility for recurrent thefts. The argument was that the "voivod had lost control of his people."

The designation of the local Gypsy Self-Government's elected president as a voivod was misleading. First, the term "voivod" was historically used to designate the leaders of Vlach Gypsy communities. Romungro (Hungarian-speaking Romani) communities such as Gyöngyöspata's did not have a voivod to lead them. Second, Gyöngyöspata's Romani population did not invest their elected leader with the power to settle internal disputes. This fact, however, was not acknowledged by members of the ethnic majority, who expected the president to police the behavior of "his community." He himself saw the title as a source of symbolic power, which could be used to attract external resources for his extended family. (He was not alone: self-appointed or elected political entrepreneurs in the Northeast began vindicating the title at approximately the same time with the same purpose in mind.) In exchange, he agreed to act as arbiter between Roma and non-Roma in cases of disputes. I learned that, in 2006, a house in the Vári street had caught fire. The house had been recently purchased by a local Romani family whose members planned to move back from Budapest after their business went bankrupt. Romani informants told me that the head of the family—who carried the nickname "Devil"—was widely loathed and feared for his irreverence and thievery. I was also told that the street's non-Romani inhabitants had contacted the voivod to ask him not to make a fuss about their plan to prevent the family from moving into the newly purchased house. (The family decided to move to another village in

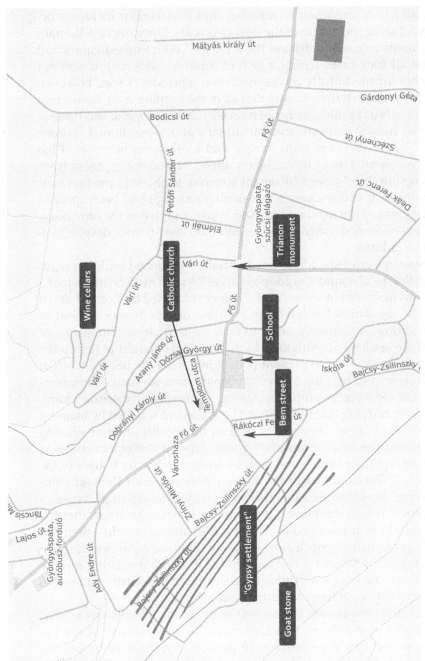

Map 2.2. Map of Gyöngyöspata featuring the "border zone" (marked with stripes) and other landmarks. © OpenStreetMap contributors, CC BY-SA license.

the end.) It is important to mention that four similar incidents occurred during the course of the next two years. Since my non-Romani informants refused to discuss the topic and police investigators had closed all four cases (citing a lack of forensic evidence), it was not possible for me to fully reconstruct these episodes. I was, however, able to establish with certainty that all of the families were Roma; two out of the four families were not native to Gyöngyöspata; and three of the four houses were situated outside the above-mentioned "border zone."[30] It is also important to note that local Roma interpreted the fires as willful acts of intimidation aimed at preventing them from moving into the "village." Romani informants also told me that in at least one of the four cases, a threatening message had been sprayed on the gates of the newly purchased house. In three of the four cases, the new owners decided to move into their new homes despite feeling intimidated.

These episodes shed light on the briefly mentioned building regulation that local councilors adopted in 2007 to ban modifications to the built environment in streets of the village inhabited by Roma. I noted that the regulation hindered the building of new homes as well as renovations and improvements to built property in and in the vicinity of the settlement. Although local councilors sought to justify the measure as an effort to prevent poor Roma from the nearby town of Gyöngyös from moving to Gyöngyöspata, non-Romani commoners cited the measure as primarily aiming to prevent "recalcitrant families" from moving into the village. The argument was that by banning the building of new houses (as well as the modification of existing structures) the local community could prevent settlement-dwellers from selling their homes and thereby from purchasing houses in the "village." The examples of the above-mentioned four Romani families show, however, that this mechanism of segregation and control was not flawless. Moreover, if we are to believe the claim that the fires should be interpreted as willful acts of arson—as I do—then this warrants a further conclusion—namely, that the local non-Romani population, or at least a key segment of it, felt that existing mechanisms were no longer adequate for ensuring their security and began to search for novel ways to buttress the social order.

Our effort to uncover the context of frictions pitting Roma against non-Roma in the streets that separated the settlement from the village showed that non-Roma were particularly appalled by the behavior of families whom they had previously gotten along with. The dominant grievance cited was petty theft and young men's failure to show respect and deference toward elderly residents. We noticed that elderly Romani women labored hard to prevent the explosion of accumulating tensions. Having formed durable bonds of reciprocity with non-Romani neighbors, they actively sought to appease them through practices of gifting and the verbal downplaying of frictions. These women also used their authority to persuade young men in their families to adopt a more reverent behavior toward neighbors. Although they were not entirely unsuccessful as "interethnic arbiters," there was little they could do to preempt thefts, which non-Roma became increasingly exasperated with.

The fragile equilibrium characterizing the interethnic relationship in the border zone was not only strained by recurrent thefts but also by the sporadic eruption of collective episodes of violence. The first fight broke out in the Bem street (see map 2.2) in 2006 after children from the settlement deflated the tires of the car belonging to the president of the local winemakers' association. The conflicting recollections of the incident make the story difficult to reconstruct, but here is my reading. The car owner startled one of the children involved in damaging the tires, who fell and hit himself. Seeing the blood on the child's face, his grandmother cried for revenge. In minutes, an angry crowd of Romani men had gathered outside the house where the president had taken refuge, calling on him to come out. Fearing the reactions of the crowd, the president called his friends to ask for help. As soon as they arrived, a fight broke out, which was broken up by the forceful intervention of a police unit that promptly arrived at the scene. In addition to the physical injuries sustained by both sides, the most important consequence of the incident was political. A village meeting was held at which anti-Romani passions flared for the first time and were immediately echoed by councilors, whom we later identified as belonging to the Friends of Gyöngyöspata Circle.

One year later, another violent incident was sparked by an event that our non-Romani respondents remembered as a "Magyar boy being narrowly hit by a Gypsy car." (The claim was that local Roma men who were driving a car at great speed in the village narrowly lost control of the vehicle and came close to hitting a boy who was playing in the street.) The men who recognized the driver and went to the Bajcsi street to ask for an explanation were allegedly beaten up by settlement-dwellers. The incident was reported to the police, but the charges were quickly dropped, provoking another village meeting and a demonstration in front of the voivod's house.

A third incident, which occurred in 2009, took place in the local school. A teacher—who lived on the Bajcsi and was married to a prominent member of the Friends Circle—was physically assaulted by an angry grandmother after her grandson was allegedly beaten in class. It was at this point that the local school became implicated in ethnic skirmishes as a "second frontline."

In 2010, a violent confrontation between a policeman and settlement-dwellers celebrating their children's graduation from the local elementary school was narrowly evaded thanks to the intervention of a police dog. Finally, in December 2010, Romani children beat up the son of Oszkár Juhász, Gyöngyöspata's would-be mayor, who was then known as the head of the Jobbik Party's local chapter.

These physical confrontations took place in an atmosphere that was turning hostile toward not only "unruly" families but increasingly toward the local Romani community as such. Although this is an issue I will deal with in the next chapter, it is important to highlight that the involvement of prominent members of the Friends of Gyöngyöspata Circle was no accident. Not only were the association's key representatives—who owned vineyards and/or lived in the border zone—personally interested in policing "unruly Gypsies"; the association, as I will go on to show, also played a key role in creating a situation wherein "neither accommodation nor assimilation is seen as being desirable [and] every measure to hold the groups apart and restore the morally sanctioned hierarchy between them becomes legitimate" (Wimmer 1997: 31; see also Wimmer 2002). What I find important to emphasize here is that the will to undermine the position of the mayor and his local allies was born out of the conviction that the "old" ways of dealing with settlement-dwellers were no longer practicable. I use the example of the local school to demonstrate this.

Our interviews with members of the local elite (councilors, teachers and school principals, members of local associations, clergymen) revealed that the emergence of the elementary school as a site of friction was born out of a conflict that pitted the proponents of integration against the defenders of segregation. Both groups saw the emergence of aggression within the walls of the school as a sign of looming chaos and "Gypsyfication." Our discussions with their leading representatives revealed that they were acutely aware that Gypsyfication posed a threat to the social reproduction of groups who could not afford to send their children to private schools and would also face hurdles in getting them accepted in Gyöngyös's public schools. They also voiced their fear that the school's transformation into a ghetto-school would deal a heavy blow to the village's reputation and thereby negatively affect its ability to retain high-status groups. While certain teachers, led by the principal, believed that the best way to prevent this scenario was to adopt the left-liberal government's integration policy (which relied on the assumption that segregation was the main cause of disharmony), others sided with a prominent member of the Friends Circle (a teacher who was later elected principal) who proposed to enforce segregation and strengthen the authority of teachers to discipline unruly students.

In the 2006–2010 electoral cycle, this conflict between the proponents of integration and segregation progressively evolved into a political conflict focused on the future prospects of the local community. Leading representatives of the Friends Circle accused the mayor and his supporters of refusing to acknowledge the existence of a "ticking time bomb" and of "sticking their heads in the sand." They used the criminal report to portray local power-holders as the allies of left-liberal politicians who "emboldened" criminal offenders. This is why the report should not only be seen as a window onto social experience but also as an instrument for underpinning proto-political claims and enlisting support from the local population. Such an effort to shift the balance of power on the local level by building a popular front against an unholy alliance of "unruly Gypsies" and "disconnected elites" was still novel at that time. Because of this, Gyöngyöspata provides a unique opportunity to study the emergence of popular anti-Gypsyism as a social force. In this chapter, I sought to show how this force emerged out of everyday frictions that were themselves generated in the midst of economic pressures and the government's simultaneous effort to undermine local mechanisms of segregation and control. In the next chapter, I will show how it was transformed by particular actors into a political movement and how different actors in the political field responded to the unprecedented rise of political anti-Gypsyism.

Concluding Remarks

This analysis has linked the emergence of popular racism to the structural forces that I highlighted in the previous chapter. With the help of statistics and ethnographic material I highlighted two structural particularities that plausibly played into the emergence of racist sensibilities in deprived northeastern microregions.

The first had to do with the regional particularities of agricultural production. While the Northern Hungary region resembled others in terms of the dwindling contribution of agricultural production toward added value and the steep drop in the number of people employed in the sector, it stood out in terms of the high ratio of microentrepreneurs. Although many individual producers gave up agricultural production—Northern Hungary actually ranked second in terms of the decline of the number of individual agricultural producers in the 1991–2007 period (see table 2.2)—the ratio of microenterprises remained above average.[31] In 2007, the region still ranked third in terms of the number of individual producers in stark contrast to the role of agriculture: the region ranked second lowest in terms of added value and the number of agricultural employees. One of the causes of this discrepancy was the high ratio of part-time producers.[32] This may well have been connected to the lack of alternative livelihood strategies in deindustrialized corners of the Northeast. Although Gyöngyöspata differed from other deprived microregions in this respect—it was situated in a region where industrial capacities had been relatively well preserved—I also found evidence for "involuntary entrepreneurship" among local producers. Ethnographic evidence presented in this chapter reveals that microproducers who remained active in the viticultural sector—which was negatively affected by the sluggish rise of the price of wine grapes in the 2001–2010 period (see table 2.1)—were especially frustrated with their predicament.

The second structural particularity I highlighted was the concentration of the surplus population in northeastern zones of deprivation. A study funded by the National Development Agency in 2010 revealed that forty-four localities in Heves county (that is, every third locality) had a "Gypsy or poor settlement" in its center, periphery, or vicinity (Domokos 2010). The study found that in 2010 approximately three hundred thousand people (3 percent of Hungary's population) lived in segregated settlements; that there were 1,633 settlements in the whole country; and that every fourth Hungarian locality had a settlement in its center, periphery, or vicinity. Approximately two-thirds of settlement-dwellers lived in the Northern Great Plain and Northern Hungary regions, where respectively every second and third locality had a settlement. Gyöngyöspata is, again, to some extent exceptional in this regard, due to the fact that local power-holders managed to prevent the influx of deproletarianized workers from the nearby town in the post-1989 period. However, the life that settlement-dwellers were forced to live resembled the predicament of the rural surplus population in many other corners of the northeastern periphery. Gyöngyöspata can thus be seen as one node in a territorially uneven web of "zones of relegation" where the surplus population found itself trapped and subjected to informal mechanisms of segregation and control.

The Northeast thus stood out as the region where both the post-peasantry and the surplus population were simultaneously facing a crisis of social reproduction (of different proportions, of course). This crisis was manifested on the one hand by the post-peasantry's inability to reproduce its form of life (which was tied—both materially and symbolically—to agriculture) and the out-migration of young people from deprived rural localities. On the other hand, it was also manifested in the surplus population's dwindling capacity to take advantage of tightly controlled channels of social mobility. Decreasing demand for unskilled labor in the deactivated and depeasantized agricultural sector prevented the building of patron-client ties between deproletarianized workers and post-peasants. Research conducted by sociologists in other rural areas—notably Southwestern Hungary, where Roma are also present in large numbers—shows that patron-client relationships played a decisive role in the stabilization of socioethnic hierarchies (see Feischmidt 2008; Kovács et al. 2013; Virág 2010). They achieved this by providing a minimum of security to unskilled workers who had lost their jobs after regime change, and by harnessing this newly freed labor force to post-peasant economic initiatives, which emerged after the privatization of agricultural collectives and state farms. Thus, one way to read my material is to argue that the presence of a surplus population constitutes a key condition of possibility of popular racism. This structuralist interpretation is in line with Ladanyi and Szelényi's (2006) reliance on the concept of the "underclass" to explain deep-seated historical shifts in interethnic relations. My retrospective microhistory of Gyöngyöspata, however, reveals the picture to be more complex and offers a more dynamic and relational reading of frictions. Although clientelism played only a small role in stabilizing the livelihoods of the surplus population in microregions where the agricultural sector was hit particularly hard by capitalist transformations, our fieldwork showed that it nevertheless played a key role in stabilizing the new social order. This was because it offered the only hope for crossing the invisible wall that separated the surplus population from mainstream society.[33] I showed that clientelism—legitimized through the hegemonic discourse of "worthiness"—faltered not only as a result of structural pressures but also the culturally misplaced integration initiatives pursued by the local elite. My own participation in the elaboration and implementation of local development projects in the depressed Mezőcsát microregion in 2008–2009 showed that in the 2006–2010 period, local power-holders still had access to state resources that allowed for the implementation of culturally informed and democratically negotiated development initiatives, and that these could exercise a beneficial impact on communal relations (see Szombati 2011). This contrast between my experiences in the villages of Igrici and Gyöngyöspata underscores Rebel's (2010) theorization of culture. Rebel's main point is that the unexpected return of old cultural codes or templates is not driven by some internal logic of a putatively self-referential cultural sphere, but by the needs, interests, and aspirations of specific social actors. While these are also shaped by past experiences and symbolizations, they arise within the domain of everyday life—that is, in the course of the negotiation of interpersonal relationships.

A focus on local communities' ability to opt between a given range of economic and cultural programs should not, however, distract our attention from the systemic constraints under which local actors operate. My findings warrant the conceptualization of racism as a popular countermovement galvanized by large-scale socioeconomic dislocations and political pressures that were acutely felt in "zones of deprivation," where the post-peasantry found itself compelled to adopt a strategy of "voice" (Hirschman 1970) in the face of the—partially real, partially imagined—threat of inundation and the bleak prospect of a further decline in its economic prospects, social status, and political influence. The importance of the countermovement concept resides in its ability to highlight the role of translocal forces in the emergence of socioethnic antagonisms. In this respect, it is important to emphasize that post-peasants' disenchantment with their place and trajectory in the liberal democratic regime was exacerbated by the "undeserved" attention and support that liberal elites granted the Romani minority. My analysis of the Jászladány case reveals that integration policies pursued by the left-liberal government were interpreted as a sustained effort to erode their positions vis-à-vis "Gypsies." They were, importantly, also seen as an integral element of a broader political economic shift. The post-communist elite's willingness to heed the expectations of European elites instead of the needs of "worthy citizens" was interpreted as part of a turn toward Brussels and Big Capital. From the perspective of mainstream groups, the decline of the rural economy and the emancipation of Roma appeared as two sides of the same coin. Michael Stewart was therefore right to highlight the link between European integration and a newfound insistence on ethnocultural solidarities (see Stewart 2012). His insistence on cultural dislocations, however, misses the crucial import of the crisis of social reproduction—and concomitant experiences of disempowerment and fears of losing ground—affecting peripheral populations who were negatively affected by heightened global competition and simultaneously felt abandoned by elites who had failed, in their view, to defend their interests. My claim, in other words, is that the disenfranchisement of the countryside was experienced in zones of deprivation as a simultaneously economic, cultural, and political process. In the next chapter, I will seek to extend this interpretation in time by showing how politically-oriented actors used the crisis of hegemonic Hungarianness in zones of deprivation to harness emergent racist sensibilities to a series of—partially overlapping, partially conflicting—power projects and how this led to the rise of political anti-Gypsyism in the 2006–2010 period.

Notes

1. In 2007, the left-liberal government decided to launch a complex scheme to develop the country's most depressed microregions, which it identified based on economic, social, and infrastructural indicators. A financial envelope, including funds from various EU-sponsored operational programs, was set aside for each microregion in the programming period of 2007–2013. The decision to earmark development funds was justified on the following grounds: "In international comparison, these microregions are characterized by low levels of employment, non-competitive educational institutions, and a high rate of [household] indebtedness. These processes especially impinge on the Roma population, fostering tendencies of segregation and discrimination." See "LHH kistérségek felzárkóztatási programja a kormány cselekvési tervében" (The Most Disadvantaged Microregions program is part of the government's strategic action plan), The Hungarian Government's website for Development Programs, 22 April 2009, accessed 20 December 2017, https://www.palyazat.gov.hu/lhh_kistersegek_felzarkoztatasi_programja_a_kormany_cselekvesi_terveben.
2. The rest were involved in trade (121), transportation and communications (52), and other services (172).
3. The village had a population of 2,729 in 1990. The 809 "inactive earners" were pensioners (who derived income from the social security system) and landowners (who were paid rent by those who used their land).
4. Besides cellars, the Goat Stone also accommodated "holiday houses," where owners (who lived mostly in Gyöngyöspata or in nearby villages) would come with their families to spend their free time.
5. The "Act on Partial Compensation of Damage Unjustly Caused to the Property of Hungarian Citizens by the State" (known as the First Compensation Act) was adopted by right-wing parties—among them the Independent Smallholders' Party—who had won the parliamentary elections of 1990. Acting on public pressure to return land "stolen by the communists," the government sought to compensate former landowners (or their heirs). The Act, which was passed by parliament in 1991, created a uniform legal basis for the compensation of those who had been affected by the nationalization of private property after 8 June 1949. It called for the creation of Land Compensation Committees, which were charged with the task of designating pieces of land that cooperatives would have to let go of and organizing auctions where these pieces of land would then be offered for sale. Thus, instead of returning lands to earlier owners, beneficiaries were handed "compensation coupons," which could be used to bid for land. The sharp drop in the price of land was linked to the fact that a large number of beneficiaries were looking to sell their "coupons."

6. Statistics compiled by the Central Statistical Office show that the ratio of people employed in the agricultural sector dropped from 15.5 to 4.9 percent between 1990 and 2005. In Northern Hungary, the respective percentages were 13.6 and 3.7 percent. See KSH 2008: 56.

7. The region is actually in the northeastern part of the country; it is formed by Borsod-Abaúj-Zemplén, Heves, and Nógrád counties.

8. The Gyöngyös microregion is one of the two microregions that have been classified (based on socioeconomic development indicators) as "developing" in the Northern Hungary region. While the neighboring Eger microregion is Northern Hungary's only "dynamically developing" microregion, the remaining twenty-two microregions are classified as "de-developing."

9. Nonetheless, the number of "commuters" dropped from 829 to 554 between 1990 and 2011. (Out of these 554 people, 341 worked in construction or industry, 194 in services, and 19 in agriculture.) This probably resulted from the closing of coal mines, which led to the collapse of demand for unskilled labor.

10. The 1990 census registered forty-six unemployed local residents. Most of these were probably unskilled Roma workers, who were the first to be laid off from industrial workplaces such as the mine that was closed in neighboring Gyöngyösoroszi in 1986.

11. The representative "Gypsy survey" conducted in 2003 by Kemény and his colleagues showed that only 19.7 percent of Romani men were officially employed in counties in the North, and the same ratio was 14.2 percent in the East (see Kemény et al. 2004: 102–103).

12. This was in some cases also true for the inhabitants of "poor settlements" whose population was uniquely composed of landless non-Romani agricultural workers (Kovács et al. 2013).

13. Anthropologist Michael Stewart (1997) wrote an ethnography of one of Gyöngyös's Vlach Romani communities based on fieldwork he conducted between 1984 and 1986. Stewart focused on Roma who were involved in horse-trading and other part-time business ventures that provided them not only supplementary income but also allowed them to maintain ethnic distinction through such practices of demarcation. My research did not focus on Gyöngyös, but it is worth noting that the community Stewart studied has become powerfully polarized along class lines since regime change. While some of the part-time entrepreneurs Stewart wrote so eloquently about converted themselves into full-time entrepreneurs (and became wealthy), many others became impoverished after they lost their industrial workplaces. Their economic predicament does not differ much from the Romungros I got to know in Gyöngyöspata, with the exception that there are more economic opportunities available in an urban environment.

14. See the previous chapter for a discussion of the broader forces driving intraregional migration.

15. Up until now I have mostly used the term "surplus population" to refer to people who found themselves excluded from the primary labor market and quality schooling, and were also physically segregated from mainstream society. In this chapter I will mostly refer to them as "settlement-dwellers." One of my arguments for sticking to the emic term is to highlight the experience of being physically segregated and trapped as the key experiential dimension of exclusion. The other argument for avoiding the use of more generalizing terms is to highlight locally imposed, informal mechanisms of segregation and control whereby local elites attempted to limit contact between marginalized and mainstream groups and to uphold certain privileges for the latter, while ensuring control over the former.

16. A report commissioned by the Heves County Council in 2003 showed that this practice was far from being unique to Gyöngyöspata. The report arrived at the conclusion that

98 percent of students enrolled in special care classes were of Romani ethnic descent. See "Heves megyei indokolatlan fogyatékossá nyilvánítás" (Heves County's Unjustified Disability), Chance for Children Foundation (CFCF) website, n.d., accessed 09 February 2016, http://cfcf.hu/heves-megyei-indokolatlan-fogyatékossá-nyilvánítás. In a recent ruling (dated March 2016) the Tribunal of Eger ruled that the practice violated the rights of Romani children and that the Ministry for Human Resources bears responsibility for practices of discrimination.

17. The Hungarian state granted parents the right to freely choose the school in which they wish to enroll their children in 1985.

18. The status of "escapees" resembled that of the few "poor peasant" families who sustained themselves by taking up seasonal work in the vineyards of post-peasants and performing other household chores on an ad hoc basis. These families were not identified as "Gypsies" because everybody knew that they were of "Magyar" descent. But they were also looked down upon due to their "uncivilized demeanor" and form of life, which was said to resemble that of Roma. It is also worth noting that children born into these families were sometimes grouped together with settlement-dwellers in the "B" classes and that intermarriage between poor peasants and settlement-dwellers entailed ostracization. A man who had married a Gypsy woman (and moved to the settlement) was said to have been "Gypsyfied." This shows that poor non-Roma families were not totally exempt from mechanisms of segregation and control.

19. I note that repeasantization also occurred through another process: the inflow of city-dwellers. Above, I alluded to one young family who had moved from Budapest to Gyöngyöspata to become winemakers.

20. See "Évek óta hiába kértek segítséget a cigánybűnözőktől rettegő gyöngyöspataiak" (The terrified citizens of Gyöngyöspata have been pleading for years in vain for help), website of the Jobbik Party's Gyöngyös chapter, 19 March 2011, accessed 20 December 2017, http://gyongyos.jobbik.hu/content/c%C3%ADmlap-exkluz%C3%ADv-dokume ntumok-évek-óta-hiába-kértek-seg%C3%ADtséget-cigánybűnözőktől-rettegő-gyöng.

21. According to the census of 2001, people above the age of sixty constituted 21.9 percent of the local population. The census of 2011 showed that their share had increased to 24.3 percent. This means that in 2006 their share should have been somewhere between these two numbers. It is safe to assume that at least one person out of every ten inhabitants who were below the age of sixty owned a piece of land around the village. This means that the ratio of elderly people (above the age of sixty) and landowners must have been around 30 percent.

22. György cites a musician going by the name "Luigi" to highlight this strategy: "They also started to rap because they wanted to tell people how much they suffered from their minority position. They were in a minority in America and we are in a minority here in Hungary. So rap had a political edge; it was a form of revolt when black people went out to the streets to rap. The same thing is happening in Hungary . . . Roma are shunned at work, in the school, here and there. I can't get together with a girl because she is not Roma but I am and that's a problem" (György 2009: 130–131, translation mine).

23. In an interview conducted and published by Pál Molnár, a prominent right-wing intellectual, in 2000, the minister responsible for overseeing secret services (Ervin Demeter) claimed that the previous left-liberal government had adopted the concept of "livelihood criminality" to placate left-wing popular constituencies whom Demeter obliquely referred to as "groups who would be negatively affected by a policy of zero tolerance." See "Igényes nemzetközi szövetség egyenrangú tagjai vagyunk" (We are respected members of an outstanding international association), Hungarian Electronic Library website, n.d., accessed 6 January 2016, http://mek.oszk.hu/01900/01989/01989 .htm.

24. The first amendment to the penal code that raised the threshold in question had in fact been introduced in 1993 under József Antall's conservative government (act 1993/ XVII). The next amendment—raising the threshold set in 1993 from 5,001 forints to 10,001 forints—took place under Viktor Orbán's first government (act 1999/CXX), which followed the socialist-liberal government led by Gyula Horn. Subsequently, the threshold was raised to 20,001 forints under the second socialist-liberal government led by Ferenc Gyurcsány (2004–2008), and most recently to 50,001 forints under Viktor Orbán's second government (2010–2014).

25. See Cohen's (2002: xlii) introduction to the third edition of *Folk Devils and Moral Panics*.

26. Quote from a parliamentary statement pronounced on 19 March 1996 (original in Hungarian, translation mine). See "75. felszólalás, 158. ülésnap, azonnali kérdések és válaszok órája (2190), Dr. Keresztes Sándor (KDNP) kérdése a belügyminiszterhez a szatymazi és budafoki templombetörésekről" (75th statement on 158th plenary at the hour of immediate questions and answers [2190] to the question submitted by Dr. Sándor Keresztes [Christian Democratic People's Party] on the issue of the church lootings in Szatymaz and Budafok), the Hungarian Parliament's official website, n.d., accessed 11 January 2016, http://www.parlament.hu/naplo35/158/1580075.htm. Interior minister Kuncze's statement relied on the representation of the Gypsy as "poor brother" and critical sociologists' conceptualization of the poverty-criminality nexus: the claim that criminality among impoverished minorities is the result of their social predicament.

27. Kovai's (2013) ethnographic account of a village that resembles Gyöngyöspata in many regards also emphasizes that local power-holders were able to legitimize the unequal distribution of opportunities and collective resources without having to openly discriminate against Romani families.

28. The case can be summed up as follows. In 1997, the municipality of Székesfehérvár decided to evict thirteen Romani families from a building that contained flats that the municipality rented as social housing. The municipality argued that the tenants had failed to pay public utility bills and that this gave it the right to evict these "illegal tenants." The protests of human rights organizations, however, forced the municipality to modify its plans. At first, the mayor proposed to move the families to a settlement situated outside the city's perimeters. Following neighboring municipalities' protestation, the mayor proposed to move the families into large metal containers. Unfavorable media reports and pressure from representatives of the left-liberal government—which sought to prevent the episode from making international headlines—compelled the municipality to scrap the plan and grant the families money to purchase property instead. (It is worth noting that a representative survey found that 90 percent of Hungary's adult population had heard of the case and 63 agreed with the plan to move the Roma into containers.) Although the families managed to buy real estate in a few neighboring villages, the local population prevented them from moving into their new houses. In the end, the Székesfehérvár municipality was forced to accommodate the families in the same kinds of flats it had sought to evict them from. This short description relies on Bernáth and Messing's analysis (1998) of the case.

29. The European Roma Rights Center compiled a useful overview of the case. See "Legal but Illegitimate: The Gypsy Minority Self-Government in Jászladány", European Roma Rights Center website, 7 February 2004, accessed 13 January 2016, http://www.errc.org/article/legal-but-illegitimate-the-gypsy-minority-self-government-in-jaszladany/1302.

30. Two of the newly purchased houses were located in an ethnically mixed street: the Arany János street. One was on the main street, which was exclusively inhabited by "peasants." The last one was located right next to the voivod's house (itself situated on the edge of the settlement).

31. The ratio of microenterprises (whose income was less than 600,000 forints—2,000 euros—in 2007) was 90.6 percent in Northern Hungary as compared to the national average of 85.1 percent. See KSH 2008: 172. This explains why the average income (81,000 forints, which is 270 euros) of those working full-time in the agricultural sector was lowest in the Northern Hungary region.

32. In 2007, the ratio of full-time producers was lowest in Northern Hungary and the Northern Great Plain regions (39 percent). See KSH 2008: 29.

33. Options that were more readily available to the unskilled workforce in regions that were closer to Western consumer markets and centers of accumulation were not so readily available in the Northeast. These included taking up formal wage work in newly implanted factories that took advantage of Hungary's cheap labor force. This strategy played an important role in the Southwestern Ormánság region, where the implantation of several multinational companies provided unskilled Romani workers access to the formal labor market (see Feischmidt 2012), although this trend was broken by the recent global economic crisis (Váradi and Schwarz 2013). In my Transdanubian field site I found evidence for the conversion of deproletarianized workers into petty entrepreneurs (on which more in chapter 5). While these two strategies were not altogether absent in the Northeast, they were often impractical due to the relative weakness of industrial capacities and distance from Western markets.

Chapter 3

REDEMPTIVE ANTI-GYPSYISM

The Transposition of Struggles
from the Social to the Political Domain

In the preceding chapter, I built on our collaborative fieldwork in Gyöngyöspata to formulate the claim that popular anti-Gypsyism emerged as a potent social force in regions where the combination of economic decline and left-liberal integration policies undermined local regimes of segregation and control, indirectly strengthening the hand of actors who proposed to take action against "unruly Gypsies." In this chapter, I will complement this analysis by focusing on the actors who played a key role in the "naming and blaming of Roma" as a menacing collectivity. As two anthropologists who conducted fieldwork in a northeastern village (that is in many respects similar to Gyöngyöspata) argued, the "Gypsy" category "has the potential to condense and make explicit the experience of losing both self-confidence and ground" (Horváth and Kovai 2010: 41, translation mine). However, a great amount of work was required to turn this potentiality into an active force—first and foremost, a discourse capable of signifying heterogeneous popular grievances and displacing the hitherto dominant representation of the Gypsy as the "poor brother." I will begin by analyzing how a new redemptive discourse emerged in the course and context of a local power struggle that was waged over the desirable future path of Gyöngyöspata by two elite factions.[1] I then extend my analysis to another northeastern microregion, where local power-holders used a similar discourse to formulate claims and demands that were—for the first time—directly addressed to the national political elite. Finally, I move to the national level to show how the strategies of intellectuals, journalists, and far-right activists contributed to the transposition of small-scale local conflicts into an abstract and irreconcilable Manichean struggle between "Gypsies" and "Magyars." This effort to unveil micro-macro linkages will focus on relational processes and strategies that played a central role in upward scale shift, which I—following McAdam, Tarrow, and Tilly (2001)—see as a central driver of political radicalization: the shift of first the electorate, then politicians, toward increasingly exclusionary and authoritarian demands and initiatives.

Pragmatists versus Ethnotraditionalists

In the aftermath of regime change, local political life in Gyöngyöspata came to be dominated by petty entrepreneurs who relied on the economic and social capital they had accumulated in the late socialist period to establish connections to regional politicians who played a key role in the effort to modernize Hungary after the change of regime (see Kovách 2012). In a recent publication (Feischmidt and Szombati 2016), my colleague and I called these actors "pragmatists" because they were led by the conviction that Gyöngyöspata's future depended on its ability to fully integrate into European economic networks and maintain close relationships with the actors responsible for the management of state-administered development funds with which they hoped to develop the local economy. The group received the backing of two institutions—the Catholic Church and the Association of Local Entrepreneurs—that played a key role in local public life. Both threw their weight behind a local entrepreneur who was elected mayor in 1990 and retained this position until 2006. This political continuity—not uncommon in the period—reflected widespread popular support for the deagrarianization of the local economy. The mayor's success in enlisting popular support hinged on initiatives such as the development of the gas and telecommunications networks and the building of a swimming pool (an unusual step for such a small town). It was mainly thanks to his efforts that Gyöngyöspata managed to attract infrastructural development funds in the 1990s. However, efforts to attract resources floundered in the last decade—as epitomized by the mayor's failure to create an industrial park and a ski slope in the critical 2005/2006 period.

The second elite group—whom we called "ethnotraditionalists"—was formed by a new generation of entrepreneurs involved in winemaking and agrotourism, with one exception: an entrepreneur making a living through the commercial sale of security systems (including

CCTV cameras). It is they who brought to life the Friends of Gyön-gyöspata Circle with the aim of creating an alternative to the modernization project that had been promoted by the pragmatists. This rival vision was founded on the rediscovery of local cultural heritage and its instrumentalization for the reconstruction of the village economy. While the pragmatists drew on the well-established canon of patriotic symbols and ideals to inscribe the locality into the national community, their would-be successors stressed continuity with nineteenth-century village traditions and proposed to revive peasant economic activities in order to revitalize the local economy in a period when the left-liberal modernization project was showing signs of running out of steam. Their plan was to integrate Gyöngyöspata into the regional touristic network and reinvent the locality as a Palóc village.[2] Their most important cultural intervention was the organization of the "Palóc Days," an annual festival (first organized in 2007) where villagers were encouraged to display local traditions (folk costume, folk dance, handicrafts, special dishes, etc.) in order to attract visitors and revenue. The Friends Circle built on the example of the nearby village of Hollókő—which was proclaimed a UNESCO World Heritage Site in 1987 and is widely considered to be one the most successful attempts to promote ethnotourism in Hungary—as a model for reenvisioning Gyöngyöspata's future. The ethnotraditionalist project can broadly be characterized as a "repeasantization" initiative. Ethnotraditionalists pursued this goal through variegated initiatives that relied on the cultural memory of the peasant economy to elaborate innovative livelihood practices that sought to improve the terms of trade and ensure the autonomy of petty agricultural producers and touristic entrepreneurs through the creation of short and decentralized exchange circuits that directly connected them to consumers. In the beginning of the previous chapter, I noted that these initiatives—especially those focused on the revitalization of winemaking—had been quite successful and that this gave representatives of the Friends Circle, whom one could describe as the organic intellectuals of the post-peasantry, a degree of self-confidence and legitimacy to step up as the spokespersons of the "native" population.

I also explained that ethnotraditionalists had become convinced that the local Romani community constituted a menace to their plan to reinvent Gyöngyöspata. This conviction was founded on two critical experiences. First, members of the Friends Circle had played a key role in the previously mentioned attempts—the broom-making and the community gardening initiative—whereby they sought to integrate settlement-dwellers into their project. Second, key members of the association had been implicated in the physical confrontations that erupted in the "border zone" after 2006. The president of the local winemakers' association (whose tires Romani children had deflated) was one of these people. These experiences played powerfully into the rearticulation of post-peasant identity. They compelled ethnotraditionalists to make a concerted effort to persuade villagers that the "Gypsy problem" required urgent attention and intervention and that local Roma posed a threat to the future of the community. The compilation of the previously mentioned criminal report constituted the mantelpiece of this effort to build a new narrative that linked the experience of decline to the presence of a "problem population": "Due to the continuous perpetration of crimes, the despairing owners of orchards, weekend houses and cellars have abandoned their properties; they no longer have enough energy to rebuild what has been destroyed; thefts and acts of vandalism have forced them to renounce the legacy of their parents and grandparents" (translation mine).

What we see here is the reimagination of the post-peasantry as the victim of the surplus population. The concomitant claim is that communal revival can only come about through the eradication of culturally or biologically encoded[3] criminal behavior. This stood at odds with the convictions of the pragmatist camp. The latter sought to downplay these frictions based on the hope that the interethnic relationship could be managed within prevalent (formal and informal) arrangements. One former mayor told us that he and his allies in the local council based their conduct on the assumption that structurally generated tensions could only be eased through centralized state efforts and that all they could do was to ensure that frictions would not "cause a fire." The text suggests that ethnotraditionalists initially believed that institutional pressures would be sufficient to bring about this behavioral change. "Bad Gypsies" could, in other words become "good" again if authorities would only change their laissez-faire approach, which—as the report claimed—"emboldens criminals and sows distrust and skepticism among decent people."

This new redemptive discourse constituted a radical reimagination of the figure of "the Gypsy." Although pragmatists preferred not to utter the "G word," the regime of segregation and control they operated was founded on the representation of Roma that the Communist Party had codified in 1961. The new discourse decisively broke with the representation of the Gypsy as the "poor brother" by subverting the hitherto dominant conceptualization of the poverty-criminality nexus. While Communist ideologues claimed that widespread criminality among impoverished minorities was a result of their social predicament, the report returned to the interwar period's dominant discourse: "Recidivists are unmoved by judicial sentences; they live as they please. They are not given real sentences; the law acquits them of responsibility because they have children. The only task of these people is to procreate in order to reproduce *criminal society*" (translation and emphasis mine). In this passage, the author drew on the historic representation of Roma as preferring idleness over hard work and as being prone to criminal behavior. This traditional image was, however, complemented by the novel claim that "lazy, thievish Gypsies" present a threat to the community of "decent citizens." In other words, the report infused the historic representation of cultural incompatibility with the idea of menace.

In the report, the non-Romani community was not (yet) alluded to in a positive form—it only appeared as the mirror image of "unruly" and "unworthy" Gypsies. However, the organization of the Palóc Days—together with the effort to bring the folk costume back into use—in the year following the report's publication highlighted the effort to reinforce Gyöngyöspata's image as a "peasant village." Set against the prospect of demographic change ("Gypsyfication") and the declining social power of the post-peasantry, the return to ethnic traditions presented an opportunity to restore "peasant pride" and shift attention to the needs of the "majority." Traditions, in other words, served as a vehicle for the restoration of social power and the reaffirmation of "natural" hierarchies. As for the discourse that asserted "parasites must be punished to ensure our survival," it derived its force not only from the prospect of restoring harmony through the purging of bad apples but also from the fact that it offered a meaningful explanation for the social inequalities that were being made in front of people's eyes (or rather, with their participation) and exempted non-Roma from any responsibility for the plight of the Romani community. The new discourse not only magnified the injuries of the majority but also silenced painful experiences of exclusion on the other side of the reemergent ethnic divide. By blaming Roma for communal decline, ethnotraditionalists diverted attention away from destructive socioeconomic processes that the pragmatists had hitherto acknowledged as the real causes of frictions.

This combination of anti-Gypsyism with the reinvention of ethnic traditions proved to be an effective tool for entrenching the group as a key player in local public life. The Friends Circle, whose president compiled the criminal report just before the municipal elections of 2006, managed to get some of its representatives elected to the local council. Although in 2006 its mayoral candidate was narrowly defeated by the pragmatist opponent, the group forced the new council to implement discriminatory measures to tame "thievish Gypsies." One of these initiatives involved the installation of CCTV cameras on the border between the "village" and the "Gypsy settlement." The association also purchased two properties that had been offered for sale in the border zone to prevent Roma from moving into "the village." These initiatives were financed through a peculiar financial arrangement. Councilors affiliated with the Friends Circle persuaded their peers to transfer their monthly honorarium to the association's private bank account. This allowed the municipality to outsource the exercise of control over the private housing market to a voluntary association and thereby evade the scrutiny of state institutions that the left-liberal elite had put in place to combat discrimination against the Romani minority.

Although the discourse and initiatives promoted by ethnotraditionalists were popular,[4] the group drew criticism for spending the money transferred by the local council in a nontransparent way. This, I was told, played an important role in the defeat of the ethnotraditionalists' preferred candidate at the race for the mayor's seat in October 2010. The newly elected mayor, who enjoyed the backing of the pragmatists, chose to pursue the earlier strategy of non-action. One of the cornerstones of this strategy consisted in enforcing the taboo on publicly "naming and blaming the Gypsy" based on the calculation that the structurally rooted "Gypsy problem" could not be solved on the local level. The only action the new mayor did take was to end the channeling of local councilors' fees to the Friends Circle, thus robbing the ethnotraditionalists of a key resource. The latter responded by further whipping up anti-Gypsy sentiment in public life. This deadlock was broken by a young man who stepped onto the political turf as Jobbik's candidate in 2010. He was a lone wolf and looked down upon by both elite factions because of his lower-class status. This was the main reason why in October 2010 he managed to obtain only 5.8 percent of votes at the mayoral race. However, growing tensions between ethnotraditionalists and the new mayor's pragmatist supporters positioned him as a potential sidekick whom the ethnotraditionalists sought to instrumentalize to pile pressure on their opponents. Instead of becoming their henchman, he ended up occupying the seat they coveted. This was thanks to Jobbik's success in wresting the initiative from place-based actors by "invading" Gyöngyöspata in the spring of 2011 as part of its renewed national campaign against "Gypsy criminality" (see chapter 4 for a detailed discussion).

Ethnotraditionalists' effort to reinstate ethnic forms of solidarity and identification was not unique to Gyöngyöspata. Evidence presented by other researchers shows that similar cultural agendas—seeking to draw power and resources through a newfound insistence on territorialized ethnic solidarities—emerged at roughly the same time in other corners of the countryside. Margit Feischmidt and her colleagues (see Feischmidt et al. 2014) drew attention to an important shift from political toward ethnic conceptualizations of nationhood among everyday citizens in the decade that followed Hungary's accession to the European Union. Citing the work of a previous generation of researchers, they show that this was paralleled by a shift in the object of national pride. While between 1995 and 2004 Hungarians based their pride on the country's economic and democratic credentials, in the last ten years this has been replaced by a focus on history (Feischmidt et al. 2014: 31). Relying on focus group interviews conducted with right-wing youth in rural towns, the researchers call attention to the proliferation of cultural associations involved in the protection of (both local and national) cultural heritage. They interpret this emergent cultural agenda, together with disaffected youth's interest in patriotic rock music and the commemoration of the "Trianon-trauma," as a reaction to precarity, and disillusionment with the left-liberal project as a whole. Their ethnographic investigations showed that cultural and political entrepreneurs not only took advantage of this spontaneous interest in ethnonational culture and history but also played a key role in creating linkages between associations active on the local, regional, and national level. This claim echoes Douglas Holmes's (2002) finding that regional politicians played an important role in articulating "integralist" alternatives in Italy's Friuli region. Holmes (2002: 4) emphasized that these actors "drew on adherents' fidelity to specific cultural traditions and sought to recast these traditions within a distinctive historical critique and an exclusionary political economy." This shows that emergent right-wing cultural agendas may be energized by dislocations affecting rural communities (outmigration, the disappearance of jobs, etc.). The "return to traditions"—emerging out of a conservative critique of individualist, consumerist, and multiculturalist liberalism—may thus be seen as responding to wider structural dislocations. Our fieldwork in Gyöngyöspata showed that this movement could become wedded to an exclusionary discourse (that presented only one part of society as worthy of social protection) and the reinforcement of historical ethnic hierarchies in rural localities where the post-peasantry was facing a crisis of social reproduction and saw its aspirations and projects threatened by the surplus population. However, for "the Gypsy" to take center stage, spontaneously emergent cultural and ideological currents needed to be articulated within an explicit political agenda. In the next section, I will show how mayors operating in the Northeast elevated the "Gypsy issue" into the political public sphere, thereby setting the stage for the emergence of new forms of political contention.

The Mayors' Revolt

Sociologist János Zolnay (2012: 26) has argued that "local politicians have largely been responsible for introducing aggressive racist terms into public discourse," adding that the "statements of mayors have strongly shaped the topics of public political discussion during the last two or three years." Although his analysis mostly deals with mayors' opposition to top-down efforts to enforce desegregation in the school system, Zolnay—citing the example of the village of Monok—also highlighted that mayors in the Northeast took advantage of the decentralized distribution of social assistance to discriminate against "welfare-scroungers." He failed, however, to highlight that attempts to prevent the abuse of the welfare regime or to tie social benefits to obligatory community work may have actually responded to grassroots pressures. This is what the analysis of Virág (2010)— who conducted fieldwork in the northeastern Cserehát region, one of the country's poorest regions and the epicenter of rural ghettoization—suggests. She found that poor pensioners and public servants employed at the minimal wage were deeply angry with the left-liberal government, which had implemented a welfare reform that benefited the poorest segments of society in 2007.[5] One of the consequences of the reform was that it equalized the incomes of families in which adults were out of work and of families in which one adult was employed on the minimal wage. Virág, quoting local informants, claims that the reform poisoned the relationship of the unemployed and the working poor. She goes on to argue that feelings of injustice among the latter (fed by the conviction that the government had provided an unjust advantage to welfare recipients) led the mayors of Monok and other villages situated in the neighboring Szerencs microregion to call for new types of sanctions in order to "establish control over 'work-shy' individuals—most notably through the implementation of workfare measures" (Virág 2010: 150, translation mine). The decree adopted by the municipality of Monok in May 2008, stipulating that only unemployed welfare claimants who signed up for community work would henceforth be entitled to benefits, was followed by a petition that carried the title "Mayors' Initiative to Make Our Society Work Better."[6] Signed by eighteen mayors of the Szerencs microregion, the document articulated the need for a radical overhaul of the welfare regime based on the example set by Monok, and called on parliament and the government to draw up legislation that would put an end to the "distribution of free handouts" and ensure Hungary's transformation into a "work-based society":

> We, the mayors of the Szerencs microregion and the legitimate representatives of 50,000 citizens, who labor to fulfill our duties at the lowest rung of the administrative hierarchy—and remain open to the initiatives of national power-holders—believe that the time has come to state loud and clear: we are heading in the wrong direction. The country is heading in the wrong direction and yet we refuse to search for the true causes of our problems. The decisions that have been taken [by the government] have deepened the crisis that we experience and must deal with [in our localities] . . . It is imperative to *change the politics* that exacerbates economic problems and in 10–15 years' time could entirely ruin certain regions and even cause a national security threat. *The key to change is in the hands of legislators.* Self-governments are only governments in name because they have been stripped of meaningful regulatory powers. (translation mine, emphases in original)

The text goes on to enumerate the problems that the mayors saw as the most direct causes of the crisis their communities were facing: (a) the family support system "accelerated the demographic dynamism of undersocialized masses"; (b) the system of welfare benefits "incentivizes work-shy behavior" and undermines efforts to create a work-based society; (c) unchecked loan sharking "exacerbates and reproduces poverty" and contributes to the spread of asocial behavior among youth; (d) the government increased the burden weighing on disadvantaged local municipalities by forcing them to pay part of the extra costs associated with its welfare reform; and (e) the insufficient policing of rural areas contributes to the spread of criminality in communities and violence in schools.

If one puts Virág's (2010) analysis and the petition next to each other, both the motivation and the goal of local mayors become clear. Mayors—some of whom were affiliated with the Socialist Party—sought to pile pressure on the central government to implement measures that would calm constituencies who were growing impatient with both Roma and the left-liberal elite. The text shows that local power-holders felt that they lacked the means to control anti-Gypsy sentiment and were afraid of losing their power. This fear is also evident from the text's warning that the executive's failure to act would "tip the balance toward the masses who know nothing about civilized morals and the culture of coexistence," as well as the use of an argument that resembled the one we already encountered in the criminal report: the mayors claimed that non-action on behalf of the central government would lead to the "depopulation of *our* villages" and "annihilate *our* millennial culture" (translation and emphases mine).

My interviews with the two people who acted as Ministers of Social Affairs in the turbulent 2008–2010 period revealed that the revolt of provincial mayors convinced the government to radically change its course. Erika Szűcs, who was minister between May 2008 and April 2009, told me that by the turn of 2008/2009 the leadership of the Socialist Party had become so terrified of losing its bastions in the Northeast that it decided to break with its progressive reform agenda and to convert the workfare measures advocated by the mayors into official policy. In January 2009, the second Gyurcsány government launched the Road to Work Program with the aim of putting the labor of the surplus population to the service of local communities. The government reduced the amount of benefits unemployed citizens were eligible to claim and forced them to accept unprestigious community work. The new policy provided mayors with the regulatory powers they deemed necessary for taming the surplus population by granting them a key role in the distribution of community work (to which benefits had been tied in the framework of the program). The policy, a radical variant of which still constitutes the cornerstone of the right-wing government's social policy (see chapter 4), constituted the first major step toward the dismantlement of universal citizenship in Hungary.

Although the program met the demands of popular constituencies, it did not allow the Socialist Party to repair the dent that unpopular austerity measures had left on its credibility.[7] Sensing that the tide had turned their way, provincial mayors began to lobby for the reallocation of further discretionary powers to the local scale. In July 2009, the mayor of Monok sent a new proposal to Prime Minister Gordon Bajnai (who had replaced Ferenc Gyurcsány in April 2009). The mayor proposed to alleviate popular feelings of injustice in relation to welfare-scrounging by transforming social assistance into an in-kind payment. (The idea was to transfer welfare benefits to a "social card" that could only be used in local shops and could not be used to buy alcohol or cigarettes.) Although the government refused to introduce the "social card" based on the argument that it violated the rights of beneficiaries, in October 2009 the municipality of Monok decided that it would implement the measure anyway. Its example was followed by a few other municipalities. The new minister of social affairs, László Herczog, responded by initiating a constitutional review. Although the Constitutional Court struck down these local decrees, the conflict pitting mayors against the government allowed right-wing opposition parties to side with popular opinion. The leader of the alliance of cities enjoying county status—a prominent member of Fidesz—declared his support for the Monok model. And Fidesz leader Viktor Orbán adopted the mayors' call for building a "work-based society" (see chapter 4).

I find the revolt of the mayors significant for three reasons. First, it reinforced the symbolic link between the decline of the countryside and the "Gypsy menace." While this link had been established by local actors beforehand, it was significant that elected officials (some of whom were associated with the Socialist Party) legitimized this articulation in the political public sphere. Students of racism have argued time and time again that the official certification[8] of racism does not simply legitimize its everyday manifestations but may also radicalize public opinion. While this is not possible to prove in this particular case, mainstream parties' response to the mayors' revolt highlighted another type of impact—namely, that the espousal of redemptive anti-Gypsyism contributed to the radicalization of the political right (on both the discursive and programmatic level), whose representatives sought to align themselves with rightward-drifting publics. Finally, the event also played a role in the delegitimation of the political left, which abandoned its erstwhile social policy agenda and adopted exclusionary proposals that resonated with right-wing ideas.

Scripting Local Conflicts into National Struggle: Right-Wing Intellectuals and the "Gypsy Menace"

While the conflict pitting mayors against the central government received widespread publicity in the national media, it was overshadowed by other events that played an even more important role in the reimagination of Roma as a threat to the *national* community. Media analysts have highlighted a number of ways in which the media contributed to the perception that "Gypsy criminality" had become rampant after the infamous Olaszliszka incident that took place on 15 October 2006 in a village situated in the Tokaj hills (Hungary's most famous wine region). A passing car nearly hit a local Romani girl who had been walking on the street. When the driver, a teacher named

Lajos Szögi, stopped to see if the girl was alright, members of the girl's family and other Romani neighbors who had witnessed the event beat the driver to death. The murder, which was witnessed by the driver's two children, quickly became known as the "Olaszliszka lynching."

The term "lynching" was introduced into public discourse by a right-wing journalist (and Fidesz founder) named Zsolt Bayer, who was renowned for his frontal attacks on political correctness and occasional anti-Semitic diatribes. While in the 1990s he had worked for liberal papers, he joined his friend Viktor Orbán's epic journey to the political right. In an opinion piece published in the country's main right-wing newspaper (*Magyar Nemzet*) two days following the incident in Olaszliszka, Bayer launched an unprecedented attack against the Romani minority. Using dehumanizing language that emphasized the racial differences between Roma and Magyars, his hugely influential article amounted to a clarion call for the nation to take up arms against "Gypsy criminality":

> Yes, America has arrived in Hungary. There are spaces—inhabited by particular races—where the state cannot guarantee the security of citizens in this country. In these spaces everyone looks after oneself as he deems right . . . . The souls of the two children cry for revenge. Zero tolerance, may this be our motto. For there is no one to defend our rights but ourselves. If the Gypsies responsible for lynching [Lajos Szögi] get off the hook, then we can only blame ourselves. And that will mean that anything can be visited upon us.[9] (translation mine)

Bayer's article is the first known formulation of "redemptive anti-Gypsyism" as a project for "remodeling the nation" (Efremova 2012). Using the example of the "criminal report," I showed that this discourse first emerged as a political instrument in the context of local power struggles. (The report, I stress, was compiled before the topos of "Gypsy criminality" emerged in the political public sphere.) The key difference between the intervention of the Friends Circle (in the context of a local struggle against pragmatist opponents) and Bayer's article (which intervened in a broader struggle between the left-liberal and right-nationalist political camps) is that the latter operated with an abstract representation of "the Gypsy," one that was void of any concrete meaning and thus—paradoxically—beyond falsification.

This kind of symbolic work reminds me of Stanley Tambiah's (1996: 192) analysis of the ways in which the particulars of local disputes become assimilated "to a larger, collective, more enduring and therefore less context-bound cause or interest." Tambiah proposed the concept of "transvaluation" to highlight the process whereby the original petty discords are absorbed into burning issues of race, religion, or ethnicity, which attract all the more hostility in the measure they are abstract and unconditional. Based on Bayer's example, I prefer to think of transvaluation as a strategy of "abstraction" that harnesses local events to the goals of political actors operating in the national political arena. Abstraction, I argue, not only played an important role in the elaboration of novel representations of the other, but also offered a weapon for party political struggle (on which more below).

The mainstream media continued Bayer's work of unmooring local events from their contexts. Vörös (2009: 20) has credited the media for recasting Olaszliszka into a general symbol of "Gypsy criminality" by publishing dozens of news items that in some way resembled the original incident: "Olaszliszka . . . gave a name to events that appeared similar to the original one . . . It has thus become a sort of archetype through which journalists interpret these events" (translation mine). While Vörös's analysis highlights the role of the main right-wing daily (*Magyar Nemzet*), two other sociologists who analyzed the representation of Roma in the mainstream media came to the conclusion that commercial media outlets also fueled the public's fear of Roma (see Bernáth and Messing 2012).[10] These studies echo the conclusions of international studies focusing on the media's role in "moral panics," which have highlighted the mainstream media's critical role in agenda-setting and issue-framing (see Hervik 2011).

The complicity, largely involuntary, of editors and journalists in the reproduction and circulation of symbolically loaded frames and images should not, however, be confused with the symbolic efforts of intellectuals. To stress this point, I bring the example of another figure who labored to abstract a conflict from its immediate context in order to promote the national redemptive narrative. This is filmmaker Gábor Kálomista, who produced a documentary titled *Country Stabbed in the Heart* after Romanian handball player Marian Cozma was murdered in front of a nightclub in Veszprém on 8 February 2009. The film—which was later aired on state television and even projected in the European Parliament on the initiative of Fidesz's representatives—portrayed Cozma, and through him the Veszprém Handball Club (which functioned as a metonym for Hungary), as a martyr who had died at the hands of barbaric "Gypsy criminals." Kálomista's symbolic strategy differed slightly from Bayer's and recalls Marshall Sahlins's (2005) analysis of the amalgamation of personalized local disputes into Manichean struggles. Focusing on the structural-cum-symbolic amplification of difference, Sahlins argued that relational relays of various sorts may endow opposing local

parties with collective identities, and opposing collectives with local or interpersonal sentiments. Of the three cases he discusses, there
is one that bears direct relevance to the documentary. Citing a letter written by the British Consul in Honolulu in 1841—in which the
gentleman complained about "some person or persons . . . building
a wall near the end of the bowling alley belonging to Mrs Mary Dowsett"—Sahlins (2005: 6) shows how small issues can be turned into
Big Events in cases when relatively trivial disputes over local matters get articulated with greater political and ideological differences:
"By nationalizing the personal relations in the case of Mrs Dowsett's
bowling alley, and thereby personalizing the national relations, the
British consul hoped to create an international showdown." In a similar vein, Kálomista's film deliberately fueled anti-Gypsy passions
by portraying the murder as the stabbing of a whole country in the
heart. This shows how higher-level oppositions could be interpolated
in lower-level conflicts—and vice versa—without the necessary me-
diation of journalists.

These two examples highlight right-wing intellectuals' active involvement in the transposition of small-scale local conflicts into an irreconcilable struggle between the forces of good and evil. Respected
figures' espousal of the "Magyar cause" was important for two reasons. First, it legitimized efforts to deliver justice through informal
rather than institutionalized forms of action. (In the next section, I
will show how Jobbik took advantage of this to mobilize rural constituencies with the help of paramilitary proxies against "Gypsy criminals.") Second, the Bayer-Kálomista duo's espousal of redemptive
anti-Gypsyism placed Fidesz on an ideological platform that did not
substantively differ from the one that Jobbik espoused. Had leading
right-wing intellectuals proposed a more nuanced (i.e., nonbinary)
representation of Roma and local conflicts, the main right-wing opposition party could have occupied the middle ground between the
(increasingly half-hearted) emancipatory politics of the left-liberal
camp and the racist extremist platform of the far-right. Since there
was no such ground to occupy, the Fidesz leadership was incentivized to retreat from the ideological battle ground, thus leaving Jobbik
facing a severely weakened and divided left-liberal camp.

Jobbik at the Helm of the Racist Insurgency

Jobbik was initially founded as a youth organization by students of
ELTE University's Arts and Humanities Faculty in 1999 with the aim

of bringing together young people who shared Christian conservative values. While the founders initially held deep sympathies for Viktor Orbán (who served as prime minister between 1998 and 2002), they became bitterly disillusioned with Fidesz after the party lost the parliamentary elections in 2002. This was because, in their view, Fidesz had abandoned its right-wing supporters, who occupied one of Budapest's main bridges to demand the recount of votes. More importantly, they accused Orbán of progressively abandoning the Civic Circles he had called into life in order to reorganize the "patriotic political side" in the 2002–2006 period.[11] They concluded that the main right-wing party was not prepared to represent Hungarian interests without hesitation and compromise. This led them to form their own political party. On 24 October 2003 they founded the Movement for a Better Hungary (Jobbik), which they defined as a "national-Christian" force and tasked with leading the nation back to the road of "freedom and self-determination."

The new party initially struggled to garner attention and gained only 2.2 percent of the votes at the parliamentary elections of 2006,[12] mostly due to the lack of access to mainstream media outlets, which—following the political strategies of the two dominant parties (the Socialist Party and Fidesz)—erected a *cordon sanitaire* around the new party. Jobbik was lucky enough to be thrown a lifeline by Prime Minister Ferenc Gyurcsány, whose infamous Őszöd speech[13] sent a shockwave through society and generated unprecedented street protests in the capital. Jobbik's leadership jumped on the bandwagon to present itself as the leading voice of the protest movement. This effort received a boost from the police, whose heavy-handed clampdown on unarmed demonstrators generated widespread sympathy for right-wing protesters who confronted an authoritarian government.

Having successfully entered the national political arena in the autumn of 2006, Jobbik was determined to remain in the spotlight. In order to achieve this, the party had to find a way to keep the initiative after the protests died down around Christmastime. Here is how the party's current president, Gábor Vona, remembered the conundrum four years later: "I realized that . . . it would not be possible to continue building the party in the same way as before. . . . We needed something that would make Hungarians get off the couch and actually do something."[14] This "something" was the Hungarian Guard (Magyar Gárda), a uniformed organization that Vona founded and tasked with taking part in charitable missions and disaster prevention. While the Hungarian Guard engaged in such activities too, it mainly attracted media attention with its marches through rural communities plagued by "Gypsy criminality." Under the pretext that the police force was unable or unwilling to maintain the social order in these rural communities, paramilitary members, wearing a uniform and symbols reminiscent of the Arrow Cross Party,[15] began to conduct marches in rural localities demanding the restoration of public order in the countryside.

In the interview I conducted with Jobbik founder Csanád Szegedi—who left the party in July 2012—the former vice-president highlighted a disagreement on the framing of the Hungarian Guard's interventions. Fellow vice-president József Bíber—a former member of the anti-Semitic Party of Hungarian Life and Justice (MIÉP)—proposed to connect the struggle against "Gypsy criminality" with the struggle against Zionism. He proposed to portray Roma as a "biological weapon" that the "Jewish" (left-liberal) elite had unleashed on Hungary with a view to weakening resistance to the country's pillaging by Israeli and Jewish-American investors. Szegedi contested the viability of this frame. Relying on first-hand experiences gained in his native Miskolc—where the "Gypsy issue" first emerged as a site of political contention in 1989 (see Vermeersch 2006: 123–132)—he argued that the discourse would be more attractive to the public if "the Jews were left out of the picture." Instead, he proposed to adopt Bayer's definition of the "Gypsy issue" and to use the Hungarian Guard as a proxy to organize a nationwide rolling campaign against "Gypsy criminality."[16] It was his vision that prevailed.

The leadership's decision to send the Hungarian Guard into villages where socioethnic tensions were running high sparked tensions between moderate and radical representatives within Jobbik's leadership. Party president Dávid Kovács left the party with his supporters because he believed that the Hungarian Guard was uncontrollable and that it would take Jobbik too far from the political mainstream. The decision was indeed a risky one. By portraying Roma as culturally and/or genetically prone to criminal behavior, Jobbik was not only contesting the dominant liberal discourse on poverty but its own Christian teachings, including the moral command to help those in want.

The first of these marches took place in the village of Tatárszentgyörgy in December 2007. In the eighteen months that followed, the organization paid visits to hundreds of localities plagued by socioethnic frictions in an effort to get its message ("'Gypsy criminality' is happening in the whole country → it can happen to you → the law and the state will not help you → but we will!") through to the public. Although the ritualized delivery of substantive justice through marches and patrols also aimed to enlist local communities as allies (this was important to legitimize interventions), the leadership's main goal was to establish a chain of equivalence between decontextualized events in order to foster perceptions of "rampancy" and "threat." In other words, the rolling anti-Gypsy campaign's goal was to create the impression that there were hundreds of small Olaszliszkas in the country and that it was imperative to do something about Gypsies before it was too late. To foster this perception, Jobbik's leaders devised a blueprint for the Hungarian Guard's interventions.

The first task was to legitimize local interventions by portraying the interethnic relationship in a particular locality as being "untenable" (due to the presence of "Gypsy criminals") and to highlight the fact that the local Magyar population was pleading for help. In this preliminary phase, the key role was assigned to formally independent bloggers and pseudojournalists. While analysts have highlighted that the Kuruc.info blog (registered in the United States) played a key role in the circulation of symbolically loaded topoi (see Bíró and Róna 2011a), such as "Hungarian-hatred," "politician criminality," and "Gypsy criminality," regional bloggers' role in issue-framing has largely gone unnoticed. The "Gypsy stories" posted on these blogs were invariably built from the following symbolic building blocks: the description of Roma as a collective exhibiting "animal behavior"; the narrativization of events as threatening (often through the familiar expression "things got out of hand"); obligatory references to the "pleas of the local Magyar population" and the inevitable condemnation of "irresponsive authorities" coupled with the call to support "helpless mayors." After writing their stories, far-right bloggers pitched them to journalists who worked for respected regional papers in the hope that the latter would reproduce (or at least draw on) their accounts. Taking advantage of the mainstream media's scarce resources (which often prohibited fact-finding) and hunger for sensational news, these bloggers were often successful in achieving a wider circulation for stories whose audience would otherwise have been restricted to the locality or microregion where they took place. This is what happened in both of my field sites. In Gyöngyöspata, Barikád TV (an online blog that was controlled by Jobbik) published a video report titled "Gypsy Terror—Heves County on the Brink of Civil War" two days after an older non-Romani resident of the Bajcsi street committed suicide. The report contained segments of an interview with Jobbik's local leader who declared that the old man had taken his life because he could not stomach the "relocation of Gypsies into the village." In Devecser, the script was basically the same. One week after a Romani and Magyar family got into a fight, Jobbik MP Gábor Ferenczi convened a press conference, inviting bloggers and journalists to talk to one of the "Magyar victims." The journalist of the regional paper (*Veszprémi Napló*) published a report that used the same term as Ferenczi—"lynching," an idiom, which, as explained above, had appeared in the far-right dictionary after Olaszliszka—to describe the conflict between the two families.[17] These two cases support the claim that the far-right blogosphere played a key role in framing local events as instances of the countrywide "Gypsy menace" and in providing greater visibility to these "Gypsy stories."[18]

The next phase—that of mobilization—consisted in sending paramilitaries and party activists into these localities with the professed aim of restoring public order. To this end, they sought to mimic the police force both with regard to attire (boots and uniform) and conduct (patrols). However, paramilitaries also sought to provoke the local Romani population in the hope that violent counterreactions would justify further radical interventions. While most of these actions lasted only a couple of hours (as in Devecser), on a few occasions (as in Gyöngyöspata) paramilitaries attempted to stay in a locality for a longer period of time with a view to maximizing media coverage. Both types of interventions were preceded or followed by speeches or party communiqués, which sought to abstract local events from their contexts and connect them to Big Issues. This was achieved through the deployment of generic language ("Gypsy criminals," "the elderly victim," "unresponsive authorities," etc.) in order to create the impression that the case at hand was part of a general pattern and sequence. Communiqués often used concepts and metaphors that were deliberately double-edged—for instance, by talking of their effort to reestablish cohesion within "the community." Another strategy included the magnification of stakes or achievements. In Gyöngyöspata, for instance, Jobbik legitimized its intervention by pretending to prevent the outbreak of a "civil war." However, the most frequently used tactic was to directly emphasize the link between events unfolding on the local and the national level. When paramilitaries began to patrol a certain area, Jobbik politicians made an effort to stress that their actions were part of a campaign aiming to cleanse the whole country of "Gypsy criminals," and portrayed the locality as but one battleground of a nationwide struggle.

Stewart (2012: xxxvii) rightly stressed that Jobbik used the "Olaszliszka lynching" to legitimize its violent interventions and to radicalize public opinion by generating "social situations in which citizens had to 'take sides.'" The Jobbik leadership deliberately sent its paramilitary allies to localities where one part of the local population could be mobilized to legitimize (and in some cases materially support) the intervention. To this end, they sought to gauge local public opinion before local interventions by gathering information through activists. In cases when leaders were not fully certain of being able to mobilize the local population, they only issued communiqués (but did not appear on site to hold speeches or give interviews). Longer campaigns were carried out only in localities where the local population was expected to overwhelmingly support intervention.

Szegedi told me that the leadership's initial main concern was that the mainstream media—which was under the influence of mainstream elites—would impose an embargo on news related to the Hungarian Guard. Mainstream parties' successful effort to build a cordon sanitaire around MIÉP showed that this concern was well-founded. The important thing to note in this regard is that the political right abandoned this strategy—which had also been instrumental in relegating Jobbik to the sidelines in the 2002–2006 period—in the aftermath of Olaszliszka. Key right-wing media outlets—first and foremost *Magyar Nemzet*—continued to publish "Gypsy stories" and frame them as instances of "Gypsy criminality" even after it became clear that this strategy would help Jobbik make further inroads into rural Hungary. This makes it hard to argue that Fidesz began to adopt elements from the far-right discourse only after the genie of anti-Gypsyism escaped from the bottle. After all, Bayer and Kálomista helped Jobbik circumvent the cordon sanitaire and place the "Gypsy issue" firmly on the political agenda. I suggest that Fidesz quietly abandoned the cordon sanitaire in the hope that Jobbik would lure former left-wing voters away from the Socialist Party in its northeastern bastions where socioethnic tensions were on the rise. This suggestion finds indirect support in the important speech Viktor Orbán gave at the gathering of right-wing intellectuals in the village of Kötcse on 5 September 2009.[19] Here, he voiced for the first time his aim to transform Hungary's bipolar party structure by occupying the middle ground between the "extremist" poles represented by the Socialists and Jobbik. Although Orbán did not clarify how he intended to foster the creation of a "centralized power field," Fidesz's maneuvers in the 2009/2010 campaign period showed that the party adopted a largely passive strategy that involved the acknowledgement of the reality of the "Gypsy problem" and a simultaneous retreat from the political battle, thereby leaving a weakened left to battle the racist tide. In the next chapter, I will address the first element of the strategy by focusing on Orbán's rhetoric and arguing that he adopted elements of the far-right discourse. Here, I would like to focus on the left's response to the far-right challenge.

The success of the Hungarian Guard's rolling campaign became evident from the growing number of people attending party rallies and the mushrooming of local Jobbik organizations. In the span of one year—between 2008 and 2009—the number of Jobbik chapters grew from 70 to 249 (see Róna 2015: 79). Until January 2009, Jobbik's popularity had hovered around 1 percent, but then it began to climb sharply.[20] While the Cozma murder certainly played into the spectacular shift in the party's fortunes, there are indications that the left's strategy had an even more significant impact. As noted above, the government announced its Road to Work Program in January 2009. This was preceded, however, by another important initiative. In December 2008, the Attorney General's Office initiated a procedure to ban the Hungarian Guard. The move was paralleled by an unprecedented attack in the left-wing media against the far-right. Newspapers and radio and television stations affiliated with the left branded the Hungarian Guard and Jobbik as neofascist organizations. This coordinated attack was, however, severely hampered by the emergence of dissent from within the left-liberal camp. On 3 January 2009, the police chief of Miskolc, Albert Pásztor, publicly declared that robberies in Miskolc were committed by Gypsies: "I must say that Magyars would only rob banks or gas stations; all other robberies are committed by [Roma]."[21] When the minister of interior announced the sacking of the police chief, a demonstration was immediately organized in support of Pásztor. The mood of the local public was captured by the fact that the local representatives of all parliamentary parties made clear that they supported Pásztor. In the end, the government was forced to backtrack and reinstate Pásztor into his function. Another newsworthy incident that took place three months later highlighted the lack of consensus on the "Gypsy issue" among key left-wing intellectuals. In a public debate, the general ombudsman, Máté Szabó, asserted his conviction that "'Gypsy criminality' is a special form of 'livelihood criminality'" that could be identified based on the individual or collective nature of acts committed by criminals. Szabó stated his belief that Roma are more prone to committing crimes in groups due to the "collectivist, almost tribal" organization of their communities, which "stands opposed to advanced individualization within Hungarian society."[22]

In the first serious attempt to dissect the "Jobbik phenomenon," two political scientists stressed that hostile reporting did not hurt the Far Right. To the contrary, it helped Jobbik entrench the "Gypsy issue" as a topic of political contention and boost its populist credentials (see Karácsony and Róna 2010). The left-wing response was also hampered by its own legitimacy deficit. Appearing not only fragmented but also increasingly out-of-touch with popular concerns did not help its effort to discredit the Far Right. Jobbik used the spotlight to portray itself as the antipode of the left-liberal establishment by promising to unleash a "cleansing storm that would wash away everything that is stinky and rotten."[23] Jobbik party manager Gábor Szabó later acknowledged that left-liberal journalists' concerted attack on the Hungarian Guard had boosted his party during the European election campaign. This assertion recently found an echo in the scholarship on moral panics. Howarth (2012: 227), summarizing key findings on the subject, noted that "a parallel system of argumentation [may emerge and challenge] elite consensus in [a] conditio[n] of uncertainty and distrust of elites." We have, in sum, good reasons to believe that attacks conducted by the representatives of the discredited left-liberal elite helped Jobbik establish itself as a popular movement braving to speak (popular) truth to (elite) power.

The far-right surge was also foreshadowed in opinion polls. While the public was initially frightened by the Hungarian Guard (a poll conducted shortly after the its first marches showed that 38 percent of respondents thought that the organization was dangerous and 21 percent found it outright frightening[24]), the ratio of respondents who shunned the organization had significantly dropped by the spring of 2009 (when a poll revealed that 38 percent of respondents believed that the Hungarian Guard was pursuing the right ends with the wrong means and only 53 percent claiming that everything was wrong with the organization[25]). At the European parliamentary elections organized on 7 June 2009, Jobbik succeeded in achieving an extraordinary breakthrough. The party received 14.77 percent of the vote and came in third place just behind the Socialists (17.37 percent). The consensus among political scientists is that this breakthrough was based on its deftness in elevating the "Gypsy-issue" into the political debate.[26]

> Prevailing anti-Romani sentiments in Hungarian society alone would not have brought 427,000 votes and three seats in the European Parliament. Jobbik had to demonstrate that it was the most competent political player on the Roma issue, which dominated the political agenda in the first half of 2009. According to a survey conducted in 2009, more than twice as many people thought that Jobbik was the party that could best handle the Roma issue than the number of those who actually ended up voting for the party. This was undoubtedly thanks to the Hungarian Guard and, more broadly, to the appropriation of the Gypsy question. This proved to be the main cause of Job-

bik's stunningly rapid success in 2009, as well as the ideological cement of its constituency. (Bíró and Róna 2011a: 247, translation mine)

The results of the election appeared to confirm the calculation that Jobbik's rise would hurt the Socialist Party foremost. The far-right party obtained better results than the Socialists in seven counties—of which six were situated in Northeastern Hungary, which had hitherto been the left's most important bastion outside the capital city.[27] In the nine months that separated the European and the national parliamentary elections, Jobbik was able to maintain its momentum. This had, in fact, been so powerful in the Northeast that the party threatened to outperform certain Fidesz candidates. Although Fidesz stuck to its passive response, there was one candidate who broke the mandatory silence. On 3 September 2009, the mayor of a small northeastern town, Edelény, declared that "in the localities that are predominantly inhabited by Roma . . . [women] deliberately take pills so that they give birth to mentally retarded children, which entitles them to claim double family allowance."[28] Fidesz's leadership responded first by attempting to drown out the issue and then by accusing the Socialist Party of shielding its own racist candidates. In the end, the leadership dropped the racist candidate. The latter, however, ended up running as an independent (with Jobbik's support) and won the mandate in the Edelény district.

The results of the European parliamentary elections further boosted Jobbik. In 2010, more members joined the party than in the six years following its foundation. By 2010, Jobbik had eight hundred local organizations and eleven thousand members, which prompted researchers to argue that "regarding organizational reach Jobbik could compete [with the Socialists] who had been in government for 12 years out of the last 20" (Bíró and Róna 2011b: 4). At the parliamentary elections of April 2010, Jobbik came in third position (16.67 percent), not far behind the Socialists (19.30 percent). Although its leaders were disappointed with the result, it was nevertheless a spectacular achievement.

Despite its success in rallying insecure social strata in 2010, the majority of voters shied away from supporting a young extremist party. This was even the case in microregions where members of the ethnic majority fantasized about Gypsies inundating local schools and village centers, ravaging orchards, and getting mayors elected. Fidesz outperformed its right-wing rival in all electoral districts with the exception of Edelény. This was not surprising given that Jobbik was led by inexperienced politicians who lacked an encompassing program and support among elite groups. This, together with the Far

Right's somewhat obsessive focus on "Gypsy criminality," made it relatively easy for Fidesz to portray Jobbik as an extremist party that could not be trusted with the reins of power in the midst of a global economic storm. In order to secure a parliamentary supermajority in April 2010, Orbán only had to promise to bring the country back from the brink of insolvency and address popular concerns related to justice, order, and security. Under the circumstances of a full-fledged economic crisis, his modest promise to restore public order in the countryside and clamp down on welfare-scroungers even contented the majority of voters in electoral districts situated in the deprived Northeast.

Concluding Remarks

Political scientists who analyzed the shift of the Hungarian party structure have voiced puzzlement with regard to Jobbik's stunningly rapid rise and breakthrough. Enyedi and Benoit (2011: 39) have, for instance, noted that "Jobbik's success is difficult to explain" (translation mine). Lacking the tools to analyze political contention as a multi-scalar relational process, they could only go as far as to argue that "the fact that Jobbik gained almost fifteen percent in the course of a few months in early 2009 points with particular clarity to the relevance of events" (Enyedi and Benoit 2011: 24). In this chapter, I sought to show that the far-right party's breakthrough resulted from the explosive combination of the agendas that actors (local mayors, right-wing intellectuals, media elites, and mainstream and far-right politicians) operating on different levels and pursuing divergent—partially overlapping—strategies had adopted. The evolution of the public debate on the "Gypsy issue" in the 2007–2010 period exhibited all of the essential features of the definition that was proposed by the father of "moral panic theory":

> (i) Concern (rather than fear) about the potential or imagined threat; (ii) Hostility—moral outrage towards the actors (folk devils) who embody the problem and agencies (naïve social workers, spin-doctored politicians) who are "ultimately" responsible (and may become folk devils themselves); (iii) Consensus—a widespread agreement (not necessarily total) that the threat exists, is serious and that "something should be done." The majority of elite and influential groups, especially the mass media, should share this consensus. (iv) Disproportionality—an exaggeration of the number or strength of the cases, in terms of the damage caused, moral offensiveness, potential risk if ignored. Public concern is not directly proportionate to objective harm. (Cohen 2002: xxvi–xxvii).

In the introduction to the third edition of *Folk Devils and Moral Panics*, Cohen (2002: xxxvii) noted that "successful moral panics owe their appeal to their ability to find points of resonance with wider anxieties." His conceptual framework, however, provides no space or tools to analyze the dynamic of these anxieties. Instead, Cohen focuses attention on the mainstream media. By publishing alarmist reports and fitting heterogeneous events into a unitary interpretive frame, mainstream media outlets play a key role in creating the perception that a particular social group poses a fundamental threat to the social order. This dynamic, in turn, sways public opinion toward the authoritarian pole, leading to calls for the deployment of what Bourdieu (1994) called the "right hand of the state." If the pressure is sustained for long enough (this usually requires the politicization of the phenomenon—i.e., the organization of dissent) ruling elites are pushed to acknowledge the reality of the problem and may even be compelled to implement some of the authoritarian measures demanded by pressure groups. This, in turn, can trigger a negative feedback loop whereby the growing visibility of the problem leads to the identification of an increasing number of cases, leading to further pressure and authoritarian measures. If the dynamic reaches this stage, it usually leaves a long-lasting and decisive mark not only on social memory but also institutions and actors. This interpretation is not wholly misplaced, but it underplays the significance of the social contradictions that feed moral panics, as well as the political mechanisms whereby panics are sustained.

My reconstruction of Gyöngyöspata's microhistory shows that anti-Gypsyism had raised its head at the moment when particular segments of rural society were gripped by a powerful sense of loss and insecurity with regard to their personal outlooks and the future of their communities. It is difficult, in other words, to imagine how ethnotraditionalists' and paramilitaries' effort to lay the blame squarely on Roma could have succeeded without such fodder to feed on. Redemptive anti-Gypsyism and the promise to return the state to its rightful owners spoke in the most powerful way to the inhabitants of the country's northeastern periphery, which bore the brunt of the global economic crisis and where socioethnic frictions were rife.[29]

My analysis warrants the characterization of Jobbik supporters as people who are "rather secure but objectively can still lose something" (Minkenberg 2000: 187). Political sociologists have labeled this social stratum "modernization losers" who are likely to support the Far Right because they see it as an appealing counterweight to neoliberal policies (see Kalb 2011) and to the fragmentation of established cultural milieus (Holmes 1989, 2000). My ethnographic description of deprivation and abandonment (in chapter 2) and subsequent analysis of the politics that took root in this fertile soil (in this chapter) warrants the conclusion that it may be better to identify this social category as "insurgents" who have an objective stake and symbolically expressed interest in recapturing the state from cosmopolitan elites and handing it to nationalist politicians in the hope that the latter will transform the state-citizen nexus to their advantage.[30]

The moral panic around "Gypsy criminality" should therefore be seen as an ideological manifestation of deep-seated antagonisms that emerged at the junction of largely invisible forces that piled pressure on the interethnic relationship at a particular moment in time and in particular spaces. This interpretation draws on Hall et al.'s (1978) reinterpretation of Cohen's concept but breaks with his understanding of moral panics as necessarily refracting the interests of political elites. I have made an effort to follow the unfolding of the political process from the sites where external pressures entered everyday experience by working "up and outwards": following the actors who made efforts to symbolize lay experiences with a view to creating political effects. Focusing on noninstitutionalized forms of political agency (which fall below the radar of political scientists) and conventional political initiatives, I sought to identify strategies that played a central role in upward scale shift, which I see as key for understanding the radicalization of the electorate and the success of authoritarian right-wing parties (i.e., Fidesz and Jobbik) in 2010. The relational strategies I highlighted—abstraction and polarization—played a key role in transposing small-scale local conflicts into an irreconcilable Manichean struggle between "Gypsies" and "Magyars."

As far as know, Margit Feischmidt and I were the first to highlight the role that local elites played in the elaboration of a novel redemptive discourse (Feischmidt and Szombati 2016). In this chapter, I broadened this analysis by showing that their strategy of polarization—forcing public opinion into a pro- and an anti-Romani camp—was adopted by actors operating on the national level. I took this analysis one step further by highlighting right-wing intellectuals' role in abstracting local events and repackaging them into a national narrative. This analysis recasts the media as but one—albeit important—actor that encouraged the electorate's radicalization. My analysis specifies the media's role by highlighting that it increased the visibility of the "Gypsy issue" in the political public sphere and thereby contributed to upward scale shift. My analysis also adds a key factor that was overlooked by both Cohen and Hall but has become commonplace in political science: the interaction between radical and mainstream parties as a key element of radicalization. I argue that the shift of both politicians and the electorate toward increasingly exclusionary and authoritarian demands and initiatives was greatly helped by the main right-wing party's strategy. It is to this key issue that I now turn.

Notes

1. This part of my analysis draws on a coauthored article in which Margit Feischmidt and I tried to show how the rearticulation of the "Gypsy" and "Hungarian" categories allowed one of these elite factions to gain the upper hand over its rival. See Feischmidt and Szombati 2016.
2. Although their origins remain unclear (historians have variably described the Palóc as the descendants of the Khazars, Kabars, Avars, Szeklers, or Cumans), ethnologists generally refer to them as a Magyar subethnic group that retained a few cultural distinctions, such as a recognizable dialect and folk costume.
3. During our fieldwork, we encountered cultural, moral, and biological arguments to substantiate the need to discipline Roma, including the widespread use of the argument that Roma have a very different history and special traditions that are incompatible with the norms of the majority; the even more widespread claim that Roma are immoral because they prefer idleness over hard work and have little respect for private property; and the rarer biological analogy between Roma and animals (mostly rats). The cultural, moral, and biological arguments buttressing popular anti-Gypsyism—though unique in maintaining the biological distinction—show some important similarities with the ways minorities have been reimagined in Western Europe. Verena Stolcke (1995) pointed out already two decades ago that the new rhetoric and politics of exclusion increasingly rely on the representation of immigrants as being culturally incompatible with the native population and the concomitant argument that they pose a threat to ethnonational dominance. A recent analysis of discourses circulating in the political public sphere confirmed that both Islamophobia and anti-Gypsyism tend to be articulated along both "cultural" and "racial" lines (Vidra and Fox 2012).
4. Our discussions with local residents a few years later revealed that families who suffered from the decline of the rural economy supported the group's plan to revive peasant traditions. On the other hand, landowners, pensioners, and inhabitants of the border zone also supported the group's intransigent stance toward Roma.
5. The reform centralized welfare transfers and raised them in order to ensure what Hungary's leading social policy practitioner—who took part in the reform's elaboration—called a "social minimal" (a guaranteed minimal income for all families) for the first time in Hungary's history. See Zsuzsa Ferge's defense of the reform in the main left-of-center daily: "Rögös út a munkához" [The bumpy road to work], *Népszabadság*, published 13 April 2008, retrieved 11 November 2015 from http://www.fergezsuzsa.hu/docs/rogos_ut_a_munkahoz.pdf.
6. See (in Hungarian) "Önkormányzati kezdeményezés társadalmunk jobbá tétele érdekében" (Municipal initiative to make our society better), *Borsod Online*, n.d., retrieved 23 April 2015 from www.boon.hu/2008/06/s1.pdf.
7. By the time the eighteen mayors presented their proposals, the government's and the prime minister's popularity were already at a historic low. A poll published in May

2008 showed that only 19 percent of respondents wished to see the prime minister in an important political role in the future and 56 percent of respondents wanted early elections. See (in Hungarian) "Még sosem utálták ennyire Gyurcsányt" (Gyurcsány has nevery been so much hated), *Index*, published 29 May 2008, accessed 4 November 2015, http://index.hu/belfold/median8609/.

8. McAdam, Tarrow and Tilly (2001) define certification as the validation of actors, performances, and claims by external authorities. They argue that certification operates as a powerful selective mechanism in contentious politics "because a certifying site always recognizes a radically limited range of identities, performances, and claims" (158).

9. See (in Hungarian) Zsolt Bayer, "Cigányliszka" (Gypsyliszka), *Magyar Nemzet Online*, 17 October 2006, accessed 1 October 2013, http://mno.hu/velemeny/ciganyliszka-473730.

10. Bernáth and Messing's (2012) study compared the representation of Roma in the mainstream media in 2010/2011 and previous years (1988, 1993, 1997, 2000). They found a clear shift toward representations forged in the context of criminality to the detriment of other contexts (poverty, self-governance, human rights, etc.).

11. See Greskovits 2017 for a highly illuminating analysis of the Civic Circles' role in the making of right-wing hegemony and Halmai 2011 for an ethnographic analysis of local Circles in two Budapest working-class districts. It is also worth noting that Jobbik's current president, Gábor Vona, had been a member of the Circle that was led by Orbán.

12. The party formed an electoral alliance with the anti-Semitic Party of Hungarian Life and Justice (MIÉP) party. Although MIÉP was on the decline, it possessed infrastructural capacities that were valuable to Jobbik.

13. The speech was delivered by the prime minister in Balatonőszöd in May 2006 to an audience of Socialist MPs. The meeting was supposed to be confidential, but Gyurcsány's speech was taped by an unknown source and broadcast on public radio on 17 September 2006. In a key passage, the prime minister acknowledged that the Socialist Party had misled voters to win the parliamentary election of 2006: "There isn't much choice because we screwed it up. Not a little, but big time. No European country has done something as stupid as we have.... We have obviously been lying throughout the past one and a half or two years. It was perfectly clear that what we were saying was not true. We are beyond the country's [financial] possibilities to such an extent that would have been inconceivable under the previous Socialist-Liberal government. And in the meantime, by the way, we did not do anything for four years. Nothing. You cannot name one significant governmental measure that we can be proud of, apart from the fact that in the end we managed to bring the country back from the brink. Nothing. If we have to give an account to the country of what we have done in four years, what are we going to say?" See (in Hungarian, translation mine) "A teljes balatonőszödi szöveg" (The entire Balatonőszöd speech), *Népszabadság* archive, n.d., accessed 11 May 2015, http://nol.hu/archivum/archiv-417593-228304.

14. Excerpt, translation mine, from Jobbik's self-documentary titled *Jobbik Nemzedék* (Jobbik generation), produced by Jobbik, Movement for a Better Hungary, 2010, accessed 14 October 2014, https://vimeo.com/10279639.

15. The Arrow Cross Party was a national-socialist party that rose to power in October 1944 with the help of Nazi Germany, which invaded Hungary in March 1944. During its short rule, which lasted until the country's liberation by Soviet forces in early 1945, more than ten thousand Jews were murdered by Arrow Cross paramilitary militias in Budapest, and tens of thousands were sent on foot to the Austrian border in so-called "death marches."

16. Szegedi told me that he had adopted the term "Gypsy criminality" from Bíber. While this may well be true, it is important to mention that it has a longer history. In chapter

1, I noted that the link between Gypsyness and criminality had already been established in the early twentieth century. Here I add that the term also appeared in the informal jargon of criminal investigators in the Socialist period (see E.Z. Tóth 2012). It was appropriated much later—in 2005—by a far-right activist nicknamed "Tomcat" and subsequently by Bíber to signify problems related to the coexistence of Roma and non-Roma in the contemporary period (Juhász 2010).

17. The text of the original article was posted by Ferenczi on Jobbik's webpage: "Ferenczi Gábor: Nagyobb biztonságra van szükség Devecserben" [Gábor Ferenczi: More security is needed in Devecser], Jobbik Magyarországért Mozgalom, published 2 August 2012, accessed 13 January 2013, https://www.jobbik.hu/rovatok/alapszer vezeti_h%C3%ADrek/ferenczi_g%C3%A1bor_nagyobb_biztons%C3%A1gra_van_ sz%C3%BCks%C3%A9g_devecserben.

18. Research focusing on the hurdles faced by emergent antiestablishment parties has highlighted the importance of visibility. Researchers who have analyzed the media's role in the emergence of radical right-wing parties have forcefully argued that the mass media plays an increasingly pivotal role in elevating new issues and parties into the public sphere (see, for instance, Koopmans 2004). Hervik (2011) has, moreover, shown that the rise of tabloid newspapers—which have a financial interest in focusing on conflicts and scandals—has fueled moral panics and provided visibility to far-right political entrepreneurs who seek to ride the waves panics create. Plasser and Ulram (2003) have argued that visibility provided by the media is especially important in the early phases of party-building, when new movements struggle to make themselves seen and heard.

19. See (in Hungarian) "Megőrizni a létezés magyar minőségét—Orbán kötcsei beszéde szóról szóra" [To preserve the Hungarian quality of existence—Orbán's speech at the Kötcse gathering word-by-word], *HírExtra*, 18 February 2010, retrieved 13 March 2014 from http://www.hirextra.hu/2010/02/18/megorizni-a-letezes-magyar-minoseget-orban-kotcsei-beszede-szorol-szora/.

20. See (in Hungarian) "Jobbkanyar: pártok és politikusok népszerűsége" (Right turn: popularity of parties and politicians), *Medián*, published 25 February 2009, accessed 4 September 2014, http://median.hu/printcikk.ivy?artid=4c6342ea-f8cf-40ea-a9b1-de6ede194f27.

21. See (in Hungarian, translation mine) "Leváltották a cigányozó rendőrkapitányt" (Gypsy-bashing police chief sacked), *Index*, 30 January 2009, accessed 31 January 2009, http://index.hu/belfold/paszt0130/.

22. See (in Hungarian, translation mine) "Szabó Máté: figyelmeztetni kell a cigány-bűnözésre" (Máté Szabó: we must call attention to Gypsy criminality), *Figyelőnet*, published 2 April 2009, accessed 23 February 2015, https://24.hu/belfold/2009/04/02/szabo_mate_figyelmeztetni_kell/.

23. Excerpt, translation mine, from Jobbik's self-documentary titled *Jobbik Nemzedék* (Jobbik generation), produced by Jobbik, Movement for a Better Hungary, 2010, accessed 14 October 2014, https://vimeo.com/10279639.

24. See (in Hungarian) "Ki mint fél, úgy ítél: a radikális jobboldal megítélése" (How we fear is how we judge: public opinion on the radical right), *Medián*, published 30 August 2007, accessed 19 September 2009, http://www.median.hu/object.9eeed0a8-efc2-4286-81ea-4fe22cc801af.ivy.

25. See (in Hungarian) "Magyar Gárda megítélése: egzisztenciális félelmek erősítik a szélsőségeket" (Public opinion on the Hungarian Guard: existential fears strengthen the extremists), *Publicus*, published 17 May 2009, accessed 19 September 2009, http://www.publicus.hu/blog/magyar_garda/. The Budapest Tribunal's decision on 2 July 2009 to ban the Hungarian Guard (on grounds that its marches disrupted social peace and violated Roma citizens' right to safety) was supported by a similar mar-

gin: 53 percent supported the ban, while 37 percent rejected it. See (in Hungarian) "Nem a ruha teszi: Felmérés a Magyar Gárda feloszlatásáról" (It is not about the clothes: Survey of public opinion on the Hungarian Guard's dissolution), *Medián*, published 9 July 2009, accessed 19 September 2009, http://www.median.hu/printcikk .ivy?artid=12f8a53b-1583-49ec-8820-ef67a68c500f.

26. Jobbik essentially proposed a program of "reverse affirmative action" (Zaslove 2004): the reintroduction of segregation in schooling, the incarceration of "Gypsy criminals," and the scrapping of child benefits above the second child. (The latter proposal first appeared in the mayors' above-mentioned petition.)

27. Borsod-Abaúj-Zemplén, Szabolcs-Szatmár-Bereg, Hajdú-Bihar, Jász-Nagykun-Szolnok, Heves, and Nógrád counties.

28. See (in Hungarian, translation mine) "Cigányellenes kijelentései miatt feljelentik az edelényi polgármestert" (Edelény's mayor taken to court for anti-Gypsy comments), *Origó*, published 3 September 2009, accessed 30 September 2009, http://www.origo .hu/itthon/20090903-ciganyellenes-kijelentesei-miatt-feljelentik-az-edelenyi-polgarm estert.html.

29. A study published by a political geographer who sought to draw a link between socioeconomic and political trends found that Jobbik made its greatest advances between the parliamentary elections of 2006 and 2010 in electoral districts where the ratio of the Romani population exceeded the national average by 17 percent (Vécsei 2011). Of the localities where Jobbik made the greatest leaps, 72 percent were situated in either the Northern Hungary or Northern Great Plain regions. This first cluster stood out in terms of unemployment and poverty rates: the ratio of youth unemployment exceeded the national average by 31 percent and the ratio of people receiving social assistance by 32 percent. The study also found that Jobbik made significant—but lesser—advances in another cluster of localities where the ratio of the Romani population exceeded the national average by 7 percent. Of the localities that belonged to this cluster, 85 percent were located in the eastern part of the country. These localities were also slightly worse off than the national average in terms of employment and income levels but were altogether close to the average. The two clusters also stood out in relation to criminality and out-migration. Whereas crime against property decreased nation-wide in the 2006–2010 period, it grew in the two clusters where Jobbik made significant gains. The ratio of population loss (due to out-migration) was by far the worst in the cluster where Jobbik achieved its best scores. In the other cluster, the previously positive migration trend was reversed in the period. The factors that Vécsei highlights are the same ones I identified in Gyöngyöspata, where the number of unemployed people increased between 2008 and 2010 (see table 2.4), and which lost 4 percent of its population between 2001 and 2011. The only dimension in which Gyöngyöspata stands out is in relation to the criminality rate. The data provided by the Interior Ministry (see table 2.5) do not show a clear increase in the number of crimes committed against property (spikes in 1995, 1999, and 2007 were followed by drops). I note that local informants strongly disputed official statistics, suggesting that the police had refused to conduct criminal investigations in a significant number of cases. This suspicion, as explained above, found expression in the "criminal report."

30. See Friedman 2010. This claim is at odds with the interpretation of political scientists who have sought to discredit Jobbik's representation as the party of "losers . . . subjected to material deprivation, crime and humiliation" (Karácsony and Róna 2010: 22, translation mine) based on reference to a lack of a strong correlation between personal income level and far-right party preference (see, for instance, Bíró and Róna 2011a: 265). The main problem with these studies in my view is that they operate with an overtly objectivist definition of "loss," which misses the centrality of the contexts and relationships out of which feelings of loss and insecurity emerge.

View of Gyöngyöspata's center from the Vári wine cellars, with the Goat Stone in the background. © Photo by Polina Georgescu.

Romani women enrolled in the public works program clean the flower beds opposite Gyöngyöspata's landmark cultural symbol, the Catholic church. © Photo by Polina Georgescu.

Winemaker Bálint Losonci posing in front of an old wine cellar with a bottle of a 2015 Parola, his signature wine. © Photo by Polina Georgescu.

The house of winemaker and local patriot Magdolna Bernáth, who came in second place as the "ethnotraditionalist" candidate in the 2011 by-election. © Photo by Polina Georgescu.

A traditional "Szekler gate" guards the entrance of the house of the head of the local winemakers' association in the Bem street, where a fight broke out in 2006. The following motto is carved above the entrance: "Our past is from our Hungarian ancestors. Our future depends on our Hungarian children." © Photo by Polina Georgescu.

A house on the Bem street near the "border zone," featuring barbed wire and a sign reading "Careful, electricity!" © Photo by Polina Georgescu.

A girl poses for a picture in front of her house, situated right next to the Rédei Creek on the "Gypsy settlement." © Photo by Polina Georgescu.

A typical house on Gyöngyöspata's "Gypsy settlement," with the Goat Stone in the background. © Photo by Polina Georgescu.

The younger János Farkas, former head of the local Gypsy Self-Government, in his house. © Photo by Polina Georgescu.

People living on the "Gypsy settlement" gather to discuss the results of the by-election, which the Jobbik candidate won on 17 July 2011. © Photo by Polina Georgescu.

Éva Dezső, the former principal of the local elementary school and a proponent of integrated instruction, standing in front of her house. © Photo by Polina Georgescu.

Kids leaving the local elementary school. © Photo by Polina Georgescu.

Former Gypsy councilor Pál Farkas's children pictured in front of their house on the Bem street in 2011, a few months before the family moved to Canada. © Photo by Polina Georgescu.

The remnants of former Gypsy councilor Pál Farkas's house five years after the family moved to Canada. © Photo by Polina Georgescu.

The Trianon memorial on Gyöngyöspata's main square, with the Catholic church in the background. The inscription reads, "Under the protection of the Sacred Crown. This is how things were and this is how they will be. 3 June 1920"—a reference to the Trianon Treaty, which deprived Hungary of two-thirds of its former territory. © Photo by Polina Georgescu.

The new Turul statue built to commemorate the civilian victims of the two world wars (except for Holocaust victims whose names figure on a plaque in the Jewish cemetery situated on Devecser's outskirts). © Photo by Polina Georgescu.

View of Devecser's center from the memorial park dedicated to the victims of the red mud spill. © Photo by Polina Georgescu.

Agribusinessperson and former Jobbik councilor György Kozma standing in front of his house in what was once a typical "peasant street." © Photo by Polina Georgescu.

Teacher, amateur historian, and local patriot József Czeidli posing in front of the Turul statue that was inaugurated in 2014 in the memorial park. © Photo by Polina Georgescu.

Former teacher Katalin Mester standing in Devecser's old cemetery, which she fought to save from the hands of the local priest who removed several old tombstones to make way for new graves. © Photo by Polina Georgescu.

Massage therapist, fortune-teller, and Jobbik councilor Anikó Bognár standing in front of her house where the "neighbor feud" took place in 2012. © Photo by Polina Georgescu.

Former lower school principal Katalin Simon, a proponent of integrated tuition, in her home shortly after she was removed from her position by the head principal in 2017. © Photo by Polina Georgescu.

Typical square houses in one of Devecser's "clean streets." © Photo by Polina Georgescu.

Houses on the edge of the "new colony" that was designed by Hungary's leading organic architect and is now the home of red mud victims who chose to stay in Devecser rather than to start a new life elsewhere. © Photo by Polina Georgescu.

Musician Tibor Orsós holding a brick from what was once his house on the Dankó settlement, which was washed away by the red mud spill. © Photo by Polina Georgescu.

A house belonging to a Romani family, with the Somló hill in the background. © Photo by Polina Georgescu.

Lomis trader Alfréd "Johnny" Király and his wife, Ildikó, standing in front of their house on Devecser's main square. © Photo by Polina Georgescu.

Lomis trader Rajmund Fodor in front of his "bungalow" (shop) on Devecser's used goods market. © Photo by Polina Georgescu.

Lomis traders on Devecser's used goods market on a typically uneventful autumn market day. © Photo by Polina Georgescu.

School attendant Mónika Pitzinger, a member of the clan that was involved in the 2012 "neighborhood feud," in her food stall on Devecser's used goods market. © Photo by Polina Georgescu.

– Chapter 4 –

RIGHT-WING RIVALRY
AND THE DUAL STATE

ℰ⁓

In this chapter, I analyze the impact of right-wing rivalry (in the context of the moral panic on "Gypsy criminality") on the politics of governmental power, and argue that it played a key role in the liberal state's transformation in an authoritarian direction under the new Fidesz government in the 2010–2014 period. I begin by highlighting Jobbik's effort to stabilize its support after its parliamentary entry by returning to the "Gypsy issue" and organizing a major mobilization campaign in Gyöngyöspata. I then analyze the government's response by highlighting a series of tactical maneuvers, which—together with a number of unenforced errors—undermined the far-right's effort to establish Gyöngyöspata as a model town. I then analyze more thoroughly Fidesz's long-term strategic response by arguing that the party first incorporated elements of the new racist common sense into its own hegemonic project and, once in government, went on to implement an anti-egalitarian vision of the "work-based society." The ruling party achieved this through the separation of the "Normative State" (which holds jurisdiction over "homogenous society") from the "Prerogative State"[1] (which is provided special means to discipline "heterogeneous groups"). In the final part of the chapter, I argue that this dualization of state functions helped the ruling party retain its hold over a radicalized political center and defuse the moral panic on "Gypsy criminality." In this I seek to move beyond Cohen's emphasis on volatility as a key element of moral panics. While a panic may "dissipat[e] suddenly and without warning" (Cohen 2002: xxvii), I will seek to draw a link between the new politics of governmental power and decreasing perceptions of threat in rural society.[2]

Jobbik's Return to the Streets

After its entry into parliament, Jobbik found itself in a difficult situation. The party had to find its place within the parliamentary framework, which it had routinely criticized and on occasion called into question. While participation in parliamentary politics risked undermining the party's antiestablishment image, its rejection would have questioned the legitimacy of the political strategy Jobbik had followed. The definition of the party's relationship to conventional forms of politics was confounded by the unexpectedly sharp rightwing turn of Viktor Orbán's new government. The prime minister announced his desire to build a new political regime that broke the mold of consensual elite politics. The ruling party single-handedly rewrote the country's constitution and robustly defended the new Fundamental Law and accompanying cardinal laws against political criticisms and legal infringement procedures initiated by the European Commission. On top of this "freedom struggle," Fidesz also adopted a series of laws (granting dual citizenship to ethnic Hungarians living abroad, introducing a Trianon memorial day, adopting a "three strikes" penal policy, etc.) that had initially been proposed by its far-right rival. These circumstances led to a decline in Jobbik's popularity, which translated into weak results at the municipal elections of October 2010. The latter, in turn, generated a conflict between representatives of the party's moderate and radical wings—a conflict that found a form of expression in a split within the legally disbanded Hungarian Guard's successor organization: the New Hungarian Guard Movement (hereafter NHG).[3]

After a period of debate and wavering, the party leadership decided that the most pressing imperative was to reaffirm the party's political identity and reassure its core voters. Following Vice President Csanád Szegedi's suggestion, Jobbik returned to the anti-Gypsy street politics that had catapulted it into the spotlight. The move also allowed the party to take advantage of a new window of opportunity. Between the first and second rounds of the 2010 parliamentary elections, Viktor Orbán—looking to steal a few thousand extra votes from Jobbik with a view to securing a two-thirds parliamentary majority—had promised to restore security in rural localities. After taking office, Interior Minister Sándor Pintér concretized that pledge by promising to restore order "in two weeks' time."

The return to the by then well-rehearsed mobilization blueprint took place in the village of Lak (Borsod-Abaúj-Zemplén County) where an 81-year-old woman was murdered on 23 January 2011. Relying on rumors that the perpetrators were four Romani adolescents, Jobbik organized a march against "Gypsy criminality" in the village. In the speech he gave at the event, party leader Gábor Vona outlined a new proposal to separate Gypsy children from their families at a young age and to send them to boarding schools because "this is the only way to teach them how to behave normally and integrate into society."[4] He also announced that he would be attending the opening day of the new parliamentary session in the uniform of the disbanded Hungarian Guard. This symbolic gesture allowed Jobbik to focus the political debate on its favorite theme—law(lessness) and (dis)order—and to criticize the governing coalition for failing to live up to its pledge to restore order in the countryside.

Polls conducted in February 2011 showed that the party's popularity had stopped declining. This encouraging sign may have led Jobbik's leaders to conclude that anti-Gypsy mobilization could indeed stabilize the party's support and possibly allow it the regain lost ground. Vona's strongly worded speech in Lak and his announcement on wearing the uniform of a banned organization was also designed to test the reactions of the new government—but also the press—to the revival of racist rhetoric. Although the media proved receptive to the decoy, the local mayor and councilors did not respond favorably to the framing of the murder as an ethnic issue. Jobbik's leaders therefore embarked on a search for another locality where socioethnic frictions could be instrumentalized. In the beginning of February, a resident of the Bajcsi street (see chapter 2) called the party president to inform him of the flaring of anti-Gypsy sentiment in Gyöngyöspata. The party leadership decided to use the opportunity to launch a campaign in Vona's own electoral district where the Jobbik leader was looking to get himself directly elected in 2014.[5]

In the autumn of 2010, the houses of two Romani families were damaged by the flooding Rédei Creek, which separated "the village" from the "Gypsy settlement." A representative of the Red Cross offered to clean the creek bed and asked the head of the organization's unofficial Romani division to find new homes for affected families in the village. The organization planned to move a family of eight and a family of fourteen to two streets that were part of what I called the "border zone" (where a few Romani families had bought houses in recent years). Although the larger family did not wish to accept the property offered by the Red Cross, news quickly spread among local residents that one of the most "unruly" families would be moving to the Bajcsi. At the meeting of the local council on 31 January, outraged residents (who later appeared in media reports as the victims of "atrocities" committed by Gypsies) demanded that councilors find a way to prevent the relocations from taking place. It is most probably as a result of this meeting that the village's mayor decided to persuade the Red Cross to change its plans. The organization, bowing to pressure, decided to withdraw its offer to buy the houses in the second half of February.

As noted above, Jobbik's leadership was informed of the situation in early February by a local resident. Although party delegates later denied that the leadership had prepared the "invasion of Gyöngyöspata," evidence collected by the parliamentary committee that was set up on the ruling party's initiative in May 2012 revealed that the leaders of Jobbik and the NHG had jointly planned the intervention.

The opportunity to launch the campaign arose on 22 February 2011, when an elderly resident committed suicide in the Bajcsi street. Two days following the incident, a far-right blog published a video report wherein Jobbik's local leader, Oszkár Juhász, declared that the old man had committed suicide because he could not stomach the "relocation of Gypsies into the village." (Most of our informants linked the suicide to the man's health condition.) On 1 March 2011, members of the NHG appeared in the uniform of the newly created For a Better Future Civic Guard Association (hereafter FBF)[6] with the professed aim of supporting the work of the police by conducting patrols in Gyöngyöspata's "crime-infested streets." On 6 March 2011, Jobbik organized a mass rally on the village's main square, calling on residents to demonstrate against "Gypsy terror." Party leader Vona spoke of rampant crime and the government's inability to "bring Gypsy criminals to justice." Between fifteen hundred and two thousand people attended the event; approximately one-third to one-half of them were local residents in the estimation of my colleague Margit Feischmidt and myself. At the end of the rally, the crowd marched to the settlement where Oszkár Juhász handed a text titled "Code of Coexistence" to the leaders of the Gypsy Minority Self-government.

The events that followed the demonstration were closely followed by the Hungarian press. While journalists had made only sporadic appearances in the village before the rally, this drastically changed after it became clear that the paramilitaries were planning to stay. For ten days, the members of FBF patrolled the streets day and night. The police force, which maintained a continuous presence, did not prevent activists clad in black boots and uniforms from following Romani residents who left their homes. These activists were provided accommodation by local residents—some of them members of the Friends of Gyöngyöspata Circle—who supported the campaign.

Although paramilitaries were most warmly welcomed by the residents of the streets surrounding the settlement, their presence was supported by a much wider segment of the local population. Close to a thousand local residents signed a petition requesting that members of FBF stay in the village after its leader finally decided to leave Gyöngyöspata on 16 March 2011.

The departure of paramilitaries did not mark the end of the intimidation campaign. Members of two other extremist paramilitary organizations—the Outlaw Army and the Defense Force—appeared in the village just before FBF's departure with the aim of maintaining pressure on the Romani community. The tension grew day by day, but representatives of the government remained silent, despite the fact that the interior minister had previously signaled that provocation on behalf of paramilitary organizations would not be tolerated. Human rights organizations, frustrated by authorities' unwillingness to step up against hate groups, decided to intervene. In a joint letter, the Hungarian Civil Liberties Union, the Helsinki Committee, and the Legal Defense Bureau for National and Ethnic Minorities declared that the patrols constituted a deliberate attempt to provoke ethnic violence and signaled that the police should have broken up the 6th of March rally because its organizers had violated local Roma citizens' basic rights.[7] The Civil Liberties Union filed complaints in three cases where it believed that the harm inflicted on Roma individuals and hate motives could be verified.[8] The qualms formulated by human rights groups were confirmed in the report released on 19 April 2011 by the parliamentary commissioner for minority rights. Although the authorities mentioned in the report (interior minister, national chief of police, justice minister, state prosecutor's office, secretary of state responsible for social inclusion) did not officially react to the commissioner's allegations, their responses incorporated some of the recommendations he put forward: a proposal to create a task force responsible for preventing and mitigating local ethnic conflicts; and an amendment to the governmental decree on minor offenses, which allowed authorities to impose fines on civic guards that organized patrols without previously signing an agreement with local councils and chiefs of police. These measures showed that the government was mainly concerned with preventing the appearance of civic guards linked to the far-right in other localities. This fear was vindicated by the appearance of FBF in the town of Hajdúhadház, situated 150 kilometers east of Gyöngyöspata, on 11 April 2011. Representatives of the organization announced their plan to replicate their Gyöngyöspata campaign based on the claim that it had yielded positive results and could thus be used as a model to intervene in other "crime-infested" neighborhoods.

At roughly the same time, members of the Defense Force reappeared in Gyöngyöspata and announced their plan to organize a military training on a property located right next to the "Gypsy settlement." Although the majority of the local population (and even those who had supported the patrols) condemned this novel intimidation campaign, Gyöngyöspata's mayor—whose authority had been severely undermined by the mentioned petition—resigned three days after the announcement. It is at this point that the local Romani population's fear culminated. In the face of panicked reactions, an American businessman and philanthropist who had arrived in the village to discuss the possibility of launching a community garden and an after-school program decided to give women and children the opportunity to leave the village for a few days. Images of Romani women and children leaving on buses rented by the American philanthropist created a political sensation and generated a row between the government and left-of-center parties. On the left (and in the international media), the action was interpreted as the legitimate "evacuation" of a threatened community. On the right, it was presented as an "Easter vacation" and simultaneously condemned as a political ploy to undermine the government's reputation.

The last actors to influence events were a handful of Budapest-based liberal intellectuals belonging to the Dignity for All Movement. The group staged its first demonstration on 15 March 2011, the anniversary of the revolution of 1848 (which some members celebrated together with Romani families in Gyöngyöspata). Following this event, the One Hundred Thousand for Gyöngyöspata Facebook group—composed of young Budapest-based activists who were loosely linked to the Dignity for All Movement—organized two successive demonstrations in front of the interior ministry, demanding that authorities step up against paramilitaries. The Romani activists present at these events developed close ties with Gyöngyöspata's Gypsy Minority Self-government, which was led by a young man named János Farkas. Another group of young activists organized vigils in the village in the period when paramilitaries were the most active. Besides them, the director of an organization specializing in peaceful conflict resolution (Partners Hungary Foundation) also made sporadic visits to the village to initiate a dialogue between local Roma and non-Roma. These actors—as opposed to their predecessors (see my discussion of the beneficial impact of European accession on local antisegregationist struggles in chapter 2)—failed to significantly influence the course of events. Representatives of the right-wing government neglected activists' calls to clamp down on paramilitaries—a decision that was probably based on their assessment that expressing solidarity with the local Romani population could alienate Fidesz's voters. The only meaningful action the police did take was to arrest the members of the Defense Force on 22 April 2011 in order to prevent the organizing of the above-mentioned military training.

The last noteworthy event occurred on the night of 26 April 2011, when members of the Defense Force (who had just been released from custody) returned to Gyöngyöspata and provoked a violent confrontation with settlement-dwellers. It was after this incident that the prime minister declared, "Our patience has ended." In the interview he granted to a commercial television channel, Viktor Orbán acknowledged the police's sluggish response but argued that the authorities had to wait for public opinion to catch up with events before intervening.[9] This comment lends support to the claim that the government's reticence to face down Jobbik was based on its fear of losing support at a moment when the moral panic on "Gypsy criminality" was in full swing.

Although this was the only violent incident that occurred during the campaign, the relationship between Roma and non-Roma did not improve afterward in Gyöngyöspata. The fear and terror gripping Roma gradually subsided, but many could not come to terms with the fact that several non-Romani families had supported the groups who "terrorized" their children. Collective action against the far-right intervention was hampered by the lack of ethnic solidarity within an externally homogenized, but in reality fragmented, community. The socioeconomic and cultural gulf between integrated families who lived in the village and settlement-dwellers acquired a political dimension in the period of the conflict. As I explained in chapter 2, "integrated families"—instead of contesting the ethnicization of social relations—accepted the new discourse promoted by the Circle but simultaneously attempted to deflect blame onto "settlement-dwellers" by splitting the Gypsy category and blaming "unworthy Gypsies" for the arrival of FBF based on the argument that this would not have happened if they had not "misbehaved." This did not turn out to be a particularly effective strategy because those who considered themselves "worthy" could also not escape the negative consequences of ethnic stigmatization. One of our informants formulated this thusly: "I have been working since the age of sixteen and have not even stolen a needle. So why do I have to suffer for the deeds of children who stole some vegetables?" These families have been particularly badly

hit by the conflict because winemakers were reluctant to employ
Roma even on an ad hoc basis out of fear that they would be accused
of siding with the enemy.

Although the far-right intervention satisfied the majority's thirst
for substantive justice, non-Romani residents were angered by the
media's portrayal of the village. Those living in or in the proxim-
ity of the conflict zone were outraged by what they considered bi-
ased reporting, in particular the media's unwillingness to evoke the
antecedents of the conflict directly relevant to their experience: the
devastation of the Goat Stone, the bullying of old people by Romani
youth, and other factors undermining peaceful coexistence between
members of the minority and the majority.

The "cold peace" descending on the village fell in line with the
interests of Jobbik. Local leader Oszkár Juhász launched his bid to
become mayor by proposing to emulate the "model of Érpatak" (on
which more below), which he presented as an experientially proven
method for restoring public order in the countryside. He cleverly
identified himself as a radical but realist candidate by distancing
himself from the captain of the Defense Force, who also announced
his candidacy for the vacated mayor's seat. His main rival, the vice-
mayor, who was widely expected to win the electoral contest, presented herself as the candidate of reconciliation. Her position was,
however, weakened by the government's largely passive response to
events, notably its failure to preserve the state's monopoly over the
use of physical coercion.

The government did, however, launch a political offensive in the
national political arena. In early May, it announced the creation of an
ad hoc parliamentary committee with the professed aim of "investigating the events in Gyöngyöspata and the background of uniform-
related crime, and facilitating the elimination of uniform-related
crime." Although committee president Máté Kocsis (Fidesz) presented his task as a fact-finding mission, his real aim was to lay the
blame for the outburst of ethnic tensions in Gyöngyöspata on Jobbik, while also presenting left-wing parties and human rights groups
as bearing a degree of responsibility for the damage inflicted on the
country's reputation.[10] The government's focus on managing the fallout of events on the national level allowed Jobbik to maintain the initiative on the local level. This indirectly contributed to its candidate's
surprise victory at the by-election organized on 17 July 2011. Oszkár Juhász, running on a ticket of "zero tolerance against destructive
behavior," obtained 33.8 percent of the vote. Despite his high score,
Jobbik's candidate could have been beaten if voters had rallied be-

hind a unity candidate. The Fidesz-backed vice-mayor (who received 26 percent of the vote) was robbed of victory by the unexpectedly strong performance of a winemaker who was a leading member of the Friends Circle (21.4 percent). Although ethnotraditionalists had gained leverage and momentum, they were not strong enough to win the election. This had mainly to do with the fact that Jobbik had successfully appropriated their radical discourse and proposals. Many local inhabitants were grateful to paramilitaries for "restoring public order" and hoped that Jobbik would find a permanent solution to the "Gypsy problem." The far-right party's authority was thus—here as elsewhere—grounded in a successful mimicry of state functions and symbolic confrontation with the dangerous classes (see Friedman 2004). In addition, Jobbik's candidate managed to position himself as a man who, once in power, could count on substantial support from his political hinterland. It is also worth mentioning that the captain of the Defense Force received 10.5 percent of the vote. This means that close to half of Gyöngyöspata's politically active citizens supported extreme racist candidates at the by-election—in stark contrast to the municipal election of October 2010, when Oszkár Juhász had received only 5.8 percent of the vote.

The Failure of the "Model Town"

At the official ceremony of investiture, the new mayor pledged to bring an end to "Gypsy criminality" and to restore the values of work and respect of the law to their rightful place. In practice, this meant an increased presence of the police and the immediate and severe sanctioning of minor offenses. The mayor's main source of inspiration and point of reference was the so-called "Érpatak model," a system of repressive measures that had been elaborated and put into practice by the mayor of the village of Érpatak, situated 200 kilometers east of Gyöngyöspata.[11]

During one of the visits he paid to Gyöngyöspata during the local election campaign, Érpatak's mayor described the core of the "model" as a concerted effort, through the deployment of excessive bureaucratic pressures, to prevent "uncooperative individuals and families" from engaging in "destructive" behavior. This approach built on the ideological premises of the "culture of poverty thesis"—namely, that asocial behavior is rooted in a deviant subculture whose negative effects can only be neutralized through punitive initiatives that are amenable to correcting "anti-communitarian" behavior. Such initiatives were to be jointly implemented by the local council and public authorities (such as the Child Custody Office, the public notary, etc.) who have the competence to impose severe demands and sanctions on welfare claimants. More narrowly defined, the Érpatak model corresponds to decree No. 2/2011 (II. 14), adopted by the local council of Érpatak, which made the receipt of welfare benefits dependent on recipients' willingness to keep their environment (sidewalk, garden, and house) clean and orderly.[12] In case of noncompliance with local regulations, the municipality has the right to withhold welfare payments. The imposition of such harsh preconditions was permitted by the decentralization of the welfare regime, which began in 2008/2009 (see the previous chapter for details), when mayors where handed discretionary powers to withhold welfare payments in case of noncompliance with certain obligations.[13] The process, however, gathered real momentum after the adoption of a new law on social welfare (Act CLXXI/2010) under the new Fidesz government (on which more below).

Under the broadest definition, the Érpatak model can be conceptualized as an authoritarian social policy regime created with the intention of disciplining the dangerous classes. The approach pioneered by the mayor defined poverty as a moral predicament and prescribed a paternalistic carrots-and-stick methodology for ensuring that the poor do no harm to others. It was this methodology—harassing "destructive" and rewarding "constructive" social elements—that Gyöngyöspata's new mayor put into practice after his victory. A newly created law enforcement unit (the "field patrol") was charged with the task of preventing petty theft. According to the local newspaper, the unit had by January 2012 "successfully pushed out crime-prone individuals from the outskirts of Gyöngyöspata and taken an important step in the creation of the promised complex defense net." A second element of this "defense net" consisted in the sanctioning of welfare claimants who were enrolled in the new centrally administered public works program that was officially launched by the interior minister in Gyöngyöspata in August 2011. The mayor supplied superintendents with video cameras to control the work of the forty individuals (the great majority of whom were Roma) who were employed between August and November 2011 in the program. Three individuals were charged with disorderly conduct and expelled for three years from the program (resulting in the suspension of their right to receive welfare benefits for the same period of time). Those who were lucky enough to evade this severe sanction were harassed by the police,[14] which conducted a large number of controls and fined

Roma for minor offenses (such as throwing cigarette stubs on the pavement, burning leaves on days disallowed by the local council, or using bicycles that had no lights).

In their speeches, Jobbik's politicians often referred to the "Gyöngyöspata model" as a method for restoring trust and harmony in lawless communities. Jobbik's strategic aim—as I learned from former Vice President Csanád Szegedi—was, however, to cleanse Gyöngyöspata of "destructive" elements with a view to proving that Jobbik had a practical solution to the "Gypsy problem." Pressured by the mayor, the notary, and the police, seventy to eighty members of the local Romani community left the locality and flew to Canada to request political asylum. While the local mayor hailed this as a success—publicly claiming that "families prone to criminality have moved their seat to Canada"—it was in reality "integrated families" who had left Gyöngyöspata, leaving the most destitute members of the surplus population behind. While landowners and inhabitants of the frontline were relieved to see Romani families leave the village, Jobbik found it difficult to present its local activities as a success story outside Gyöngyöspata.

The reputation of the "Gyöngyöspata model" was also tarnished by other factors. The owner of the largest local enterprise (who had been paying between 70,000 and 100,000 Euros in local business tax, which amounted to more than 5 percent of Gyöngyöspata's annual revenues) decided to move his transportation company's headquarters to another locality. The decision was partially motivated by the desire to avoid sponsoring an extremist municipality, which—in his view—was hacking away at the fabric of local society. Thus, while the new mayor had promised to attract new investments to the locality, his politics had actually exercised an adverse effect on the local economy. The one improvement he was able to highlight was the inauguration of a new community garden with the help of the revamped public works program. Although the community garden was a success (especially when compared to local elite groups' erstwhile efforts to integrate settlement-dwellers into the local economy; see chapter 2), Jobbik encountered difficulties in claiming ownership of the project, which the interior minister actively promoted as one of the government's solutions to the "Gypsy question."

Jobbik's effort to present its local initiatives as a model also foundered on the mayor's personal credentials. Oszkár Juhász's rhetorical skills did not match those of his Érpatak colleague. As opposed to the latter, he could not be used as a traveling agent to promote Jobbik's agenda and achievements. Although the party leadership realized early on that Juhász was a "loose cannon" in need of guidance, the overseer who had been appointed as his chief-of-staff did not succeed in preventing the mayor from embroiling himself in image-bashing activities. Although the mayor initially got away with a series of blunders—such as sending an intimidating Christmas postcard (picturing him in the company of armed field patrollers) to "destructive families"—in April 2012 a recording of a phone conversation featuring his voice was released to the press. In the conversation, he and another man are heard discussing the possibility of initiating a civil war with a view to grasping governmental power. The recording received wide publicity and elicited responses from both Fidesz and Socialist party leaders. (Jobbik attempted to defend its mayor by claiming that the recording captured a private conversation and accusing Fidesz of using the secret services to eavesdrop on the opposition.) Then, in September 2012, news emerged that police investigators were accusing Juhász of orchestrating a fake assassination attempt. (At the time, the mayor had claimed that he had been fired upon after leaving his office in the early hours of 29 November 2011. Police investigators came to the conclusion that Juhász could not have been fired upon at the time and place he had indicated to police agents.) These missteps led to the resignation of two councilors in September 2011, and of another two in April 2012, cementing the impression that the mayor had lost control of the municipality. These events played a key role in the Fidesz candidate's victory at the municipal elections of October 2014. The governing party's delight at the fall of Jobbik's symbolic bastion was manifested in the local Fidesz MP's triumphant words: "Jobbik's leaders may have been pleased by the model they attempted to sell in the course of the last campaigns. The residents of Gyöngyöspata were apparently not so impressed with this model. They just declared the end of an epoch characterized by dissent, intimidation and division."[15]

Fidesz's Strategic Response: The "Work-Based Society" and Anti-egalitarian Populism

The series of tactical moves highlighted above (the launching of the expanded public works program in Gyöngyöspata, the deployment of the secret service, the use of defamation tactics to pile pressure on local councilors), together with a number of unenforced errors committed by the local Jobbik mayor, discredited the Far Right's effort to establish Gyöngyöspata as a model town. Alongside these maneuvers, Fidesz's leadership also worked out a more encompassing strategy whereby it sought to take the wind out of Jobbik's sails and prevent the Far Right from parading as the defender of the "abandoned countryside." In what follows, I will first highlight the ideological foundations of this strategy and then analyze the social policies implemented by the new government.

I begin by returning to the speech Viktor Orbán gave in front of the right-wing cultural elite at the Kötcse gathering in 2009. In the previous chapter, I used the speech to highlight Fidesz's new political strategy of occupying the center ground, which was shifting rightward in the tumultuous 2007–2010 period.[16] Here, I would like to use the same speech to argue that the Fidesz leader was looking to harness the moral panic on "Gypsy criminality" to his own ends by incorporating some elements of the far-right discourse into his own hegemonic project:

> A power bloc needs three sources to sustain itself: money, ideology and votes. The Socialists first used privatization as a source of money and then—when there was nothing else to sell—turned to foreign loans to finance their power bloc. They also built a media [empire] and surrounded themselves with a group of intellectuals who set out to convince voters that leftism is the natural condition of man; that everything associated with the left is self-evidently modern and part of the future.... As for the votes, they came up with an intellectually stimulating but incredibly harmful method to secure them. The crux of this strategy was to withdraw the state from all of the areas where it would have been needed (market expansion, health care, education, etc.) but at the same time to increase the number of citizens who are dependent on the state.... They naturally tried to deny the existence of this group and refused to accept any responsibility for its creation or recreation. So in this respect we can speak of a hidden society of several million people whose livelihood depends on state transfers ... instead of market-based achievements. It would, of course, be wrong to claim that these people were offered a bright perspective but even dim perspectives have to be appreciated these days, especially when they provide security. And this is precisely what [the Socialists] offered the group of people who depended on the state. The bargain can be summed up thusly: "although you will not climb higher, you will also not slide down" [the social ladder]. This is not a mindset that would allow a nation to achieve success in the midst of a dynamic and competitive global environment. It is in no way synonymous with a nation's competitiveness. [17]

This key passage highlights Orbán's dualistic vision of society (itself relying on the axiom that "welfare-dependent" citizens fundamentally differ from "hard-working" citizens and require different treatment) and his conviction that "welfare-dependency" powerfully undermines economic competitiveness. Orbán's diagnosis already contained the antidote to the ailments of Hungarian society: the remnants of an already curtailed welfare state must be dismantled to boost competitiveness in an era of heightened global competition. Such a strategy necessitated a clear break with the approach of post-1989 elites. Social democrats and Orbán's conservative predecessors had agreed—at least in principal—on the need for a minimal welfare state with a view to preventing the marginalization of underprivileged citizens. The postsocialist state's welfare policies fell increasingly short of this constitutionally protected goal. Neoliberal policies pursued by both left-wing and right-wing governments in the 1990s had already pointed in the direction of a "dual welfare state,"[18] and this dualization process progressed significantly after the introduction of workfare in 2008.[19] The latter generated a heated debate on the Center-Left, with certain politicians advocating for the disavowal of the republican discourse that emphasized the need for solidarity within the political community. Sensing the turning of the tide, Orbán mounted a wholesale attack against the republican approach. Fidesz's election manifesto stated the party's desire to "swap the benefit-centered approach [of the Socialists] for a work-centered approach."[20] While leaving voters in the dark about his concrete reform plans, he used public appearances to emphasize the link between "welfare-dependency" and criminality and to clarify that Jobbik was not alone in being serious about tackling criminality within the Romani community. In one of the key speeches he gave during the otherwise uneventful parliamentary election campaign, he declared that

> one of our greatest common goals—wherewith every honest, law-abiding Hungarian surely agrees—is to restore public order and security. No one wants to live in fear and everyone is angered when vandals are given free rein. This, in other words, is a national cause, which—I am sure—the majority will support, especially if the new government makes serious efforts to banish fear from our streets, squares and homes. . . . A weak government equals weak security. This is why criminality is rampant. And this is why we have to say loud and clear: we must fight criminals no matter who they are. It does not matter what their income situation is, whether they belong to the minority or the majority. Criminals must be brought to justice and judged expediently. The time has come for order to return to Hungary![21]

These words were echoed in Fidesz's election manifesto, which castigated the Socialists for weakening the criminal code, and promised to send more people to jail and impose workfare inside prisons (in line with Jobbik's proposal). The promise to clamp down on criminality and to reintegrate inmates into the "work-based society" reminds me of Jessop and his colleagues' (1984: 52) portrayal of the

New Right in Britain as being "concerned with managing the political repercussions of an 'underclass' whose existence is taken for granted rather than seen as a rebuke to society's conscience." Orbán, like Thatcher, came to the conclusion that the surplus population has to be politically regulated in order to enlist support from the lower-middle class, which both leaders heralded as the beating heart of the nation and whose moral and physical health they promised to protect from the dangerous classes.

The parallel with Thatcherism does not end here. Hungary's New Right emerged under similar conditions to Thatcherism, whose rise Hall situated at a historic conjuncture of three trends: the long-term structural decline of the British economy synchronized with the deepening recession of the world economy; the collapse of the third postwar Labour government and the disintegration of the whole social democratic consensus, which had provided the framework of British politics since 1945; and the resumption of the Cold War. These factors resemble the conditions in which Fidesz came to power: the structural decline of the Hungarian economy, exacerbated by the impact of the global economic crisis; the disintegration of the Socialist Party together with the post-1989 liberal democratic consensus (built on the ideological pillars of capitalism, liberal democracy, European integration, and minimal social security); the resurgence of Russia as a regional player and the escalation of East-West tensions. It is not just that widespread perceptions of crisis helped the two right-wing parties score decisive victories in 1979 and 2010 respectively. More importantly, the collapse of left-of-center hegemony granted both governments enough maneuvering room to reorganize the state and implement wide-ranging reforms that fundamentally redefined the state-citizen nexus.

Although both leaders have been accused of pursuing a crude version of power politics, I see their characterization as being solely concerned with the retainment of power misleading. To be sure, both Thatcher and Orbán exhibited ruthlessness—in relation to the surplus population and political opponents—in the pursuit of their hegemonic projects. But this should not distract us from seeing that they also sought to offer workable and lasting solutions to the economic woes of their countries. As Jessop et al. (1985: 97) noted,

> Thatcherism does have an explicit economic strategy. This goes well beyond control of the money supply and aims to restructure the British economy as part of a re-invigorated, post-Fordist international capitalism. In particular, Thatcherism has adopted a neo-liberal accumulation strategy premised [sic] on the deregulation of private capital, the privatization of significant parts of

the public sector, and the introduction of commercial criteria into the residual activities of the state sector. This strategy also implies commitment to an open economy. Indeed, the Government has encouraged outward investment and an export drive . . . . At the same time the Government has encouraged multinationals to invest in Britain. Typically these will draw upon and reproduce the low-wage economy of postwar Britain and exploit its accessibility to the rest of the European Community.

Although he did not draw inspiration directly from her (but rather her continental followers), Orbán drew heavily on the premises of the Thatcherite neoliberal credo to redefine his party's social vision and economic strategy. Just like Thatcher, he also considers that a nation's survival depends on its economic competitiveness, and that the historic mission of the political right is to liberate those who produce value from unnecessary burdens, and to reestablish work as society's foundational pillar. The picture is more shady when it comes to political instruments, but there are also parallels on this level. Orbán adopted Thatcher's view that the best means to reinvigorate an ailing economy—besides exercising fiscal restraint—is to unleash the creative power of private enterprise through the reduction of taxes and incentives for productive investment, and to extract the maximum amount of labor from the workforce by drastically reducing unemployment benefits, stigmatizing and punishing idleness, and rewarding those who take up work in low-wage sectors of the economy.

There are nevertheless clear differences between the SNC and Thatcher's politics of governmental power. The Orbán government has rightly been accused of *étatisme*.[22] Its interventions can indeed be qualified as unorthodox in that they do not form part of the conventional arsenal of neoliberalism. This, however, should not blind us to the fact that besides redistributing resources to key players within the ruling power bloc (first and foremost, the national bourgeoisie), they also serve the same goal as more conventional instruments: to boost competitiveness and ensure stable growth—the final guarantee of political power. Moreover, the myth that neoliberalism equals lesser state intervention has been debunked decades ago. Not incidentally, it was Thatcher's critics who remarked that her "two nations" approach required state intervention to create the conditions favorable to greater production. And, insofar as this hurt marginalized groups, it required increased repression and police measures (Hall et al. 1978). In the same way, the reorganization of the state under Orbán has also involved the "policing of the crisis" (on which more below).

Orbán has also harnessed the state apparatus to the project of organizing his power bloc to an extent that Thatcher could not have imagined possible. In this regard, he has also gone much further than neoliberal politicians in Eastern Europe who have experimented with clientelism but not in the systematic way that Orbán has attempted to feed the national bourgeoisie (while also throwing crumbs to the lower-middle class). The Hungarian prime minister palpably also believes much less than Thatcher (or right-wing politicians in Central Europe) in the credo that markets will autonomously generate domestic expansion without any substantial governmental direction or coordination. His government's effort to reduce the influence of foreign capital in certain sectors of the Hungarian economy reveals a *dirigiste* tendency that was mostly foreign to British liberalism. Last but not least, Orbán has begun to experiment with corporatism—for instance, by introducing obligatory membership in newly created state-controlled syndicates for teachers, lawyers, and other intellectual professions. This, and efforts to indoctrinate youth—through state-controlled educational curricula—exhibit authoritarian tendencies that were largely anathema to the British Right.

There is another limitation to the parallel with Thatcher. Namely, that the Tories did not have to reckon with a serious right-wing rival. In the previous chapter, I argued that Fidesz had tacitly supported the emergence of a rival to its right with a view to securing its hold over a radicalized political center. While the strategy proved successful on the electoral level, it also had a downside. By giving Jobbik space and failing to draw a clear demarcation line between itself and the far-right party, Fidesz condemned itself to making constant adjustments to its politics whenever the war of maneuver turned to its disadvantage. This is exactly what happened when the government let Jobbik parade as the defender of the countryside during the Gyöngyöspata campaign. In what follows, I will highlight encompassing modifications to the social policy regime whereby the ruling party sought simultaneously to further Orbán's economic goals and limit the Far Right's appeal by preventing it from making further inroads into the countryside.

The Dual State and Its Political Dividends

Although Fidesz's leader did not make his plans explicit during the parliamentary campaign, once in power he acknowledged that his plan to "create a work-based society instead of the Western welfare state"[23] required "the reorganization of the country's internal resources" in a way as to preserve the country's financial independence and boost

economic productivity.[24] One part of the Fidesz government's strategy consisted in the implementation of policies that were designed
to make life as satisfying as possible for "hard-working" citizens. The
main instrument for attracting the lower-middle class was the promise of material rewards to those who were already at work: cutting
the income tax, freezing the family allowance, and introducing tax re-
bates, and introducing tax relief for families with children. The other
part of the strategy consisted in making life as unbearable as possible
for those situated outside the sphere of formal work. Although he
drew inspiration from the New Social Policy (Nová sociálna politika) implemented under Mikuláš Dzurinda, Orbán went further in
replacing the diminished welfare state with a workfare state than
Slovakia's prime minister. In what follows, I provide an overview of
this cornerstone of the SNC in order to highlight how it relied on the
principle of the "work-based society" to discipline both the working
and the nonworking poor.

While his liberal predecessors had already taken significant steps
away from welfare as a universal right—first by separating the services offered to impoverished citizens and to the surplus population,
then by linking social assistance to community work in the frame of
the Road to Work Program (see chapter 3)—Orbán took that logic to
another level when he removed the right to social security from the
constitution. According to the new Fundamental Law, the Hungarian
state will only "strive to provide social security to all of its citizens"
(article XIX, par. 1).[25] Moreover, the "nature and extent of social measures may be determined in an Act in accordance with the usefulness
to the community of the beneficiary's activity" (article XIX, par. 3).
Thus, since the Fundamental Law came into force on 1 January 2012,
citizens are entitled to social rights only if they fulfill this responsibility. In accordance with the introduction of this new principle, the
government made the receipt of unemployment benefits conditional
on participation in centrally financed but locally administered public works programs. It also took the unprecedented step of reducing
eligibility for unemployment insurance from nine months to a maximum of three months.[26] Workless citizens who wish to receive social
assistance after the ninety days expire are obliged to join the public
works program for at least thirty days (Act CVI/2011). The same law
also gave the government the mandate to set the minimum wage for
public work. The government used this opportunity to introduce a
substandard minimum wage for public workers. (This is currently set
at 75 percent of the standard minimum wage.) Furthermore, public
workers are no longer protected by the new Labor Code adopted in

2012.[27] The intention to increase the punitive character of the public works program is also visible from the fact that its supervision has been moved from the Ministry of Labor to the Ministry of Interior. Drawing inspiration from the Érpatak model, parliament also passed a new law on the provision of social services and benefits (Act 2010/CLXXI), granting local municipalities the power to make the receipt of unemployment benefits conditional on "dutiful conduct." Local governments have been granted the power to impose fines on citizens who do not fulfill this obligation. A more recent modification of the act (introduced in September 2013) allows for the exclusion of beneficiaries whose children miss too many days of school.

One of the consequences of these reforms was an increase in the ratio of people who do not receive any social assistance from 40 to 52 percent (among the total number of unemployed citizens) between 2010 and 2012 (Cseres-Gergely et al. 2013:). This, combined with the fact that the family allowance (the last remaining bulwark of the universal welfare state) has not been indexed since 2009 (resulting in a loss of 20 percent of its value by 2014), has led to a deterioration of the situation of the most vulnerable social groups.

A comprehensive survey of Hungarian households (see Szívós and Tóth 2015) revealed that income poverty[28] steadily increased in the 2007–2012 period (the ratio of affected households grew from 12.6 to 17 percent) and then stagnated in the 2012–2014 period.[29] When one examines poverty in absolute rather than relative terms—in terms of material deprivation[30]—the picture is somewhat different: the ratio of citizens living in severely deprived households significantly decreased between 2012 and 2014 (from 37.3 to 28.3 percent) to below 2009 levels (33.7 percent). The authors of the report claim that this was due to the significant improvement of the situation of the lower-middle class: low-wage earners in stable jobs (not public work) who typically live in cities (not the countryside) and have one or two children (not more). In households characterized by low or very low "work intensity" where the breadwinner holds an elementary school degree, and among families with at least three children, severe material deprivation actually increased in the 2012–2014 period. This is in line with the report's claim that participation in the public works program only allows poor households to evade sliding further down but *not* to climb out of material deprivation or income poverty.

A comparative study focusing on pre- and post-crisis levels of income inequality and the percentage of people at risk of poverty or social exclusion in the Visegrád group showed that Hungary was the only country in the region where the gap between the incomes earned by the highest and lowest twenty percent of earners *and* the percentage of citizens at risk of poverty or social exclusion increased after 2010.[31]

The recent decline in the percentage of middle-class citizens suffering from severe material deprivation can be directly linked to targeted governmental policies (although a pick-up in economic growth after 2012 also played a role). The government forced banks to take on a significant share of indebted households' debt burden (which increased due to the depreciation of the Hungarian forint against the Swiss franc and the Japanese yen), resulting in a 10 percent decline in the number of citizens who could not pay mortgages or consumer debts (Tárki 2015: 55). Moreover, the government also adopted a generous tax-credit system that provided substantial financial relief for lower-middle-class families with children. Following the example set by Slovakia, Fidesz made this tax-credit scheme only available to families where at least one adult was in gainful employment (i.e., not employed in the framework of the public works program). As a result, families with one or two children could increase their income by 7 percent of the average salary after every child, while larger families could increase it by 23 percent (Szikra 2014: 10). This measure was part of a large-scale overhaul of the tax regime, whose central element was the introduction of a 16 percent flat personal income tax rate that mostly benefited top earners.[32] To counteract the negative effects of the new system (e.g., the termination of earlier compensation for low-income earners), the government directly intervened in wage setting by developing a compensation scheme for low earners (Szabó 2013). In the public sector, this took the form of direct subsidies from the central budget to service providers, whereas, in the private sector, the cost of compensation was expected to be borne by employers.

Szikra (2014: 7) found that the post-2010 welfare reforms were distinctive due to "the inordinate scale of cuts, the nearly total replacement of active labour market policies with a punitive public works programme and the fact that its principles have been included into the new constitution." Without contesting her conclusion, I will lay the stress elsewhere—namely, on the reforms' social and political outcomes.

First, the measures described above rendered hundreds of thousands of families dependent on the goodwill of local mayors and municipalities. My discussion of the takeover of local power by Jobbik in Gyöngyöspata showed what this could mean in practice for those who found themselves stripped of their most basic social rights. It is not far-fetched to claim that the reforms I analyze contributed powerfully to the stabilization of neo-feudal local hegemonies that are antithetical to the logic and ethos of democratic citizenship. Although it would be wrong to claim that the kind of dependencies I encountered in Gyöngyöspata materialized after 2010, one can assert that the reforms of the Orbán government cemented the previously contested ties that hitherto bound the surplus population to local elites. Dependence on local power-holders, together with the punitive reform of the criminal code and the reinforcement of the police force in rural regions, prevented the main losers of the reform—the long-term unemployed—from staging a revolt. The revamped public works program (which set a new minimal wage for citizens locked out of the primary labor market), the new welfare regime (which excluded citizens refusing to work on a substandard wage and granted mayors the power to withhold social assistance from citizens refusing to abide by "norms of coexistence"), the legalization of segregation in schooling through creative means (which led to the emergence of substandard depot schools), and the "three strikes" rule (which allowed the state to permanently lock up criminals) mesh together into a disciplinary iron cage that confines the surplus population to zones of relegation and places them under a strict regime of forced labor, moral control, and penal surveillance.

Second, although social policy experts have highlighted the reforms' impact on the poor, the disciplinary regime imposed on the surplus population also served to demonstrate that the government had delivered on its promise to make life easier for "hard-working citizens" and difficult for "social parasites." In other words, the drastic measures substantiated the anti-egalitarian populist ideology,[33] which Fidesz had deployed during the election campaign. My interlocutors—especially people employed on the minimum wage (who lost out on the introduction of the flat tax if they did not have at least two children)—in both of my field sites lauded the government for putting idle welfare-scroungers to work. By disciplining the idle (subtext: Roma), Orbán had—following Dzurinda's example—found a way to legitimize a massive redistribution of income from the bottom to the top and middle of the income ladder, the further weakening of labor, and the renunciation of the state's obligation toward the poor. In this it could count not only on popular support but also on a lack of meaningful counterinitiatives on behalf of labor or parties in opposition. Unions, as Szikra (2014: 2) noted, "have been pacified by small concessions concerning the originally much more severe Labour Code and social insurance legislation." As for the Socialist Party, its critique of workfare was tainted by its active role in the implementation of the same principle in the framework of the Road to Work program (see chapter 3).

Third, the subjection of the surplus population to workfare, moral control, and penal surveillance undermined the Far Right's effort to position itself as the guarantor of justice and order. The ritualized delivery of substantive justice through intimidation campaigns had allowed Jobbik to outmaneuver liberal political elites, who were widely seen as having abandoned their obligations to ordinary citizens. The same strategy proved powerless in the face of symbolic and material steps towards the reestablishment of "natural" privileges and hierarchies. As I argued above, Jobbik's attempt to establish Érpatak and Gyöngyöspata as micromodels of a "better future" failed. While the effort to ethnically cleanse these localities faltered, the promise to make unemployment benefits dependent on public work[34] was effectively converted into national policy within the framework of the revamped public work program. Despite far-right mayors' effort to build workable local models, these were incorporated into Fidesz's hegemonic project of transforming Hungary into a society where "the strength of community and the honor of each man are based on labor" (preamble of the Fundamental Law, official translation).

Finally, the war on the poor also appears to have born electoral fruits for the government. At the parliamentary elections of April 2014, the ruling party stood its ground against Jobbik in the counties where the far-right surge had been the most pronounced in 2010 (Szabolcs-Szatmár-Bereg, Jász-Nagykun-Szolnok, Heves, and Borsod-Abaúj-Zemplén counties). Fidesz performed especially well in predominantly rural depressed northeastern electoral districts where Jobbik had successfully magnetized disgruntled citizens in 2010.

Concluding Remarks

In this chapter, I argued that, after some hesitation and a series of tactical maneuvers, the new right-wing government formulated a coherent response to Jobbik's successful return to racist street campaigning. Citing Viktor Orbán's speech at the Kötcse gathering in 2009, I claimed that the leader of the main opposition party was seeking to incorporate elements of the emergent racist common sense into his own hegemonic project, which was built on the dual pillars of *dirigiste* neoliberalism[35] and anti-egalitarian populism. Orbán's attempt to harness the moral panic on "Gypsy criminality" to his own hegemonic project reminded me of Stuart Hall's (1983) analysis of Thatcher's effort to instrumentalize a sequence of moral panics (around the issues of race, law and order, permissiveness, and social anarchy) to win for her political project the gloss of populist consent at the 1979 election. Hall's insistence on authoritarian populism as a prime vehicle for generating mass electoral support for right-wing political projects is particularly important for understanding the form that ideological struggles have lately taken in Eastern Europe. Neoliberal politicians such as Dzurinda have idealized work as the cornerstone of a new moral economy and castigated welfare-scroungers for presenting an unbearable burden on the national economy. The first to notice that the "two nations populism" pioneered by Margaret Thatcher was being adopted on the eastern periphery was anthropologist Nicolette Makovicky (2013), who showed how in 2004 the Dzurinda cabinet successfully countered popular opposition to its neoliberal welfare reform by fanning moral outrage against "Gypsy welfare scroungers." This strategy, Makovicky (2013) argues, allowed the right-wing cabinet to prevent the "national-socialist" opposition from enlisting lower-middle-class citizens who were negatively affected by the reform. In a similar vein, Kalb (2015b) has recently argued that liberal strategies of Othering—centered on the derision of primitive "claiming behavior"—play a key role in generating electoral support for neoliberal governments in Central Eastern Europe and the Baltics. Orbán, however, did not deploy the "moral calculus of work" (Makovicky 2013: 84) in the same way as these neoliberal politicians. His combination of the neoliberal concern about economic competitiveness with the rhetorical protection of Hungarians (against internal and external enemies) redefined the nation as the community of "hard-working" citizens, minus "unpatriotic" liberal elites and "welfare-scroungers." Orbán's vision of the "work-based society" thus resembled to a great extent the Far Right's conceptualization of the nation, with the caveat that Orbán for the most part eschewed direct references to ethnicity and race (be it "Gypsy criminals" or "Jewish conspirators"). This two-pronged articulation of nationhood was designed to entrench Fidesz as the par excellence populist force and to prevent both the left and Jobbik from parading as the spokespersons of the people.[36] It also responded forcefully to a political conjuncture that was overdetermined by the impact of global economic pressures—in the form of austerity measures imposed through an IMF bailout—and a domestic moral panic against the racialized dangerous classes.

The outcome of the critical 2010 parliamentary election largely depended on which political camp would be able to impose its vision

of economic recovery and a just society (see chapter 3). The failure of
the left-liberal modernization project guaranteed a historic defeat for
the Socialists and their liberal allies. The ideological similarity of the
two right-wing parties foreshadowed strong competition between
Fidesz and Jobbik. This, however, only materialized on the country's
internal periphery where the "Gypsy issue" appeared as a pressing
concern to the majority of citizens. Elsewhere, most voters refused
to ally themselves with an inexperienced young party that they did
not trust with steering the country in the midst of a global economic
storm.

In the last part of the chapter, I showed how the Fidesz government
drew on Orbán's anti-egalitarian populist vision to take the wind out
of a resurgent Far Right's sails in the aftermath of the Gyöngyöspata
campaign. I argued that Jobbik's effort to promote the localities it
took control of as micromodels for solving the "Gypsy issue" largely
fell on deaf ears in the context of the systemic effort to reconstruct
the Hungarian state through the bifurcation of state functions and
citizens' rights. Matching Orbán's dual vision of society, the Fidesz
government concocted a dual strategy for ensuring citizens' compli-
ance with and participation in the rebuilding of society. One key pillar of the government's strategy consisted in the implementation of
policies that were designed to make life as satisfying as possible for
"hard-working citizens." The other consisted in making life as unbearable as possible for those situated outside the sphere of the formal economy. This was achieved by curtailing the state's "left hand"
and strengthening its "right hand" (Bourdieu 1994).

The coherence and radical thrust of the reforms I analyzed underscores Tamás's (2000) insightful conceptualization[37] of the New Right
as working toward the separation of the "Normative State" (which
holds jurisdiction over "homogenous society") and the "Prerogative"
State (which is provided special means to discipline "heterogeneous
groups"). By restricting social rights and enacting special obligations
for those out of gainful employment, Hungary's new authoritarian
rightist political class has actively sought to exclude the surplus population from key rights and resources in order to maintain the privileges of "the rightful owners of the state":

> Neo-Victorian, pedagogic ideas of "workfare," which declare unemploy-
> ment implicitly sinful, the equation of welfare claimants with "enemies of the
> people," the replacement of social assistance with tax credits whereby peo-
> ple beneath the category of taxpayers are not deemed worthy of aid, income
> support made conditional on family and housing practices believed proper
> by "competent authorities," the increasing racialization, ethnicization, and

sexualization of the underclass . . . the replacement of the idea of emancipation with the idea of privileges . . . arbitrarily dispensed to the deserving poor
. . . all this is part of the post-fascist strategy of the scission of the civic-cum-
human community, of a renewed granting or denial of citizenship along race,
class, denominational, cultural, ethnic lines (Tamás 2000, sec. "Varieties of
Post-Fascism," par. 3).

Relying on Lipset's (1988: 132) claim that "extremist ideologies and
groups can be classified and analyzed in the same terms as democratic groups, i.e., right, left, and center,"[38] Tamás (2000) was among
the first to argue that since "there is nothing of any importance on the
political horizon but the bourgeois center, therefore its extremism is
the most likely to reappear," citing Jörg Haider and Viktor Orbán as
exemplary cases. While I find his concept of post-Fascism somewhat
misleading—because the practices he identifies, as Tamás himself ac-
knowledges, do not necessarily threaten "liberal and democratic rule
within the core constituency of 'homogeneous society'"—the theoretical thrust of his analysis is illuminating.

In Hungary, the Dual State emerged out of a "passive revolution"
in response to the electorate's radicalization (itself a reaction to a
global economic storm and the catastrophic governmental record of
left-liberal predecessors) and competition from a far-right rival. It is
the result of a political alliance between a New Right (that has dissociated itself from the previous liberal consensus) and a popular movement (that has come to see itself as a victim of liberal elites and the
racialized dangerous classes). While Orbán presents the Dual State as
a key instrument for boosting economic competitiveness in an era of
heightened global competition, economic trends show that his government has failed to improve the competitiveness of the Hungarian
economy and that the country is falling behind its regional rivals.[39]
The Dual State has, however, proven its *political* effectiveness. While
Fidesz's landslide victory at the last parliamentary elections (held in
April 2014) can be attributed to a multiplicity of causes, election results and polling data suggest that the ruling party's ability to retain
hold over a radicalized political center may have at least partly to do
with the dismantlement of social rights and welfare, which allowed
it to take credit for disciplining "work-shy" citizens.[40] The analysis
I present in the next chapter will offer further evidence in support
of this claim. I proceed by moving back from the national to the local level in order examine how Fidesz's politics of governmental
power—in conjunction with other factors—helped local actors defuse socioethnic frictions in a region where Jobbik sought to export
its racist-extremist agenda and tactics in 2012.

Notes

1. I derive the concepts of the "Normative State" and the "Prerogative State" from Fraenkel (1969).
2. To be fair, I note that, in the introduction to the third edition of *Folk Devils and Moral Panics*, Cohen (2002: xxxix) pointed in what I see as the right direction by arguing that "moral panics have their own internal trajectory—a microphysics of outrage—which, however, is initiated and sustained by wider social and political forces."
3. The first split within the Hungarian Guard occurred in 2008 when the organization's leader—citing ideological differences with Jobbik—founded a rival organization called the Hereditary Hungarian Guard. (The latter organization adhered to a neo-Nazi ideology and built strong ties to two neo-Nazi organizations: Pax Hungarica and the Hungarian National Front.) The second split occurred in 2010 within the NHG, which had been created by Guard members who remained loyal to Jobbik. In a move that mirrored the first split, the NHG's newly elected captain left the movement to create a rival organization called the Hungarian National Guard and negotiated a merger with the Hereditary Hungarian Guard. The split necessitated the reorganization of the NHG under a new leadership. The latter, bowing to demands from Jobbik's leaders, resumed the organization of anti-Gypsy street campaigns under the cloak of a new proxy organization: the For a Better Future Civic Guard. (In 2012, the latter organization began to distance itself from the NHG, and in 2013 it changed its name to For a Better Future Hungarian Self-Defense to demonstrate its independence.) Despite these splits, the successor organizations of the Hungarian Guard cooperated on an ad hoc basis. While neo-Nazi splinter groups were most active in the organization of anti-Semitic campaigns, the NHG organized anti-Gypsy campaigns together with the For a Better Future Civic Guard, the Outlaw Army, and the Sixty-Four Counties Youth Movement. The NHG discontinued its participation in racist campaigns from December 2013. This decision resulted from pressure exercised by Jobbik party leaders who were keen on transforming the party into a more moderate nationalist force (see chapter 6). This strategy required the renunciation of hate campaigns and greater distance from paramilitary organizations. Jobbik did not, however, go as far as retracting the cooperation agreement it had signed in 2009 with the Outlaw Army and the Sixty-Four Counties Youth Movement, with a view to keeping radical supporters by its side.
4. See (in Hungarian, translation mine) Judit Doros, "A laki szorító—egy gyilkosság, négy cigánygyerek és a Jobbik" (The Lak trap—one homicide, four Gypsy kids and the Jobbik Party), *Népszabadság*, published 11 February 2011, accessed 14 December 2012, http://nol.hu/archivum/20110212-a_laki_szorito-977451.
5. The Gyöngyös district was easily won by Fidesz in April 2010. In the first round of the parliamentary elections of 2010, Vona came in third place (just behind the Socialist candidate) with 26.10 percent of the vote. In Gyöngyöspata itself, the party president came in second place with 35.42 percent of the vote.
6. The NHG took advantage of a loophole in the regulatory framework governing the activities of so-called civic guards (i.e., unarmed voluntary associations that had been brought to life in the 1990s to help the under-financed police force maintain public order and combat crime in rural localities) to create the FBF. The association was led by Attila László Tibor, the former captain of the Hungarian Guard.
7. Human rights organizations based their assessment on the Budapest Tribunal's verdict in the case of the Hungarian Guard, which claimed that targeted Roma populations constituted "captured communities."
8. See "Shadow Report about the Events at Gyöngyöspata", Hungarian Civil Liberties Union website, published 14 November 2011, accessed 5 January 2013, http://tasz

.hu/en/news/shadow-report-about-events-gyongyospata. The cases were first transferred by the Heves County Police to the Gyöngyös Police, then qualified as "minor
offenses," which did not necessitate investigation on behalf of a criminal court.

9. In the interview broadcast live on TV2 on 28 April 2011, the prime minister stated the
following: "What had to be done was already evident weeks ago. But, as you know,
those who provoke the people who live there try to hide behind the right of assembly.
And if you step up too quickly, in a hasty manner, then people's reflex will be that you
have violated the right of assembly. . . . So you cannot make a number of decisions
as fast as you would like to. In Hungarian politics, it is imperative to have a sense
of rhythm. A tough decision has to be made at the moment when the whole country
believes that that decision really needs to be taken. But if you make that decision a bit
too early, then the whole country will say 'You should not have intervened.' So the
moment has to be well chosen" (translation mine). See "Frizbi Hajdú Péterrel" ('Fris-
bee' with Péter Hajdú), *TV2*, published 28 April 2011, accessed 2 May 2011, https://
tv2.hu/musoraink/mokka/67028_orban_viktor_gyongyospatarol__az_ero_nyelven_
kell_az_allamnak_beszelni.html.

10. This was already evident in the formulation of the committee's goals. One of the key
questions to be elucidated was, "Did the parties in opposition contribute to the unsettling of public safety and social peace in the country, and if yes, with what intent?"
See (in Hungarian) "Az egyenruhás bűnözés folyamatát, hátterét és a gyöngyöspatai
eseményeket feltáró, valamint az egyenruhás bűnözés felszámolását elősegítő eseti
bizottság jelentése" (Report prepared by the ad hoc parliamentary committee tasked
with investigating the events in Gyöngyöspata and the background of uniform-
related crime, and facilitating the elimination of uniform-related crime), official website of the Hungarian Parliament, n.d., accessed 30 April 2012, http://www.parlament
.hu/irom39/06574/06574.pdf.

11. It is worth noting that Érpatak was—similarly to Gyöngyöspata—situated in a relatively prosperous microregion that was bordered by two others belonging to the
thirty-three most depressed microregions of the country.

12. The specific provisions defining cleanliness and orderliness contain the prescription
of removing weeds from the sidewalk lining recipients' homes and the obligation to
produce vegetables and fruit on 25 percent of the garden's surface.

13. Gyöngyöspata's mayor, who resigned under paramilitary pressure, had taken advantage of the reform to adopt a decree that allowed the local council to withhold welfare
payments from households that did not pay their utility bills.

14. The reason Gyöngyöspata's new leadership could count on the backing of the local
police force was that the latter sought to restore its tarnished credibility by severely
sanctioning petty offenders.

15. See (in Hungarian, translation mine) "Fidesz: Szimbolikus győzelmet arattunk Gyön-
gyöspatán" (Fidesz: We scored a symbolic victory in Gyöngyöspata), *HírTv*, published 14 October 2014, accessed 16 October 2014, http://hirtv.hu/ahirtvhirei/fidesz-
szimbolikus-gyozelmet-arattunk-gyongyospatan-1253286.

16. Two political scientists who conducted an empirical analysis of voters' ideological
self-placements on the left-right scale showed that the "median voter" moved sharply
to the right after 2008 (Enyedi and Benoit 2011). They claim that the key factor underpinning this realignment was the Socialist Party's delegitimization in the eyes of
the electorate as a consequence of corruption scandals, a deteriorating economic situation, and difficult-to-swallow austerity measures, which had been imposed by the
International Monetary Fund (IMF) after Hungary was forced to apply for a rescue
package in 2008.

17. See (in Hungarian, translation mine) "Megőrizni a létezés magyar minőségét –
Orbán kötcsei beszéde szóról szóra" [To preserve the Hungarian quality of ex-

istence – Orbán's speech at the Kötcse gathering word-by-word], *HírExtra*, 18 February 2010, retrieved 13 March 2014 from http://www.hirextra.hu/2010/02/18/megorizni-a-letezes-magyar-minoseget-orban-kotcsei-beszede-szorol-szora/.

18. Szalai's (2005: 4) concept of dualization highlights a key policy change after the collapse of state socialism: "Although the rapid *decomposition* of the old institutions was a unanimous claim articulated by all the major political actors at the start of the transition, it has led, however, to unforeseen troublesome results. The process quickly turned to the *desertion* of the state, and simultaneously, to the strengthening of sharpened social struggles over its remnants. A most serious consequence of these developments has been the evolvement of a dual structure with ever more deeper captivation of the coexisting corporatist and liberal drives to utilize the state's power and resources for providing protection on the market, and simultaneously, 'freeing' the state from its classical welfare commitments toward the poor. Soon these developments have concluded into the effective ghettoization of welfare, which in turn, has accentuated the processes of marginalization and social disintegration" (emphases in original). Elsewhere Szalai (2002) has argued that the dualization of welfare fostered a dual vision of society as being composed of two coexisting but separated groups: "ordinary people" and "the incapable poor."

19. Between 2004 and 2007, Hungary witnessed a short-lived effort to build a genuine Keynesian welfare state under Zsuzsa Ferge's programmatic, and Ferenc Gyurcsány's political, leadership. This effort was, however, undermined by the global economic crisis and the rise of popular anti-Gypsyism. As I explained in chapter 3, the effort to move in the direction of a universal social policy regime was overturned under the second Gyurcsány government, which introduced workfare measures with a view to curbing the disintegration of the Socialist Party's voter base in the Northeast.

20. Excerpt from the 2010 election manifesto (p. 79, translation mine). See (in Hungarian) "Nemzeti Ügyek Politikája—2010" (The Politics of National Causes), the Fidesz Party's archives, n.d., accessed 7 January 2014, http://static-old.fidesz.hu/download/481/nemzeti_ugyek_politikaja_8481.pdf.

21. The quote is from Viktor Orbán's 2010 "state of the country" address. See (in Hungarian, translation mine) "Újjá kell építeni Magyarországot" (Hungary needs to be rebuilt), Prime Minister's website, published 5 February 2010, accessed 29 October 2012, http://2010-2015.miniszterelnok.hu/beszed/ujja_kell_epiteni_magyarorszagot.

22. Without seeking to provide an exhaustive list, I want to highlight the renationalization of strategic companies (providers of critical public services and energy companies) with a view to guaranteeing low consumer prices; the rewriting of public tendering procedures and the channeling of European development funds to the national bourgeoisie; the redistribution of land leasing rights and licenses to sell tobacco products to political cronies; the selective imposition of "crisis taxes" on foreign companies in sectors (mainly retail and banking) where the government wishes to decrease the presence of foreign capital and increase the leverage of the national bourgeoisie; and the reform of the banking sector with a view to decreasing citizens' and companies' exposure to foreign currency loans, providing space for a looser monetary policy and incentivizing lending.

23. See (in Hungarian, translation mine) "Orbán: Nem jóléti állam, hanem munka alapú társadalom épül" (Orbán: We are building a work-based society, not a welfare state), Fidesz Party website, published 19 October 2012, accessed 13 March 2014, http://www.fidesz.hu/hirek/2012-10-19/orban-nem-joleti-allam-hanem-munka-alapu-tarsadalom-epul-kepek/.

24. See (in Hungarian, translation mine) "Munkaalapú társadalom felépítése a feladat" (The goal is to build work-based society), Fidesz Party website, published 20 Janu-

ary 2014, accessed 13 March 2014, http://www.fidesz.hu/hirek/2014-01-20/munkaala
pu-tarsadalom-felepitese-a-feladat/.
25. See "The Fundamental Law of Hungary", official website of the Hungarian Government, published 25 April 2011, accessed 14 March 2014, http://www.kormany.hu/
download/e/02/00000/The%20New%20Fundamental%20Law%20of%20Hungary.pdf.
26. This is currently the shortest period within the European Union. See Blaskó and Fazekas (2016: 21).
27. Social policy practitioners have characterized the new Labor Code as ardently em-
ployer-friendly (Szabó 2013). The new code undermined employee rights by rede-
fining the labor contract as a civil law relationship, assuming equal power relations
between employers and employees (A. Tóth 2012: 9). According to the new legislation, individual work contracts and collective agreements can now set lower standards than the Labor Code. There are several areas where employers can lower work
standards even without the rubber stamp of individual work contracts or collective
agreement modifications. For example, the new legislation stipulates less favorable
overtime compensation for employees, and employers can terminate work contracts
while the employee is on sick leave (A. Tóth 2012: 5).
28. Income poverty is defined as having an equivalized disposable income (after social
transfers) below the at-risk-of-poverty threshold, which is set at 60 percent of the national median equivalized disposable income (after social transfers).
29. In the 2012–2014 period, there appears to have been a slight improvement in the depth
of income poverty: the distance between the median income of relatively poor households and the median income of other households somewhat decreased.
30. Material deprivation is defined as the inability to afford at least three (and severe material deprivation as the inability to afford at least four) of the following nine items:
(1) pay rent, mortgage, other debt obligations, or utility bills; (2) keep the home ade-
quately warm; (3) face unexpected expenses; (4) eat meat or proteins regularly; (5) go
on holiday; (6) own a television set; (7) own a washing machine; (8) own a car; (9) own
a telephone.
31. See Szívós 2014: 58–62.
32. The highest tax rate was previously 32 percent.
33. My concept ("anti-egalitarian populism") takes inspiration from the debate around
Hall's (1983, 1985) conceptualization of authoritarian populism (see also Jessop et al.
1984, 1985). Although I see parallels between his conceptualization of Thatcherism
and my reading of Orbán's policies, I prefer the term "anti-egalitarian" to stress Orbán's break with republican ideology.
34. The part of Jobbik's election manifesto that dealt with social policy carried the telling
subtitle "Work instead of benefits: we won't feed those who refuse to work!" See
(in Hungarian) "Radikális változás: A Jobbik országgyűlési választási programja a
nemzeti önrendelkezésért és a társadalmi igazságosságért" (Radical change: Jobbik's
election manifesto in the service of national self-determination and social justice), Jobbik Party website, n.d., accessed 12 October 2012, https://jobbik.hu/sites/default/files/
jobbik-program2010gy.pdf.
35. Greskovits and Bohle (2012) have contrasted Fidesz's "disembedded neo-liberalism"
to the "embedded neo-liberalism" of left-liberal predecessors.
36. This malleability of the conception of peoplehood reflects the nature of populism,
which is "neither a set of particular ideological contents nor a given organizational
pattern, but rather a discursive logic" (Stavrakakis 2004: 256), leaving it open to "con-
tradictory articulating attempts" (Laclau 2005: 41).
37. I note that Tamás (2000) also relies on Ernst Fraenkel's pathbreaking study of Nazi
law (see Fraenkel 1969).

38. Lipset (1988: 131–132) claimed that the dominant view of extremism as a phenomenon belonging to the ends of the left-right continuum and being foreign to the political center is an error. Using the example of interwar Fascism, he argued that "Fascist ideology, though antiliberal in its glorification of the state, has been similar to liberalism in its opposition to big business, trade-unions, and the socialist state. It has also resembled liberalism in its distaste for religion and other forms of traditionalism. And ... the social characteristics of Nazi voters in pre-Hitler Germany and Austria resembled those of the liberals much more than they did those of the conservatives" (p. 133).

39. The European Commission's recent review of Hungary's macroeconomic imbalances recorded a considerable (23 percent) decline of export market shares between 2008 and 2012. Although this trend was reversed in the 2012–2014 period, the prices of Hungarian export products progressively declined throughout the 2008–2014 period. This stands in stark contrast to Poland, the Czech Republic, and Slovakia (where export prices have risen by around 30 percent). The Commission's experts see this phenomenon as being linked to "Hungary's inability to improve the quality of its products, albeit from a comparatively high initial level. The traditionally significant weight of high-technology products in the Hungarian export sector has been declining since the last decade. The share of high and top quality products in export value decreased from around 30 percent in 2009 to 23 percent by 2014, while the quality distribution shifted towards the middle with a potentially greater exposure to cost competition" (European Commission 2016: 19).

40. It is worth citing an opinion poll (published in October 2015), which revealed that Fidesz was perceived as the party that offers the most workable solutions to "conflicts between Gypsies and the majority." Of the respondents, 26 percent stated that Fidesz offered the best solutions, while 19 percent sided with Jobbik, 9 percent with the Socialists, and 2 percent with the greens (LMP). See (in Hungarian) "Jobb félni? Median-felmérés a menekültválságról" (Better be afraid? Median poll on the refugee crisis), *Median*, published 7 October 2015, accessed 8 October 2015, http://median.hu/object .c38fa2c9-5bc2-40c9-ae38-bab515a5f172.ivy. If we compare the results of this poll with the results of the 2009 European Election Survey (see Karácsony and Róna 2010), we find that the percentage of respondents who believe that Jobbik offers the best solutions to this issue has not increased (19 percent chose Jobbik in 2009). However, Fidesz was seen by a much smaller percentage of respondents as offering the best solutions (41 versus 26 percent). It is also worth noting that the ruling party lost a lot of support in—and in the vicinity of—less depressed (but neither dynamic) counties, such as Baranya, Zala, Somogy, and Tolna, where citizens were probably expecting the government—in vain—to deliver on its promise to kickstart the engine of the economy, and were probably much less impressed with the public works program. In these counties both the left-wing opposition and Jobbik significantly improved their scores. The left made a comeback in urbanized counties (e.g., Baranya) and the far-right made significant gains in predominantly rural counties (e.g., Zala, Somogy, Tolna). For exact numbers see (in Hungarian) "Választás '14" (Election '14), *Republikon*, n.d., accessed 15 January 2015, http://republikon.hu/media/9504/valasztasok_2014_ri.pdf.

– Chapter 5 –

THE LIMITS OF RACIST MOBILIZATION
The Case of Devecser

In this chapter, I rely on fieldwork conducted in the town of Devecser to explain the absence of an organic racist countermovement in the 2006–2010 period and to highlight the limitations of racist mobilization in the 2010–2014 period in a region that markedly differed from the northeastern periphery. I will use the method of "retrospective micro-historical reconstruction" (Handelman 2005) to identify key similarities and differences between Devecser and Gyöngyöspata, which I treat as exemplary cases of their wider regions. Concerning similarities, I will emphasize the salience of insecurities and feelings of deprivation among semiskilled blue-collar workers in connection to the restructuring of the local economy within the wider process of European enlargement. In Devecser, as in Gyöngyöspata, these experiences found expression in increasingly angry complaints with regard to local Roma (who made up approximately 30 percent of the local population in my Transdanubian field site). However, in Devecser, neither the local elite nor key social groups had an interest in "cleansing" the town, as opposed to the post-peasantry, whose leading representatives perceived presence of Roma as a threat to their ethnotraditionalist project in Gyöngyöspata. This was partly thanks to the successful conversion of unskilled workers of Romani origin into petty traders who provided cheap access to durable goods and spent considerable effort on maintaining peaceful coexistence with members of the majority. Non-Romani workers' access to Western labor markets and the preemptive politics of the local mayor (which stood in stark contrast to the politics of non-action pursued by Gyöngyöspata's "pragmatist" elite) also undermined the emergence of popular racism.

However, as I go on to show, a major industrial disaster that struck the town in October 2010, destroying the local Gypsy settlement, restructured the social fabric and generated powerful tensions between "natives" and inhabitants of the Dankó settlement who were relocated to the town center. Jobbik sought to take advantage of this tense atmosphere in August 2012 by organizing a "blitz campaign" that followed the blueprint of the Hungarian Guard's previous interventions. As I go on to show, there were three tendencies that allowed local power-holders to obstruct the Far Right's effort to divide the local community along ethnic lines. First, far-right activists could not count on organically formed local racist sensibilities. Second, the local Fidesz mayor took advantage of the new policies adopted by the Orbán government to mitigate feelings of abandonment among the local population. Finally, petty traders of Romani descent also played a role in preventing the homogenization and criminalization of the Romani community in the way we witnessed in Gyöngyöspata. Although on the surface the two communities played a similarly passive role during the anti-Roma mobilization campaign, merchants' response to the racist mobilization effort highlighted their ability to preempt the radicalization of the non-Roma population.

The Contradictions of Modernization in a Transdanubian Town

Devecser (see map 5.1) is a small town in Veszprém County,[1] situated on the Transdanubian plain at the foot of the Somló Hill, a former volcano that offers ideal conditions for viticulture. Although wine made by peasants from the local Juhfark grape variety had for centuries attracted merchants from Budapest and Vienna, the small size of the area suited for grape-growing prevented viticulture from acquiring the role it played in Gyöngyöspata (and the Mátra region). The local economy was dominated by traditional agricultural activities—cereal and wood production—until the advent of industrialization at the end of the nineteenth century. Within the agricultural sector, the Esterházy family, the largest landowners in the country, occupied a predominant position even after the abolition of serfdom (and the partition of commonly used pastures and woodland between peasants and the landowning nobility). The severe land shortage result-

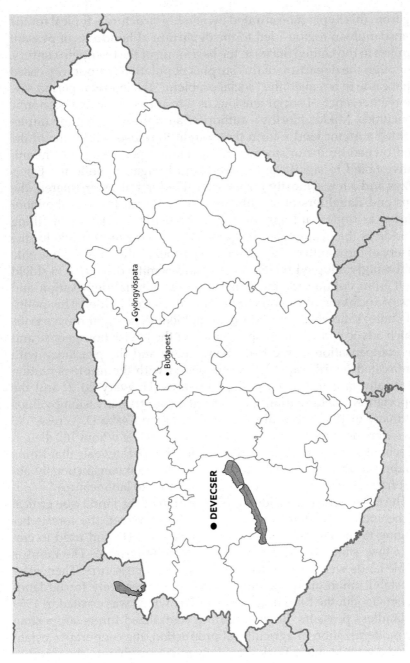

Map 5.1. Map of Hungary featuring Devecser. © Wikimedia Commons, Commons, CC BY-SA license.

ing from this hyperconcentrated ownership structure—typical for the Transdanubian region—led to the departure of hundreds of peasant families to the United States in the beginning of the twentieth century. Although the departure of this surplus population temporarily eased what came to be called the "social problem," the interwar period saw the reemergence of social tensions as a result of persistent economic difficulties. Miklós Horthy's authoritarian right-wing regime implemented a minor land reform that sought to redistribute some of the land owned by the aristocracy to the landed peasantry, but the initiative failed to significantly curb "land hunger."[2] While the Esterházys and a few—mostly Jewish—local industrialists prospered, the sons and daughters of smallholders were forced to enter the labor market as underpaid agricultural or industrial workers. Unwilling to address the deep-seated inequalities that were responsible for the misery of the country's "three million paupers," the conservative elite increasingly adopted the Far Right's anti-Semitic discourse to shield itself from critique for the persistence of material deprivation and lack of social mobility at the bottom of the social ladder. This political strategy, however, ended up strengthening far-right movements, which advocated for the dispossession of the Jewish bourgeoisie and the compensation of the petty bourgeoisie and the peasantry with confiscated Jewish capital. The era ended with the implementation of racially targeted social policy measures (Ungváry 2012) and the deportation of Hungarian Jews after the country's invasion by Nazi Germany in 1944. According to local historian Csaba D. Veress, 195 Jews were deported from Devecser in June 1944, of whom 162 died in Auschwitz. A report published in the local paper[3] reveals that Roma residing in the Devecser district—who had been conspicuously absent from earlier reports—were also deported to labor camps.[4]

The Communists considered the solution of the land issue critical to the success of their political project. In Devecser, the forests belonging to the Esterházys were confiscated in 1945 and used to create a new state-owned company: the State Enterprise. The family's arable lands were distributed among the local peasantry. Then, after the stabilization of the regime, the party progressively forced landowners to join the Blooming Cooperative, which was created in 1959 by landless peasants. Benefiting from centralized funds supporting the modernization of agricultural production, the cooperative established a sizable sheep flock that allowed it to grow into the county's second and the country's seventh largest agricultural cooperative (employing more than five hundred people). As for the State Enterprise, it created the county's largest cow farm in 1974, which allowed the company to employ more than five hundred people in its hey-day. The reorganization of agricultural production had two main consequences. First, the new enterprises provided for the first time a decent income to the agricultural population, allowing the formerly marginalized agricultural proletariat to integrate into mainstream society. Second, the landowning peasantry lost its dominant role in public life.

The new agricultural enterprises, which initially formed the back-bone of the local economy, were also instrumental in the integration of marginalized Roma who lived on the outskirts of Devecser and had hitherto been largely neglected by authorities. The above-mentioned local history monograph first alludes to Roma in the context of a Catholic survey conducted in 1817, which mentioned an unspecified number of "Gypsies" living on the edge of town. In his memoirs, the son of the local rabbi (Linksz 1990) remembered one or two Hungarian-speaking Romani families from the beginning of the twentieth century who earned a living by playing music in local taverns. Although he did not mention them, it is plausible that a sizable Beash-speaking community of woodcarvers already resided in the area at the time the Linksz family arrived in Devecser. Uncle Lajos, one of the oldest members of the community, told me that his forebears had been brought to Devecser by the Esterházys, who allowed them to dig huts in the Baláca forest where the material necessary for carving tubs and cutlery was abundantly available. A photograph he keeps in his pocket depicts forty closely huddled huts—each housing a nuclear family—in the middle of a clearing.

The turning point in the life of Lajos and his tightly knit community came in 1967, when the local party committee decided to build new houses for Baláca residents. Construction of the first houses in the Dankó street—a segregated row of houses that resembled Gyön-gyöspata's Gypsy settlement—began in May 1967. By June 1970, most of the twenty-six families (115 people) who lived in the forest had moved to "the Dankó" (and a few families moved to a newly opened street on the opposite side of town). In exchange for receiving a plot and building material, the newcomers were required to take up jobs in one of the two agricultural enterprises. Adjusting to a new form of life was difficult for Uncle Lajos, who had grown up without knowledge of Hungarian and was oblivious to the existence of "things modern" (such as radio receivers). While "Hungarian came easily" and television was fun (although not for everyone: Lajos told me that an old man got himself electrocuted when he opened the TV set to look for "the small man who had disappeared from the screen"), spending time between four walls and getting up at the same time every day were difficult to get used to. But after a few months, Lajos "got used to the new life and forgot about the forest." He first worked as a firefighter, then became a member of the much-dreaded Workers' Militia before finally being employed as a tractor-driver in the Blooming Cooperative. He, like most other members of his community, was happy to take up the socialist state's integration offer in the hope that the he and other Roma would be accepted as new Magyars. (I am sure he did not carry the photograph depicting the huts back in those days.)

The Beash were not the only Roma who lived in Devecser. As noted in chapter 1, the early socialist regime's effort to extract income from the landowning peasantry had serious repercussions for rural Romani traders and craftsmen who earned a living by providing goods and services to peasants. Their predicament was also worsened by the imposition of strict regulations on itinerant trade in the 1950s. This forced merchants and service providers from the Lovara group (who call themselves "Vlach Gypsies") and Sinti (who call themselves "knife-whetters") to move into Devecser. These newly arrived Roma found themselves pressured to give up the trades of their forebears (blacksmithing and horse trading in the case of Vlach Gypsies, knife-whetting and showmanship in the case of knife-whetters) and to find a job in the industrial plants in neighboring Ajka, which was transformed into a regional industrial center and also acquired the title of district seat.[5] My discussion with the descendants of these forcibly integrated families revealed that they were—unlike the Beash—not only unhappy to enter a regimented labor regime; these families looked for a way to safeguard their form of life and identity in their new environment that was dominated by the Gadjo gaze. I found only one family that managed to pursue its traditional economic activity in a legal manner in the period. Members of this showman family (who identify themselves as knife-whetters) earned a living by organizing village fairs (*búcsú*) in Western Hungary until the demise of these rituals in the 1980s (a symptom of the decline of traditional village life) and the emergence of new economic opportunities after 1989. Vlach Gypsy families bowed formally to the pressure of proletarianization but sought to combine obligatory industrial labor with informal "Gypsy work." The latter was pursued "after work and after dusk," discretely, with a view to eluding the gaze of authorities who were keen on eradicating all traces of a once flourishing ethnic economy. According to Michael Stewart (1997), who lived in a Vlach Gypsy community in Gyöngyös, some of these apparently unlucrative activities[6] mainly served the purpose of maintaining collective bonds and providing a sense of self-worth in a period characterized by the uprooting and forced assimilation of Roma. My Vlach Gypsy informants also sought to maintain a degree of distance vis-à-vis out-groups. Strategies of cultural demarcation and boundary-making included the practice of the Romani language (Lovari, a dialect of Vlax Romani[7]), adherence to certain cultural practices, and endogamy. The knife-whetters I got to know were well on the way to assimilation. They had already abandoned their language (Sinto, a dialect of Northern Romani[8]) before regime change, adopted "the Hungarian way of life," and no longer enforced (or even demonstrated a preference for) endogamy.

In the late 1980s, Devecser also suffered from the crisis that gripped the Hungarian economy. However, it managed to evade the kind of free fall that was experienced by localities where the economy had been dominated by state enterprises (that were often dependent on COMECON exports). This was largely thanks to the efforts of Endre Tornai, a peasant landowner who had been elected president of the Blooming Cooperative in 1960. Between 1969 and 1977, Tornai negotiated a series of mergers with cooperatives established in six surrounding villages. The strategy, which gave the local cooperative access to higher quality lands and allowed for the diversification of production, fit into the new national economic strategy that replaced the "new economic mechanism" (introduced in 1968) in 1972. The return to the classic road of building socialism favored large state-owned enterprises, which, in return for capital injections, were expected to modernize their production and boost exports. Taking advantage of this modernization drive, Tornai launched new export-oriented industrial activities within the gates of the cooperative. In 1974, he opened a metal production unit that supplied steel tanks for spraying machines to the Soviet Union. Then, in 1979, he founded a small workshop where local women sewed cardigans and pullovers for the Soviet market. His son, Tamás, who was given the task of running these industrial start-ups in 1985, told me that close to half of the cooperative's income derived from its new branches. Foreseeing the collapse of demand from the Soviet Union, Tamás took advantage of the relaxation of regulations on trade and the possibility of traveling abroad to secure new contracts in West Germany. By 1989, building on his newly acquired connections, he worked himself into the role of an "integrator" who not only negotiated contracts for himself but also for other large state enterprises that were seeking to replace Soviet with Western European export markets.

The Cushioned Transition:
When "Ethnicity" Cuts across "Class"

Although Devecser was—mostly thanks to Tamás Tornai's foresight-edness—better prepared than Gyöngyöspata to face the winds of change, it could not exempt itself from the most powerful economic pressures of the time. Sluggish agricultural prices and the imple-mentation of the Compensation Act forced the Blooming Cooper-ative into bankruptcy in 1991. The 3,097 hectares (amounting to 25 percent of the cooperative's land holdings) that were auctioned off in the course of the compensation procedure constituted the most fertile and precious parcels of land. Most of these parcels were pur-chased at low prices—often for no more than a third of their face value—by the cooperative's managers and agronomists. The latter had up-to-date information on the lands worth bidding for and were regularly informed by members sitting on the local "land committee" on which lands would be coming up for sale. As for the State En-terprise, Tamás Tornai let its "irrecoverable agricultural units" drift into bankruptcy and focused on the reorganization of its industrial units into a separate enterprise called Somló Coop. He managed to persuade an Austrian and a Dutch partner to invest in the production of "big-bags"—industrial containers that were in great demand in the Netherlands and Germany—in one of the dilapidated buildings that the new company acquired in the course of the cooperative's "restructuring."

The unskilled workers who lost their jobs when the agricultural enterprises went under found themselves excluded from regular work, forced to live off increasingly meager welfare benefits and badly paid seasonal work (in the Somló vineyards).[9] By the time I began my research, many of them had already died, most of them before reaching the age of 65. I knew this from their children, who live on the settlements situated on the outskirts of town. These set-tlements had initially been built by the Esterházys for the non-Roma maids and servants who worked on their estate. Some of them were occupied by the forest-dwelling Beash after the estate's dismember-ment in 1945, but they had (with the exception of one) been aban-doned by the end of the 1970s (in parallel with the building of new homes on the Dankó). After 1990, these substandard dwellings were reoccupied by unskilled (both Romani and non-Romani) agricultural workers who found themselves locked out of the primary labor mar-ket. In 2010, a survey compiled by the National Development Agency found seven hundred people—15 percent of the town's total population—living on the six settlements.[10] (One had an estimated population of 5–45, three of 45–75, and two of 250.) While most of the people who lived here were the descendants of the Beash, there were also non-Roma (the children of estate maids and servants). I found the lives and moods of racialized and non-racialized segments of the re-emergent surplus population greatly similar. The predicament of the few pensioners who are still alive is best characterized by the figure of Uncle Lajos. When I met him, he lived as a recluse, keeping contact only with his two brothers. During our conversations he refused to talk about the present ("What is the point of talking about something there is nothing you can do about?") and kept coming back to stories dating back to the time when the cozy community he had grown up in was still intact. He became enthralled with a movie I showed him: a short film titled "Gypsies," shot in documentary style in 1962, featuring traditional Romani forms of life.[11] After one of our projections he told me, "I used to be so much ashamed of where I came from but that has changed. I now think this was the only time when we lived in our own world. You know, sometimes I wish the Communists hadn't come to take us away."

This testimony, together with the photograph he carries in his pocket, highlights the process of re-ethnicization in the post-1989 period. While for Lajos it was the dream of becoming a "proper Magyar" that ended with the collapse of the Blooming Cooperative, for younger settlement-dwellers—be they Beash or non-Roma—it was the dream of "having a normal life." I was told that holding an identity card featuring the name of a settlement (or of one of the roads that led to a settlement) in the "permanent address" rubric almost certainly entailed being shut out of "normal" (that is, formal) work. It also symbolized the radical impermanence and insecurity that characterized the predicament of the surplus population. Since settlement-dwellers did not own the houses they lived in, the prospect of eviction permanently hung above their heads.[12] Under these conditions, the relationship that settlement-dwellers entertained with the mayor (and local bureaucrats who dealt with welfare-related matters) was of paramount importance. Their fate depended on the goodwill of these actors. This was all the more so after the introduction of the Road to Work program and the latest social policy reforms (see previous chapter).

The great difference between the predicament of the surplus population in Devecser compared to what I found in Gyöngyöspata was that regime change offered new opportunities to those who possessed entrepreneurial skills. During a visit to kin living in Eastern Austria in the end of the 1980s, Uncle Ottó, the now-deceased head of the above-mentioned showman clan, realized that the Austrian middle class had acquired a habit of throwing away household appliances that would certainly not have been considered junk in Hungary. Capitalizing on the relaxation of border controls, the ambiguity of the legal framework regulating the collection of used items within the European Economic Community, command of the German language, and the networks of Austrian kin, male members of his clan began to collect used household appliances (lawnmowers, furniture, coffee makers, toys, refrigerators, vacuum cleaners, etc.) and other items of value (for example, bicycles, motorcycles, tires, skiing equipment). Benefiting from the scarcity of durable consumer goods on the Hungarian market, they then sold these items with a huge profit margin in their home town. They became known as "lomis," and their business quickly grew into an important pillar of the local economy. Those who are still in the business talk of the 1990s as "the golden age" when the middle class still had savings (which could be spent on obtaining material goods that satisfied the desire to discover and consume the "cargo" of the developed West; see Kovács 2000), when Austrians were looking to demonstrate solidarity with Hungarians whom they perceived as "poor cousins" in need of help, and when Austrian authorities were not yet worried about reusable raw materials leaving the country. One member of a lomis family I got to know particularly well—a man in his late thirties—told me that if one was agile, hardworking, and lucky, it was possible to make a monthly profit of two thousand euros in the 1990s. This naturally attracted a significant number of entrepreneurial Vlach Gypsy families from nearby villages, leading to a substantial increase in the number (and ratio) of Romani families in Devecser.

Although the business was dominated by knife-whetters and Vlach Gypsy families (who could rely on regional kin-based networks and entrepreneurial skills), its lucrative nature also attracted Beash. One such person was a man I will call W. He was born on the Dankó and lived there until 1988. He dropped out of school at the age of sixteen when he was offered the chance to accompany a Vlach Gypsy lomis who needed someone to help him load and unload his van during weekly trips to Austria.[13] His case is somewhat unusual because most lomis prefer to take along younger cousins (or other male relatives) in order to keep income inside the family (clan) circle. However, it is not always possible to find a willing relative, and some lomis actually prefer to hire people outside the family based on the claim that "strangers do not talk back," meaning that they are easier to discipline. W got involved in what he also referred to as the golden years, "when there were far more seals than hunters," and managed to put enough money aside to move into his own house by the time he was eighteen. His case was not unique. I got to know other Beash and even some non-Roma aides who had managed to gain enough money and experience to lease a van and begin making trips on their own.

By the beginning of the new millennium, Devecser had come to be widely recognized as the "capital of the lomis."[14] In its heyday, the business permitted more than two hundred local families to make a living. While some men became professional traders, others looked upon "the lomi" as an escape route in times when the labor market underwent a crisis. In the beginning of the 1990s, and then after Hungary's accession to the European Union, the business offered refuge to families who would otherwise have faced extreme hardship. This is not to say that anyone could enter the business. Families who did not own vans, could not rely on family members for help (with collecting, storing, selling), or did not have access to up-to-date information (on the best places to collect items, changes in the legal regime, etc.) found it increasingly hard to stay in the business. True, some of these hurdles could be overcome through the pooling of resources within clans. Families belonging to the same clan often travel in convoys and redistribute collected goods to compensate those who were less lucky than others. Information on the most secure routes connecting collection sites to Devecser is also widely shared on the market. This has acquired increasing importance due to two interrelated developments. By the early 1990s, the areas closest to the border had been depleted of useful items. Lomis responded by moving further west (toward Styria, Carynthia, and Tyrol). This movement, however, elicited a counterresponse on behalf of Austrian authorities. Pressured by local communities (who feared the infiltration of "Hungarian thieves"[15]) and the central government (which was looking to curb the exportation of reusable raw materials), local police began imposing substantial fines on the lomis, especially in Burgenland and Lower Austria. These fines forced poorer families out of the business and compelled others to relocate their activities to Germany, Italy, and the Netherlands. The greater distance between collection sites and Devecser led to a decline in profitability. In the words of a non-Roma lomis, "The tide is rising and many cannot swim." The consequence of the tide is a process of polarization inside the—predominantly Romani—lomis community. While families integrated into well-organized clans continue make a decent living (earning more than one thousand euros—double the wage of a skilled worker and four times the wage of a semiskilled worker), the "smaller fish" who were forced out of the business find themselves engulfed in a vicious cycle of poverty and marginalization. This is best exemplified by the fact that some of these families have been forced to relocate to the settlements I mentioned above.

If access to Western European markets fostered a process of polarization among the lomis, access to the Austrian labor market led to similar consequences in the ranks of the—predominantly non-Romani—blue-collar workforce. Skilled workers who spoke German could take up jobs in Eastern Austria. While several people I got to know relied on this opportunity as a safety mechanism to obtain extra income in times of personal hardship (which tended to correspond to phases of contraction on the Hungarian labor market), there were also dozens of families where men took up regular jobs in Austria. The gradual opening of Austria's gates (the country was forced to revoke the last administrative limitations on Eastern European labor in 2011) also had a beneficial impact on the salaries of skilled workers who held jobs in multinational companies (e.g., the automotive industry) implanted in Transdanubia. The same could not be said for the majority of semiskilled workers who worked on assembly lines in the French and Austrian multinational companies that moved production to places like Ajka or in the businesses of the budding "Tornai empire."

The big bag venture Tamás had built with the participation of Austrian and Dutch investors turned out to be a financial success, allowing him to accumulate enough capital to purchase a factory in Turkey. This profit was then used to modernize the metal workshop and to launch new ventures: a chips factory and the Tornai vinery. According to my local informants, the "Tornai empire" employed almost half of Devecser's working-age population until Hungary joined the European Union. (This was confirmed by Tamás, who told me that, until 2001/2002, Somló Coop employed sixteen hundred people.[16]) Besides helping Tamás rise into the ranks of the country's economic elite (in 2014, a newspaper cited him as Hungary's seventy-ninth wealthiest citizen), the companies he controlled played a key role in reducing the local unemployment rate, which had peaked at 20 percent in 1994–1996 but had dipped below 7 percent by 2001.[17]

This period of relative stability ended, however, on 31 December 2004, when import quotas on Chinese products were annulled from one day to the other with a view to bringing legislation in line with

Table 5.1. Number of people unemployed in Devecser (2000–2013); growth
years in italic and inflection point underlined.

2000	2001	2002	2003	2004	2005	2006
241	232	202	*218*	*229*	*292*	*338*
2007	**2008**	**2009**	**2010**	**2011**	**2012**	**2013**
344	333	<u>*471*</u>	435	327	241	223

the *acquis communautaire* (which Hungary had to abide by after its
accession to the European Union). Tamás, foreseeing that neither
Somló-Zsák (the manufacturer of big-bags) nor Admirer (the textile
factory) would be able to withstand competition, moved production
to Ukraine. This led to a sharp and persistent rise in the number of
people who were out of work between 2004 and 2009 (see table 5.1).

While the people who were fired faced extreme hardship, those
who were lucky enough to retain their jobs also found themselves under a great amount of pressure. One female worker I got to know (she
was in her late fifties and worked in an Austrian factory in Ajka) told
me that working conditions in her factory significantly deteriorated
after 2004. Workers were being constantly monitored, and the smallest mistake could get someone fired. (I learned from her that one of
her colleagues had been fired a couple of weeks before reaching the
so-called "protected age."[18]) The relevance of the issue she raised in
our private discussions was demonstrated by the publication of a
short report—boldly titled *21st Century Slavery*—in the local paper
(which was not renown for raising such contentious issues) in September 2007. Although the article did not mention the even more contentious issue of wages, I knew that semiskilled workers employed in
Ajka were—with very few exceptions—employed at the minimum
wage, which was 65,500 forints (worth 250 euros) at the time. My
discussions with blue-collar workers five years later revealed their
deep dissatisfaction with the stagnation of wages (I note that, in 2016,
the minimal wage was 111,000 forints, which is 230 euros) as well as
their anger with politicians who let people believe that the transition
would lead to convergence between Hungarian and Austrian wages.
True, the convergence that politicians had in mind can be achieved
through geographic mobility—but not for those who lack skills and
command of German.

It is hard to overestimate the importance of the availability of cheap
consumer goods in a low-wage economy. When I asked blue-collar
workers to tell me when and how they had bought refrigerators, car

tires, stoves, or other appliances, the stories this query prompted revealed that they could not have afforded these purchases if they would have had to buy durable goods elsewhere. I learned from the lomis themselves that they had deliberately frozen prices (around 2006–2007) in order to keep business flowing. This beneficial relationship did not, however, prevent "certain Magyars from beginning to see lomis as a thorn in their side"—as one of my informants put it. In the next section, I will say more about the nature of that thorn and about how its removal was successfully negotiated in the years that preceded my research.

Experiences of Deprivation and Popular Anger with the Lomis

It was W who helped me understand the predicament of a group whose members earn a living from a semilegal trade, lead a particular form of life that is characterized by a much larger degree of freedom than is the case of most other locally available professions, maintain a certain distance from mainstream groups—partially through the maintenance of ethnic cultural traditions—and are themselves frowned upon by certain segments of homogeneous society. One of the first things he told me was that he had grown fond of his itinerant form of life, which allowed for a degree of freedom that had been unimaginable for his parents (who had been forcibly relocated from the forest to the Dankó in the 1960s). The sweetness of this freedom, as I gathered, was greatly enhanced by the fact that it was not only unavailable to earlier generations but also to most members of mainstream society: "Magyars are jealous because we are our own masters. No one tells me when to open the gates of my shop, but they have to be at their workplace every day at 8:00." Freedom, in other words, was not only valuable on its own terms but also because it was something that significant outgroups did not enjoy.

Members of homogenous society label the lomi "Gypsy work." The consequences of this stigma were highlighted by the small number of non-Roma who had entered the business. Most of them began their lomis career by working as the aides of Vlach Gypsy families in the early 1990s. By the end of the decade, they had not only achieved independence but also made enough profit to invest into ventures that did not carry a stigma. However, the pursuit of such conversion strategies required a significant amount of effort. One of my interlocutors told me that it had been difficult for him to establish a new "clean" business because a lot of potential partners and clients were reluctant to associate themselves with someone who had been involved in the lomi. His attempts to cleanse himself of his past through rituals of purification—participation at community events, gestures of goodwill toward partners and clients, etc.—highlight the treatment of lomis as an outgroup on behalf of the local elite (on which more later). This distance also finds expression in the absence of marriages between lomis and non-Roma who occupy positions of prestige: teachers, agronomists, agricultural entrepreneurs, skilled workers, etc. "Decent girls"—a teacher told me—"do not marry lomis [men]."

As noted above, the majority of lomis families were the descendants of knife-whetters and Vlach Gypsy tradesmen who—as far as I can tell (based on discussions with members of the older generation)—had moved to Devecser in the 1950s. Although the second generation continued to safeguard certain ethnic practices—which they kept hidden from the Gadjo gaze[19]—a certain cultural rapprochement had taken place in the span of the last decades. While Vlach Gypsy families first settled on the edge of town (in the streets bordering what was to become the Dankó), their children had relocated to the center by the 1990s. This geographic movement coincided with the lomi's golden age. It was upwardly mobile lomis families who could afford to buy a house in the center. These families (who made up approximately twenty percent of the center's population) had a vested interest in establishing relations of familiarity and trust with the non-Romani environment. They invested considerable time and resources into maintaining friendly relationships with neighbors. This effort was not in vain. Most of my non-Romani interlocutors who live in ethnically mixed streets told me that they had gotten used to living side by side with these "decent families." The dozen or so mixed marriages that have been sealed between "wealthy lomis men" and "poor Magyar girls" attest to the fact that these wealthier families are well on the path of integration—that is, toward bridging the gap between their (high) status in the class hierarchy and their (lower) status in the prestige hierarchy.

Relations between lomis of lower standing—whose fathers were born in the forest—and non-Roma were much more problematic. The example of W shows that wealth and independence had given birth to the aspiration of being recognized as "being no worse than Magyars," as he put it to me. This kind of recognition had fallen squarely outside the realm of the thinkable in previous historical periods. My research showed that non-Roma were not only unwilling to revisit this boundary but were becoming impatient with the lomis. In February 2008, I paid my first visit to Devecser to investigate the circumstances of a demonstration that the lomis had organized on 14 January on the main square. The mobilization had been prompted by the local municipality's decision to ban the sale of secondhand goods in private yards and to relocate the lomis to a former army base situated on the outskirts of Devecser at the end of 2007. Lacking local knowledge and access to key informants, I was able to elicit only the official narrative on what I recognized as a major conflict in the life of the local community. Mayor László Holczinger explained to me that "non-Roma had become fed up" with the illegal disposal of hazardous waste (and the occasional burning of used tires), as well as the traffic jams that were caused by clients flocking to Devecser on weekends. His reluctance to back down in the face of the counter-demonstration—which was attended by 150 lomis—eventually paid off. The mayor enlisted a shrewd Romani politician as an ally (awarding him the title of "market manager"[20]) who by the time of my visit (in February 2008) had persuaded the great majority of lomis to relocate their activities to the army base.

I got the chance to revisit this important episode during my fieldwork in 2014. I used my third meeting with Holczinger, which followed two formal interviews, to inquire about the circumstances of the enforced relocation. More specifically, I asked the former mayor to comment on one sentence (highlighted in italic in the text below) of a longer interview (printed in the local paper) in which he explained why the lomis issue was causing a headache for the municipality:

> The illegal sale of secondhand goods has created powerful social tensions that require immediate action. . . . Devecser has been for quite some time now the "capital of the lomis," who specialize in the sale of secondhand goods. Among the 5,400 citizens of this town, 210–250—mostly Romani—families are involved in this business. The lomis do not sell their goods on the market, but stock and sell them in their yards. On weekends hundreds—on occasions thousands—of customers roam the streets, blocking circulation. *Devecser's local council is currently facing difficult material, moral and social tensions.* We cannot wait any longer, we must address these problems now with the means at our disposal. We have the option of using drastic and arbitrary measures, but we would wish to avoid such a situation. (translation and emphasis mine)

Reflecting on events that took place seven years earlier, the former mayor told me that he had found himself forced to act because of the eruption of "popular anger" with lomis, which ostensibly took him by surprise. When I inquired about the source if this anger, Holczinger told me that it was, in his view, rooted in "social tensions," calling my attention to the fact that it was the fifth consecutive year when the unemployment rate had risen. He then went on to argue that people who had lost their jobs in the factories had become impatient with "irreverent lomis violating basic norms of coexistence"—for example, by burning hazardous waste. His analysis confirms the argument I formulated in chapter 2 in connection to the possibilities of an organic racist countermovement in Gyöngyöspata. One of my key claims was that material insecurities generated in a period of capitalist restructuring play a crucial role in natives' turn against "deviant" social elements. Evidence collected in Devecser shows that a similar process was set in motion after the relocation of semiskilled jobs to Ukraine.

One of the reason I cited the report on "21st Century Slavery" was to argue that the publication of such a contentious piece (with such a controversial title) was motivated by the deepening of insecurities generated by the restructuring of the labor market in the aftermath of European accession. Here I would like to take this argument one step further by highlighting the reactions that the article elicited. After its publication (in September 2007), the owner of the company (which had not been named but could nonetheless be easily identified) called the author and demanded that she pay a visit to the factory to reassess her claims. (She had claimed that female workers had to work three shifts, that they were only given a fifteen minute and a five minute break during each eight hour shift, and that they were frequently humiliated and terrorized by male bosses.) Having agreed to the invitation, the author produced a new—intriguingly ambiguous—piece. This second article restated the author's opinion that the work on the assembly line was monotonous and dehumanizing. However, she went on to acknowledge that the owner provided extra benefits for afternoon and night shifts and concluded her piece by quoting a female employee: "All this is part of the package. You have to accept [these conditions] when you sign the contract . . . . All-in-all, we are happy to have work, close to our homes and in such a clean environment." The last sentence sums up perfectly one of the cornerstones of local common sense. Namely, that the contestation of labor relations is futile and can only get one fired (see the example of the woman who was laid off shortly before reaching the protected age). The fact that the company boss had the article "corrected" only confirmed local entrepreneurs' determination to prevent the public articulation of grievances related to work. This determination may, I argue, have contributed to the displacement of frustration and insecurity and may thus help us account for the emergence of "popular anger" against the lomis who (as W made clear) were their own bosses. Although my forays into local microhistory did not allow me to identify the segments of the local population who had pressured the mayor to act, they did shine light on an intriguing episode. In February 2008, the local paper published another opinion piece titled "To My Roma Friend!" It turned out that the piece—which exhorted Roma to change their "work-shy, arrogant" behavior—had been published on a far-right blog (associated with Jobbik) and that a non-local party activist had sent it to the local paper in the hope that the editor-in-chief (who had only recently replaced the previous editor and was still considered a novice) would publish it. The ruse worked (and got the inattentive editor fired). By publishing the opinion piece, the "politically independent" local paper had provided visibility and legitimacy to a redemptive racist narrative that had been absent from local public discourse.

The "Red Mud Disaster": A Natural Desegregation Experiment

By relocating the lomis, Mayor Holczinger had drawn a symbolic demarcation line between their territory and that of homogeneous society. The underlying message was that the center would remain under Magyar control. As far as I was able to tell, the move played a certain role in preempting the spread of feelings of abandonment. This dynamic was, however, overwritten by an event that will surely go down as one of the most important episodes in the history of the local community. In the early afternoon hours of 4 October 2010, a reservoir belonging to MAL Hungarian Aluminium (see endnote 5) burst, releasing one million cubic meters of red sludge, a toxic by-product of aluminum production. The spill took place the day after the local Fidesz candidate—agronomist Tamás Toldi—scored a decisive victory at the municipal elections. (It is worth noting that the lomis community had played an important role in the election by rallying behind Toldi. The four to five hundred votes they controlled were instrumental in defeating Holczinger, who lost by a margin of 307 votes.)

The red mud contaminated a huge area and damaged hundreds of houses in Devecser and the neighboring village of Kolontár. The death toll reached ten (the victims being from the neighboring village), but the number of people who sustained serious physical injuries was much higher. The industrial disaster, the worst of its kind in Hungary's history, left an indelible mark on the locality. First, the sludge washed away the Dankó and half of Devecser's old center, rendering hundreds of citizens homeless. Second, it led to the departure of close to one thousand people—that is, one fifth of the town's population— among whom members of the cultural elite and skilled blue-collar workers were heavily overrepresented. Third, the compensation policy adopted by the government only indemnified people who had lost their houses or had been physically injured by the toxic sludge. The government gave these "primary victims" the choice between financial indemnization and moving into new houses that were to be built in a "new colony" (see map 5.2). Close to one hundred families chose the latter option. This generated deep tensions between acknowledged victims and those who had not received compensation for their losses and injuries. (People who had not sustained material injures were equally hit by the collapse of property prices and the high concentration of toxic particles in the air.) Because of these reasons, unacknowledged victims not only felt unfairly treated but also often trapped in a locality that some no longer recognized as their home.

Besides being angry with the government and the prime minister (who had promised to fully compensate victims), locals were are also outraged by the "overcompensation" of certain families. The most widespread complaint was that residents of the Dankó had been "overcompensated." As I later learned, the question of what to do about the settlement's residents—that is, whether to give them money to purchase a house in the town proper or to compensate them based on the market value of their shabby houses, thereby indirectly forcing them to relocate to villages where real estate was cheaper— was debated at the highest levels of government. In the end, it was decided that Dankó residents would be given a choice between buying a house in Devecser with the help of the state or moving to a new colony where houses were to be built by the government. The overwhelming majority chose the former option, as a result of which low-status Beash families moved into "clean streets" (that is, streets that had been inhabited only by non-Roma).[21]

In essence, the red mud disaster amounted to an experiment in residential desegregation, which had very few antecedents in Hungary. The Communists, as discussed in chapter 1, had made an altogether successful attempt to improve the housing conditions of the Romani population but did not believe that either they or the non-Romani community was ready to share living quarters. Data gathered in the framework of surveys that were carried out by Kemény et al. (2004: 58) showed a clear trend toward resegregation in Hungary between

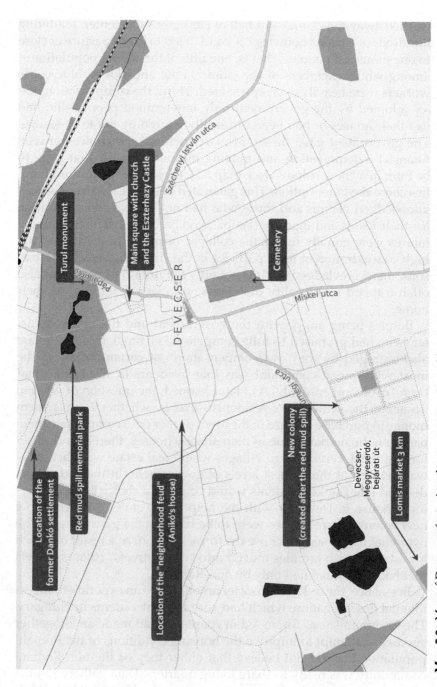

Map 5.2. Map of Devecser featuring the area contaminated by the "red mud spill" (marked with stripes) and other landmarks. © OpenStreetMap contributors, CC BY-SA license.

1993 and 2003. The only attempt to mitigate this trend was undertaken under Ferenc Gyurcsány's social-liberal premiership (2002–2009), but this amounted to no more than a small number of local experiments that were designed to test how rural communities would react to the relocation of the surplus population into the centers of villages and smaller towns. Virág (2010) showed that these experiments usually ended with the departure of higher-status (non-Roma and Roma) families, thus paving the way for the "Gypsyfication" of villages.[22] Anthropologist Judit Durst (2015), who conducted fieldwork in the poorest parts of the Northeast, showed that the departure of higher-status groups worsened the situation of those who were down and out because they could no longer rely on everyday forms of solidarity, which higher-status groups had cultivated with a view to maintaining social peace in peripheral communities. These experiments and findings showed that localized and limited state intervention (targeting only one component of rural marginality) was likely to do more harm than good.

There were also a few precedents for spontaneous residential desegregation, such as the one that took place in the northeastern village of Olaszliszka after a local flood. This particular case showed that a sudden and drastic change in the ethnic composition of the local population or the geography of ethnic cohabitation could generate fears of inundation and social breakdown, converting affected localities into hotbeds of ethnic strife. A similar dynamic was set in motion in Devecser in the postdisaster period. My discussions with the inhabitants of previously "clean" streets revealed that the arrival of "shack-dwellers" (i.e., Dankó residents) had generated frustration and anger. When I asked these "natives" what bothered them about the "newcomers," residents mentioned seemingly trivial problems, such as the playing of loud music, quarrels, dogs being walked without a leash, litter lining the street, and shack-dwellers' unwillingness to move aside to let others pass on the sidewalk. Research conducted by anthropologists in social contexts that differ from the ones I worked in has highlighted similar issues in relation to problems of coexistence between Roma and non-Roma. Giovanni Picker—who conducted research in Cluj and Pescara—highlighted, for instance, the popularity of the trope of disturbing behavior, quoting informants' complaints about Roma "disturb[ing] the environment around them" (head of municipal office of Cluj, quoted by Picker 2014: 9) and "playing music at a loud volume" (local politician from Pescara, quoted by Picker 2014: 12).

While in the previous section I stressed the importance of economic downturn and concomitant experiences of deprivation in the context of capitalist restructuring, here I have emphasized that the actions (together with the perceived intentions) of local power-holders and the central government fostered a sense of abandonment among mainstream groups. While in Gyöngyöspata it was non-action, in Devecser it was the "overcompensation" of "unworthy shack-dwellers" and the state's failure to live up to the prime minister's promise to fully compensate the local population that fostered a powerful sense of abandonment among certain segments of the local population (first and foremost the "native" inhabitants of the center). In the next section, I will show how Jobbik sought to take advantage of this situation to strengthen its positions in a locality that its leaders identified as a key target and a potential bastion in a region where the party had failed to make significant inroads in 2010.

The "Neighbor Feud" and the Devecser "Blitz Campaign"

On 21 July 2012, the head of the already mentioned showman clan, Ferenc Horváth, got into a verbal row with a middle-aged woman named Anikó Bognár, who was known as the local massage therapist. A client of Anikó's had parked his car in a way that prevented Ferenc from passing with his own vehicle. As it later turned out, Ferenc was in a hurry, on his way to his brother-in-law who lay gravely ill in his home. Anikó, who was known as a quick-tempered woman, started shouting with the 56-year-old man because—in her view—there was plenty of space for anyone to pass. While Ferenc later claimed that Anikó called him a "dirty Gypsy," the latter claimed that the man had badmouthed her. Be that as it may, Ferenc did not intend to do anything about the incident because he had known Anikó for nearly thirty years and had never quarreled with her. His daughter, the head of the local Romani Self-Government, thought otherwise. She showed up at Anikó's house later that day to tell her that she could not mistreat an older man the way she had done. (I note that most of my Romani acquaintances had told me that they would have done the same because mistreating an older man, especially the head of a family, is unacceptable. The victim, moreover, was known in the neighborhood as an extremely courteous person.) The two women got into a verbal row that ended after a few minutes. Two days following this incident, the above-mentioned brother-in-law died, and the clan was preparing to watch over the body of the deceased in the neighboring village of Somlóvásárhely. Sometime in the afternoon, the younger son of the Magyar family and the children of the Romani family got into a brawl on the street. It was this brawl that escalated into a physical clash—involving the use of baseball bats on the Romani side—in front of Anikó's house. The husband who came out of his house to help his son was severely injured. There were also lighter injuries on the Romani side.

Having talked to members of both families who had been involved in the incident—which is now referred to as the "neighbor feud"—I came to the conclusion that its key theme was respect and its context the contradiction between social class and prestige in an ethnically mixed street. This street was inhabited by wealthier Romani lomis and non-Roma petty entrepreneurs and white-collar workers (who were financially worse off than most of their lomis neighbors). The conflict involved two families whose breadwinners—Anikó and Ferenc—had both fought hard to be accepted as respected members of the community. While Uncle Ottó's descendants had sought to earn respect by achieving material success and playing the role of interethnic arbiter, Anikó did not recognize them as being different from "any other Gypsies." She told me that they behaved in the same way as the "newcomers"—alluding, among other things, to the fact that they always listened to loud music—and also mentioned that lomis do not pay their taxes. Members of the showman family, on the other hand, saw Anikó as a "dirty-mouthed bus driver" (her initial profession). This public representation—which she was well aware of— offended Anikó's sense of pride. Having fought hard to shield her family from impoverishment (her husband had lost his job some time earlier), she saw herself as a woman worthy of recognition. Our conversations also revealed a deep sensitivity to being treated as a "stupid female bus driver." Respect, in other words was a symbolic asset both sides had fought hard to earn and neither wanted to lose.

The yearning for recognition also played a role in the escalation of the conflict. Anikó told me that Mayor Toldi and the chief of police had visited her on the eve of the fight to try to dissuade her from notifying the police. On her account, both men were afraid that an official investigation could fire the passions and lead to the outbreak of a local "ethnic war." The effort backfired. Anikó wanted nothing more than for truth to prevail and for justice to come down on those who had wounded her husband. Recognizing that public officials could not be counted on as allies, she began to look for alternatives. Jobbik MP Gábor Ferenczi—a native of neighboring Ajka who also had family roots in Devecser—heard her story. He contacted Anikó, offering legal help to the family. The latter accepted, agreeing in return to help Jobbik organize an anti-Romani demonstration in Devecser.

On 5 August 2012, eleven days after the incident, the Far Right organized a rally under the title Live and Let Live! Demonstration in Favor of Rightful Magyar Self-Defense. The event[23] drew approximately one thousand demonstrators, the great majority of whom were activists of Jobbik and far-right paramilitary groups[24] who had traveled from places as far as Szeged to attend the event. The crowd gathered in the early afternoon on the main square under paramilitary banners before marching to the beat of live patriotic (or "national") rock music (see Feischmidt and Pulay 2017) to the house of the "victimized Magyar family." The ritual occupation of the square was followed by speeches pronounced from a makeshift podium erected in front of the Catholic church. One of the speakers was FBF president Attila László, who had played a key role during the "occupation of Gyöngyöspata." He identified participants as the "brave supporters of the dispossessed countryside, which is being exploited and drained of its last energies" by an unholy alliance of unpatriotic governments and unruly hordes of "criminal Gypsies." He reminded his audience that the governments of Italy and France had already been forced to clamp down on "Gypsy criminals" and had recognized decent citizens' right to self-defense. Since these governments had responded positively to pressure from their citizens, Magyars must learn to overcome their differences and "unite to sweep the scum out of this country!" His words were echoed by Jobbik MP Ferenczi, who, before asking the crowd to begin its march toward the place where "eighty armed Gypsies attacked three Magyars," reiterated his belief that "honest, patriotic, conservative Christian people" stood at the crossroads of history. Mentioning a "recent brutal attack committed by Gypsies against a German couple" in the nearby village of Jánosháza, he sought to connect the dots between the local, national, and European level by portraying the local incident as part of a wider regional trend. The Jobbik MP then reiterated Jobbik's demand for the reintroduction of the death sentence and greater financial support for local police forces as a means of combatting "Gypsy criminality." The next speaker, László Toroczkai, president of the Sixty-four Counties Youth Movement, warned the crowd that the embattled Magyar folk had three options: emigration, becoming the slaves (*csicska*) of the Gypsies, or taking up the fight against "Gypsy criminality." He also warned Magyars not to hide behind the illusion that they can duck "Gypsy criminality" since the latter was present on every square inch of Hungary's territory.

The speeches given by Outlaw Army leader Zsolt Tyirityán and Jobbik regional vice-president Imre Orbán in front of Anikó's home departed from the carefully constructed canon of political anti-Gypsyism, which unequivocally named the enemies of the nation but refrained from inciting physical violence in order to stay within the legal boundaries of free speech. The inflamed crowd then began to make its way back toward the main square through the ethnically mixed streets of the town center. It is at this moment that a handful of demonstrators began to taunt Roma ("Come out, dirty Gypsies!") and to throw rocks into the yards of certain houses. (I later learned that a local sympathizer had identified the homes of those he considered the most "recalcitrant families.") One of the stones hit a left-wing activist who had come to demonstrate solidarity with the local Romani community and was inside one of the yards that were targeted. Another right-wing demonstrator hit Ferenczi by accident on the head. The police responded by barricading the gates of the houses and forcing the crowd to move toward the main square. After a number of tense face-offs between officers and demonstrators, the crowd finally reached the main square, where the rally ended with the music of the Wolves, the band whose heavy guitar riffs activists had initially gathered to.

The Local Elite against the Far Right

When I began my fieldwork in February 2013, I was first and foremost interested in gauging the local elite's response to Jobbik's attempt to ignite anti-Gypsy passions in Devecser and the wider region. One of my first findings was that local power-holders actively sought to undermine the far-right narrative, which stressed that local Roma had "gotten out of hand" and that there was an urgent need to "put them back in their rightful place."

Before highlighting the key elements of this counterstrategy, I would like to call attention to the fact that the far-right account was strengthened by a local narrative. When I inquired why one would reach the conclusion that local Roma presented a threat to the collectivity, some of my non-Romani informants used the figure of the *csicska* (slavey) to convey their conviction that inaction on behalf of "the majority" would be interpreted as a sign of weakness by Roma and that the latter would seek to take advantage of this weakness to "make a Gypsy town out of Devecser." In everyday usage, the word *csicska* referred to poor Magyars who—because they had no

198 | *The Revolt of the Provinces*

marketable skills and no kin to turn to in times of need—were offered shelter and food by wealthier Romani families in exchange for
assistance with household chores.[25] However, in my informants' narratives, the term became divorced from its everyday connotation and
infused with new meaning by way of a connection with the generalized discourse of the "Gypsy menace," which had by then become a
familiar element of public culture. This connection was established
by reference to key events (the "Olaszliszka lynching" or the "Veszprém murder") or figures (Lajos Szögi or Marian Cozma[26]) whose
evocation conjured the specter of a nationwide Manichean struggle
pitting "Gypsy criminals" against "decent Magyars." The figure of
the *csicska* acquired its new meaning within this interpretive frame. It
also came to stand for Magyars who refused to heed the ineluctable
imperative to take sides in the conflict. Its public evocation amounted
to a proto-political speech-act: members of the audience found themselves under pressure to certify the threat of "Gypsyfication" and
symbolically distance themselves from "cowards" and "Gypsy-loving
traitors."

The local elite's counterstrategy aimed to undermine the plausi-
bility of the racist Manichean eschatology on which Magyars would
either reestablish control over "unruly Gypsies" or face the inevitable
prospect of being turned into *csicskas*. One of the core elements of this
strategy was to rely on the local media to directly refute the far-right
framing of local circumstances and events.

During the course of the Devecser blitz campaign, Jobbik followed
the same script that had worked in Gyöngyöspata. The obligatory first
step in these campaigns was to frame a local incident as a manifestation of the countrywide "Gypsy menace." As explained in chapter 3,
the key role in the phase of issue-framing was assigned to far-right
bloggers who were tasked with conjuring the specter of rampant
Roma criminality by creating the impression that a "small Olaszliszka" was in the making. However, when party leaders deemed a
locality or incident of strategic importance, they charged a regional
politician to take issue-framing into his own hands. This is what happened in Devecser. On 31 July 2012 (one week after the incident in
front of Anikó's house), Gábor Ferenczi invited regional journalists
to talk to one of the "Magyar victims" and to inform them of Jobbik's
plan to organize a rally. The regional paper (*Veszprémi Napló*) published a report that used the same term as Ferenczi—"lynching," an
idiom, which (as explained in chapter 3) had appeared in the far-
right dictionary after the Olaszliszka case—to describe the conflict
between the two families.[27] The wider circulation of the far-right in-

terpretive frame was, however, undermined by the regional newspaper's editor-in-chief, who had the initial report removed from its website. The modified version essentially relied on Mayor Toldi's evaluation of the rally that was to be staged five days later: "The collective display of force is not a solution. These people will leave, but we will stay here with the task of finding a solution to problems."[28] It is noteworthy that the paper returned to the "neighbor feud" eight days after the rally with the aim of presenting the episode from the perspective of the Romani participants. This approach, when contrasted with reporting during the Gyöngyöspata conflict, shows that regional media outlets had developed a certain resilience to instrumentalization by the Far Right.[29]

Just as Jobbik incorporated the figure of the *csicska* to buttress its frame, the opposition—led by Mayor Toldi—also relied on elements of common sense to undermine the far-right frame. One of these elements was the widely shared story of the demonstration of solidarity on behalf of lomis in the immediate aftermath of the red mud disaster. Lomis used their vans to transport people and assets to safe ground from the area that was affected by the toxic spill. My informants, even those who despised Roma, acknowledged that it was not ill-prepared authorities but lomis who had saved the day. My non-Romani interlocutors also praised the lomis community's "cool-headed" response to the Jobbik rally. In the days preceding the rally, the representatives of the most powerful lomis families and the local Fidesz leadership held a meeting on the premises of the market. The meeting was initiated by Mayor Toldi, who wanted to convince "proud Beash families" and the market manager to call off a counterrally wherewith they wanted to demonstrate the local Roma community's refusal to bow to intimidation. The mayor argued that a counterdemonstration risked escalating tensions and that it was better for Roma to ignore the provocation so everyone could return as soon as possible to normal life. He was backed by Vlach Gypsies and knife-whetters, who also believed that it would be better to "leave the street to Jobbik" based on the conviction that this would send an unequivocal message to the Magyar community: that local Roma wanted to live in peace. According to informants who had participated in the meeting, representatives of the most powerful Vlach Gypsy and knife-whetter families also used the occasion to blame Beash families for the escalation of tensions and to warn them that further "provocations against Magyars" would only worsen the situation. Beash representatives apparently left the meeting fuming in anger. The next day, the market manager called off the counterdemonstration. The public narratives of these two events supported the mayor's key argument that "local Roma cannot be placed in one basket; there are a very large number of Roma who want to integrate."[30]

Using the State and Civil Society to Defuse the "Gypsy Menace"

My fieldwork in the 2013–2014 period also allowed me to identify the strategic initiatives whereby the mayor sought to defuse the "Gypsy issue" in the run-up to the local elections of October 2014. One of the elements of the strategy consisted in using some of the private donations that poured into Devecser (mainly from Hungary and Austria) after the red mud disaster to foster the integration of the families who had moved from the Dankó to the center. Money provided by the Soros Foundation was used to create a Sure Start Center—where mothers with small infants received free food and counseling—in 2013. The municipality also teamed up with Tamás Tornai to establish a vocational school for pupils from disadvantaged backgrounds. The school opened its doors to twenty-six students—of whom twelve were training to become welders and sixteen nurses at the time of research—in September 2013. Both institutions are run by the Order of Malta, a charitable Catholic organization, which has become Fidesz's favored partner in integration initiatives. Although both institutions emphasize the principal of inclusiveness, their activities mainly seek to help relocated Dankó residents adopt the form of life of the majority.

Mayor Toldi also used his party connections to reinstate Devecser as the seat of the newly established Devecser district (*járás*) after the central government implemented a nationwide territorial reform in 2013. Although I initially dismissed the importance of this move—which compensated the local population for the loss of the district seat in 1971 (see endnote 5)—I later realized that it provided a potent response to the far-right claim that Devecser had stepped on the path of "Gypsyfication." The importance of symbolic compensation was also recognized by Michel Wieviorka, who conducted sociological research in the towns of Roubaix, Mulhouse, and Marseille in the early 1990s. In his analysis, Wieviorka (2004: 57–58) associated racism with fears linked to the downward spiral of peripheral urban collectivities:

> Roubaix is an industrial town where, in the space of a few years, the social fabric had rapidly deteriorated while, at the same time, the socio-political system formed by the three main actors in the town (the employers, the trade unions

and the local authority) had collapsed. The most dynamic part of the population abandoned the town, while immigrants came there in considerable
numbers in search of cheap housing and social welfare. In Roubaix, I formed
a group of about ten people, some of whom were poor people stuck in council (HLM) housing in a peripheral working-class area with a bad reputation.
Others who were not so poor lived in the town centre and were extremely
apprehensive about the downward spiral of the town . . . . [Our sociological
analysis] demonstrated that, quite apart from its social sources, racism may
also be closely associated with a crisis in the cultural, regional community and
the feeling of being in danger of being excluded from modernity.

Under Toldi's leadership, the municipality proceeded with the local
adaptation of the policies I analyzed in the previous chapter. In discussions that turned around national politics, many of my informants
shared their view that the new right-wing government had taken the
right track when it reinstated the obligation to work in exchange for
social solidarity in the framework of the revamped public work program and capped welfare benefits (with a view to preventing welfare
claimants from receiving a higher income than employees earning
the minimal wage). The local Fidesz mayor was also credited for introducing a "code of coexistence" (inspired by the Érpatak model)
with a view to disciplining unruly social elements. Most importantly,
the local municipality took advantage of the central government's
educational reform to break with the integration policy of its pre-
decessor. Under the second Gyurcsány-government (2006–2009), the
local elementary school had participated in the special integration
program that aimed to end the segregation of children coming from
socially disadvantaged backgrounds.[31] Although ministry officials
had been highly satisfied with the program's local implementation,
the ratio of Romani students gradually increased, reaching 50 percent in 2010 and 60 percent in 2012.[32] I found that teachers had become increasingly demotivated and unhappy with being trapped
in a low prestige institution (where many were likely to end their
careers). The "Gypsyfied" school, I was told, could no longer carry
out its mission: to overwrite the "backward," "destructive," and
"antisocial" cultural baggage of disadvantaged students: the use of
dirty language, insolent behavior toward teachers, a precocious and
"aberrant" interest in sexuality, etc. One frequently cited story that
enjoyed wide circulation among teachers epitomized the "triumph
of barbarism over civilization." A year before I arrived, an "uncontrollable child" convinced one of his classmates (a "kind and warm-
hearted child" who lived in one of the segregated settlements outside
Devecser and was "suffering from deep psychological injuries") to

break the windshields of cars parked in front of the school. Teachers were not only shocked by the act of vandalism itself but much more by the fact that the child whom they had worked so hard to educate had "succumbed to the little devil's influence." Mayor Toldi responded to the spread of "destructive" and "anti-communitarian" behavior—which many teachers blamed on the "overpermissive" integration policy—by reinstating segregation in the local school right before the local elections of October 2014. Taking advantage of the Fidesz government's educational reform (that allowed principals to circumvent formally retained integration policies[33]), he proposed to separate incoming students into "clean" and "mixed" classes. The move met the expectations of lower-class Magyars (who could not afford to send their children to private schools[34]) but failed to prevent the local elementary school from becoming a "depot."[35]

The lomis community tacitly supported the local leadership's efforts to check the spread of "anti-communitarian behavior" in Devecser. Although the lomis had benefited from (and supported) the integration policy, they did not oppose the reintroduction of segregation in the local school. (Instead, as noted above, many of them took their children to another school.) Neither did they contest the adoption of a municipal decree that strictly regulated acceptable forms of social behavior following the guidelines of Érpatak's far-right mayor. Many of my lomis interlocutors also declared their support for the government's workfare policy, arguing that taxpayers were right to expect the unemployed to work for the community. Their backing of new mechanisms of control and segregation should, I contend, be seen as a maneuver aimed at securing the favor of the non-Romani elite together with communal peace. This instance of interethnic alliance-building was nevertheless not without its victims. While the lomis were largely spared from sanctions, and former residents of the Dankó were subjected to a relatively mild carrots-and-sticks assimilation regime, the inhabitants of the satellite settlements found themselves relegated to a depot school and subjected to a new disciplinary workfare regime. It was they who paid the price for the successful containment of racist mobilization.

Concluding Remarks

The effort to build Devecser into a contrastive case highlights the salience of my earlier remarks concerning social reproduction. My material shows that an organic racist countermovement failed to emerge in an environment where access to Western commodity and labor markets allowed some Roma and Magyars to shield themselves from the negative impacts of economic restructuring (in the period of European accession). This is not to say that anti-Romani sensibilities were not palpably present in Devecser but rather to claim that the "Gypsy issue" did not become a central feature in local public life. The only exception to this—the 2007 episode that ended with the lomis' relocation to the army base—highlighted local power-holders' ability to play a proactive role in the mitigation of popular anti-Gypsyism. Although feelings of deprivation and abandonment were not as widespread and profound as in Gyöngyöspata (and, by extension, the Northeast), it is important to highlight the difference between Mayor Tábi and Mayor Holczinger. While the former sought to enforce the taboo on "Gypsy-talk," the latter risked conflict with the lomis (later losing the election partly because of this). By relocating them outside the center, Mayor Holczinger—as my informants put it—had "removed a thorn from the side of the Magyars." Under Mayor Toldi, the local municipality adopted a different but similarly coherent strategy to prevent tensions caused by the government's failure to fully compensate red mud victims and residential desegregation from exploding. To summarize, we can say that local power-holders—enjoying the support of the central state and civil society—successfully diffused simmering tensions through the symbolic separation of the lomis from homogeneous society; then, later, through the symbolic reaffirmation of hegemonic Hungarianness and an effort to incorporate relocated settlement-dwellers into homogeneous society; and, finally, through the reinstitutionalization of mechanisms of segregation and control targeting the surplus population (in accordance with policy changes on the national level in the 2010–2014 period).

The success of this effort—led by the local Fidesz mayor—was predicated, on the one hand, on the availability of state capacities. The central state had made more than five million euros available for the reconstruction and development of the town in the 2010–2014 period. This allowed not only for the reparation of damages but also for the building of a new police station and the creation of a new memorial park (dedicated to the victims of the red mud spill). My description of conditions in the local school highlighted that the reinforcement of state capacities pertained only to the "right hand of the state" (Bourdieu 1994). The local municipality was, however, lucky enough to be able to enlist private donors (the Soros Foundation and Tamás Tornai) and service providers (the Maltese Order) who offered services (vocational training, early childhood support) that the Dual State (see previous chapter) no longer seeks to provide to those 'down and out'. My case is clearly exceptional in this regard, since most local municipalities cannot rely on civil society organizations to supplant the weakened "left hand of the state" to foster social cohesion. My material nevertheless highlights mainstream groups' positive reaction to the local mayor's effort to mitigate feelings of abandonment through a combination of compensatory and repressive measures that followed the logic of anti-egalitarian populism and relied on the dualization of state functions. It is important to note that this strategy of polarizing society along the lines of social class did not map neatly onto the ethnic divide in this locality (and many other localities in Transdanubia). This strengthened the mayor's argument that "local Roma cannot be placed in one basket" and weakened Jobbik's attempt to polarize the local community along ethnic lines. In the next chapter, I will go on to show how the local Fidesz chapter nevertheless lost its credibility in the eyes of local citizens and how Jobbik took advantage of the delegitimation of the political elite to mount a challenge to the ruling party.

Notes

1. The town had a population of 4,676 inhabitants according to the census of 2011, of whom 550 inhabitants (11.7 percent) declared themselves "Gypsy/Roma."
2. The failure of the 1920 land reform was also visible in Devecser. In 1896, the earl Ferenc Esterházy owned an overwhelming 79 percent of the land around Devecser (43 percent of arable farmland and 90 percent of forests). This left the 487 smallholder peasant households (who owned 38 percent of arable farmland but less than 1 percent of woodland) in a precarious situation, especially taking into consideration that the arable lands were mostly of poorer quality and the most valuable local resource was wood. Between 1910 and 1941, the Esterházy estate's total share of locally owned land dropped to 55 percent, mainly as a result of the land reform. However, the number of mid-size farmers (who owned between 10 and 100 hectares) also dropped from 115 to 85 in that period. This shows that the reform failed to strengthen the positions of the "peasant-bourgeoisie" (Veress 1996: 174–201 and 273–287).
3. The local paper—the *Devecseri Újság* (Devecser Journal)—was founded in 1927. Publication ceased in 1949, but after a long period of slumber the paper was refounded in 1994 by a group of local intellectuals who enthusiastically embraced the project of regime change. Although the editorial board depended financially on the local municipality, it acted relatively independently of the mayor. This changed in 2010, when the newly elected Fidesz mayor appointed a new editor and fired the "old guard." The deeply symbolic move was paralleled by a change in name. The paper was renamed the *Új Devecseri Újság* (New Devecser Journal).

4. A local census conducted in 1941 identified only three "Romani-speaking" individuals living in Devecser at the time. However, the number of individuals identified as "Romani-speaking" may actually have been accurate considering the fact that most "musicians" spoke Hungarian and woodcarvers spoke Beash, an archaic Romanian dialect. Nevertheless, there may have been a more sinister reason for the small number of Romani-speaking individuals recorded in the census. By 1941, people must have been reticent to identify themselves as members of the Romani-speaking minority due the criminalization of Gypsyness in public discourse and increasingly frequent police raids on "vagrant" communities. As noted in chapter 1, vagrants were branded in the 1930s as presenting a threat to public security and subjected to harsh administrative controls. I do not know if Vlach Gypsy traders and craftsmen (who generally moved from one place to another after having satisfied local demand for their products or services) resided in Devecser at that time, but my interviews with Vlach Gypsy families revealed that some of their relatives had been among the victims of the Porajmos. I spoke to members of two families whose forebears had been deported by the military police (*csendőrség*) to the Komárom fortress (from which they did not return).

5. State planners had destined Devecser to remain an agricultural town. They proposed to develop the neighboring village of Ajka, where an alumina plant and aluminum furnace had been completed during the Second World War. After its defeat at the hands of the Red Army, Hungary agreed to pay one part of the reparations that were due to the Soviet Union in alumina because bauxite (the basis of alumina production) was the only natural resource abundantly available and relatively cheaply extractable in the country. This is why MAL Hungarian Aluminium—the name of the holding that regrouped the different subdivisions of alumina-aluminum production—received substantial investment funds all along the socialist period. In 1971, urban planners recognized the dominance of the town—which by that time had a total of thirty-two factories and a population four times as large as Devecser's—by moving the district seat from Devecser to Ajka.

6. Not all of these activities were unlucrative. A member of a Lovari family who had severed ties with most members of his family told me that his kin had been engaged in the trade of illicit goods since the 1970s and had managed to evade judicial pursuit by investing considerable resources into the maintenance of amicable relationships with authorities. The story was confirmed by a retired policeman and a state prosecutor whom I interviewed later.

7. Lovari is a Vlax Romani dialect, which developed in Romania in the long period when Roma were subject to slavery (thirteenth to nineteenth century). It was initially spoken only by members of the Lovara group, who were mostly involved in horse-trading. Since Vlach Gypsy groups spent many years together under slavery, the different Vlax Romani dialects were all heavily influenced by Romanian, which allows for a certain degree of mutual intelligibility. Lovari, however, was more recently also influenced by Hungarian, which is not a surprise considering that Vlach Gypsy communities have been present in Hungary since the nineteenth century. Today, Lovari is the most widely spoken Vlax Romani dialect in Hungary (and is—together with Kelderash—also one of the most internationally spread Vlax Romani dialects). Its dominance is not only the result of the demographic weight of the Lovara group in Hungary but also thanks to its recognition as a "foreign language," which has now been taught for more than two decades at universities. According to a survey carried out by Kemény et al. (2004: 39), the ratio of Romani speakers among the Roma population sharply declined between 1971 and 1993 (from 21 to 4 percent) but then rebounded (to 8 percent in 2003). We have good reasons to believe that this rebound was caused by this "renaissance" of Lovari following regime change.

8. Sinto (or Sinto-Manush) is a Northern Romani dialect, which is spoken by a hetero-geneous group who are referred to under a wide variety of regional names but most often as "Sinti" (or "Sinti Roma"). Historians have established that the Sinti arrived in Germany and Austria in the sixteenth century along with other Roma from India, eventually splitting into two groups: the Eftavagarja ("the Seven Caravans") and Estraxarja ("from Austria"). The two groups then expanded into other countries. The Eftavagarja arrived in France, Portugal and Brazil, where they are called "Manouches" (Manush, Manuš, Manus), and the Estraxarja moved into Italy and Central Europe. The few thousand Sinti who live in Hungary today (and refer to themselves as "knife-whetters," "showmen," "German Gypsies," or "Sinti") are the descendants of the Estraxarja who migrated here at the end of the nineteenth and beginning of the early twentieth century (see Szuhay 2003 for an ethnographic account of the life of one contemporary community). The loss of the Sinto language had partly to do with the fact that there are only a few hundred families in the country who continue to speak this dialect, which is not fully intelligible to speakers of other dialects. This stands in stark opposition to Lovari (see previous note).

9. Although reliable statistics are available from only 2000 onward, reports published in the local paper allow for an estimation of the number of people affected. These show that the number of unemployed people peaked at six hundred (amounting to approximately 20 percent of the total working-age population) between 1994 and 1996. Altogether three hundred people had been laid off in 1994 and 1995 from the local unit of the Bakony Factories, a large company specializing in electrical supply systems that had opened a plant producing ignition switches for Dacia and Fiat in Devecser in 1976. (As opposed to the unskilled agricultural workers who lost their jobs, most of the semiskilled workers of the Bakony plant eventually found jobs in nearby towns—first and foremost Ajka, where both alumina production and aluminum manufacturing survived the change of regime.) This means that the number of agricultural workers who had been fired from the cooperative and the state enterprise must have also been close to three hundred (approximately 10 percent of the local workforce). It is significant that the local paper did not report on the fate of those who lost their jobs as a result of the "restructuring" of the cooperative. (The term was used by Tamás Tornai, whom I interviewed in 2015.)

10. See Domokos 2010.

11. *Gypsies*, a documentary directed by Sándor Sára in 1962, constituted the first attempt to portray the predicament of Roma in socialist Hungary by focusing on the material and cultural distance separating traditional Romani communities and mainstream society and by highlighting the difficulties of enforced assimilation. Sára returned to the topic in a highly influential fiction film (*The Upthrown Stone*, 1969) to highlight the ruthlessness of the early socialist state's policies in relation to the Romani minority. Sára's critical vision exercised a decisive influence on progressive intellectuals and played a key role in entrenching the "Gypsy issue" as a normative yardstick for evaluating the political class among young dissidents, who later went on to play a key role in cultural and political life after regime change.

12. At the time of my research, the inhabitants of one of these settlements (called Szék-puszta) were facing precisely this prospect. They were unfortunate enough to live next to a major road that authorities were planning to expand in width. Settlement-dwellers had heard that they would be kicked out of their homes and that their homes would be destroyed. Under current legislation, neither the local municipality nor the state have an obligation to provide new homes to tenants.

13. These trips usually lasted one or two days in the 1990s but subsequently got longer due to the greater distance lomis had to travel. Today, most journeys last at least three to four days and involve strenuous physical labor. It is not unusual for lomis to un-

load their van three times a day (a procedure that can easily take an hour). This has to be done at least once every evening, since lomis spend the night in the compartment of their vans to save money. Because of this it makes sense to hire an aide.

14. It is important to note that Devecser is not the only town that has a lomis presence in Transdanubia. While the greatest number of lomis reside in Devecser, there are also smaller lomis communities in the following towns: Csorna, Kapuvár, Keszthely, Sárvár, Sümeg, and Zalaegerszeg. The ten to thirty lomis families who live in each of these towns sell the items they collect on the market of Devecser or the markets of other towns: Celldömölk, Pápa, Tapolca, or Veszprém. Of these, only the Veszprém market is on par with the one in Devecser, but the latter is still the largest and most important, drawing resellers from as far as Western Romania and Western Ukraine. According to the estimate of János Kozák, who managed the Devecser market between 2008 and 2014 and also initiated the foundation of a national lobby group representing all lomis active in Hungary, there were approximately one thousand to fifteen hundred families involved in the business in Hungary at the time of research.

15. My lomis acquaintances sadly acknowledged that by the early 1990s, signs with the words "Don't steal, Hungarian!" had become a normal feature of the Austrian landscape and that citizens and mayors had become suspicious of vans with Hungarian license plates driving around villages. It is worth noting that while most of the waste collectors active in Austria were from Western Hungarian towns, the business attracted people from faraway places. According to data collected in the frame of an EU-financed project (that aimed to assess the state of informal waste collection in Central and Eastern Europe), in 2010, 69 percent of waste collectors active in Austria came from Hungary. Another 19 percent were Austrian, 4 percent Slovak, 3 percent Bulgarian, 2 percent Czech, 2 percent Slovene, and 1 percent Romanian. See website of the TransWaste programme, 2009–2012, n.d., accessed 25 March 2016, www.transwaste.eu.

16. According to the census of 2001, there were 3,401 people aged fifteen to sixty-four who lived in Devecser. (Although not all of the sixteen hundred people employed by Tornai were from Devecser, most of them were from the town.)

17. The National Employment Service registered 232 people out of work in Devecser (see table 5.1). The 232 unemployed people correspond to an unemployment rate of 6.8 percent.

18. The Hungarian labor code offers protection against the dismissal of employees who are within five years of the retirement age.

19. There was one Vlach Gypsy family whose private life I got a chance to peek deeper into. Participation at family meals showed that they spent a significant amount of effort on the maintenance of ties with relatives who lived in surrounding towns and villages. They participated in collective ethnic rituals, such as baptisms and funerals, and also sought to launch business ventures together with relatives with a view to maintaining their ethnic network. This clan, like most others, also sought to keep the Lovari language alive. This, however, was only partially successful. Although members of the younger generation understand the language (and some speak it), they tend to consider Lovari as a sign of cultural backwardness. The upwardly mobile Beash families I got to know preferred to speak Hungarian or a mix of Beash and Hungarian even at home.

20. János Kozák was a businessman and a member of the National Gypsy Council, an elected body that the state recognized as the official representative of Roma. He had earned his political credentials in 2006 when he played a key role in brokering a new left-leaning majority within the newly elected council.

21. It is also worth noting that several owners of houses on the Dankó had registered kith and kin (who lived in nearby villages) as official residents. The policy to compensate

all of the people who lived in houses that were destroyed by the red mud (or demolished by authorities) gave these Beash villagers the opportunity to claim new houses.

22. I am not arguing that this process—which Virág refers to as rural ghettoization—was primarily driven by state intervention, only that the latter could easily lead to the same result as spontaneous geographic mobility.

23. An hour-long video provides a good summary of the rally (which lasted approximately two to three hours): "Élni és élni hagyni – Jobbik demonstráció Devecseren" (Live and let live – Jobbik demonstration at Devecser), YouTube, published 25 August 2012, accessed 14 February 2013, https://www.youtube.com/watch?v=ggmzsGz5ypk. I myself was not present at the rally and reconstructed the event with the help of video footage as well as the detailed accounts of local citizens who were in attendance.

24. The following groups took part in the demonstration: NHG, National Guard, FBF, Sixty-Four Counties Youth Movement, Defense Force, Outlaw Army.

25. I got the chance to listen to the story of one *csicska*, a man who was from a neighboring county and claimed to have been enslaved by a criminal gang after he lost his job and home in the early 1990s. After fleeing his captors, he arrived in Devecser without a penny and was given a container to live in by one of the lomis. In exchange for accommodation and food, he is asked to help out on Saturdays and Sundays on the lomis market. As far as I could tell, he was a happy man. He told me that his "boss" (that was the word he used to describe the head of the lomis household, whom I also got to know quite well) let him do what he liked (gardening) and related to him in a kind and respectful way. His case shows that the relationships of dependency the term *csicska* refers to are not necessarily abusive.

26. See chapter 3 for descriptions of these events and figures.

27. See (in Hungarian) "Ferenczi Gábor: Nagyobb biztonságra van szükség Devecserben" (Gábor Ferenczi: There is need for greater security in Devecser), *Alfahír* (former Barikád) news website, published 3 August 2012, accessed 18 December 2012, https://alfahir.hu/ferenczi_gabor_nagyobb_biztonsagra_van_szukseg_devecserben-20120803.

28. See (in Hungarian, translation mine) Zsuzsa Tóth B., "'Lincselés'" miatt demonstrációt tervez a Jobbik Devecserbe" ('Lynching' prompts Jobbik to plan demonstration in Devecser), Veszprémi Napló Online website, published 31 July 2012, accessed 18 December 2012, http://veol.hu/hirek/lincseles-miatt-demonstraciot-tervez-a-jobbik-devecserbe-1292447.

29. The significance of the *Veszprémi Napló* reports is demonstrated by the fact that the intervention of the editor-in-chief prompted Ferenczi to file an official complaint. The latter argued that the paper violated the principle of unbiased reporting.

30. Excerpt from an interview conducted by a prominent left-wing journalist on 9 August 2012. See (in Hungarian, translation mine): "Bolgár György interjúi a Galamusban—2012. augusztus 7." (Interviews conducted by György Bolgár on 7 August 2012), Galamus blog website, published 9 August 2012, accessed 18 December 2012, http://galamus.hu/index.php?option=com_content&view=article&id=155119&catid=69&Itemid=106&limitstart=1.

31. The school in Devecser had been identified by the ministry of education as a priority target due to the high ratio of Roma children. Until the 2004/2005 school year, the local school published statistics on the ethnic background of its pupils as well as their performance. At the end of the 2001/2002 school year, the ratio of Roma children was 30.9 percent (191 students out of a total of 618). This was one of the highest ratios in Western Hungary. The ministry's interest in having the local school participate in its desegregation program was also rooted in the spectacular difference in the performance of Roma and non-Roma children. According to the statistics published in the local paper, the ratio of Roma among those who had to repeat a class generally hovered around 75 percent. Their performance stood in stark contrast to non-Roma

students. Local students' participation in countrywide surveys showed that the local school was among the best in the country in terms of student performance. (A nationwide mathematics survey conducted in 2001 showed, for instance, that local students were in the top ten percent of students.)

32. This was mainly the result of demographic trends (i.e., a gap between the fertility rates of Romani and non-Romani women and the influx of Romani families from nearby villages). However, there was another factor in play. From the middle of the last decade—when the ratio of Roma children surpassed 40 percent—a few wealthier non-Roma families moved their children to schools in Ajka. Their example was later followed by wealthier lomis families.

33. From 2013, beneficiaries of child protection benefits are, for instance, no longer considered "socially disadvantaged." This minor modification makes it easier for state-run schools to observe legislation that stipulates that the difference in the ratio of students coming from a socially disadvantaged background between different classes cannot exceed 25 percent (within a specific grade).

34. After 2010, the Fidesz government decided to hand hundreds of rural elementary schools over to the Catholic and Protestant churches. The move was designed to benefit the rural middle class by allowing for "spontaneous segregation" in the countryside. Schools run by churches could choose among a number of instruments to prevent pupils of lower-class background from entering their gates. These instruments include tuition fees and selection based on achievement and competences.

35. As noted above, the local school had already been "deserted" by the local middle class a few years earlier. The reintroduction of segregation did not make the local elementary school attractive enough to allow for the return of the children whom parents had moved to Ajka.

– Chapter 6 –

FROM RACISM TO ULTRANATIONALISM

Jobbik's Transformation through an Ethnographic Lens

The Devecser "blitz campaign" was Jobbik's last noteworthy attempt to use redemptive anti-Gypsyism as a vehicle for forging a popular anti-elitist alliance in disaffected rural communities. Its failure strengthened the hand of moderates, who dominated the leadership and sought to substantially modify the party's ideology, program, and image with a view to establishing Jobbik as a credible challenger to Fidesz. In this chapter, I use ethnographic material gathered during the parliamentary and local election campaigns (that spanned the 2014 election year) in Devecser to identify two key conditions of possibility for Jobbik's successful transformation into an ultranationalist party: the collapse of left-wing networks of support and the delegitimization of Fidesz. I then go on to highlight the ideological, programmatic, and stylistic innovations that allowed Jobbik to project the image of the "true nationalist force" and successfully attract orphaned left-wing and disillusioned right-wing constituencies in a formerly left-leaning town. This strategy, which reflected the party's national strategy, allowed it to first increase its share of the popular vote by 8.5 percent at the parliamentary elections (from 24.9 to 33.4 percent between 2010 and 2014), then to snatch the mayor's seat from Fidesz and thereby acquire its first bastion in Transdanubia.

Political Orphans

In Devecser, the postcommunists managed to evade the kind of wipe-out they had suffered in many other rural areas (including

Gyöngyöspata[1]). Although the Socialist Party performed poorly at the parliamentary elections of 1990, it recovered lost ground in the subsequent years, arriving in first place in 1994, 1998, and (after finishing a close second in 2002) in 2006. The postcommunist left's influence was also manifested in the outcomes of local elections. The two independent mayors who led Devecser between 1990 and 2010 both entertained close ties with the political-economic bloc that stood behind the Socialist Party: the *nomenklatura*.[2] This was most evident in the case of István Jokesz (1990–2002), who had headed the local council in the last years of the Kádár regime (between 1987 and 1990). His successor, László Holczinger (2002–2010), also depended on the benevolence of regional left-wing politicians, who played an instrumental role in securing the state-administered development funds that allowed for the reconstruction of the sanitation system and the building of the gas network during his first term in office. Holczinger's second term was marked by the exhaustion of development funds,[3] a 40 percent increase in the number of unemployed people (see table 5.1), and growing insecurity in connection to the Socialist-backed caretaker government's austerity policies.

These negative trends disproportionately affected the blue-collar workforce. My discussions with people who worked for Tamás Tornai, Austrian and French manufacturers in Ajka, and Audi (in Győr) revealed that most of them had supported the Socialist Party until 2006. I was told that "this was normal" because leaders like Gyula Horn (who had been foreign minister in 1989 and then prime minister—and Socialist Party president—between 1994 and 1998) represented continuity with the communist system, which had done a great deal for workers. Continuity was far less clear in the policy domain, but my informants believed that the Socialists were still better than the other parties because they did not only cater to middle-class constituencies. There were, however, a number of issues that affronted them—first and foremost the privatization of state assets under Horn's premiership. The privatization of the cooperative's auxiliary units by Tamás Tornai was, of course, a recurrent story. While many workers were bitter about this, they conceded that Tornai had at least made an effort to safeguard local jobs (even if he failed). What my informants were unequivocally angry about was the privatization of the recreation facilities that had been owned and run by trade unions. The importance of these facilities resided in their central role in providing affordable holidays to working-class families. It was not only that workers could no longer afford a proper family holiday after these facilities (typically situated on the shores of Lake Balaton) were sold, often to businessmen entertaining close ties with the Socialists. It was also that in the absence of these institutions, it was much more cumbersome to maintain kinship ties. The privatization of these welfare institutions not only caused the thinning of horizontal ties, but also generated suspicions in relation to Socialist politicians. Feelings of suspicion were transposed into anger after Ferenc Gyurcsány's years in office (see chapter 3). The workers I talked to still spoke in scathing terms about the former prime minister, whom they referred to as a "crook" or "traitor." While they were united in their distaste for Gyurcsány, my in-depth conversations yielded insights into cultural, ideological, and political divisions within the left-wing electorate.

Pensioners, having experienced at least three political upheavals (1956, 1989, 2010), were generally distrustful of politicians who promised a better deal for the "little man." While most held a positive memory of the Kádár era (which had brought material security), they had grown powerfully disillusioned with the Socialists after the party's neoliberal turn under Gyurcsány. This disillusionment did not, however, push them into the arms of the right. They remained skeptical of Fidesz, which they described to me as an elitist party—and found Jobbik's racism overblown and unappetizing. Having no one to trust, they drifted further and further away from party politics.

Although their children were also critical of politicians, they appeared to be more hopeful with regard to the possibility of a brighter future. The six skilled workers whom I talked to (they held better paying jobs in the automotive sector or worked in Austria) had all—with one exception—become Fidesz supporters by the time I began research. They presented this shift in their political allegiance as the outcome of a rational decision to support a party that appeared to be serious about redressing the dire state of the Hungarian economy and keeping the country on the course of "development." When I inquired about their view of Jobbik, they told me that its politicians were too inexperienced and foolhardy to be trusted with the reins of power. This view tended to be contested by peers trapped in low-paid (yet physically demanding) jobs, as well as those out of work. These unskilled workers held pronounced antiestablishment attitudes and tended to lean toward Jobbik.

The deep material and ideological rift between insecure and secure segments of the blue-collar workforce had been concealed by their mutual allegiance to the Socialists until 2006. The party's leaders were able to uphold this heterogeneous electoral alliance after that tumultuous (and politically devastating) year only in localities where the local economy had weathered the economic crisis relatively well.

One such place was the town of Ajka. Elsewhere, as in Devecser, support for the party collapsed at the parliamentary elections of 2010. In Devecser, the once-dominant Socialists were relegated to third place (with 23.8 percent of votes) behind Jobbik (24.9 percent) and Fidesz (45.2 percent).

While the demise of the Socialist Party was clearly linked to the legitimacy crisis that became manifest after the Őszöd speech (see chapter 3), my fieldwork allowed me to highlight the sociological dimension of this demise. The fact that there was more than politics (in the conventional sense) involved was driven home to me after I got to know an older worker whom I will refer to as L.

L was born in 1945 into a poor Magyar family with eight children. Both his parents were brickmakers who "lived a vagrant Gypsy life": they stayed in a town or village only for as long as there was demand for the bricks they made from mud (a freely available resource). The family arrived in Devecser in 1948 and decided to stay because the newly nationalized brick factory (which had belonged to the Esterházys) offered a permanent position to both his father and mother. L trained to become a blacksmith between 1959 and 1962. He then worked for three years as a blacksmith in a nearby bauxite mine until an accident killed three of his comrades. Having vowed to never again set foot in a mine, he asked to be transferred to the brick factory in Devecser, where he was initially employed as a repairman. One of the party cadres noticed L's interest in politics and his belief in the communist cause. He allowed himself to be persuaded to join the Workers' Militia, an armed force that was created after 1956 to prevent the outburst of another popular revolt. In 1970, he began to attend the "party school" and was promoted to the position of foreman based on his political credentials. Although he did not finish the school, his superiors in the militia trusted him with the task of organizing local commemorations. This allowed him to get to know influential people, including the county state prosecutor, the county party leader, and even First Secretary János Kádár. Although he was happy with the new job, he asked to be demoted after a bruising fallout with his boss, who feared that L would use his connections in the Workers' Militia to obtain a leading position in the factory. The move was fortunate in that it allowed L to keep his job after regime change.

On the occasion of our second meeting, L told me that he wished to trust me with a painful secret he had been carrying for seventeen years. In 1996, he was arrested for drunk driving. Here is how he described the incident and its fallout:

There was a conflict in which my wife was involved in the brick factory. I heard it in the [local pub] and went out to see what was happening. The manager of the factory called the police . . . . I was sentenced to one hundred days of community work but the prosecutor, that son of a bitch, appealed the verdict. I got six months in a high security prison. . . . They took everything away from me, including my medication. I was put in solitary confinement and stayed there for four days. I thought I was going to go mad. The lieutenant-colonel couldn't believe I had been given such a harsh sentence for drunk driving. This was thanks to my work for the party. They made me sit for all the community work I had invested myself in. That is when I began hating the Socialists. I realized I had put my energies into feeding an elite that did not deserve to be fed. (translation mine)

Our following discussion of politics in the liberal democratic era revealed that L still believed that the socialist regime had done a great deal for people like him. But he had grown to mistrust and despise postcommunist politicians, who had first instrumentalized, then disavowed him. There is, however, another way to read L's story—namely, to see it as an episode in the transformation of a political-economic network—the nomenklatura—that emerged in the late socialist period and had to undergo certain fixes to continue functioning after 1989. On this reading, the theme of L's story is (ritualized) sacrifice. The disavowal of former militiamen (who constituted a political liability for the nomenklatura) can be interpreted as an act of destigmatization that was necessary for the political-economic network to survive.

By the time I began fieldwork, the nomenklatura was suffering from problems that were of a different nature and magnitude than the legitimation crisis of the early 1990s,[4] which was successfully resolved. The first problem was that the red mud disaster had decimated the network: the so-called "scientific intelligentsia" (agronomists, engineers, planners, etc.) took advantage of the government's generous compensation policy to leave Devecser in droves (and start a new life in the county seat or the capital). The second problem was that after scoring a historic victory in 2010, Fidesz party leaders decided that the time was ripe to uproot the nomenklatura. My left-leaning informants told me that certain companies and individuals were "blacklisted"—that is, denied access to national or European development funds. This "total warfare" was apparently unprecedented. Informants familiar with the history of tenders told me that Toldi's left-leaning predecessors had channeled a part of the public resources they controlled to companies and individuals that had coalesced around Fidesz in the 1994–1998 and 2002–2010 periods (when the Socialists occupied seats of governmental power).

The most important consequence of the nomenklatura's "suffocation" was that it created a social vacuum. The pipes of the network had been oiled with money (orders for entrepreneurs, per diems for experts, fees for lawyers). Without it flowing through them, these pipes became corroded and began to leak. My informants had a number of ways to explain the reduction in the intensity of exchanges within the network. Some of them told me that people had become greedy and self-centered and that this diminished their appetite for social interaction outside the tight-knit family. Others observed that people had become more inward-looking and prone to psychological illness. A handful admitted that they were far less willing to invest time and energy into relationships that would yield far less material benefit than before. While these explanations were in and of themselves interesting, my attention was grabbed by the fact that many of my left-leaning informants had retreated from politics. While most retained an intellectual interest in social issues and political events, many lost their appetite for voting or any other form of political agency. This was not true for everyone. L, for instance, reacted to his traumatic experience by shifting his allegiance to the right. I first met him at a Jobbik meeting (hosted by party president Vona on 2 October 2014), where he engaged in a long and passionate anti-Gypsy tirade. In the course of our private discussions, he confided that while he sympathized with Jobbik's program, he believed that a strong and experienced leader like Viktor Orbán was better placed to combat greedy bankers and the Brussels elite. He also confided that he had been personally hurt by a prominent Jobbik politician, who reprimanded him for entering the Workers' Militia. However, by the time of my research, he had also grown disillusioned with Fidesz's local faces and practices. He had shown up at the Jobbik meeting where I got to know him to gauge whether he should give the party a second chance.

Disillusionment with Fidesz

The first two years of Tamás Toldi's mayorship were dedicated to the mitigation of the direct impact of the red mud disaster. Generous support from the central government and an unexpectedly large amount of private donations trickling in (from both Hungary and Western Europe) allowed the local council to finance a large number of initiatives that went far beyond the reparation of damages inflicted on infrastructure and the physical environment. The government, however, committed two serious mistakes. The first was to channel monetary private donations into a centrally controlled reconstruction fund. The government decided that this public fund could not be used to compensate for damages inflicted on private property (with the exception of housing). This, as noted beforehand, generated feelings of rancor among those who had lost "only" their private possessions (such as vehicles). Second, although the local municipality organized public hearings where locals could formulate an opinion on the centrally coordinated reconstruction plan, there was a general feeling that authorities did not take the local population's needs and opinions sufficiently into account. Several of my informants voiced complaints about the decision to demolish houses that had suffered only minor damages. I also detected considerable irritation with the decision to spend a considerable amount of money on the creation of a "memorial park"—together with artificial lakes—on the premises where the houses had stood. The breadth of feelings of abandonment was rendered apparent when more than a thousand residents (a third of the local adult population) signed a petition to voice their opposition to the relocation of the central bus stop in 2014. While for some the petition was only about the bus stop, for others it offered an avenue for venting their anger with the local Fidesz chapter. The nontransparency of the process whereby central funds were allocated to different reconstruction projects fueled accusations of corruption. The mayor was himself accused of having abused his position. I was told that the new "colony"—destined to accommodate homeowners whose houses had been destroyed or demolished and who chose to stay in Devecser—was built on a parcel of land that belonged to the mayor's relatives. Some locals also accused the mayor of clientelism, arguing that the state had "overcompensated" Dankó residents (see previous chapter) because Toldi's reelection depended on Roma votes.

My discussions related to local politics also highlighted a source of critique that was largely independent of the red mud disaster. Nobody drew as much criticism as Vice-Mayor László Kovács, whom Toldi had charged with running the daily affairs of the municipal apparatus. Kovács—who was only referred to by his nickname ("Kokó")—was widely considered a ruthless opportunist who would do anything to enhance his power and improve his status. While locals praised the mayor's unassuming style and civilized demeanor, they could not stand Kovács's "arrogance." The latter was also accused of embezzling a chunk of the international donations that poured into Devecser after the disaster. The story about how he had supposedly guided a truck bound for the town hall to his backyard and amassed stolen goods on the premises of the former army base was recounted to me on at least a dozen different occasions. Locals also despised him for branding his opponents "commies." Not only did my informants find his use of the term indiscriminate—the vice-mayor had accused practicing Catholics of having sided with "the reds"—but also laughable. As a councillor, Kovács had worked closely together with the nomenklatura. It was an open secret that he had solicited the favors of regional Socialist politicians on several occasions.

While accusations of "arrogance" were leveled at leading Fidesz personalities, their practices were labeled "partisan" and "one-sided." In the aftermath of Toldi's victory, the new Fidesz leadership quickly moved to replace the heads of key public institutions: the school, the kindergarten, the cultural house, etc. The new appointees were perceived as lacking leadership experience and as having been chosen based on their unconditional loyalty to Fidesz. The replacement of respected managers (such as the school principal) with "foot soldiers" carried the message—this, at least, is how it was decoded by my informants—that the governing party had the authority to totally redraw the political playing field. This was not an insensible strategy. During the run-up to the parliamentary elections of April 2014, I met several people who told me that they would vote for Fidesz despite the fact that they considered its local leaders more arrogant than their left-wing predecessors. This was because they believed that the country needed a strong leader like Viktor Orbán to steer it through—and shield it from the worst effects of—a global storm. L, for instance, told me that "in times of crisis we must all pull together and unite behind our leaders," and conveyed his frustration with left-wing politicians' attacks against the country's leader in the European parliament. The prime minister's discourse on the need to defend Hungary from foreign enemies and domestic traitors thus appears to have resonated with certain voters.

However, even Orbán's aura was not enough to evade defeat at the municipal elections of October 2014. While Fidesz supporters were prepared to stomach certain side effects of authoritarian rule because they believed the prime minister had delivered on his promise to protect Hungary, they were not prepared to do the same for local leaders who appeared to care more about their own livelihoods than the needs of local citizens. The facade of authoritarianism—which had become Fidesz's hallmark—crumbled, revealing a reality that no amount of political spin could conceal: corruption, opportunism, nepotism, mediocrity, and an insatiable lust for power.

From Gypsies to the Turul

Given my assessment of the nomenklatura's situation, it is not surprising to see that it did not play a role in organizing opposition to Fidesz in the 2010–2014 period. Jobbik, on the other hand, succeeded in organizing an electoral alliance of disillusioned citizens of all stripes and colors. There were few precedents for the far-right's managing to unite citizens of different "class position" and political affiliation prior to 2014. The only places where it did achieve this had been peripheral localities such as Gyöngyöspata, where the "Gypsy issue" became number one priority for diverse segments of the ethnic majority. This, as explained beforehand, was not the case in Devecser (or most other localities situated outside the country's northeastern periphery). In what follows, I would like to highlight the ideological, programmatic, and symbolic innovations that allowed Jobbik to build a broad oppositional alliance in the two years that followed its failed racist mobilization campaign.

The first thing I must note is that Jobbik's national leadership drew the right conclusions from the failure of the Devecser blitz campaign. In 2013, political analysts noticed an important change in the public relations materials that were released by the party, noting that the new billboards and videos reflected the ambition to shed Jobbik's aggressive hypermasculine image. This was interpreted as being part of a broader attempt to break out from the extremist quarantine and to refashion the party—following the example set by the Front National and the Freiheitliche Partei Österreichs—into a mainstream nationalist force capable of attracting broad popular constituencies. This interpretation—that Jobbik wanted to move from the margins toward the center—was also supported by the eschewal of racist rhetoric and the espousal of new programmatic themes, most importantly job creation and the improvement of public services.

Jobbik's local campaign activities followed the new guidelines set by the national leadership. In his opening remarks at the party's kickoff campaign meeting for the parliamentary elections of April 2014, mayoral candidate Gábor Ferenczi described Jobbik as a party that belonged to the "patriotic political side" (i.e., the political right) but also emphasized that it was the only genuinely popular political force:

> Looking back at the 24 years which have passed since the stolen transition what we see is that so-called right-wing and left-wing governments who succeeded each other have robbed the country, leaving behind a mountain of debt and massive poverty. This diagnosis can be expanded. 95 percent of the

nation's wealth has been sold off to the benefit of private interests. Successive governments have acted as the agents of foreign capital, implementing neo-liberal policies that are detrimental to Hungarian entrepreneurs. The multi-national companies who benefit from these policies exploit employees. There are 3 million people living below the poverty line and hundreds of thousands of our compatriots have been forced to flee the country as economic migrants. There are a minimum of 150,000 families who are unable to pay the interests of their foreign currency loans. Life expectancy is low and very few children are born in Hungary. Undeniably, there is a need for a radical change, for something more than a simple change of government. What we need is a real regime change. Therefore, the only acceptable outcome of this election is if the Movement for a Better Hungary [Jobbik] wins.[5]

Although most Hungarian political commentators label Jobbik an "economically left-wing" (or even "anti-capitalist") party, this is an inaccurate description. Ferenczi, in line with the national directive to vamp up social populist rhetoric, pledged to use the taxes levied on multinational corporations to improve local health services and to supply poorer families with subsidized wood (for heating). This pledge, however, was accompanied by the promise to decrease the local business tax and to reduce welfare scrounging by terminating the payment of child benefits to families with unemployed adults and more than two children. The program that Jobbik proposed was essentially no different from Fidesz's anti-egalitarian populism (see chapter 4): carrots for the deserving, sticks for the undeserving poor. Instead of pledging to fight for higher wages and to rebuild the welfare state, Jobbik pursued the far-right's traditional strategy of attracting petty entrepreneurs by promising tax relief and attracting the working poor by identifying them as morally superior to welfare scroungers and promising to institutionalize the principle of prefer-ential treatment. What is true, though, is that this program resembled the policies of the late Kádár era and that it proved attractive to peo-ple like L who had experienced material and/or symbolic dispossess-sion after 1989.

To make Jobbik attractive to petty entrepreneurs, blue-collar work-ers, and poor pensioners, the local Jobbik chapter needed to distance itself from its extremist discourse and actions. Demonstrating a break with the party's past did not necessitate a fundamentally new ap-proach to the "Gypsy issue." While overtly racist speech-acts had to be abandoned, destigmatization did not require the eschewal of the kind of moralizing language that was instrumental in driving a wedge between deserving and undeserving citizens. All party representa-tives had to do was appropriate the symbolic arsenal that the mayor of Érpatak had created through years of painstaking work.[6] The key piece of this arsenal was the constructive/destructive dichotomy, which allowed enunciators to defend themselves against accusations of racism via the claim that there were destructive elements within both the Magyar and Gypsy communities. Thus, instead of laying the blame squarely on Romani culture or gene pool, the Érpatak discourse castigated criminal elements, together with the liberal elites whose policies had putatively emboldened destructive forces within Romani communities. This rearticulation of political anti-Gypsyism presented a more benign and potent alternative to the crude racism that had characterized Jobbik's earlier campaigns (see chapter 4). In this it resembled the "new" ("cultural," "differentialist") racism that had displaced the "old" ("biological," "hierarchical") racism in Western Europe two decades ago (see Barker 1981; Stolcke 1995; Taguieff 1988).

I got the chance to see how this modified approach to the "Gypsy issue" functioned in practice during a campaign meeting that was hosted by party president Gábor Vona in October 2014. The event began with the mayoral candidate's presentation of his political program and continued with a speech by Vona, in which he framed the stakes of the local election as the "chance to elect Jobbik's first city mayor west of the Danube." Both speeches included pledges to introduce policies (e.g., the death penalty and the scrapping of universally distributed family allowances) that the party had hitherto presented as instruments to combat "Gypsy criminality" and "welfare-scrounging." It was not only the first time I heard Jobbik politicians deliberately eschewing justification of these policy instruments on ethnoracial grounds; it was also the first occasion on which I witnessed party representatives confronting racist hate speech—Vona's surprising intervention came shortly after he opened the floor to questions from the audience, which the thirty to forty sympathizers used to voice complaints about "stinky" and "thievish" Gypsies. After listening to these laments (voiced, among others, by L), Vona explained that "Jobbik does not discriminate between citizens based on ethnic descent. We only make a distinction between those who are worthy and respectable people and those who are not."

A month earlier, the local Jobbik chapter had demonstrated that it was serious about overwriting the memory of the blitz campaign. On 6 September 2014, Jobbik's mayoral candidate hosted a "family day" in the park of the former Esterházy castle. Gábor Ferenczi had decided to invite a pedagogical assistant of Beash origin who had been one of the faces of a nationwide Roma integration project to act as moderator. He also asked one of the most respected Vlach Gypsy

lomis to bring his mobile food stall to the event. The decision to extend a friendly hand precisely to these individuals was an ingenious
move. Ferenczi knew not only that these "integrated" individuals
were respected in the community but also that they had had personal conflicts with the local Fidesz leadership. While both hesitated
to accept Ferenczi's invitation, the desire to "get even with Fidesz"
(as one of them put it) trumped their aversion. The participation of
two esteemed Roma individuals sent a powerful message to the local
community—namely, that Jobbik had made a decisive break with its
extremist past.

This message was not primarily intended to reach Roma ears. Ferenczi knew well that Jobbik did not dispose of the means to break
the alliance that had been forged between mayor Toldi and the lomis
(see previous chapter). His intention was rather to persuade disillusioned center-right and center-left voters of the sincerity of Jobbik's
transformation into a more moderate nationalist force. As opposed
to Gyöngyöspata, where key members of the local elite felt that their
plan to strengthen cultural tourism was fundamentally threatened
by the surplus population, the elite in Devecser did not have a personal stake in castigating "Gypsies." Its representatives lived in relatively "clean" streets. Lomis did not present a threat to their careers
or income, and they had the means to send their children to study
in the schools of neighboring towns (and the universities of Budapest). This did not mean that they were not troubled by the prospect
of "Gypsyfication." But, while agreeing that this was a problem that
needed to be dealt with, they believed that Jobbik and its paramilitary allies had gone too far. Councillors, teachers, and entrepreneurs
I talked to several months after the blitz campaign still recalled being
ashamed of the transformation of their quiet little town into a space
where visceral hatred reigned, even if for one day only. By engaging
in physical violence, the far-right had soiled the town's reputation.
This elite view, as far as I could tell, was partially rooted in the inte-
riorization of what we could call the "imagined gaze of the civilized
West." This became clear to me after a discussion with teachers two
years following the August rally. A teacher who voiced her opinion
that the brutality of paramilitaries had been exaggerated by Jobbik's
local opponents was contradicted by a colleague who explained that
the men clad in black had violated a deeply rooted cultural code:
that of nonviolence, which constituted the barrier between Eastern
barbarity and Western civility. The six or seven other teachers present in the staff room were quick to espouse the latter view. One of
them recounted how embarrassed she had felt when she was asked

to explain the reasons for the rally to an official visitor from Austria. (Such allusions to "Western values" were tellingly missing from elite narratives in Gyöngyöspata.)

Thus, in order to expand its base, Jobbik had to persuade voters that Ferenczi could purify local politics without setting the town on fire. One of the ways the party sought to achieve this was to combine the by-then-familiar message of "radical change" with the reassuring vision of communal harmony. This was precisely why the party decided to turn its final campaign event into a family outing. Although the program also provided space for parading symbols of self-determination and self-defense (the Warriors of Attila, an association involved in the protection of Magyar cultural heritage, organized an archery training for local children), these were considerably toned down and blended with the display of local traditions and conservative values. Ferenczi invited two respectable local associations—the Autumn Light Pensioners' Club and an association regrouping local dog trainers—to perform at the event. This demonstration of commitment to communitarian ideals stood in stark contrast to earlier campaigns.

In this regard it is important to note that the blitz campaign of August 2012 was not the only event that shaped Jobbik's local image. Starting in 2009—when the local party chapter was created[7]—Jobbik held yearly commemorations of the "red terror" of 1919. Led by Ferenczi, whose grandfather had been among the five local victims of the Commune,[8] these demonstrations were attended by leading Jobbik politicians and uniformed members of the Hungarian Guard. Although the presence of paramilitaries irritated local Roma (who, based on the previous episodes in Northeastern Hungary, believed that their intention was to provoke them and divide the local community along ethnic lines), the main aim of these commemorations in my view was to discredit the Socialist Party by emphasizing the historic sins of the "antipatriotic left." Demonstrating commitment to communal peace and harmony was especially important in light of these antecedents.

In order to prove that it was serious about recasting itself into a party of unity, Jobbik needed to match its new rhetoric and image with new programmatic initiatives and new faces. Ferenczi's local program—carrying the slogan "Order, Livelihood, Requital: Radical Change for a Livable Town!"—foregrounded the creation of new jobs, the compensation of red mud victims for "secondary damages" and greater accountability in public administration. As I learned from Jobbik's local president and vice-president, these new elements were chosen with a view to diversifying the topics the party dealt with—which they saw as key for making a successful overture to new constituencies. After careful deliberation, the party also chose to stick to some of its old guns in order to preserve its appeal among more radical voters. This was manifested in Ferenczi's promise to re-store segregated tuition (or, as he called it, "positive segregation") in the local school and public security in the streets of the town. His program thereby blended elements of the "old" racist strategy with new postracial initiatives—without seeking to resolve the tension be-tween these. The same strategy prevailed with the party's local rep-resentatives. Jobbik did not drop Anikó, the victim of the "neighbor feud," who clearly represented the "old" face of the party. Ferenczi, however, managed to persuade a local councillor named György Kozma to join Jobbik in the summer of 2014. The latter had been one the founders of the moderate right-wing party (the Hungarian Dem-ocratic Forum) that dominated political life in the first parliamentary cycle (1990–1994) and had strong roots in Veszprém county.

I interviewed Kozma in the period when he was still hesitating to accept Jobbik's nomination to run for a position on the local council. He told me that his hesitation was rooted in a "discomfort with grand ideologies." When prompted to elaborate, he explained that although his family history "rooted him on the political right," the "violence of history" had made him suspicious of radical political projects. To give an example of what he meant, he told me that "the whites" had in 1919 executed his paternal grandfather's cousin, who had been a member of the Workers' Council in the town of Pápa. In an attempt to link these events to the present, he narrated how he had warned Ferenczi that the "Gypsy card" was an unjust and dangerous political tool that had attracted the wrong kind of people to the party. Label-ing the 2012 rally as a "rampage of football hooligans," he explained to me that intelligent people recognize that there are only problems with a criminal group within the Roma minority and that these prob-lems derive from irresponsible social policy, not "bad blood." When I asked him to explain Jobbik's attractiveness in the face of these short-comings, he highlighted two factors that made him consider joining.

The first was disillusionment with the project of liberal democratic transformation, of which he had been one of the local protagonists in the 1990s. He told me that the young people who participated in the founding of new political parties believed that they would be able to shape the social model Hungary would build in the postsocialist period. This was naïve because these people—himself included—did not see behind the facade of the democratic process where the in-

224 I The Revolt of the Provinces

visible hands of global capital had already dictated the key institutional arrangements to the country's new elite. All that was left to this elite, in his view, was the option of creating a clientelistic machinery, which allowed them to siphon off one part of the profits that escaped the country. "I believed in democracy, but it turned out that it was not about people's rule." This a posteriori assessment brought him close to Jobbik, which he presented as "the only party that talks honestly" about this problem. His second argument for joining was that he saw Jobbik as the only party that recognized that the Common Agricultural Policy pursued by the European Union is built on a quasi-clientelistic, perverse redistribution of capital from taxpayers to the largest landowners who dominate the agricultural sector. This mattered to him because in 1991 he decided to reclaim the lands that had been confiscated from his grandparents. His success as a self-made agricultural entrepreneur[9] earned him a solid reputation and a seat on the local council. As a former councillor, he had proven his ability to work across party lines for the common good.

Kozma's decision to accept Jobbik's nomination to the local council a few weeks after our discussion was a powerful blow to Fidesz. Jobbik had found a moderate and respectable candidate who had the pedigree to contest the party's characterization as inescapably brutish.

The last thing Jobbik needed was a symbol capable of condensing its new politics in a way that would maximize its appeal. The solution was provided by a member of the local council who was officially affiliated with Fidesz but privately sympathized with Jobbik. This councillor proposed that the municipality erect a monument to commemorate the victims of the two world wars. The construction of such memorials was no neutral affair in a town where the memory of 1919 was much more vivid than elsewhere and where the Second World War ended with the deportation of one tenth of the local population (see previous chapter). In 1943, the local council had already commissioned a monument to commemorate the victims of the First World War. The monument was decorated on its sides with representations of the mythic Turul bird, which had become the symbol of Hungarian supremacy in the Carpathian basin.[10] I learned from a local teacher that these plaques had been removed in the 1950s. Also, in 1959 the local council decided that the monument would henceforth be dedicated to the memory of the victims of the "white terror" of 1919.[11] In 1997, councillors decided to build a new statue to the victims of the two world wars on the town's main square. It was this monument that mayor Holczinger proposed to replace with a new one, based on the claim that there was a discrepancy between the aesthetic qualities of the "old" monument and the weight of the historic losses that the country suffered during the world wars. Although the local council set aside 800 thousand forints to cover construction costs, the money was used to cover more urgent expenses. The newly elected Fidesz majority, as noted above, had other priorities than the building of monuments in the first years of its reign.

In 2013, Councillor Zoltán Rosta—a petty entrepreneur who owned a food delivery business and a flower shop—dug up Holczinger's proposal and complemented it with the innocent suggestion that the new statue comprise a Turul bird with a view to establishing continuity with the first monument (the one erected in 1943). The councillor persuaded three young craftsmen to volunteer their services to the community. The latter came up with a visual design and submitted it to Mayor Toldi in early 2014. Although the submitted design carried the heading "monument to the victims of the two world wars," its visual elements resembled the close to two hundred Turul statues that have sprung up in the last decade all over the countryside. Although a few of these are also dedicated to the victims of the world wars, the overwhelming majority have a much narrower meaning. They commemorate the losses suffered by Hungary after the imposition of the "Trianon diktat." Anthropologist Margit Feischmidt highlighted the role of Trianon in the recent wave of memory politics initiated by the neonationalist right:

> Radical right-wing organizations' effort to construct novel lieux de memoire and a counter-hegemonic memory-politics . . . was centered on the resurrection of the Trianon-trauma through local commemorations of the anniversary of the Trianon Treaty, which had been banned under the state socialist period and continued to be neglected by left-liberal elites after the "change of regime." . . . This strategy was greatly helped by popular forms of memory-politics—ranging from the publication of semi-professional historical periodicals to the creation of historical memory sites. These played an important role in the rehabilitation of a historically loaded symbolic tool kit, which enabled Trianon to become the "mythical motor" . . . of Hungarian neo-nationalism. They achieved this by sidelining professional historiography and creating space for a historicizing identity politics. The latter was enacted by—typically young—activists associated with the Jobbik party and revisionist movements who began to organize commemorative events in local communities from the beginning of the past decade. (Feischmidt n.d.: 12)

According to Feischmidt, the popularity of the "Trianon-cult" is rooted in the widespread need for personal pride and collective self-esteem in communities that suffered material and symbolic injuries in the aftermath of the change of regime. My own research in a community that also recently suffered significant material, as well as symbolic, damages underpins this claim.

Jobbik's newly recruited candidate, György Kozma, was one of the main supporters of the Trianon memorial. He told me that the construction of Turul statues in the countryside is the best way to open the eyes of Hungarians who have been fooled by manipulative elites. It was, in fact, his son, a woodcarver by profession, who had volunteered to create the statue with the help of a blacksmith and a mason. Kozma's father, who still remembered the old monument of 1943, publicly voiced his joy to "see the Turul fly again over the ridges of the Carpathian homeland." The traditionally right-wing Kozma family was not alone in supporting the monument. A local teacher, who (having published several essays on the town's cultural history) is widely recognized as Devecser's cultural ambassador and renowned for his dedication to the social democratic cause, was also counted among prominent supporters. At the town hall meeting held on 7 July 2014, where Mayor Toldi announced the council's decision to support construction, the teacher voiced his hope that the monument would heal the wounds that plagued the local community. He praised the young craftsmen for playing such a constructive role in the rebuilding of the "fractured community." An older man seated in the audience responded to these eloquent words by declaring that those who wanted to heal the community should look for a way to "punish the lousy Gypsies," adding that the monument would surely be vandalized. Mayor Toldi quickly stepped into the fray by highlighting the council's plan to install CCTV cameras and arguing that Roma cannot be collectively blamed for the deterioration of public security.

Recognizing the power of the discourse and associated symbols, Viktor Orbán entrenched the commemoration of the "national tragedy" as a cornerstone of his government's memory-politics. The new law, whereby parliament declared the fourth of June the Day of National Cohesion (Act No. 45 of 2010) calls the Peace Treaty signed in 1920 "one of the greatest tragedies of Hungarian history" and emphasizes the "political, economic, legal, and psychological problems [that] remain unresolved to this day" (translation mine). According to Feischmidt, this is without doubt the most significant change in the public memory of Trianon and, in her view, part of a more general shift in the direction of an ethnic conception of Hungarian nationhood. She demonstrates this by highlighting a speech given by Prime Minister Orbán at the Ópusztaszer memorial (where one of

the memorials commemorating the "millenium"—see endnote 10—
had been erected in 1896). Viktor Orbán, alluding to the bird's role in
healing the Trianon-trauma, claimed that

> [the Turul] reminds us that every Hungarian is responsible for every other
> Hungarian. The Hungarian nation is a world nation because the boundaries
> of the country do not coincide with those of the nation. . . . This statue tells
> us that there is only one country, which is capable of uniting all Hungarians
> on both sides of the Trianon border into a single community." (quoted by
> Feischmidt n.d.: 5)

Refusing the "grassroots proposal" to place the bird on top of a
war memorial would therefore have raised uneasy questions about
the credibility of Fidesz's memory politics and also undermined the
party's claim of supporting popular initiatives. However, by bowing to the demand to build a Trianon memorial on the main square,
Mayor Toldi allowed Jobbik to demonstrate its influence over the
Fidesz-dominated council and to parade as the healer of communal
wounds.

Four months later, Ferenczi won the local election with 54.2 percent of the vote (against Toldi's 45.8 percent). It would, of course,
be erroneous to claim that giving green light to the construction of
the new memorial played a decisive role in this outcome. The fallout
of the industrial disaster, together with local Fidesz representatives'
arrogant and authoritarian style, played a much more significant
role in Ferenczi's victory. It is, however, fair to say that Jobbik's new
symbolic politics were instrumental in uniting a divided opposition.
By appropriating the Turul, Jobbik could simultaneously claim the
mantle of the "credible nationalist force" and rally enough orphaned
left-wing voters to beat the incumbent candidate. This was no trivial
feat given that Fidesz's national leaders had made abundantly clear
that central resources earmarked for regional development would be
withheld from towns that chose the wrong (political) colors.

Concluding Remarks

In this chapter, I showed how Jobbik refashioned its program, image, and symbols to better adapt to a rural environment where the
post-peasantry did not regain its former economic, cultural, and political clout after 1989 and where the project of social modernization
(framed in the collective imaginary as "Europeanization") had not
lost (all of) its appeal among blue-collar workers.

My description of the nomenklatura's demise recalls Wieviorka's analysis of the simultaneous decline of the French Communist Party and the rise of the far-right in municipal councils during the 1980s. Neoliberal reforms in both France and Hungary slowly but surely eroded the social networks that supported left-wing power blocs on the local level. My working-class informants recalled how the change of regime had destroyed social institutions, such as labor unions, that had played a key role in the reproduction of egalitarian ties and solidarities. The oral history interview I conducted with one of them revealed how expulsion from the nomenklatura engendered social dislocation and also confirmed that the victims of material and/or symbolic dispossession sought to redress their battered self-esteem through comparisons with a negatively valued reference group: "Gypsies." In Devecser, where the local economy weathered the change of regime better than in most other places, I found that such traumatic material and symbolic injuries were relatively rare in comparison to Gyöngyöspata. Adopting the repertoire of redemptive racism was, moreover, problematic, in an environment where local experience did not correspond to racist stereotypes, which had been abstracted from deprived environments where "class" overlapped with "ethnicity." It is also important to note that the local elite—keen on projecting a civilized image of the locality—had shunned demonstrations of crude racism and affirmed the possibility of peaceful coexistence between Roma and Magyars (while also taking care to stigmatize the marginalized surplus population). Because of this, frustrations generated first by wage stagnation and a harsh labor regime, then by the material damages and symbolic devaluation suffered after the red mud disaster, turned the local community against the left-liberal elite whose representatives had steered Hungary in the post-1989 period.

Local Fidesz representatives initially benefited from popular disgruntlement with the political left and successfully portrayed themselves as the spokespersons of the new anti-liberal consensus. The party's local and regional leaders also sought to suffocate the nomenklatura (through the reorientation of state-administered development funds) with a view to supporting Viktor Orbán's ambition of preserving Fidesz's dominance through the durable transformation of a bipolar party structure into a tripolar one (see chapters 3 and 4). This part of the strategy was thoroughly successful. By the time of my fieldwork, the center-left political-economic network (which had erstwhile demonstrated a high degree of cohesion) had collapsed—as evidenced by the left's inability to field a mayoral candidate in a previously left-leaning town at the municipal elections of 2014. But

Fidesz's mishandling of the long-term fallout of the red mud disaster, together with the perceived rapacity and arrogance of its local leaders, gradually undermined the ruling party's carefully crafted plebeian image. Popular demand for strong-handed leadership in the midst of a global economic storm and a pan-European political crisis (which the state's propaganda machine constantly kept on the political agenda) allowed Fidesz to retain its lead on both the national and local level at the parliamentary election of April 2014. But it was not enough to secure Mayor Toldi's reelection in October 2014.

In the last part of the chapter, I argued that, in the presence of popular grievances, symbolic interventions acquired a central role in local public life. Power-holders saw these as vehicles for uniting members of a damaged and divided community behind their power projects. While Margit Feischmidt (n.d.: 11) is right to claim that "Hungarian society turns to historical symbols in situations of crisis," we may add that distrust between townsmen and the lack of tangible local solidarities also played a role in the resurgence of memory as a central feature of local politics in Hungary. Feischmidt (n.d.: 11) was also right to claim that "when a new generation of politicians sets out to define its position within the Hungarian political arena, it . . . chooses historical symbols to achieve its goals." This is exactly what happened in Devecser, which Jobbik's national leaders had identified as a prime target in their quest to establish a strong presence in the Transdanubia region, where the party had struggled to make inroads in 2010.

My analysis of the grassroots effort to build a memorial to the "Trianon diktat" on the town's main square just before the municipal elections highlights Jobbik's skill in tapping into the Trianon discourse. The latter can be portrayed as a redemptive discourse that presents an alternative to "Gypsy-talk" in relatively deprived environments where Roma cannot be straightforwardly blamed for the plight of the "hard-working majority." My discussions with the discourse's main promoters showed that they saw it as an avenue for creating a popular countermovement uniting disaffected voters of all colors and stripes. While Gypsy-talk expresses discontentment with the unjust redistribution of material and symbolic rewards in a liberal polity, Trianon can be used to highlight the ways in which the new right-wing elite ravages the local (and, by extension, national) community.

While the need for personal pride and collective self-esteem was certainly pronounced in this particularly damaged and divided community, the symbol's ability to convey the desire for radical social change and combine this with an emphasis on community-building may have made it attractive to a broader spectrum of relatively de-prived rural communities. The Turul should, of course, be seen as but one element of an encompassing shift in Jobbik's political identity and strategy as part of an effort to transform the party into a main-stream nationalist force. My political ethnography of the last local election campaign showed that the success of this strategy depended on the one hand on the absence of credible left-wing opponents and the diminishment of the ruling Fidesz Party's plebeian credentials, and, on the other hand, on far-right politicians' ability to adopt a less confrontational vocabulary, incorporate new programmatic themes, enlist respectable spokespersons, and find a multivocal symbol that both reflected and fostered their ambition to recast Jobbik as the party of national unity. This strategy found confirmation not only in Devecser but also in the nearby town of Tapolca, where Jobbik first won the mayor's seat (in October 2014) and then won its first directly elected parliamentary seat at a by-election (held in the spring of 2015). Its advantages over the earlier racist extremist strategy became apparent in light of the setback that Jobbik suffered in Gyöngyöspata in October 2014 (see chapter 4).

Notes

1. In Gyöngyöspata, the Socialist Party (the successor of the Hungarian Socialist Work-ers' Party) received 3.3 percent of the vote at the parliamentary elections of 1990. Al-though the party improved its score at the next three elections (respectively obtaining 16.4 percent, 20.6 percent, and 36.9 percent of votes at the parliamentary elections of 1994, 1998, and 2002) the majority of local voters supported right-wing political par-ties throughout the liberal democratic period (1990–2010). Right-wing dominance was thus achieved early compared to other localities. It is also worth noting that radical right-wing forces—the Independent Smallholders' Party (FKGP), the Party of Hun-garian Life and Justice (MIÉP), and, later, Jobbik—received above-average support in Gyöngyöspata in the period.
2. Imre Kovách (2012) argued that political parties began to play a dominant role in the distribution of regional development resources (which made up 6 to 8 percent of GDP) after 1996. Because of this, local political life became increasingly dependent on emergent political-economic networks: "multiparty democracy and the market econ-omy did not foster the emergence of local forms of autonomy; political institutions and parties organized on the national level exercised decisive influence on local and regional politics" (Kovách 2012: 115, translation mine).
3. In the 2006–2010 period, only one significant development took place in Devecser with the help of the state: the reconstruction of the local elementary school.
4. I know from other members of the nomenklatura that the period between 1990 and 1994 had been difficult to survive. As one key member told me, "We did not attend

any social events—weddings, parties, even funerals—in this period. We felt isolated." Such a feeling of isolation called for strategies and rituals of self-purification.

5. Source: Gábor Ferenczi's Facebook page, posted on 6 April 2014, translation mine.

6. The mayor had been invited to attend Jobbik's closing campaign meeting during the parliamentary election campaign of 2014. In his address, Jobbik's celebrity mayor gave a condensed outline of his take on the "Gypsy issue." A far-right activist filmed the whole event and posted it on YouTube: Balázs Bognár, "Lakossági Fórum Devecser," YouTube video, published 5 April 2014, accessed 19 September 2014, https://www.youtube.com/watch?v=mtSPIwwOP88.

7. Jobbik's local chapter was formed on 7 August 2009. I was not able to collect reliable information on membership or activities between 2009 and 2012. It is, however, very likely that there were only a handful of active members until the party leadership decided to stage a blitz campaign in Devecser on 5 August 2012. (Jobbik opened its local office in February 2012, and the local chapter launched its Facebook page in March 2013.) The vice-president of the local chapter told me that the number of members hovered around fifty to sixty (in October 2014).

8. On 5 May 1919, news reached Devecser that the Communist-led government had fallen in Budapest. The local population—led by a local teacher, two peasant landowners, and a blacksmith—declared the victory of the "counterrevolution." The news turned out to be a false alarm, and Devecser was occupied by red guards sent from the nearby towns of Pápa and Veszprém. Three "whites" (counterrevolutionaries) were hanged on the main square, and two collaborators were shot in the local cemetery. Following the Commune's collapse (on 1 August 1919), twenty-three "reds" were shot in a forest near Devecser in reprisal.

9. Kozma did not belong to the same social group as the winemakers and touristic entrepreneurs I met in Gyöngyöspata. As an agricultural entrepreneur, he was—as he himself recognized—powerfully dependent on the European market and European subsidies allocated by the Hungarian state. This differentiated him from the entrepreneurs I met in Gyöngyöspata, who tried to distance their agricultural and touristic ventures from both international markets and the state (but remained dependent on local communal relations, as well as the village's reputation). In contrast to them, Kozma's livelihood was in no way threatened by the local presence of Roma, and this probably played a role in his rejection of political anti-Gypsyism.

10. Although the Turul is considered to have played an important role in premodern Magyar mythology, it acquired a political meaning after representatives of the Hungarian state decided to build seven large statues to celebrate "1,000 years of Hungarian statehood" in 1896. These monuments were built in the following localities: Devin, Nitra, Мукачеве, Brasov, Земун, Pannonhalma, and Pusztaszer. Four of these localities—Devin, Мукачеве, Земун, and Brasov—were situated on the borders of the Hungarian state. Three of the monuments—the ones in Nitra, Мукачеве, and Земун—exhibited the Turul. The placement of these statues on the country's "hard" borders (with Russia, Romania, and Serbia) warrants the claim that they symbolized the historic Hungarian state's strength and integrity in the face of foreign enemies. After the loss of large swaths of territory as a result of the Trianon treaty (1920), the meaning of the Turul was slightly modified. The bird became a symbol of Hungarian irredentism—that is, of the desire to reconquer lost territories.

11. See note 8 for a very brief description of the "white terror." The monument in question was torn down in 2013.

EPILOGUE

In the conclusion of his magisterial overview of interwar fascism, Michael Mann (2004) ventured on the minefield of historical prognosis. Pondering the prospects of the rebirth of fascism on the continent's eastern periphery, he wrote,

> Authoritarianism is not openly proclaimed in Eastern Europe; it is denied. Nor is it likely to be openly proclaimed as long as regimes desire entry into the EU or NATO or as long as they desire resources from the EU, the United States, or international financial institutions. Around the fringes of the continent, the EU requirement of democracy for entry has remained influential. Though in a sense we once again have "two Europes," the western part is now larger, it combines Social, Christian, and liberal democracy, and it is now dominant over the other Europe of dual states. Hungary, closer to the European Union, does not seem set to recreate its interwar trajectory . . . . It is possible to envisage (e.g., in Russia) a future radical rightist movement that would combine elements of nationalism and communism to proudly proclaim extreme nation-statism. This would be much closer to fascism—though almost certainly without the name. (Mann 2004: 371)

At the moment of Mann's writing, this appeared to be a sensible prediction. Western Europe was led by political leaders (among them, Helmut Kohl and Jacques Chirac) who embodied the two traditions—French social modernism and German Catholic social doctrine—that "defined a science, political economy, and metaphysics of solidarity that established a very specific architecture for the European project" (Holmes 2000: 25). It appeared plausible that Eastern enlargement would go hand-in-hand with greater cooperation and convergence within the process of building an ever closer union. In the course of the last couple of years, that prospect has been cast into serious doubt by the advance of nationalist forces of the right (but also the left) who reject a further weakening of the nation-state. With the rise of politicians like Marine Le Pen in France, Viktor Orbán in Hungary, Jarosław Kaczyński in Poland, and Heinz-Christian Strache in Austria, "nation-statism" (even if it is not of the extreme variety) is back in town. While we may still see the building of a political union in the core of the EU (where the establishment has thus far retained the upper hand over nationalists), countries like Hungary and Poland—led by authoritarian right-wing politicians—now appear more likely to opt out of that process even if it goes forward.

To be sure, what we are witnessing is certainly not the rebirth of classic fascism. Mann (2004: 370) was right to highlight that while contemporary rightist populists are ardently nationalist and support ethnic cleansing "in the relative mild form of orderly and either voluntary or compulsory deportations," they have no paramilitaries and are only in the vaguest sense making claims to "'transcend' class conflict." To this we may add that electoral competition can help tame extremist political movements (my analysis of Jobbik's effort to expand its constituency by breaking with extreme racist rhetoric and mobilization clearly points in this direction). Nevertheless, the transformation of European politics in the last decade—which we could summarize as the breakdown of the liberal democratic consensus on the periphery and its erosion in the core of the EU—compel us to revisit Mann's claim that liberal democracy is proof against the new rise of exclusionary nationalism (if not fascism). Episodes such as Brexit and the rise of anti-immigrant sentiment (alongside xenophobic national-populist parties) show that the vicissitudes of neoliberal globalization (first and foremost the both real and imagined betrayal of "natives" on behalf of self-serving cosmopolitan elites) creates demand for an exclusionary politics that promises a politics of "reverse affirmative action" (see Zaslove 2004). The cases of Hungary and Poland (see Koczanowicz 2016), moreover, reveal that once in power, national-populist rightists may seek to transform the state in an authoritarian and illiberal direction in order to consolidate power and to project themselves as the defenders of the good, worthy native folk. The influence exercised by national-populists on European societies now extends well beyond the policy domain and the "immigration issue." It touches on questions of identity (such as our conception of what it means to be European) and on the state-citizen nexus (such as what citizens of different standing can expect from the political community). This book has offered insights into the microfoundations of this anti-egalitarian dynamic, highlighting the role that economic dispossession, the loss of cultural pride, and, perhaps most importantly, political abandonment and orphanage played in the generation of popular insecurities and racism.[1]

I would like to close this analysis by offering some tentative thoughts on two important—and in some way ineluctable—questions that impose themselves at this critical conjuncture in relation to reemergent right-wing populist movements: (1) Why is it that national-populism has achieved dominance in Eastern Europe and—for now—only here? (2) Can Hungary's pioneering System of National Cooperation serve as a model for European nationalists? While the material I have presented does not allow me to straightforwardly answer these questions, I believe that my analysis does offer some cues for thinking productively about them.

I begin by returning briefly to Mann's claim on the implausible return of European fascism. Mann (2004: 354–355) put forward the following argument to explain the success of interwar fascism on the European periphery and to argue against its revival in the contemporary period:

> Let me emphasize: Fascism was not a crisis of liberalism, since institutionalized liberalism weathered all these crises without serious destabilization. Fascism was a product of a sudden, half-baked attempt at liberalization amid social crises. (Mann 2004: 354–355)

> I have argued in this book that institutionalized liberal democracy is proof against fascism. Postwar Western Europe has entrenched liberal democracy far too strongly for much support to be offered to neofascists or rightist populists on grounds more general than the immigration issue. Western Europe has successfully institutionalized the class conflict that helped to generate classic fascism. It is capable of institutionalizing most forms of conflict, just as it did in northwestern Europe in the interwar period. (ibid.: 370)

While in the first quote Mann makes a nod to Polányi and Gramsci (by referencing "social crises"), his argument about the resilience of liberal democracy relies primarily on the concept of the "dual state" (which has nothing to do with my concept of the Dual State; see chapter 4). The crux of the argument is that Eastern European states have differed from Western European ones throughout the course of the twentieth century and that this qualitative difference is only likely to disappear thanks to the rise of Western European hegemony in the post-1989 period. The key difference between the Eastern and Western state is that the former exhibited a duality: it was "half liberal democratic, half authoritarian. Since old regime conservatives usually controlled the executive part of the state, including its military and police, they had the option of using repression to solve crisis—reducing or overturning the power of the state's parliamentary half" (Mann 2004: 354). Building on this logic, Mann (2004: 370) then goes on to formulate the prognosis that Western liberal democratic influence will overpower "lingering authoritarianism" in the East.

Kalb and Halmai (2011) compiled an edited volume to highlight the untenability of such Orientalizing styles of argumentation in scholarship on Eastern Europe and to forge a path toward the elaboration of a common framework for analyzing neonationalist movements in different corners of the continent. One of the key lessons to take away from the volume is the need to lay legacy approaches to rest. The New Right cannot be treated as a legacy of state socialism or previous periods, for that matter (cf. Minkenberg 2009). Although its symbols hark back to the interwar period (see my discussion of the Turul in chapter 6), its politics are thoroughly modern in substance. My own analysis adds more meat to these bones by showing that those who have lost out on or feel threatened by the kind of "progressive neoliberalism" that underpinned the project of Europeanization are prone to support movements that promise a return to the bounded solidarities of the national community. They seek to overturn the emancipation of minorities and oppose the obligatory redistribution of refugees, which ruling elites of the center validate by referring to the principles of solidarity and reciprocity. Such talk fails to convince the masses who have not benefited from EU monetary transfers or the opening of borders. Due to their negative experience with Europeanization, they see "open society" as an avenue for foreign powers to exercise undue influence over their country and community. Due to the historic memory of ethnonationalist division as a source of weakness and conflict, they see "multiculturalism" as a source of danger. In the face of these threats, they demand the restoration of order and "natural" hierarchies, lend their support to authoritarian leaders who promise to check negative foreign influences, and are agnostic about the dismantlement of democratic institutions, not only because they deem them distant but also because they see them as the symbols of an ineffective pluralism. This, in my view, explains better than legacy approaches the return of nation-statism and its recent rise to positions of power in Hungary (but also Poland[2]).

In this book I have deliberately eschewed the label "fascist" to characterize the politics pursued by Hungary's new right-wing elite. One of the reasons I am reluctant to use this label[3] is that, similarly to Mann, I find important to highlight differences between interwar fascists and contemporary anti-liberal rightist insurrectionists. The latter do not strive for a new beginning and do not promise to create a new society, even less to forge a New Man (see Griffin 1991; Rydgren

2007). While national-populist politicians (e.g., Jean-Marie Le Pen)—whom I am wont to characterize as "right-wing sovereignists"[4] in order to emphasize the centrality of the state for their politics—abundantly criticize the collusion of "big business" and "big brother" and strive to repatriate some economic powers from the supranational back to the national level, they stop short of calling for a systemic overhaul of economic institutions. While they castigate the left for failing to protect workers from the excesses of neoliberal capitalism, they themselves do not seek to fundamentally alter the relations between labor and capital. Furthermore, the current political conjuncture in which the mainstream right is increasingly prone to adopting certain radical rightist proposals, but at the same time striving to safeguard liberal democratic rule, resembles less fascism and more the effort to obstruct its advance on behalf of the propertied classes.

My second reason for not "talking fascism" is that I consider the SNC a rather successful work of bricolage that answers to diverse influences, pressures, expectations, and needs. While Fidesz's politics of governmental power bears the marks of a neofascist surge[5] (which destroyed the remaining credibility of the left and compelled the main right-wing party to adopt elements of an emergent ethnoracial common sense), it also comprises neoliberal and conservative elements.[6] The SNC is, moreover, still very much a work in progress.

Since this book has been primarily concerned with explaining political racism and its impact on party politics and the state, I have not dealt with developments that occurred after 2014 when the moral panic on "Gypsy criminality" subsided. Although the country's legal-institutional framework has not changed since then, the politics pursued by the ruling party have confounded the expectations of commentators who believed that Orbán would moderate his rhetoric, tactics, and policies if he won the election in 2014. What we have seen is actually the opposite of this. Fidesz, building on Orientalist logic and clichés, capitalized on the European "refugee crisis" to instigate a moral panic against Hungary's inundation by "uncivilized Muslim hordes" (see Thorleifsson 2017), echoing rightist politicians in Western Europe and prompting the latter to recognize him (and the fence he built on Hungary's southern border) as the savior of Christian Europe (see Brubaker 2017). Most recently, he turned on investor and philanthropist George Soros, whom Hungarian state media has denounced as the man behind the European Commission's plan to distribute refugees inside the European Union and accused of sponsoring left-wing troublemakers in Hungarian civil society. These moves are designed to create a situation of permanent symbolic warfare, which

Fidesz strategists deem necessary to keep mobilized their relatively small but diehard support base (which has become much more rural in character since the elections of 2014). This has gone hand in hand with an effort to discredit the work of "political NGOs" and, following Putin's lead, to seal them off from sources of foreign funding. These developments highlight the regime's Schmittian foundations. While the friend/foe distinction is primarily used to conjure a sense of threat in the face of external enemies seeking to spread their negative influence in Hungary, it has also animated witch hunts targeting the nation's internal enemies—left-liberal philosophers, NGOs, civic activists, etc.—who are said to be financed and controlled from abroad. Thus, in the last three years, the tendency to exclude the "surplus population" from key rights and resources has been compounded by the tendency to redefine politics as the exclusive domain of the ruling majority. This means that liberal rule is now also being eroded within "homogeneous society." While it is still not clear how far the ruling party will push this dynamic, the process of de-democratization has clearly advanced and "consolidation" no longer appears as a plausible prospect.

At this point I would like to make a short but important comment about Mann's claim on the successful institutionalization of the class conflict as a key cause of the nonreturn of fascism. This book has offered evidence that appears to at least partially contradict this claim, at least in Hungary's case. Parts of the analysis I present in chapters 2, 3, and 4 demonstrate that the rise of the radical right was partly triggered by the left-liberal elite's misguided effort to pursue desegregation in parallel to neoliberal reforms, more particularly moves toward the privatization of healthcare and higher education. And, in chapter 4, I advanced the claim that after winning the elections in 2010, Fidesz reorganized the state to the advantage of the bourgeoisie and (to a lesser extent) the lower middle class, to the detriment of the most vulnerable segments of society and at the price of economic modernization.[7] Although economic elites in liberal democracies have always been in a position to exercise influence over a putatively class-neutral state, in Hungary's post-2010 "illiberal democracy," the ruling class has fully captured the state in a way as to avoid having to make any substantial concessions to vulnerable social groups. Together, these parts of the argument suggest that the rightward shift of the electorate had at least partially to do with the liberal democratic regime's *in*ability to institutionalize the "class conflict." The problem can be formulated with more clarity thusly: the crux of the issue is that in Hungary the social reproduction of middle strata is also dependent on institutionalized promises of solidarity, and the state does not have sufficient capacity to simultaneously foster middle-class formation, pursue poverty alleviation, and promote a degree of social mobility in the lower rungs of society. This situation creates powerful incentives for a kind of anti-egalitarian politics that limits access to resources for "unproductive" or "unworthy" segments of the population.

It would take a separate analysis to probe if the rise of national-populism in other Eastern European countries (such as Poland, Slovakia, the Czech Republic, and Romania) was driven by mechanisms and processes that are similar to the ones I highlighted. What is certain, however, is that Fidesz's politics of electoral support and governmental power has offered a workable model for consolidating bourgeois class power on the EU's periphery at a time of generalized crisis. The SNC offers a template for forging a new right-wing sovereignist consensus built on the pillars of neoliberalism "lite" (the classic program combined with economic protectionism and significant material concessions to the middle class), anti-egalitarian populism (which allows governments to claim to be advancing the interests of the hardworking majority), exclusionary nationalism (which offers a potent tool for valorizing the downwardly mobile and insecure lower middle class), and authoritarianism (which chokes dissent and undermines pluralism). It represents a fundamental shift in the modality through which a rightist ruling bloc attempts to construct hegemony on the European periphery—one that is clearly tilted toward the coercive rather than consensual end of the spectrum but leaves the outer forms of democratic class rule intact. It keeps peripheral economies integrated in global (mostly German-controlled) production chains by playing on the periphery's developmentalist illusions, but it does so in a different way than the previous left-liberal elite had envisioned it. Instead of emphasizing the need to liberate a backward society by dropping its retrograde cultural baggage and embracing Western values, it works through compensatory strategies that obscure the periphery's subordination to the center and emphasize the putative superiority of what Viktor Orbán dubbed the "work-based society." What remain unresolved are the byproducts and consequences of this coarser brand of class rule: weak growth, the persistence of deep social divisions, and the lack of meaningful prospects at the bottom of society. But Hungary's ruling elite has shown that it is possible to successfully defuse simmering tensions through authoritarian measures, top-down orchestrated moral panics and the pursuit of politics as a battle for nonnegotiable principles.[8]

The model's apparent stability exercises a certain appeal in a region that suffers from a series of intertwined chronic crises: negative migration flows, dependence on external capital flows, and dwindling geopolitical significance (somewhat counterbalanced by the reemergence of Russian expansionism). Fidesz's successful symbolic "freedom struggle" against "Brussels bureaucrats" and the lack of substantive critique on behalf of the German foreign policy establishment have also underscored the viability of the SNC.[9] Since 2015, Orbán can also count on the protection of Jarosław Kaczyński, the leader of Poland's Law and Justice Party (PiS), who has adopted his anti-Brussels, anti-refugee, and anti-liberal rhetoric while also moving to curb the power of the judiciary and shrink the space available for the civic and political opposition. Together, the Polish and Hungarian governments have the power to shield each other from critique formulated by the European Commission and to prevent the imposition of penalties on their countries.

We have yet to see a radical rightist party lead a government in Western Europe, yet we are already seeing concessions being made to right-wing sovereignists. This process could in principle also lead to the erosion of the liberal state and prepare the terrain for its dualization along the lines of national belonging. Yet, I believe that there are good reasons to believe that Hungary's model will not prove attractive for Western Europe, where the preservation of (some) geopolitical influence depends on continuous technological advancement, where social mobility remains a politically consequential (although increasingly illusory) social ideal, and where minorities wield significant political power.

The main difference between East and West appears to me to be twofold. It primarily has to do with the state's more restrained fiscal capacities in the East. As noted above, in countries like Hungary, the state does not have sufficient fiscal capacity to simultaneously foster the three functions mentioned above. In the core, the welfare state is still strong enough to perform these functions.[10] This may partially explain why Northwestern Europe is the only region in Europe where the radical right-wing parties failed to make further inroads into the electorate in the aftermath of the "great recession" (see Kriesi and Pappas 2015). In the core, right-wing sovereignists must compete with left-wing sovereignist rivals who agree with their critique of globalist elites but confront their effort to internally divide "the people" along ethnic or quasi-racial lines. This kind of politics, together with the remnants of classic social democracy, can still credibly claim to support the needy irrespective of status or merit through the taxation of the rich. Left-wing sovereignists and classic social democrats—and this is the second main difference I see between East and West—are much weaker in the East, not only due to the constraints imposed by diminished fiscal capacities, but also due to social democrats' previous espousal of neoliberalism (the consequences of which this book has sought to capture) in several countries. These two factors together explain, in my view better than anything else, why radical right-wing parties have managed to become the dominant political force in Hungary and Poland but not in Western European countries. It is in these countries—and these countries only—where both the propertied classes and workers have sided with right-wing sovereignists in the hope of securing a degree of protection from external and internal competitors (transnational capital and unworthy "others"). In the European core, the propertied classes continue to support the (neo) liberal status quo, primarily because they still have enough self-confidence to make it on their own.

Notes

1. This echoes Wendy Brown's recent analysis of the Trump phenomenon in which she situates "dethroned Whiteness" at the intersection of four decades of neoliberal policies and practices (that have gutted wages, benefits, pensions, job security, infrastructure, and easy access to higher education among the working and lower middle classes); three decades of financialization that exacerbated the redistribution upwards of wealth; globalization that transformed both the economies and the populations of the global North, draining them of large-scale industry and of Whiteness; and a perceived liberal political trajectory understood by Trump-voters to have demoted them and promoted historically excluded groups: women, racial and sexual minorities, the disabled, new immigrants, and, above all, African Americans. See Brown 2017.
2. See Koczanowicz's (2016) and Krastev's (2016) essays on the rise of the PiS party in Poland.
3. Commentators writing on Hungary have used the following labels to describe the regime: "illiberal" (Csillag and Szelényi 2015), "post-Fascist" (Tamás 2013), "authoritarian" (Müller 2016), "hybrid regime" (Bozóki and Hegedűs 2017), "leader democracy" (Körösényi 2015), and "mafia state" (Magyar 2016).
4. Friedman (2015) uses the term sovereignism in a similar semantic context and sense but reserves it for left-wing populists.
5. I myself would qualify the early Jobbik (2006–2012) as a neofascist movement based on the five criteria proposed by Mann (2004): (a) the party adhered to an aggressive nationalist ideology that presented the struggle against internal and external enemies as key for ensuring national survival. This was manifested in the slogan "Hungary belongs to Hungarians." Its nationalism was infused with racism (anti-Semitism, later anti-Gypsyism). The movement also exhibited minimal tolerance of cultural diversity within the national community. (b) It was certainly statist. Although its leaders were

ambivalent about the kind of state they would seek to build if they attained positions of power, in public speeches party leaders distanced Jobbik from "fascism," "communism," and "democracy." (c) Did it seek to transcend class conflict? Not really. While advocating for protectionist economic policies, the party has stopped short of advocating for a "third way" between capitalism and socialism. However, as Mann (2004: 15) himself recognized, fascists who attained positions of power always leaned "toward the established order and toward capitalism." This book has provided evidence in support of the claim that Jobbik sought to cleanse the nation of enemies (d) and that its paramilitary proxies deployed "orderly violence" to achieve this end (e). Thus, the only characteristic that the early Jobbik did not fully satisfy is that of transcending class conflict (c). The early Jobbik can therefore be portrayed in Mann's (2004: 13) terms as a neo-Fascist movement pursuing a "cleansing nation-statism through paramilitarism." In the previous chapter, I have shown that in the last couple of years party leaders have distanced themselves from paramilitarism in an effort to de-radicalize the party and attract more moderate voters.

6. For the neoliberal elements, see chapter 4. Enyedi (2015) highlights the conservative aspects of Fidesz's politics.

7. The Hungarian state, as chapters 1 and 2 have highlighted, operates one of the most ineffective and unequal systems of public services in the EU.

8. See Avishai Margalit's (2010) distinction between "politics as religion" and "politics as economics."

9. The Merkel-Macron tandem may strive to rein in Eastern European right-wing sovereignists by realizing the plan of a two-speed Europe. The rationale is that restricting development funds for Eurozone economies and encouraging investment in the core will create incentives for renitent countries like Poland and Hungary to join "first speed countries," to be led by Germany and France and policed by the Commission (to observe unified fiscal regulations and liberal democratic values enshrined in the Treaty on the European Union). It is, however, far from certain that this effort (if it goes forward) will succeed.

10. It is also worth noting that today's political conjuncture in Western Europe is shaped by a "vertical" class struggle waged by financial capital and allied political elites "from above" with a view to guaranteeing financial interests and the safety of the middle classes in the center through the imposition of austerity by the means of administrative mechanisms (see, for instance, the "European semester" mechanism overseen by the European Commission) and coercion (see the "debt deals" that have been imposed on Greece by the troika). While creditors have the ability to advance their interests without politicizing their claims, the demos' ability to advance its own interests through elections, referenda, or other democratic means are extremely limited (as became clear not only in Greece but in other countries where the banks were bailed out with taxpayers' money without citizens' approval).

REFERENCES

Archival Sources

Census data from 1990, 2000, and 2010 published by the Central Statistical Office (KSH).
Criminal statistics provided (upon personal request) by the Interior Ministry (BM).
Documentary film titled *Jobbik Nemzedék* (Jobbik generation), produced by Jobbik, Movement for a Better Hungary, 2010 (*Jobbik*).
Election results from 1939, 1945, 1990, 1994, 1998, 2002, 2004, 2006, 2010, and 2014 published by the National Electoral Bureau (NVI).
Employment statistics provided (upon personal request) by the National Employment Service (NFSZ).
Settlement data base provided (upon personal request) by the National Development Agency (NFÜ).

Newspapers

Devecseri Újság (1994–2010)
Új Devecseri Újság (2010–2014)

Books and Articles

Albert, G. 2012. "Anti-Gypsyism and the Extreme-Right in the Czech Republic: 2008–2011." In M. Stewart, ed., *The Gypsy "Menace,"* 137–165. London: Hurst.
Back, L., and J. Solomos. 2000. "Introduction: Theorising Race and Racism." In L. Back and J. Solomos, eds., *Theories of Race and Racism: A Reader*, 1–28. London: Routledge.
Baiocchi, G., and B.T. Connor. 2008. "The Ethnos in the Polis: Political Ethnography as a Mode of Inquiry." *Sociology Compass* 2 (1): 139–155.
Bale, T., C. Green-Pedersen, A. Krouwel, K.R. Luther, and N. Sitter. 2010. "If You Can't Beat Them, Join Them? Explaining Social Democratic Responses to the Challenge from the Populist Radical Right in Western Europe." *Political Studies* 58: 410–426.
Balibar, E. 1991. "Racism and Nationalism." In E. Balibar and I. Wallerstein, eds., *Race, Nation, Class: Ambiguous Identities*, 37–68. London: Verso.
Barker, M. 1981. *The New Racism.* London: Junction Books.
Bataille, G. 1993. "The Psychological Structure of Fascism." In A. Stoekl, ed., *Visions of Excess: Selected Writings, 1927–1939*, 137–160. Minneapolis, MI: University of Minnesota Press.

Benjamin, W. 1999. *The Arcades Project.* Cambridge, MA: Belknap Press.

Berezin, M. 2009. *Illiberal Politics in Neoliberal Times: Culture, Security and Populism in the New Europe.* Cambridge: Cambridge University Press.

Bernáth, G., and V. Messing. 1998. "'Vágóképként, csak némában'—Romák a magyarországi médiában" [As a cutaway, only in silent mode – Roma in the Hungarian media] Report published by the Office for Ethnic and National Minorities (Nemzeti és Etnikai Kisebbségi Hivatal). Retrieved 20 December 2017 from http://mek.niif.hu/00100/001 44/00144.pdf.

———. 2012. "Szélre tolva: Kutatási zárójelentés a roma közösségek többségi médiaképéről, 2011" [Pushed to the margins: Research report on the representation of Roma in the media]. Manuscript. Retrieved 24 April 2013 from http://www.amenca.hu/uploads/pdf/szelre_tolva.pdf.

Binder, M. 2009. "'A cigányok' vagy a 'cigánykérdés' története'? Áttekintés a magyarországi cigányok történeti kutatásairól" [The history of "the Gypsies" or of the "Gypsy question"? An overview of research on the history of Gypsies in Hungary]. *Regio* 20 (4): 35–59.

———. 2010. "A cigányokról alkotott történeti kép változása a rendszerváltás tükrében Szlovákiában és Magyarországon" [The transformation of the image of Gypsies through the lens of regime change in Slovakia and Hungary]. In T. Krausz, M. Mitrovits, and C. Zahorán, eds., *Rendszerváltás és történelem: Tanulmányok a kelet-európai átalakulásról,* 313–343. Budapest: L'Harmattan.

Bíró, A. 2013. "The Price of Roma Integration." In W. Guy, ed., *From Victimhood to Citizenship: The Path of Roma Integration,* 11–40. Budapest: Kossuth.

Bíró, N.A., and D. Róna. 2011a. "Tudatos radikalizmus: A Jobbik útja a Parlamentbe, 2003–2010" [Rational radicalism: Jobbik's road to parliament, 2003–2010]. In A. Lánczi, ed., *Nemzet és radikalizmus,* 242–283. Budapest: Századvég.

———. 2011b. "Rational Radicalism: Jobbik's Road to Parliament, 2003–2010." Paper presented at the workshop "On the Moderation and Immoderation of Religious Political Parties in Democratic Politics," University of Eichstätt, Germany, 16–18 June 2011.

Blaskó, Z. and K. Fazekas, eds. 2016. The Hungarian Labour Market—2016. Institute of Economics, Centre for Economic and Regional Studies, Hungarian Academy of Sciences Budapest. Retrieved 16 December 2016 from http://www.econ.core.hu/file/down load/HLM2016/TheHungarianLabourMarket_2016_onefile.pdf.

Bourdieu, P. 1984. *Distinction: A Social Critique of the Judgement of Taste.* Cambridge, MA: Harvard University Press.

———. 1994. "Rethinking the State: On the Genesis and Structure of the Bureaucratic Field." *Sociological Theory* 12 (1): 1–19.

Bozóki, A., and D. Hegedűs. 2017. "An Externally Constrained Hybrid Regime: Hungary in the European Union." Paper presented at the annual conference of the Council of European Studies, Glasgow, UK, 12–14 July.

Brown, W. 2017. "Apocalyptic Populism." *Eurozine,* 30 August. Retrieved 12 October 2017 from http://www.eurozine.com/apocalyptic-populism/.

Brubaker, R. 2017. "Between Nationalism and Civilizationism: The European Populist Moment in Comparative Perspective." *Ethnic and Racial Studies* 40 (8): 1191–1226.

Bryceson, D.F. 1996. "Deagrarianization and Rural Employment in Sub-Saharan Africa: A Sectoral Perspective." *World Development* 24 (1): 97–111.

———. 2000. "Disappearing Peasantries? Rural Labor Redundancy in the Neo-Liberal Era and Beyond." In D. Bryceson, K. Kay, and J. Mooij, eds., *Disappearing Peasantries? Rural Labour in Africa, Asia and Latin America,* 299–326. London: Intermediate Technology Publications.

Burawoy, M. 1998. "The Extended Case Method." *Sociological Theory* 16 (1): 4–33.

———. 2000. *Global Ethnography: Forces, Connections, and Imaginations in a Postmodern World.* Berkeley, CA: University of California Press.

———. 2003. "For a Sociological Marxism: The Complementary Convergence of Antonio Gramsci and Karl Polanyi." *Politics & Society* 31 (2): 193–261.

Burawoy, M., and K. Verdery, eds. 1999. *Uncertain Transition: Ethnographies of Change in the Postsocialist World.* Lanham, MD: Rowman and Littlefield.

Bustikova, L. 2014. "Revenge of the Radical Right." *Comparative Political Studies* 47 (12): 1738–1765.

Cohen, S. 2002. *Folk Devils and Moral Panics: The Creation of the Mods and Rockers.* Third edition. London: Routledge.

Collier, R.B., and D. Collier. 1991. *Shaping the Political Arena: Critical Junctures, the Labor Movement, and Regime Dynamics in Latin America.* Princeton, NJ: Princeton University Press.

Csalog, Z. 1984. "A cigánykérdés Magyarországon 1980 előtt" [The Gypsy question in Hungary before 1980]. *Magyar füzetek* (Párizs), 14–15: 93–137.

Csepeli, G. 2011. *Új tekintélyelvűség a mai Magyarországon: társadalmi csoportok hierarchiájának látásviszonyai* [New authoritarianism in contemporary Hungary: representations of social hierarchy]. Budapest: Apeiron.

Cseres-Gergely, Z., G. Kátay, and B. Szörfi. 2013. "The Hungarian Labour Market in 2011–2012." In K. Fazekas, P. Benczúr, and Á. Telegdy, eds., *The Hungarian Labour Market, 2012,* 18–40. Budapest: MTA.

Csillag, T., and I. Szelényi. 2015. "Drifting from Liberal Democracy: Neo-Conservative Ideology of Managed Illiberal Democratic Capitalism in Post-Communist Europe." *Intersections* 1 (1): 18–48.

della Porta, D., and M. Diani. 2006. *Social Movements: An Introduction.* Malden, MA: Blackwell Publishing.

Despres, L.A., ed. 1975. *Ethnicity and Resource Competition in Plural Societies.* The Hague: Mouton.

Domokos, V. 2010. "Szegény- és cigánytelepek, városi szegregátumok területi elhelyezkedésének és infrastrukturális állapotának elemzése különböző (közoktatási, egészségügyi, településfejlesztési) adatforrások egybevetésével" [Analysis of the geographic location and infrastructural conditions of poor and Gypsy settlements, and urban slums based on educational, health and regional development statistics]. Study commissioned by the National Development Agency.

Dupcsik, C. 2009. *A magyarországi cigányság története: Történelem a cigánykutatások tükrében, 1890–2008* [The History of Gypsies in Hungary: History in the mirror of Gypsy studies]. Budapest: Osiris.

Durst, J. 2015. "Juggling with Debts, Moneylenders and Local Petty Monarchs: Banking the Unbanked in 'Shanty-Villages' in Hungary." *Review of Sociology* 25 (4): 30–57.

European Commission. 2016. Commission staff working document. Country Report Hungary 2016. Retrieved 22 December 2017 from https://ec.europa.eu/info/sites/info/files/cr_hungary_2016_en.pdf.

Efremova, G. 2012. "Integralist Narratives and Redemptive Anti-Gypsy Politics in Bulgaria." In M. Stewart, ed., *The Gypsy "Menace,"* 43–66. London: Hurst.

Enyedi, Z. 2015. "Plebeians, Citoyens and Aristocrats or Where is the Bottom of Bottom-up?" In H. Kriesi and T.S. Pappas, eds., *European Populism in the Shadow of the Great Recession,* 235–250. Colchester, UK: Harbour House.

Enyedi, Z., and K. Benoit. 2011. "Kritikus választás 2010: A magyar pártrendszer átrendeződése a bal–jobb dimenzióban" [Critical election 2010: The transformation of the Hungarian party system along the left-right axis]. In Z. Enyedi, A. Szabó, and R. Tardos, eds., *Új képlet. Választások Magyarországon, 2010,* 17–42. Budapest: Demokrácia Kutatások Magyar Központja Alapítvány.

Essed, P. 1991. *Understanding Everyday Racism: An Interdisciplinary Theory.* Newbury Park, CA: Sage.

Éber, M.Á. 2014. "A centrum hitele" [The center's loan]. *Fordulat* 21: 64–86.

Éber, M.Á., Á. Gagyi, T. Gerőcs, C. Jelinek, and A. Pinkasz. 2014. "1989." *Fordulat* 21: 10–63.

Feischmidt, M. 2008. "A boldogulók identitásküzdelmei" [The identity struggles of strivers]. *Beszélő* 13 (11). Retrieved 9 January 2013 from http://beszelo.c3.hu/cikkek/a-boldogulok-identitas%C2%ADkuezdelmei.

———. 2012. "Kényszerek és illeszkedések: Gazdasági és szimbolikus stratégiák aprófalvakban élő romák életében" [Constraints and matches: Economic and symbolic strategies among Roma residing in peripheral villages]. *Szociológiai Szemle* 22 (2): 54–84.

———. n.d. "Memory-Politics and Path Dependency: Trianon as Mytho-moteur of Hungarian Neo-Nationalism." Manuscript provided by author based on personal request.

Feischmidt, M., R. Glózer, Z. Ilyés, V. Kasznár, and I. Zakariás. 2014. *Nemzet a mindennapokban: Az újnacionalizmus populáris kultúrája* [The nation in everyday life: The popular culture of neo-nationalism]. Budapest: L'Harmattan.

Feischmidt, M. and G. Pulay. 2017. "'Rocking the Nation': The Popular Culture of Neo-Nationalism." *Nations and Nationalism* 23 (2): 309–326

Feischmidt, M., and K. Szombati. 2012. *Gyöngyöspata 2011. The Laboratory of the Hungarian Far-Right: A Case Study of Political Mobilization and Interethnic Conflict*. Budapest: Ökopolisz Foundation. Retrieved 22 December 2012 from http://pdc.ceu.hu/archive/00006555/01/Ecopolis_Gyongyospata2012.pdf.

———. 2013a. "Cigányellenesség és szélsőjobboldali politika a magyar társadalomban. Gyöngyöspata – és a hozzá vezető út" [Anti-Gypsyism and far-right politics in Hungarian society. Gyöngyöspata – and the path leading there]. *Esély* 1: 74–100.

———. 2013b. "Rechtsradikale Mobilisierung und interetnische Konflikte: Fallanalyse Gyöngyöspata 2011" [Radical right-wing mobilization and interethnic conflict: The case of Gyöngyöspata 2011]. In Enikő Dácz, ed., *Minderheitenfragen in Ungarn und in den Nachbarnländern im 20. und 21. Jahrhundert*, 293–304. Baden-Baden: Nomos.

———. 2014. "A hagyományok visszatérése, a cigányellenesség és a jobboldali radikalizmus" [The return of traditions, anti-Gypsyism and the radical right]. In M. Feischmidt, ed., *Nemzet a mindennapokban: Az újnacionalizmus populáris kultúrája*, 371–400. Budapest: L'Harmattan.

———. 2016. "Understanding the Rise of the Far Right from a Local Perspective: Structural and Cultural Conditions of Ethno-Traditionalist Inclusion and Racial Exclusion in Rural Hungary." *Identities* 24 (3): 313–331. doi: 10.1080/1070289X.2016.1142445.

Feischmidt, M., K. Szombati, and P. Szuhay. 2014. "Collective Criminalization of the Roma in Central and Eastern Europe: Social Causes, Circumstances, Consequences." In S. Body-Gendrot, M. Hough, K. Kerezsi, R. Levy, and S. Snacken, eds., *The Routledge Handbook of European Criminology*, 168–187. London: Routledge.

Földes, G. 1995. *Az eladósodás politikatörténete, 1957–1986* [The political history of debt, 1957–1986]. Budapest: Maecenas.

Fraenkel, E. 1969. *The Dual State: A Contribution to the Theory of Dictatorship*. New York: Octagon Books.

Friedländer, S. 1997. *Nazi Germany and the Jews*. Vol. 1, *The Years of Persecution, 1933–1939*. New York: Harper Collins.

Friedman, J. 2004. "Champagne Liberals and the New Dangerous Classes: Reconfigurations of Class, Identity, and Cultural Production in the Contemporary Global System." In A. Chun, ed., *Globalization: Critical Issues*, 49–82. New York: Berghahn Books.

———. 2010. "Diametric to Concentric Dualism: Cosmopolitan Elites, Cosmopolitan Intellectuals and the Re-configuration of the State." In A. Hobart and B. Kapferer, eds., *Contesting the State: The Dynamics of Resistance and Control*, 261–90. Wantage: Sean Kingston.

———. 2015. "Global Systemic Crisis, Class and Its Representations." In J.G. Carrier and K. Don, eds., *Anthropologies of Class: Power, Practice and Inequality*, 183–199. Cambridge: Cambridge University Press.

Goldberg, D.T. 2002. "Racial States." In D.T. Goldberg and J. Solomos, eds., *A Companion to Racial and Ethnic Studies*, 233–258. Maiden, MA: Blackwell.

Greskovits, B. 2017. "Rebuilding the Hungarian Right through Civil Organization and Contention: The Civic Circles Movement." EUI Working Paper, RCAS 2017/37. Florence: Robert Schuman Centre for Advanced Studies. Retrieved 20 December 2017 from http://cadmus.eui.eu/bitstream/handle/1814/47245/RSCAS_2017_37.pdf?sequence=1.

Greskovits, B., and D. Bohle. 2012. *Capitalist Diversity on Europe's Periphery.* Ithaca, NY: Cornell University Press.

Griffin R. 1991. *The Nature of Fascism.* London: Routledge.

György, E. 2009. "A 'Nyócker' – egy városnegyed, mint reprezentációs eszköz" [The "Eighth" – a district as representational tool]. *Regio* 20 (4): 119–134.

Habermas, J. 1974. "The Public Sphere: An Encyclopedia Article." *New German Critique* 3: 49–55.

Hall, S. 1978. "Racism and Reaction." In Commission for Racial Equality, ed., *Five Views of Multi-Racial Britain*, 23–35. London: Commission for Racial Equality.

———. 1983. "The Great Moving Right Show." In S. Hall and M. Jacques, eds., *The Politics of Thatcherism*, 19–39. London: Lawrence and Wishart.

———. 1985. "Authoritarian Populism: A Reply to Jessop et al." *New Left Review* 151: 115–122.

Hall, S., C. Critcher, T. Jefferson, J. Clarke, and B. Roberts. 1978. *Policing the Crisis: Mugging, the State, and Law and Order.* London: Macmillan.

Halmai, G. 2011. "(Dis)possessed by the Spectre of Socialism: Nationalist Mobilization in 'Transitional' Hungary." In D. Kalb and G. Halmai, eds., *Headlines of Nation, Subtexts of Class*, 113–141. New York: Berghahn Books.

Hamburger, K. 2000. "Liszt könyvének magyarországi fogadtatása. Első rész, 1859–1861" [On the Hungarian Reception of Liszt's Book. Part One, 1859–1861]. *Muzsika* 43 (12): 20–25.

Handelman, D. 2005. "Microhistorical Anthropology: Toward a Prospective Perspective." In D. Kalb and H. Tak, eds., *Critical Junctions: Anthropology and History beyond the Cultural Turn*, 29–52. New York: Berghahn Books.

Hann, C. 2013. "Still an Awkward Class: Central European Post-Peasants at Home and Abroad in the Era of Neoliberalism." *Praktyka Teoretyczna* 3 (9): 177–198.

Harcsa, I. 2003 "Paraszttalanítás – egy fogalom születése" [De-peasantization – the birth of a concept]. *Századvég* 8 (29): 77–85.

Harvey, D. 2005. "Notes towards a Theory of Uneven Geographical Development." In *Spaces of Neoliberalization: Towards a Theory of Uneven Geographical Development. Hettner-Lecture 2004 with David Harvey*, 55–92. Stuttgart: Franz Steiner Verlag.

Havas, G., I. Kemény, and I. Liskó. 2002. *Roma gyerekek az általános iskolában* [Gypsy children in the primary school]. Budapest: Új Mandátum.

Havas, G., and I. Liskó. 2005. *Szegregáció a roma tanulók általános iskolai oktatásában* [Segregation of Roma students in primary schools]. Budapest: Felsőoktatási Kutatóintézet. Retrieved 29 September 2015 from http://ofi.hu/sites/default/files/attachments/266_lis kocigaltiskszegreg.pdf.

Hervik, P. 2011. *The Annoying Difference: The Emergence of Danish Neonationalism, Neoracism and Populism in the Post-1989 World.* New York: Berghahn Books.

Hirschman, A.O. 1970. *Exit, Voice, and Loyalty: Responses to Decline in Firms, Organizations, and States.* Cambridge, MA: Harvard University Press.

Hirt, S.A. 2012. *Iron Curtains: Gates, Suburbs and Privatization of Space in the Post-Socialist City.* Hoboken, NJ: Wiley and Sons.

Holmes, D. 1989. *Cultural Disenchantments: Worker Peasantries in Northeast Italy.* Princeton, NJ: Princeton University Press.

———. 2000. *Integral Europe: Fast-Capitalism, Multiculturalism, Neofascism.* Princeton, NJ: Princeton University Press.

Horváth, K., and C. Kovai. 2010. "A cigány-magyar különbségtétel alakulása egy északmagyarországi faluban" [The evolution of the Gypsy-Magyar distinction in a village in Northern Hungary]. *anBlokk* 4: 28–31.

Howarth, A. 2012. "Discursive Intersections of Newspapers and Policy Elites: A Case Study of Genetically Modified Food in Britain, 1996–2000." Dissertation defended at the London School of Economics. Retrieved 21 July 2015 from http://etheses.lse.ac.uk/388/1/Howarth_Discursive%20intersections%20.pdf.

Huszár, Á. 2011. "Társadalmi rétegződés és az egyenlőtlenségek igazolása: Sérülékeny csoportok a magyar társadalomban" [Social stratification and the justification of inequalities: Vulnerable groups in Hungarian society]. *Szociológiai Szemle* 21 (3): 107–124.

Jessop, B., K. Bonnett, S. Bromley, and T. Ling. 1984. "Authoritarian Populism, Two Nations, and Thatcherism." *New Left Review* 147: 32–60.

———. 1985. "Authoritarian Populism, Two Nations, and Thatcherism." *New Left Review* 151: 87–101.

Johnson, H. 2004. "Subsistence and Control: The Persistence of the Peasantry in the Developing World." *Undercurrent* 1 (1): 55–65.

Juhász, A. 2010. "A 'cigánybűnözés', mint az igazság szimbóluma" ["Gypsy criminality" as the symbol of truth]. *anBlokk* 1 (4): 12–19.

Kalb, D. 1997. *Expanding Class: Power and Everyday Politics in Industrial Communities, The Netherlands, 1850–1950.* Durham, NC: Duke University Press.

———. 2005. "'Bare Legs Like Ice': Recasting Class for Local/Global Inquiry." In D. Kalb and H. Tak, eds., *Critical Junctions: Anthropology and History Beyond the Cultural Turn,* 109–136. New York: Berghahn Books.

———. 2009. "Conversations with a Polish Populist: Tracing Hidden Histories of Globalization, Class, and Dispossession in Postsocialism (and Beyond)." *American Ethnologist* 36 (2): 207–223.

———. 2011. "Headlines of Nation, Subtexts of Class: Working Class Populism and the Return of the Repressed in Neoliberal Europe." In D. Kalb and G. Halmai, eds., *Headlines of Nation, Subtexts of Class,* 1–36. New York: Berghahn Books.

———. 2015a. "Introduction: Class and the New Anthropological Holism." In J.G. Carrier and K. Don, eds., *Anthropologies of Class: Power, Practice and Inequality,* 1–27. Cambridge: Cambridge University Press.

———. 2015b. "Theory from the East? Double Polarizations versus Democratic Transitions." *Baltic Worlds* 3–4: 17–29.

Kalb, D., and G. Halmai, eds. 2011. "Headlines of Nation, Subtexts of Class: Working Class Populism and the Return of the Repressed in Neoliberal Europe." New York: Berghahn Books.

Kalb, D., and H. Tak, eds. 2005. *Critical Junctions: Anthropology and History beyond the Cultural Turn.* New York: Berghahn Books.

Karácsony, G., and D. Róna. 2010. "A Jobbik titka: A szélsőjobb magyarországi megerősödésének lehetséges okairól" [Jobbik's secret: On the possible causes of the rise of the far-right in Hungary]. *Politikatudományi Szemle* 19 (1): 31–66.

Karsai, L. 1992. *A cigánykérdés Magyarországon, 1919–1945: Út a cigány holocausthoz* [The Gypsy question in Hungary, 1919–1945: The road to the Gypsy Holocaust]. Budapest: Cserépfalvi.

Kemény, I. 1972. "A magyar munkásosztály rétegződése" [The stratification of the Hungarian working class]. *Szociológia* 1 (1): 36–48.

———. 1976. "A magyarországi cigányok helyzete" [The predicament of Gypsies in Hungary]. In I. Kemény, K. Rupp, Z. Csalog, G. Havas, *Beszámoló a magyarországi cigányok helyzetével foglalkozó, 1971-ben végzett kutatásról,* 7–67. Budapest: MTA, Szociológiai Kutató Intézet.

Kemény, I., B. Janky, and G. Lengyel. 2004. *A magyarországi cigányság 1971–2003* [The Gypsies in Hungary 1971–2003]. Budapest: Gondolat. Retrieved 21 June 2012 from http://www.kallaierno.hu/data/files/magyarorszagi_ciganysag_1971_2003_A+MalB.pdf.

Kenrick, D., and G. Puxon. 1995. *Gypsies under the Swastika.* Hatfield, Hertfordshire: University of Hertfordshire Press.

Kertesi, G. 2005. *A társadalom peremén: Romák a munkaerőpiacon és az iskolában* [On the margins of society: Roma on the labor market and in school]. Budapest: Osiris.

Kertesi, G., and G. Kézdi. 2011. "Roma Employment in Hungary after the Post-Communist Transition." *Economics of Transition* 19 (3): 563–610.

Koczanowicz, L. 2016. "The Polish Case: Community and Democracy under the PiS." *New Left Review* 102 (Nov/Dec): 77–96.

Koopmans, R. 2004. "Movement and the Media: Selection Processes and Evolutionary Dynamics in the Public Sphere." *Theory and Society* 33 (3): 367–391.

Kotics, J. 2011. "Újjáéledő paraszti mentalitás? A reprivatizáció hatása a gazdálkodói stratégiákra és habitusokra" [The rebirth of peasant mentality? The impact of reprivatization on agricultural producers' strategies and habitus]. In G. Vargyas, ed., *Párbeszéd a hagyománnyal: A néprajzi kutatás múltja és jelene,* 167–181. Budapest: L'Harmattan.

Kovai, C. 2013. "Azok a 'boldog békeidők.' A magyarság mint ideál, a cigányság mint analógia" [Those "happy peace times." Hungarianness as ideal, Gypsyness as analogy]. In P. Szuhay, ed., *Távolodó világaink. A cigány-magyar együttélés változatai,* 41–55. Budapest: Magyar Néprajzi Társaság.

Kovách, I. 1997. "Posztszocializmus és polgárosodás" [Postsocialism and embourgeoisement]. *Szociológiai Szemle* 4: 19-47.

———. 2003. "A magyar társadalom 'paraszttalanítása' – európai összehasonlításban" [The "depeasantization" of Hungarian society – from a European perspective]. *Századvég* 2: 44–66.

———. 2012. *A vidék az ezredfordulón: A jelenkori magyar vidéki társadalom szerkezeti és hatalmi változásai* [The countryside at the turn of the millennium: Structural and power shifts in contemporary Hungary]. Budapest: Argumentum.

Kovács, A., ed. 1999. "A Modern Antiszemitizmus" [Modern anti-Semitism]. Budapest: Új Mandátum.

Kovács, É., Z. Vidra, and T. Virág, eds. 2013. *Kint és bent: lokalitás és etnicitás a peremvidékeken* [Outside and inside: locality and ethnicity on the margins]. Budapest: L'Harmattan.

Kovács, J. M., ed. 2000. *A zárva várt Nyugat: kulturális globalizáció Magyarországon* [Waiting in closure: cultural globalization in Hungary]. Budapest: Sík Kiadó.

Kovács, T. 2006. *Az egyéni mezőgazdálkodás és területi különbségei Magyarországon* [Individual agricultural production and its regional differences in Hungary]. Doctoral dissertation. Retrieved 3 September 2013 from http://real-d.mtak.hu/156/1/Kovacs_Terez.pdf.

Körösényi, A. 2015. "A magyar demokrácia három szakasza és az Orbán-rezsim" [The three periods of Hungarian democracy and the Orbán regime]. In A. Körösényi, ed., *A magyar politikai rendszer – negyedszázad után,* 401–422. Budapest: Osiris – MTA TK.

Központi Statisztikai Hivatal [KSH]. 2008. *A mezőgazdaság fejlettségének regionális különbségei: Változások a rendszerváltozástól napjainkig* [Regional differences in agricultural development: Changes since regime change]. Budapest: KSH. Retrieved 25 September 2013 from http://mek.oszk.hu/06800/06880/06880.pdf.

Krastev, I. 2016. "The Unraveling of the Post-1989 Order." *Journal of Democracy* 27 (4): 88–98.

Krekó P., A. Juhász, and C. Molnár. 2011. "A szélsőjobboldal iránti társadalmi kereslet növekedése Magyarországon" [Increasing demand for extreme right-wing politics in Hungary]. *Politikatudományi Szemle* 2: 53–79.

Kriesi, H., and T.S. Pappas, eds. 2015. *European Populism in the Shadow of the Great Recession.* Colchester: Harbour House.

Kuper, A. 1999. *Culture: The Anthropologists' Account.* Cambridge, MA: Harvard University Press.

Laclau, E. 2005. "Populism: What's in a Name?" In F. Panizza, ed., *Populism and the Mirror of Democracy,* 32–49. London: Verso.

Ladányi, J., and A. Horváth. 2000. "Székesfehérvár üzenetei" [Székesfehérvár's messages]. In Á. Horváth, E. Landau, and J. Szalai, eds., *Cigánynak születni: Tanulmányok, dokumentumok,* 109–113. Budapest: Új Mandátum.

Ladányi, J., and I. Szelényi. 1997. "Ki a cigány?" [Who is the Gypsy?]. *Kritika* 12: 3–6. Retrieved 2 October 2013 from http://www.adatbank.transindex.ro/html/cim_pdf443.pdf.

———. 1998. "Az etnikai besorolás objektivitásáról" [On the objectivity of ethnic categorization]. *Kritika* 3: 33–35.

———. 2006. *Patterns of Exclusion: Constructing Gypsy Ethnicity and the Making of an Underclass in Transitional Societies of Europe.* Boulder, CO: East European Monographs.

Langmuir, G.I. 1990. *Toward a Definition of Antisemitism.* Berkeley, CA: University of California Press.

Lengyel, G. 2006. "Cigánytelepek egykor és ma" [Gypsy settlements yesterday and today]. In E. Kállai and K. Törzsök, eds., *Átszervezések kora: Cigánynak lenni Magyarországon. Jelentés 2002–2006,* 56–91. Budapest: Európai Összehasonlító Kisebbségkutatások Közalapítvány. Retrieved 21 October 2013 from http://www.kallaierno.hu/data/files/atszervezesek_kora_ciganynak_lenni_magyarorszagon_jelentes_2002_2006_T2Z+8g.pdf.

Linksz, A. 1990. *Harc a harmadik halállal* [Struggle with the third death]. Budapest: Magvető.

Lipset, S. M. 1988. *Political Man: The Social Bases of Politics.* Baltimore, MD: Johns Hopkins University Press.

Magyar, B. 2016. *Post-Communist Mafia State: The Case of Hungary.* Budapest: CEU Press.

Mahoney, J. 2000. "Path Dependence in Historical Sociology." *Theory and Society* 29: 507–548.

Mahoney. J., and D. Schensul. 2006. "Historical Context and Path Dependence." In R.E. Goodin and C. Tilly, eds., *Oxford Handbook of Contextual Political Analysis,* 454–471. Oxford: Oxford University Press.

Makovicky, N. 2013. "'Work pays': Slovak Neoliberalism as 'Authoritarian Populism.'" *Focaal* 67: 77–90.

Mann, M. 2004. *Fascists.* Cambridge: Cambridge University Press.

Margalit, A. 2010. *On Compromise and Rotten Compromises.* Princeton, NJ: Princeton University Press.

Márkus, I. 1973. "Az utóparasztság arcképéhez" [A contribution to the portrait of the post-peasantry]. *Szociológia* 2 (1): 56–67.

McAdam, D., S. Tarrow, and C. Tilly. 2001. *Dynamics of Contention.* Cambridge: Cambridge University Press.

Melegh, A. 2003. "From Reality to Twilight Zones: Transition of Discourses and the Collapse of State Socialism." *Regio* 1: 170–186.

Mendras, H. 1970. *The Vanishing Peasant: Innovation and Change in French Agriculture.* London: MIT Press.

Miles, R. 1982. *Racism and Migrant Labour: A Critical Text.* London: Routledge.

———. 1993. *Racism after "Race Relations."* London: Routledge.

Miles, R., and M. Brown. 2003. *Racism.* London: Routledge.

Minkenberg, M. 2000. "The Renewal of the Radical Right: Between Modernity and Antimodernity." *Government and Opposition* 35 (2): 170–188.

———. 2009. "Leninist Beneficiaries? Pre-1989 Legacies and the Radical Right in Post-1989 Central and Eastern Europe. Some Introductory Observations." *Communist and Post-Communist Studies* 42 (4): 445–458.

Minkenberg, M., and B. Pytlas. 2013. "The Radical Right in Central and Eastern Europe: Class Politics in Classless Societies?" In J. Rydgren, ed., *Class Politics and the Radical Right*, 206–223. London: Routledge.

Mintz, S.W. 1986. *Sweetness and Power: The Place of Sugar in Modern History.* New York: Penguin Books.

Molnár, Á. 2005. "Kényszervállalkozások és előrelendülés: A mezőgazdasági kisüzemek helyzete a rendszerváltás után Kiskanizsán" [Involuntary entrepreneurs and progress: The predicament of agricultural small enterprises in Kiskanizsa after regime change]. In G. Schwarz, Z. Szarvas, M. Szilágyi eds., *Utóparaszti hagyományok és modernizációs törekvések a magyar vidéken*, 127–138. Budapest: MTA.

Munk, V. 2013. "Roma sztárok médiareprezentációja Magyarországon" [The representation of Roma celebrities in the Hungarian media]. Ph.D. dissertation defended at Eötvös Loránd University. Retrieved 16 March 2013 from http://doktori.btk.elte.hu/phil/munkveronika/diss.pdf.

Müller, J.-W. 2016. "The Problem with 'Illiberal Democracy.'" *Social Europe*, 27 January. Retrieved 9 January 2017 from https://www.socialeurope.eu/the-problem-with-illiberal-democracy.

Nagy, P. 2007. "Cigány csoportok és az együttélési modellek változásai a Kárpát-medencében a 15–20. században" [The transformations of Gypsy groups and models of coexistence in the Carpathian Basin between the 15th and 20th century]. Paper presented at the seventeenth annual conference of history teachers, Budapest, Hungary. Retrieved 13 February 2016 from http://kisebbsegkutato.tk.mta.hu/uploads/files/olvasoszoba/romaszovegtar/Cigany_csoportok_es_az_egyuttelesi_modellek.pdf.

Omi, M., and H. Winant. 2015. *Racial Formation in the United States.* New York: Routledge.

Picker, G. 2014. "Rethinking Ethnographic Comparison: Two Cities, Five Years, One Ethnographer." *Journal of Contemporary Ethnography* (Online first, 19 August). doi: 10.1177/0891241614548105.

Plasser, F., and P.A. Ulram. 2003. "Striking a Responsive Chord: Mass Media and Right-Wing Populism in Austria." In G.S. Mazzoleni, J. Stewart, and B. Horsfield, eds., *The Media and Neo-Populism: A Contemporary Comparative Analysis*, 21–43. Westport, CT: Praeger.

Polanyi, K. 2001. *The Great Transformation: The Political and Economic Origins of Our Time.* Boston, MA: Beacon Press.

Pomogyi, L. 1995. *Cigánykérdés és cigányügyi igazgatás a polgári Magyarországon* [The Gypsy question and the administration of Gypsy affairs in the bourgeois era]. Budapest: Osiris.

Prónai, C. 2008. "Kulturális antropológia és cigánykutatás" [Cultural anthropology and Gypsy studies]. *Kultúra és közösség* 12 (2): 43–49.

Purcsi, B. G. 2001. "Fekete személyi igazolvány és munkatábor: Kísérlet a cigány-kérdés 'megoldására' az ötvenes évek Magyarországán" [Black identity cards and work camps: Attempts to "solve" the Gypsy question in the fifties]. *Beszélő* 6 (6): 26–37. Retrieved 24 October 2015 from http://beszelo.c3.hu/cikkek/fekete-szemelyi-igazolvany-es-munkatabor.

Rebel, H. 2010. *When Women Held the Dragon's Tongue: And Other Essays in Historical Anthropology.* New York: Berghahn Books.

Róna, D. 2015. "Jobbik-jelenség: A Jobbik Magyarországért Mozgalom népszerűségének okai" [The Jobbik phenomenon: The causes of the Movement for a Better Hungary's popularity]. Dissertation defended at Corvinus University, Budapest, Hungary.

Rürup, R. 1987. "Die 'Judenfrage' der bürgerlichen Gesellschaft und die Entstehung des modernen Antisemitismus" [The "Jewish question" of bourgeois society and the emergence of modern anti-Semitism]. In *Emanzipation und Antisemitismus: Studien zur "Judenfrage" der bürgerlichen Gesellschaft*, 93–119. Frankfurt: Taschenbuch Verlag.

Rydgren, J. 2007. "The Sociology of the Radical Right." *Annual Review of Sociology* 33 (1): 241–262.

Sahlins, M. 2005. "Structural Work: How Microhistories Become Macrohistories and Vice Versa." *Anthropological Theory* 5 (1): 5–30.

Sághy, E. 2008. "Romapolitika Magyarországon az 1950–1960-as évek fordulóján" [Roma policy in Hungary in the 1950–1960 period]. *Múltunk* 1: 273–308.

Scheiring, G. 2016. "Sustaining Democracy in the Era of Dependent Financialization: Karl Polanyi's Perspectives on the Politics of Finance." *Intersections* 2 (2): 84–103.

Sewell, W.H. 2005. *Logics of History: Social Theory and Social Transformation.* Chicago, IL: University of Chicago Press.

Sider, G.M. 1986. *Culture and Class in Anthropology and History: A Newfoundland Illustration.* Cambridge: Cambridge University Press.

Sider, G.M., and G. Smith, eds. 1997. *Between History and Histories: The Making of Silences and Commemorations.* Toronto: University of Toronto Press.

Smith, D.N. 1996. "The Social Construction of Enemies: Jews and the Representation of Evil." *Sociological Theory* 14 (3): 204–240.

Solt, O. 1998. *Méltóságot mindenkinek: összegyűjtött írások. I. kötet* [Dignity for all: selected writings. Volume I]. Budapest: Beszélő.

Stavrakakis, Y. 2004. "Antinomies of Formalism: Laclau's Theory of Populism and the Lessons from Religious Populism in Greece." *Journal of Political Ideologies* 9 (3): 253–267.

Stewart, M. 1997. *The Time of the Gypsies.* Boulder, CO: Westview Press.

———. 2002. "Deprivation, the Roma and the 'Underclass.'" In C.M. Hann, ed., *Postsocialism: Ideas, Ideologies and Practices in Europe and Asia,* 133–156. London: Routledge.

———, ed. 2012. *The Gypsy "Menace": Populism and the New Anti-Gypsy Politics.* London: Hurst.

———. 2013. "Roma and Gypsy 'Ethnicity' as a Subject of Anthropological Inquiry." *Annual Review of Anthropology* 42: 415–432.

Stolcke, V. 1995. "Talking Culture: New Boundaries, New Rhetorics of Exclusion in Europe." *Current Anthropology* 36 (1): 1–24.

Stone, J. 1995. "Race, Ethnicity, and the Weberian Legacy." *American Behavioral Scientist* 38 (3): 391–406.

Szabó, I. 2013. "Between Polarization and Statism: Effects of the Crisis on Collective Bargaining Processes and Outcomes in Hungary." *Transfer* 19 (2): 205–215.

Szalai, J. 2000. "Az elismerés politikája és a 'cigánykérdés': A többségi-kisebbségi viszony néhány jelenkori problémájáról" [The politics of recognition and the "Gypsy question": On certain contemporary problems of the majority-minority relationships]. In Á. Horváth, E. Landau, and J. Szalai, eds., *Cigánynak születni. Tanulmányok, dokumentumok,* 531–571. Budapest: Új Mandátum.

———. 2002. "A társadalmi kirekesztődés egyes kérdései az ezredforduló Magyarországán" [Certain questions on social exclusion in Hungary after the millennium]. *Szociológiai Szemle* 4: 34–50.

———. 2005. "Poverty and the Traps of Postcommunist Welfare Reforms in Hungary: A Fourth World of Welfare Capitalism on the Rise?" Paper presented at the Annual Conference of RC19, ISA "Retheorizing Welfare States: Restructuring States, Restructuring Analysis," Northwestern University, Chicago, IL.

———. 2007. *Nincs két ország? Társadalmi küzdelmek az állami (túl)elosztásért a rendszerváltás utáni Magyarországon* [There aren't two countries? Social struggles for state (over)redistribution after the regime change in Hungary]. Budapest: Osiris.

Szelényi, I. 1992. *Harmadik út? Polgárosodás a vidéki Magyarországon* [Third way? Embourgeoisement in rural Hungary]. Budapest: Akadémiai Kiadó.

Szikra, D. 2014. "Democracy and Welfare in Hard Times: The Social Policy of the Orbán Government in Hungary between 2010 and 2014." *Journal of European Social Policy* (Online first). doi: 10.1177/0958928714545446.

Szívós, P. 2014. "A magyar háztartások jövedelme és fogyasztása nemzetközi összehasonlításban: felzárkózás vagy leszakadás?" [The income and consumption of Hungarian households in international comparison: catching up or falling back?]. In T. Kolosi and I.G. Tóth, eds., *Társadalmi riport, 2014*, 51–62. Budapest: Tárki. Retrieved 31 October 2016 from http://www.tarki.hu/adatbank-h/kutjel/pdf/b324.pdf.

Szívós, P. and I.G. Tóth. 2015. "Jól nézünk ki (…?!) Háztartások helyzete a válság után" [Looking good (…?!) The situation of households after the crisis]. Tárki monitor report, 2014. Budapest: Tárki. Retrieved 2 November 2016 from http://www.tarki.hu/hu/research/hm/monitor2014_teljes.pdf.

Szombati, K. 2011. "A részvétel problémája az akciókutatásban: a mezőcsáti fejlesztőmunka tanulságai" [The problem of participation in action research: lessons from community development in the Mezőcsát microregion]. In G. Pataki and A. Vári, eds., *Részvétel – akció – kutatás: magyarországi tapasztalatok a részvételi-, akció- és kooperatív kutatásokból*, 52–83. Budapest: MTA.

Szuhay, P., ed. 1998. *Cigány-kép, Roma-kép: A néprajzi Múzeum "Romák Közép- és Kelet-Európában" című nemzetközi kiállításának képeskönyve* [Gypsy-image, Roma-image: illustrated book of the international exhibition "Roma in Central and Eastern Europe" organized by the Hungarian Museum of Ethnography]. Budapest: Néprajzi Múzeum.

———. 2003. "'Ez egy eredeti cigányélet': Ozorai és tamási szintó cigányok" ["This is an original Gypsy life": The Sinti of Ozora and Tamási]. *Beszélő* 8 (5). Retrieved 8 September 2014, http://beszelo.c3.hu/cikkek/%E2%80%9Eez-egy-eredeti-ciganyelet%E2%80%9D.

———. 2012. "Az 1992-es 'etnikai háború'" [The 1992 "ethnic war" (of Kétegyháza)]. In *Sosemlesz Cigányország*, 26–49. Budapest: Osiris.

Taguieff, P.A. 1988. *La force du préjugé. Essai sur le racisme et ses doubles* [The strength of prejudice. Essay on racism and its doubles]. Paris: La Découverte.

Tamanoi, M. 1983. "Reconsidering the Concept of Post-Peasantry: The Transformation of the Masoveria System in Old Catalonia." *Ethnology* 22 (4): 295–305.

Tamás, G.M. 2000. "On Post-Fascism: The Degradation of Universal Citizenship." *Boston Review* (Summer). Retrieved 7 September 2010 from http://bostonreview.net/world/g-m-tam%C3%A1s-post-fascism.

———. 2013. "Once More on Post-Fascism." Lecture held on 15 March in Zagreb. Retrieved 16 September 2015 from http://eszmelet.hu/g-m-tamas-once-more-on-post-fascism-2/.

Tambiah, S. 1996. *Leveling Crowds: Ethnonationalist Conflicts and Collective Violence in South Asia*. Berkeley, CA: University of California Press.

Tarrow, S. 1998. *Power in Movement: Social Movements and Contentious Politics*. Cambridge: Cambridge University Press.

Thorleifsson, C. 2017. "Disposable Strangers: Far-Right Securitisation of Forced Migration in Hungary." *Social Anthropology* 25 (3): 318–334. doi:10.1111/1469-8676.12420.

Tilly, C. 1976. *The Vendée*. Cambridge, MA: Harvard University Press.

———. 2001. "Relational Origins of Inequality." *Anthropological Theory* 1 (3): 355–372.

———. 2008. "Why and How History Matters." In R.E. Goodin and C. Tilly, eds., *The Oxford Handbook of Contextual Political Analysis*, 417–437. Oxford: Oxford University Press.

Tóth, A. 2012. "The New Hungarian Labour Code: Background, Conflicts, Compromises." Working paper. Budapest: Friedrich Ebert Foundation. Retrieved 24 October 2015 from http://www.fesbp.hu/common/pdf/Nachrichten_aus_Ungarn_june_2012.pdf.

Tóth, E.Z. 2012. "Cigánybűnözés? – egy korjelző forrás az 1970-es évekből: Rendőrségi jelentés egy bűnözői csoportról" [Gypsy criminality? – An epochal source from the 1970s: a police report on a criminal group]. *ArchívNet* 12 (6). Retrieved 20 September 2015 from http://archivnet.hu/hetkoznapok/ciganybunozes__egy_korjelzo_forras_az_1970es_evekbol.html.

Ungváry, K. 2012. *A Horthy-rendszer mérlege: diszkrimináció, szociálpolitika, és antiszemitizmus*

Magyarországon, 1919–1944 [The Horthy-regime on balance: discrimination, social policy and anti-Semitism in Hungary, 1919–1944]. Budapest: OSZK.

van der Ploeg, J.D. 2008. *The New Peasantries: Struggles for Autonomy and Sustainability in an Era of Empire and Globalization.* London: Earthscan.

———. 2010. "The Peasantries of the Twenty-First Century: The Commoditisation Debate Revisited." *Journal of Peasant Studies* 37 (1): 1–30.

Vanhaute, E. 2012. "Peasants, Peasantries and (De)Peasantization in the Capitalist World-System." In S. Babones and C. Chase-Dunn, eds., *Routledge Handbook of World-Systems Analysis: Theory and Research*, 313–321. London: Routledge.

Váradi, M.M. 2007. "Utak, elágazások – a közelmúlt falukutatásai" [Roads, crossroads – rural research from the near past]. In É. Kovács, ed., *Közösségtanulmány. Módszertani jegyzet*, 43–68. Budapest: Néprajzi Múzeum Budapest.

Váradi, M.M., and G. Schwarz. 2013. "'És nem találok két embert, aki elmenne bejelentett munkahelyre, három műszakba dolgozni'" ["And I can't find two people willing to work three shifts"]. In K. Kovács and M.M. Váradi, eds., *Hátrányban, vidéken*, 215–218. Budapest: Argumentum.

Veress, C.D. 1996. *Devecser évszázadai* [Devecser through the centuries]. Veszprém: Devecser Nagyközség Önkormányzata.

Vermeersch, P. 2006. *The Romani Movement: Minority Politics and Ethnic Mobilization in Contemporary Central Europe.* New York: Berghahn Books.

Vécsei, P. 2011. "A 2006 és 2010 közötti területi politikai szerkezetváltozás és a területi reálfolyamatok összefüggéseinek alakulása" [The evolution of the link between socioeconomic trends and political geography between 2006 and 2010]. In R. Tardos, Z. Enyedi, and A. Szabó, eds., *Részvétel, képviselet, politikai változás*, 383–407. Budapest: Demokrácia Kutatások Magyar Központja Alapítvány.

Vidékfejlesztési Minisztérium. n.d. "Nemzeti Vidékstratégia 2012–2020, 'a magyar vidék alkotmánya'" [Rural development strategy 2012–2020, "the constitution of the Hungarian countryside"]. Budapest: Vidékfejlesztési Minisztérium. Retrieved 19 October 2015 from http://videkstrategia.kormany.hu/download/4/37/30000/Nemzeti%20Vid%C3%A9kstrat%C3%A9gia.pdf.

Vidra, Z., and J. Fox. 2012. "The Radicalization of Media Discourse: The Rise of the Extreme Right in Hungary and the Roma Question." CPS Working Paper. Retrieved 21 August 2015 from https://cps.ceu.edu/sites/cps.ceu.edu/files/cps-working-paper-media-discou rse-radicalization-2012.pdf.

Virág, T. 2010. *Kirekesztve: Falusi gettók az ország peremén* [Excluded: Village ghettos on the country's periphery]. Budapest: Akadémiai Kiadó.

Vígvári, A. 2013. "Utcaharc: Egyeztetési eljárások az egyik tiszakerecsenyi utcában" [Street fight: Negotiation strategies in a street in Tiszakerecseny]. In É. Kovács, Z. Vidra, T. Virág eds., *Kint és bent: lokalitás és etnicitás a peremvidékeken*, 303–329. Budapest: L'Harmattan.

Volkov, S. 1978. "Antisemitism as a Cultural Code: Reflections on the History and Historiography of Anti-Semitism in Imperial Germany." *Leo Baeck Institute Yearbook* 23: 25–45.

Vörös, A. 2009. "Szimbólumképződési folyamatok a médiában – Olaszliszka" [The generation of symbols in the media – Olaszliszka]. *Jel-Kép* 4: 3–31.

Wacquant, L. J. D. 1996. "L'underclass' urbaine dans l'imaginaire social et scientifique américain" [The urban underclass in the American social and scientific imagination]. In S. Paugam, ed., *L'Exclusion: l'état des savoirs*, 248–262. Paris: Éditions La Découverte.

———. 2008. *Urban Outcasts: A Comparative Sociology of Advanced Marginality.* Cambridge: Polity.

———. 2009. *Prisons of Poverty.* Minneapolis: University of Minnesota Press.

Wieviorka, M. 2004. "Researching Race and Racism: French Social Sciences and International Debates." In M. Bulmer and J. Solomos, eds., *Researching Race and Racism*, 52–65. London: Routledge.

Wilson, W.J. 1987. *The Truly Disadvantaged: The Inner City, the Underclass, and Public Policy.* Chicago: University of Chicago Press.

——. 1993. *The Ghetto Underclass: Social Science Perspectives.* Newbury Park, CA: Sage.

——. 1996. *When Work Disappears: The World of the New Urban Poor.* New York: Knopf.

Wimmer, A. 1997. "Explaining Xenophobia and Racism: A Critical Review of Current Research Approaches." *Ethnic and Racial Studies* 20 (1): 17–41.

——. 2002. *Nationalist Exclusion and Ethnic Conflict: Shadows of Modernity.* Cambridge, Cambridge University Press.

Wistrich, R. 1990. "Antisemitism as a Radical Ideology." In *Between Redemption and Perdition: Modern Anti-Semitism and Jewish Identity,* 31–41. London: Routledge.

Wolf, E.R. 1969. *Peasant Wars of the Twentieth Century.* New York: Harper & Row.

——. 1990. *Europe and the People without History.* Berkeley, CA: University of California Press.

——. 1999. *Envisioning Power: Ideologies of Dominance and Crisis.* Berkeley, CA: University of California Press.

Zaslove, A. 2004. "Closing the Door? The Ideology and Impact of Radical Right Populism on Immigration Policy in Austria and Italy." *Journal of Political Ideologies* 9 (1): 99–118.

Zolnay, J. 2012. "Abusive Language and Discriminatory Measures in Hungarian Local Policy." In M. Stewart, ed., *The Gypsy "Menace,"* 25–42. London: Hurst.

INDEX

abandonment, 3, 19–20, 21n1, 56, 77–83, 174, 203–4; political, 233; after red mud disaster, 190, 216
abstraction, 19–20, 76, 110, 122; strategy, 4–5, 10, 19, 110, 122
acculturation, 28
Act on Equal Opportunity in 2005, 82
affliction and persecution paradigm approach to Roma history, 29
agribusinessmen, 48–49; regime change and, 49
agricultural reform, 36
agricultural sector, 9
agricultural workers, 180–81
agriculture; Common Agricultural Policy, EU, 224; deagrarianization, 99; decline of, 89–90; depeasantization and, 46–47; in Devecser, 174, 176–77, 180, 205n5; in Gyöngyöspata, 56, 58–60; household, 52n23, 53n28; modernization of, 48–49; peasant, 53n29; petty agricultural production, 47–48; post-peasantry and, 48–49; producers by region, 61; in Transdanubia, 174, 176; viticulture, 56, 59–60, 62, 66–68, 137
aluminium, 205n5; MAL Hungarian Aluminium, 190
anti-capitalism, 219
anti-communitarian behavior, 151–52, 202

anti-egalitarian populism, 171n33, 204, 233; of Fidesz Party, 154–59, 219
anti-Gypsy campaigns, 113–14. See also anti-Roma mobilization; racist mobilization
anti-Gypsyism, 19, 21n2, 89, 93; in Czech Republic, 4; emergence of, 9–10; evolution of, 4; in Hungary, 4; in Northeast Hungary, 45; political, 1, 10, 197, 220, 231n9; as political movement, 4; politics of electoral support and, 4; politics of governmental power and, 17 redemptive, 5, 98–126, 210; anti-Gypsy racism, xvii. See also political racism; popular racism
anti-immigrant sentiment, 233
antiracism, 74
anti-Roma mobilization, ix, 10, 174; in Devecser, xvi, 194–97; in Gyöngyöspata, xv–xvi, 145–51; by Jobbik Party, xv–xvii, 115–16, 144–45. See also racist mobilization
anti-Roma sentiment; in Gyöngyöspata, 145; historically, ix–x, 36–37
anti-Semitism, 21n2, 23n12
Arrow Cross Party, 113, 124n15
arson, 86
assimilation, 179
assimilationist integration policy, 34; Austria, 182–84

lomis in, 207n15
authoritarianism, 217, 232, 235
authoritarian populism, 6, 171n33
Autumn Light Pensioners' Club, 222

Bajnai, Gordon, 107
Bataille, Georges, 36
Bayer, Zsolt, 109, 113, 116
Beash, 34, 178, 180; lomis, 182
behavior; anti-communitarian, 151–
        52; social, 202
Bernáth, Magdolna, 124n10, 137
black identity cards, 33
black people, 31, 41
"Blitz Campaign," Devecser, 174,
        194–98, 210; failure of, 218
blogs, 114
Blooming Cooperative, 179–80
Bognár, Anikó, 129, 194–95
Bourdieu, P., 40, 121
Brexit, x–xi, 233
broom making, 73, 100

Canada, 153
Capitalism; anti-capitalism, 219;
        liberal, 2
Central European University (CEU),
        xii
Chance for Children Foundation
        (CFCF), 82, 95n16
child protection benefits, 209n33
children, Roma, 145
church-run schools, 209n34
civil society, 221; "Gypsy menace"
        and, 200–202
class, x–xi, 11, 52n22, 55, 157, 167, 204,
        218; analysis, 23n10; conflict,
        234, 237; ethnicity and, xvii, 56–
        63, 180–86, 228; reproduction
        of, xvii, 10; struggle, 8, 10, 14,
        241n10; theory, 9
class paradigm approach to racism,
        11
clientelism, 91, 159, 224
coexistence, code of, 201
co-existence paradigm approach to
        Roma history, 29

Cohen, S., 78, 143, 168n2; Folk Devils
        and Moral Panics, 121
Common Agricultural Policy, EU, 224
Communism, 176; postcommunism,
        ix–x, 210–11
Communist Party, in France, 228
Compensation Law, 59
cordon sanitaire, 112, 116
corporatism, 159
counterdemonstration, 199
countermovement, 2–4, 7–8, 20, 30, 55,
        92, 173, 189, 202
counterrevolution, 231n8
crime, 146. See also "Gypsy
        criminality"; arson, 86; in
        Gyöngyöspata, 69–72, 152;
        "livelihood criminality," 78,
        95n23, 117; petty theft, 68,
        72, 76; property, 68, 126n29;
        uniform-related, 150, 169n10;
        violent, 87–88
critical junctions approach, 9
Csalog, Zsolt, 36–37
csicska, 197–99, 208n25
Cultural Association of Hungarian
        Gypsies, 40, 51n8
cultural heritage, 104
culture, 92, 198; ethnonational,
        104; multiculturalism, 235; of
        poverty thesis, 151–52; Romani,
        27. See also ethnic traditions;
        traditions
culture-as-template approach, 23n11
Czech Republic; anti-Gypsyism in, 4;
        Ústí nad Labem, 42
Czeidli, József, 128

Dankó settlement, 131, 174, 177;
        overcompensation of families,
        191; red mud spill and, 190–94,
        216
Day of National Cohesion, 226
deagrarianization, 53n24, 59, 99
decentralization, unintended
        outcomes of, 42
déclassement, 42
de-ethnicization, 30–37

Defense Force, 147–48, 150–51; in
    Gyöngyöspata, 148–49
delegitimation, 106, 204; of Fidesz
    Party, 21
democracy; illiberal, 237; liberal,
    223–24, 233–35
depeasantization, 3–4, 45–50, 53n24,
    67; agriculture and, 46–47;
    regime change and, 46
deprivation, 203; lomis and, 186–90;
    material, 171n30; zones of, 49,
    92–93
deproletarianization, 38–45
desegregation, 30, 203, 208n31,
    237; red mud disaster and
    residential, 190–94; residential,
    203
of schools, 80–83, 105, 208n31
destigmatization, 214; of Roma, 33–34
Devecser, Hungary, 13–15, 127,
    128, 173–209; agriculture
    in, 174, 176–77, 180, 205n5;
    "Blitz Campaign," 174,
    194–98, 210, 218; clean streets,
    130; economy, 179–80; elite
    in, 197–200; ethnographic
    fieldwork from, 17–18; Far
    Right in, local elite against,
    197–200; far-right mobilization
    in, 15–16; Fidesz Party in, 21,
    217; Gyöngyöspata and, 228;
    "Gypsyfication" and, 200, 221;
    Jobbik Party in, 21, 194–98, 210,
    218, 231n7; land ownership
    in, 204n2; land reform, 204n2;
    land use in, 176–77; left-wing
    politics in, 211; Live and
    Let Live! Demonstration in
    Favor of Rightful Magyar
    Self-Defense, 196; lomis
    in, 132–33, 183–84, 188–89;
    map of, 175, 192; neighbor
    feud, 129, 133, 194–98; "new
    colony," 130; paramilitaries
    in, 195–97; reconstruction and
    development, 203; red mud
    spill, 127, 130–31, 190–94, 200;

Romani in, 205n4; school in,
    208n31; settlement-dwellers in,
    181, 206n11; Socialist Party in,
    211, 213; surplus population
    in, 181–82; Turul statue, 134;
    unemployment in, 185, 206n9;
    violence in, 197
development resources, distribution
    of regional, 230n2
Dezső, Éva, 141
dialects; Lovari, 205nn6–7, 207n19;
    Sinto, 206n8; Vlax Romani,
    205n7
Dignity for All Movement, 148
discrimination, 25–37, 41
"double crisis" of social reproduction,
    3–4, 19–20
"double movement," 2–3, 7–8
dual citizenship laws, 144
dualization; of Hungarian state, 6,
    159–64, 166–67; of welfare,
    170n18; Dual State, 6, 204, 234
political dividends, 159–64; right-
    wing rivalry and, 143–72
dual welfare regime, 41
dual welfare state, 156
Dupcsik, Csaba, 26–29
durable goods, 185–86
Dzurinda, Mikuláš, 160, 165

Eastern Europe; EU and, xi;
    national-populism in, 234, 238;
    neoliberal globalization in, xi
right-wing sovereignists in, 241n9;
    Western Europe and, 239–40
economy; of Devecser, 179–80; ethnic,
    178; of EU, 2–3; new economic
    mechanism, 179; political,
    racism and, ix; post-peasantry
    and, 49; restructuring, impacts
    of, 203; service-oriented, shift
    to, xi
education, 141; centralization of, 3;
    church-run schools, 209n34;
    desegregation of schools,
    80–83, 105; in Devecser,
    208n31; ghetto-schools, 43;

"Gypsyfication" in schools, 88–89; "Gypsyfied" school, 201–2; Roma, 35, 51n11; segregated tuition, 223; segregation and, 64–65, 80–83, 209n35; segregation in schools, 163

elite; in Devecser, 197–200; in Gyöngyöspata, 98–105; left-liberal, 3–4, 77–83, 225, 228, 237–38; right-wing, 235

endogamy, 179

engram, 11, 23n11

"Érpatak model," 150, 164, 219–20; failure of, 151–54; "Gypsy problem" and, 152–53; social welfare in, 152

eschatology, Manichean, 198

Esterházy, Ferenc, 204n2

étatisme, 158

"eternal racism," ix

ethnic cleansing, 233

ethnic conflict, 39

ethnic economy, 178

ethnic homogeneity, xii

ethnicity, 1, 29, 39, 41, 50n2, 65, 81; class and, xvii, 56–63, 180–86, 228; interethnic alliance-building, 202; mobilizations based around, 11; race and, 11, 16, 18, 19, 25

ethnicity approach to racism, 11, 22n7

ethnic solidarity, 4, 104, 149

ethnic traditions, 39, 102

ethnographic fieldwork, 17–18

ethnography; Jobbik Party and, 210–31; political, 20

ethnonationalism, 104, 235

ethnoracial exclusion, 29

ethnoracial identity and identification, 23n10

ethnotraditionalists, 121, 151; in Gyöngyöspata, 103; pragmatists versus, 99–105

EU. See European Union

Europe; fascism in, 7–8, 232–34; postcommunist, ix–x; radical right-wing politics in, 239. See also Eastern Europe; Western Europe

Europeanization, 3–4, 19, 50, 227; progressive neoliberalism and, 235

European Union (EU); Common Agricultural Policy, 224; Eastern Europeans and, xi; economy of, 2–3; Hungary in, 189; refugees in, 236

exoticization, of Roma, 50n4

extended case method, 16

extremism, 172n38; Jobbik Party and, 219

Farkas, János, 140, 148

Farkas, Pál, 142

Far Right; in Devecser, 197–200; in Devecser, mobilization of, 15–16; in Gyöngyöspata, 150–54; Live and Let Live! Demonstration in Favor of Rightful Magyar Self-Defense, 196; public support of, 121–22

far-right politics, xvi, 11; in Hungary, 1–2; Jobbik Party, xi; racist component of, ix

fascism; in Europe, 7–8, 232–34; interwar, 234; neofascism, 240n5; rebirth of, 232–33

fascists, 235

FBF. See For a Better Future Civic Guard Association

Ferenczi, Gábor, 218–22; neighbor feud and, 195–96, 198

Fidesz Party, xii, xvii, 1, 20; adoption strategy and, 5–6; anti-egalitarian populism and, 154–59, 219; authoritarianism and, 217; delegitimation of, 21; in Devecser, 21, 217; disillusionment with, 215–17; dual citizenship laws, 144; in Gyöngyöspata, 154; Jobbik Party and, 119–20, 159, 218; nomenklatura and, 214; political strategy of, 155,

160, 166, 228–29; politics of
electoral support, 238; politics
of governmental power, 167;
popularity of, 172n40, 212; tax-
credit system, 162; work-based
society, 154–59
First Compensation Act, 93n5
Folk Devils and Moral Panics (Cohen),
121
For a Better Future Civic Guard
Association (FBF), 146–47,
168n3
France, 196, 241n9; Communist Party
in, 228; Neoliberal reforms in,
228
Freiheitliche Partei Österreichs, 218
friction, 9–10, 19, 49–50, 55–56;
border, 83–89; Gyöngyöspata
border, 83–89; post-peasantry/
surplus population, 101; Roma/
non-Roma, 29, 84, 86–87, 149;
socioethnic, 113, 121, 145, 167
Friends Circle, 87–89, 100, 102–3, 146
Fundamental Law, 144, 160

Gadjo, Gypsy/Gadjo relationship, 36
Germany, 241n9
ghetto, Székesfehérvár, 80
ghettoization, rural, 208n22. *See also*
marginalization
ghetto-schools, 43
ghetto-villages, 43, 64
The Great Transformation (Polányi), 7
Gyöngyöspata, Hungary, 12–15,
57, 136; activists in, 148–49;
agriculture in, 56, 58–60
anti-Gypsy sentiment in, 145; anti-
Roma mobilization in, xv–xvi;
border frictions, 83–89, 101;
border zone, 85, 138, 145;
crime in, 69–72; Defense
Force in, 148–49; Devecser
and, 228; elite in, 98–105;
"Érpatak model" in, 152–54;
ethnographic fieldwork from,
17–18; ethnotraditionalists
in, 103; Far Right in, 150–54;

Fidesz Party in, 154; "Gypsy
criminality" and, 146; "Gypsy
settlement," 139–40, 145, 148;
industry in, 58; Jobbik Party in,
15, 145–46; mayoral elections in,
150–51; in media, 150; NHG in,
146; paramilitaries in, 146–48;
popular racism in, 55–97; racist
countermovement in, 189;
right-wing politics in, 230n1;
Roma/non-Roma frictions
in, 84, 86–87, 149; settlement-
dwellers in, 149; Socialist Party
in, 230n1; surplus population
in, 181–82; Trianon memorial,
135; unemployment in, 62–63,
94n10; violence in, 87–88;
viticulture in, 56, 59–60
"Gyöngyöspata model," 153–54, 164
Gypsies (documentary), 206n11
Gypsy, xi
"Gypsy criminality," 6, 31, 101–2,
113, 120, 124n16, 151, 196;
combatting, 220; Gyöngyöspata
and, 146; in Lak, 145; as
"livelihood criminality," 117; in
media, 108–10, 114–16; moral
panic, 14–15, 20, 122, 143, 149,
155, 164, 236; Orbán on, 155–57
"Gypsyfication," xi, 45, 102, 193; of
Devecser, 200, 221; in schools,
88–89; of schools, 201–2
Gypsy/Gadjo relationship, 36
Gypsy/Magyar relationship, 18, 99,
114–15
"Gypsy menace," 200–202
"Gypsy music," 30, 50n3
Gypsyness, 23n11, 26, 31, 33, 39–40,
124n16, 205n4; social dimension
of, 28–29
"Gypsy policy," 36–37
"Gypsy problem," ix, 31, 33, 101, 103,
116, 151–53; "Érpatak model"
and, 152–53; public debate of,
120; "solving," ix
"Gypsy question," xiv, 28, 31–33;
Jobbik Party and, 116, 118–19,

143, 166; politicization of,
118–19
"Gypsy rap," 75, 95n22
Gypsy Self-Government, 82, 140, 146,
148
"Gypsy-talk," 21, 203, 229
Gyurcsány, Ferenc, 2, 6, 112, 124n13,
193; public opinion of, 212

Hajdúhadház, Hungary, 147
Hall, Stuart, 6, 121–22, 164–65
hegemonic Hungarianness, 25–26, 33–
34, 37, 56; advantages of, 79–80;
contesting, 72–77; polarization
and, 64–66; in postsocialist
period, 65–66
hegemony; political, ix; right-wing,
1–2; Western European, 234
Hereditary Hungarian Guard, 168n3
historic peasantry, 48
Holczinger, László, 188, 203, 225
Holmes, Douglas, 104, 122, 232
"homogenous society," 20, 27, 33, 36,
143, 166, 186, 237
Horn, Gyula, 211
Horváth, Ferenc, 194–95
human rights, 147
Hungarian Guard, 5, 13, 112–14,
116–18, 144, 168n3, 174, 222; ban
of, 117, 125n25; public opinion
of, 118. *See also* New Hungarian
Guard Movement
Hungary, ix; agricultural producers
by region, 61; agricultural
sector in, 9; anti-Gypsyism in, 4
debt crisis, 51n13; development
programs, 93n1; dualization of,
6; EU accession, 189; exports,
172n39, 179; far-right politics
in, 1–2; Labor Code, 171n27,
207n18; New Right in, 157;
post-communist, xi; racism
in, 1;right-wing hegemony
in, 1–2; Romani groups in,
xiv; Syrian refugees in, xii;
viticulture producers by region,
62; Western, 12; xenophobia

in, 1. *See also* Devecser,
Hungary; Gyöngyöspata,
Hungary; Hajdúhadház,
Hungary; Jászladány, Hungary;
Monok, Hungary; Northeast
Hungary; Southwest Hungary;
Transdanubia, Hungary;
Western Hungary

illiberal democracy, 237
immigrants, x–xi; anti-immigrant
sentiment, 233; representations
of, 123n3
income inequality, 161–62
income poverty, 171n28
income tax, 54n30
industrial disaster, 13, 174. *See also* red
mud spill
industry, 180; aluminium, 205n5;
broom making, 73, 100; in
Gyöngyöspata, 58; in Northeast
Hungary, 62; Tornai, Tamás,
184–85
integration, 19, 25, 37, 56, 88, 141,
221; assimilationist integration
policy, 34; European, 3–4, 57, 92;
policy, 83, 98, 201–2; of Roma,
32, 177–78, 220; segregation
and, 88–89; social, 68
interethnic relationship; alliance-
building, 202; after regime
change, 40. *See also* specific
subethnic groups
Internet; blogs, 114; social media, 148
interwar period, fascism in, 234
Italy, 196

Jászladány, Hungary, 81–82
Jews, 32, 113; anti-Semitism,
21n2, 23n12; deportation of
Hungarian, 176; Roma and,
51n6
Jobbik Party, xi–xii, 1, 111–20; anti-
Roma mobilization by, xv–xvii,
115–16, 144–45; csicska and,
199; in Devecser, 21, 231n7;
Devecser blitz campaign, 174,

194–98, 210, 218; ethnography
and, 210–31; extremism and,
219; FBF and, 168n3; Fidesz
Party and, 119–20, 159,
218; in Gyöngyöspata, 15;
Gyöngyöspata and, 145–46;
"Gyöngyöspata model" and,
153–54; "Gypsy question"
and, 116, 118–19, 143, 166;
Hungarian Guard and, 5; image
of, 222; neofascism and, 240n5;
Orbán and, 112; in parliament,
144; political right and, 219;
political strategy of, 210;
popularity of, 117–20, 126n29,
144–45, 172n40, 212; Roma and,
xiv–xv; Socialist Party and, 119;
transformation of, 210–31; Turul
bird and, 230; ultranationalism
and, 210
Juhász, Oszkár, 150–51, 154

Kalb, Don, 9, 13–14, 165, 235
Kálomista, Gábor, 110
Kemény, István, 38–39
knife-whetters. *See* Sinti
Kovách, Imre, 46–48, 53n24
Kovács, Dávid, 113
Kovács, László, 216–17
Kozák, János, 207n20
Kozma, György, 127, 223, 226
Kuncze, Gábor, 78

Labor Code, 171n27, 207n18
labor force; agricultural workers,
180–81; blue-collar, 212, 228;
political allegiance of blue-
collar, 212; post-peasantry,
67–68; Road to Work Program,
117, 164; Roma in, 34, 38, 52n14;
Socialist Party and, 211–12. *See
also* unemployment
labor unions, 228
Ladányi, János, 40
Lak, village of, 144–45
land ownership, 36; confiscated land,
224

land reform, 36
László, Attila, 196
Law and Justice Party (PiS), 239
left-wing politics; in Devecser, 211;
economically, 219
left-wing sovereignists, 240
Lehet Más a Politika. *See* LMP party
liberal capitalism, 2
liberal democracy, 223–24, 233; in
Western Europe, 234–35
"livelihood criminality," 78, 95n23;
"Gypsy criminality" as, 117
LMP (Lehet Más a Politika, "Politics
can be different") party, xiv
lomis, 132–33, 182–83; anti-
communitarian behavior
and, 202; in Austria, 207n15;
in Devecser, 183–84, 188–89;
experiences of deprivation
and popular anger with,
186–90; knife-whetter, 187;
Magyars and, 186, 187; non-
Roma and, 187–88; red mud
disaster and, 199; stigma,
186; in Transdanubia, 207n14;
travel distance, 206n13; Vlach
Romani, 187
Losonci, Bálint, 137
Lovari dialect, 205nn6–7, 207n19
"lynching," 109, 198. *See also*
"Olaszliszka lynching"

Magyars, 5, 95n18, 111; Gypsy/
Magyar relationship, 18, 99,
114–15; Live and Let Live!;
Demonstration in Favor of
Rightful Magyar Self-Defense,
196; lomis and, 186, 187; Roma
and, 228
MAL Hungarian Aluminium, 190
Manichean eschatology, 198
Mann, Michael, 232–34, 240n5
marginalization, 38–45; of surplus
population, 237
material deprivation, 171n30
Mátra Cooperative, 58
Mátrai Power Plant, 62

mechanisms; relational, 10, 124n8;
  segregation and control, 3, 37,
  42, 55–56, 64–66, 202–3
media; Gyöngyöspata in, 150; "Gypsy
  criminality" in, 108–10, 114–16;
  right-wing parties and, 125n18;
  social media, 148
memory politics, 225–26, 229
Mester, Katalin, 128
micro-historical reconstruction, 15
minimum wage, 160
mobilization; campaign, xv–xvi, 5, 10,
  13–14, 115, 143, 174, 218; cycle,
  18, 20
modernization; of agriculture, 48–49,
  176–79; left-liberal, 100, 166;
  "losers," 121; project, 100, 166;
  social, 53n24, 227; socialist, 52–
  53n23, 52n15; in Transdanubia,
  174–79
Monok, Hungary, 105–8
moral panic, 168n2; "Gypsy
  criminality," 122, 164, 236;
  politics of governmental power
  and, 20
theory of, 120–21; volatility and, 143
multiculturalism, 235
multi-national companies, 219
multi-scalar analysis, 8, 15
of racism, 17
music; Black Train band, 75; "Gypsy,"
  30, 50n3, 177; "Gypsy rap," 75,
  95n22; patriotic or "national,"
  104, 196–97

Nagy, Pál, 28–30
National Gypsy Council, 207n20
nationalism, 233, 240n5; racism and,
  xvii, 50n1; ultranationalism, ix,
  xii–xiii, 210–31
national populism, 234; in Eastern
  Europe, 238; politicians, 236
nation-based approach to racism, 11,
  22n8
nation-statism, 233, 235
Nazi ideology, 32
neighbor feud, Devecser, 129, 133,
  194–98

neofascism, 240n5
neoliberal globalization, 233; in
  Eastern Europe, xi
neoliberalism, 156; progressive, 235
neoliberalization, 19, 50
Neoliberal reforms, 228
neonationalist right, 225
new economic mechanism, 179
New Hungarian Guard Movement
  (NHG), 144, 168n3;
  Gyöngyöspata and, 146
New Right, ix, 166, 235; in Britain,
  157; in Hungary, 157; politics
  of, xi–xii
New Social Policy, 160
NHG. See New Hungarian Guard
  Movement
nomenklatura, 211, 230n4; demise
  of, 228; Fidesz Party and, 214;
  suffocation of, 215, 228
Normative State, 20, 143, 166
Northeast Hungary, 3, 4, 6, 12, 15, 17,
  19, 20, 38, 43–45, 52n16, 55–97,
  105–8, 119–21, 164, 170n19, 193,
  203, 222

"Olaszliszka lynching," 108–10, 115,
  198
One Hundred Thousand for
  Gyöngyöspata Facebook group,
  148
Orbán, Viktor, xii, 6–7, 18, 144, 215,
  227–28, 232; Dual State and,
  167; on "Gypsy criminality,"
  155–57; Jobbik Party and,
  112; Kötcse speech, 116–17,
  155–56, 164; on refugee crisis,
  236; Thatcherism and, 157–59;
  welfare state and, 160–61; work-
  based society, 165
Order of Malta, 200
Orsós, Tibor, 131
Othering, ix, 165
Outlaw Army, 147, 168n3, 197

Palóc Days, 100, 102
paramilitaries, 115; in Devecser, 195–
  97; in Gyöngyöspata, 146–48

pariah caste, 41
Pásztor, Albert, 117
peasantry; agriculture, 53n29;
    historically, 48; in postsocialist
    period, 47; traditions
    and, 46–47, 123n4. *See
    also* depeasantization;
    post-peasantry
petty theft, 68, 72; by settlement-
    dwellers, 76
Pintér, Sándor, 144
PiS. *See* Law and Justice Party
Pitzinger, Mónika, 133
Poland, 239
Polányi, Karl; "double movement,"
    2–3, 7–8; *The Great
    Transformation,* 7
polarization, 19–20, 122; hegemonic
    Hungarianness in response to,
    64–66; strategy, 5, 13, 19, 122,
    204
policy; assimilationist integration, 34;
    Common Agricultural Policy,
    EU, 224; "Gypsy," 36–37; New
    Social Policy, 160; social, 160–64
political economy, racism and, ix
political economy scholarship, 2–3,
    9–10
political ethnography, 15, 24n14, 230;
    racist mobilization and, 20–21
political hegemony, ix
political public sphere, 21n3
political racism, 11–12, 19, 98–142,
    220; politics of governmental
    power and, 18
political right; Jobbik Party and, 219;
    radicalization of, 108
politics of electoral support, 165; anti-
    Gypsyism and, 4; Fidesz Party,
    238
politics of governmental power, 4, 6;
    anti-Gypsyism and, 17; Fidesz
    Party, 167; moral panic and, 20;
    political racism and, 18; right-
    wing rivalry and, 143; SNC, 158;
    Thatcher's, 158
popular racism, 18, 37, 44; emergence
    of, 44, 89, 174; in Gyöngyöspata,

55–97; surplus population and,
    91
populism; anti-egalitarian, 154–59,
    171n33, 204, 219, 233;
    authoritarian, 6, 171n33;
    national, 234, 236, 238; right-
    wing, 22n5; two nations, 165
postcommunism, 210–11; in Europe,
    ix–x
post-peasantry, 3–4, 26, 45–50;
    agriculture and, 48–49; decline
    of, 66–72; disenchantment of,
    92; economic position of, 49;
    historic peasantry and, 48;
    labor force, 67–68; property
    and, 68–69; regime change
    and, 68–69; reimagination of,
    101; "return to traditions" and,
    102–4; settlement-dwellers and,
    70–71; social reproduction crisis
    of, 90–91; viticulture and, 68
postracism, 223
postsocialist period; hegemonic
    Hungarianness in, 65–66;
    peasantry in, 47; Roma in, 38–45
poverty, 40–42, 161; culture of poverty
    thesis, 151–52; income, 171n28
pragmatists, ethnotraditionalists
    versus, 99–105
Prerogative State, 20, 143, 166
Privatization; of state assets, 211; of
    welfare, 211–12
progressive neoliberalism, 235
Proletarianization, 30–37;
    deproletarianization, 38–45
provincial mayors, revolt of, 106–8
public works program, 136, 152–54,
    160–63, 172n40

racialization, xvi, 18, 31–32, 166
racism; anti-Gypsy, xvii; antiracism,
    74; class paradigm approach
    to, 11; definition of, 22n6;
    "eternal racism," ix; ethnicity
    approach to, 11, 22n7; far-right
    politics and, ix; in Hungary,
    1; multi-scalar analysis of, 17;
    nationalism and, xvii, 50n1;

nation-based approach to, 11,
22n8; official certification of,
108; political, 18, 220; political
economy and, ix; postracism,
223; redemptive, 228; scientific,
31; ultranationalism and,
210–31. *See also* political racism;
popular racism
racist countermovement, 173, 202–3;
in Gyöngyöspata, 189
racist mobilization, ix, xvi, 4, 10–11,
14–15, 18, 20, 174; limits of,
173–209; political ethnography
and, 20–21; strategy, 114–17.
See also anti-Gypsy campaigns;
anti-Roma mobilization
racist tropes, 41
radicalization, 5–6, 122–23; of political
right, 108
radical right-wing politics, 239
rational choice approaches, 10
realist strain theorists, 23n12
reconstruction; Devecser, 203; micro-
historical, 15; after red mud
spill, 216
redemptive racism, 228. *See also*
anti-Gypsyism
red mud spill, 127, 130–31, 190–94;
abandonment after, 216;
compensation for, 191,
203, 208n21, 216; Dankó
settlement and, 216; donations
after, 200; lomis and, 199;
overcompensation for, 191;
reconstruction after, 216; Toldi
and, 215–16; victims of, 191
red terror of 1919, 222
re-ethnicization, 181
"reflexive social science," xv
reforms; agricultural, 36; land, 36;
Neoliberal, 228; welfare, 105–6,
162
refugees, 235; crisis, 236; Syrian, xii
regime change; agribusinessmen
and, 49; decentralization and,
42; depeasantization and, 46;
interethnic relationship after,

40; perception of, 45; post-
peasantry and, 68–69
relational; analysis, 122; history of
Roma, 26–30; mechanisms, 10,
124n8; strategies, 4–5, 109–11,
122
repeasantization, 53n24, 95n19, 100;
strategy, 67
resegregation, 191, 193
revolt; of provincial mayors, 106–8;
Vendée, 13–14
Rights of National and Ethnic
Minorities, 79
right-wing elite, 235
right-wing hegemony, in Hungary,
1–2
right-wing intellectuals, 108–11
right-wing politics; in Gyöngyöspata,
230n1; media and, 125n18;
radical, 239
right-wing populism, 22n5
right-wing rivalry; dual state and,
143–72; politics of governmental
power and, 143
right-wing sovereignists, 236; in
Eastern Europe, 241n9; SNC
and, 238; in Western Europe,
239
Road to Work Program, 117, 164
"Roma murders," xiv
Roma/Romani; children, 145;
culture, objectification of, 27;
destigmatization, 33–34; in
Devecser, 205n4; education,
35, 51n11; exoticization of,
50n4; history, 26–30; housing
conditions, 34–35, 131; in
Hungary, xiv; integration of,
32; Jews and, 51n6; Jobbik
Party and, xiv–xv; in labor
force, 34, 38, 52n14; in late
Socialist era, 30–37; Magyars
and, 228; postsocialism, 38–45;
representations of, 124n10;
traditions, 73, 178; unemployed,
63; Vlach, 27, 34, 37, 94n13,
178–79

rural ghettoization, 208n22. *See also* marginalization

Sahlins, Marshall, 110–11
scale shift, 122; downward, 20; upward, 5
scientific intelligentsia, 214
scientific racism, 31
segregation, 43; border frictions and, 83; desegregation, 191, 193, 203, 208n31; educational, 80–83; integration and, 88–89; mechanisms of, 3, 25, 42, 55, 65, 79, 81; residential, 65; in schools, 35, 37, 64–65, 163, 209n35; tuition, 223
service-oriented economy, shift to, xi
"settlement-dwellers," 94n15, 139; in Devecser, 181, 206n11; economics, 90; in Gyöngyöspata, 149; petty theft by, 76; post-peasants and, 70–71; symbolic action for young, 76
Simon, Katalin, 129
Sinti (knife-whetters), 178–79, 182, 206n8; lomis, 187
Sinto dialect, 206n8
Sixty-Four Counties Youth Movement, 196
slavery, "21st Century Slavery," 189
Slovakia, 4
SNC. *See* System of National Cooperation
social behavior, 202
social hierarchies, 35–36
socialism, 235
Socialist era; postsocialist period, 38–45, 47, 65–66; Roma in late, 30–37
Socialist Party, 13, 157; corruption scandals, 169n16; demise of, 213; in Devecser, 211, 213; in Gyöngyöspata, 230n1; Jobbik Party and, 119; labor force under, 211–12; leadership of, 106–7; Road to Work program and, 164

social media, 148
social movement; crisis of livelihoods and, 8; scholarship, 4, 5, 9–10
social policy, 160–64
social reproduction, 202; class and, xvii, 10; crisis of, 1, 8, 31, 92; double crisis of, 3, 19; mainstream social groups of, 3, 81, 88; middle strata of, 237–38; peasantry of, 53n29; post-peasantry of, 3, 26, 48–49, 91, 104; Roma of, 38; surplus population of, 3, 26, 38, 68, 90–91; workers of, 52n22
social welfare, in "Érpatak model," 152
solidarity; ethnic and ethnonational, 4, 104, 149; institutional, 3, 8, 26, 238
Soros, George, xii, 236
Soros Foundation, 200
Southwest Hungary, 43, 91, 97n33
sovereignism, 240n4; left-wing sovereignists, 240; right-wing sovereignists, 236, 238–39, 241n9
specific subethnic groups; Beash, 34, 178, 180; Romungros and "musicians," 73, 84, 94n13, 205; Vlach Roma, 27, 34, 37, 94n13, 178–79
stigma; destigmatization, 33–34, 214; lomis, 186; moral, 41
structuralism, 10, 14, 23n12, 52, 91
struggle; civil rights, 79–83; class, 241n10; distributive, 44, 170n18; ideological, 165; "Manichean," 110, 122; party political, 110, 113–20, 150–54; symbolic, 27, 44–45; transposition of, 98–126
Sure Start Center, 200
surplus population, 94n15, 163; characteristics of, 181; concentration of, 40, 90–91; departure of, 176; in Devecser, 181–82; disciplinary regime imposed on, 163; emancipation

of, 3; ethnicity and, 18–19, 38–41; exclusion of, 166, 237; frictions between post-peasantry and, 10; in Gyöngyöspata, 181–82; marginalization of, 237; mechanisms of segregation and control targeting, 64–66, 90, 94n15, 203; petty theft and, 72; popular racism and, 91; reemergence of, 9, 181; reimagination of, 101; relocation of, 193; segregation of, 42–43; social reproduction crisis of, 38, 90–91

Syrian refugees, xii

System of National Cooperation (SNC), 20, 234, 236; politics of governmental power, 158; right-wing sovereignists and, 238; viability of, 239

Szabó, Gábor, 117–18

Szalai, Júlia, 41–42, 170n18

Szegedi, Csanád, 113, 144

Székesfehérvár ghetto, 80, 95n28

"Szekler gate," 138

Szelényi, Iván, 40

Tambiah, Stanley, 109–10

tax, income, 54n30

tax-credit system, 162

Thatcher, Margaret, 164–65; politics of governmental power, 158; two nations populism, 165

Thatcherism, 157–59, 164–65

Tilly, Charles, 25

Toldi, Tamás, 199–202; red mud disaster and, 215–16

Tornai, Endre, 179–80, 184

Tornai, Tamás, 166–67, 180, 200, 211; industrial empire of, 184–85

Trade; exports, 172n39, 179; regulations, 179

Traditions; ethnic, 39, 102; peasant, 46–47, 123n4; "return to," 102–4; Romani, 73, 178

Transdanubia, Hungary, 12–13, 20–21, 97n33, 173–209, 229; agriculture

in, 174, 176; lomis in, 207n14; modernization in, 174–79

transvaluation, 109–10

Trianon, 225; discourse, 229; memorial, 226; public memory of, 226; Turul bird and, 227

Trianon Treaty, 135, 225

Trump, Donald, x, 240n1

Turul bird, 231n10; Jobbik Party and, 230; statues, 128, 134, 225–26; Trianon and, 227

"21st Century Slavery," 189

two nations populism, 165

Tyirityán, Zsolt, 197

ultranationalism, ix; Jobbik and, 210; racism and, 210–31; xenophobic, xii–xiii

unemployment, 38, 41, 163; in Devecser, 185, 206n9; in Gyöngyöspata, 62–63, 94n10; of Roma, 63

United Kingdom; Brexit, x–xi, 233; New Right in, 157

United States; poverty in, 40; Trump presidency and, x

Ústí nad Labem, Czech Republic, 42

Vendée revolt, 13–14

"Veszprém murder," 198

Vígvári, András, 44–45

violence, 223; in Devecser, 197; in Gyöngyöspata, 87–88, 149

Virág, Tünde, 43–44, 106

viticulture, 66–67, 137; in Devecser, 174; in Gyöngyöspata, 56, 59–60; post-peasantry and, 68; producers by region, 62

Vlach Romani, 27, 34, 37, 94n13, 178–79, 207n19; lomis, 182, 187

Vlax Romani dialect, 205n7

voivod, 84, 87, 96n30

Vona, Gábor, 112, 124n11, 145, 146, 168n5, 215, 220

wage, minimum, 160

waste collectors, 207n15

welfare; centralization of, 3; child protection benefits, 209n33; decentralization of, 42; dependency, 41, 155–56; dualization of, 170n18; dual welfare regime, 41; dual welfare state, 156; in "Érpatak model," 152; Orbán and, 160–61; privatization of, 211–12; reform, 105–6, 162; social card, 107
welfare-scrounging, 220
welfare state, 160–61; dual, 156
Western Europe; Eastern Europe and, 239–40; hegemony, 234; liberal democracy in, 234–35; right-wing sovereignists in, 239
Western Hungary, xvi, 12, 207n15
Western values, 221–22

Whiteness, 240n1
Wieviorka, Michel, 200–201
winemakers, 63, 67, 79, 87, 95n19, 101, 137–38, 150–51, 231n9. *See also* viticulture
work-based society, 106, 143, 154–60
Workers' Militia, 215
workfare, 6, 105–7, 156, 164–67, 170n19, 202
World War I/II monuments, 224–25

xenophobia, xii, 1
xenophobic ultranationalism, xii–xiii

Zolnay, János, 82–83, 105
zones; deprivation, 19, 44, 49, 90–93; regulation, 49, 90, 163

DISLOCATIONS

General Editors: August Carbonella, *Memorial University of Newfoundland;* Don Kalb, *University of Bergen & Utrecht University;* Linda Green, *University of Arizona*

The immense dislocations and suffering caused by neoliberal globalization, the retreat of the welfare state in the last decades of the twentieth century, and the heightened military imperialism at the turn of the twenty-first century have raised urgent questions about the temporal and spatial dimensions of power. Through stimulating critical perspectives and new and cross-disciplinary frameworks, which reflect recent innovations in the social and human sciences, this series provides a forum for politically engaged, ethnographically informed, and theoretically incisive responses.

Volume 1
Where Have All the Homeless Gone?
The Making and Unmaking of a Crisis
Anthony Marcus

Volume 2
Blood and Oranges: Immigrant Labor and
European Markets in Rural Greece
Christopher M. Lawrence

Volume 3
Struggles for Home: Violence, Hope and
the Movement of People
Edited by Stef Jansen and
Staffan Löfving

Volume 4
Slipping Away: Banana Politics and Fair
Trade in the Eastern Caribbean
Mark Moberg

Volume 5
Made in Sheffield: An Ethnography of
Industrial Work and Politics
Massimiliano Mollona

Volume 6
Biopolitics, Militarism, and Development:
Eritrea in the Twenty-First Century
Edited by David O'Kane and
Tricia Redeker Hepner

Volume 7
When Women Held the Dragon's
Tongue and Other Essays in Historical
Anthropology
Hermann Rebel

Volume 8
Class, Contention, and a World in Motion
Edited by Winnie Lem and
Pauline Gardiner Barber

Volume 9
Crude Domination: An Anthropology of Oil
Edited by Andrea Behrends,
Stephen P. Reyna, and Günther Schlee

Volume 10
Communities of Complicity: Everyday
Ethics in Rural China
Hans Steinmüller

Volume 11
Elusive Promises: Planning in the
Contemporary World
Edited by Simone Abram and
Gisa Weszkalnys

Volume 12
Intellectuals and (Counter-) Politics: Essays
in Historical Realism
Gavin Smith

Volume 13
Blood and Fire: Toward a Global
Anthropology of Labor
Edited by Sharryn Kasmir and
August Carbonella

Volume 14
The Neoliberal Landscape and the Rise of
Islamist Capital in Turkey
Edited by Neşecan Balkan, Erol Balkan,
and Ahmet Öncü

Volume 15
Yearnings in the Meantime: 'Normal Lives'
and the State in a Sarajevo Apartment
Complex
Stef Jansen

Volume 16
Where Are All Our Sheep? Kyrgyzstan,
A Global Political Arena
Boris Petric, translated by
Cynthia Schoch

Volume 17
Enduring Uncertainty: Deportation,
Punishment and Everyday Life
Ines Hasselberg

Volume 18
The Anthropology of Corporate Social
Responsibility
Edited by Catherine Dolan and
Dinah Rajak

Volume 19
Breaking Rocks: Music, Ideology and
Economic Collapse, from Paris to Kinshasa
Joe Trapido

Volume 20
Indigenist Mobilization: Confronting
Electoral Communism and Precarious
Livelihoods in Post-Reform Kerala
Luisa Steur

Volume 21
The Partial Revolution: Labour, Social
Movements and the Invisible Hand of Mao
in Western Nepal
Michael Hoffmann

Volume 22
Frontiers of Civil Society: Government and
Hegemony in Serbia
Marek Mikuš

Volume 23
The Revolt of the Provinces: Anti-Gypsyism
and Right-Wing Politics in Hungary
Kristóf Szombati

Innovative Approaches to Anthropology!

FOCAAL
JOURNAL OF GLOBAL AND HISTORICAL ANTHROPOLOGY

Focaal is a peer-reviewed journal advocating an approach that rests in the simultaneity of ethnography, processual analysis, local insights, and global vision. It is at the heart of debates on the ongoing conjunction of anthropology and history as well as the incorporation of local research settings in the wider spatial networks of coercion, imagination, and exchange that are often glossed as "globalization" or "empire."

Seeking contributions on all world regions, *Focaal* is unique among anthropology journals for consistently rejecting the old separations between "at home" and "abroad ", "center" and "periphery." The journal therefore strives for the resurrection of an "anthropology at large," that can accomodate issues of postsocialism, mobility, capitalist power and popular resistance into integrated perspectives.

RECENT ARTICLES

Emptiness and its futures: Staying and leaving as tactics of life in Latvia
DACE DZENOVSKA

The desire for disinheritance in austerity Greece
DANIEL M. KNIGHT

Conjuring "the people": The 2013 Babylution protests & desire for political transformation in postwar Bosnia-Herzegovina
LARISA KURTOVIC

Finding a place in the world: Political subjectivities and the imagination of Iceland after the economic crash
KRISTIN LOFTSDOTTIR

Between Afropolitans and new Sankaras: Class mobility and the reproduction of academics in Burkina Faso
MICHELLE ENGELER

"Forging New Malay networks": Imagining global halal markets
JOHAN FISCHER

Shelling from the ivory tower: Project Camelot and the post–World War II operationalization of social science
PHILIP Y. KAO

The racial fix: White currency in the gentrification of black and Latino Chicago
JESSE MUMM

berghahnjournals.com/focaal

ISSN 0920-1297 (Print) • ISSN 1558-5263 (Online)
Issues 80, 81, & 82/2018, 3 issues p.a.

journals
NEW YORK · OXFORD